Martijn Icks is a Marie Curie fellow at the Ruprecht-Karls-Universität Heidelberg, Germany. He was previously Lecturer in History and Literature Studies at the University of Nijmegen, The Netherlands and obtained his PhD cum laude in 2008.

'This is a clear and well-organised account written in a lively and approachable way. It is not a routine imperial biography, but a much wider study encompassing the nature of religious belief, culture and ethnicity, the presentation of the imperial image and the response to this in Rome and the provinces. An important and original aspect is the description of the dissemination of classical culture and the reception of Rome in later periods, and in particular the changing image of Elagabalus in opera, drama and fiction.'

Brian Campbell, Professor of Roman History,
Queen's University Belfast

'I quote in elegiacs all the crimes of Heliogabalus'

William Gilbert and Arthur Sullivan, *The Pirates of Penzance* (1879)

'It is absurd, purely grotesque, this caricature we have of Antonine; perhaps that is why the world has left him alone, that they may gaze the longer on a mask that allures.'

John Stuart Hay, *The Amazing Emperor Heliogabalus* (1911)

'History is something that never happened, written by a man who wasn't there.'

Anonymous

# THE CRIMES
# OF ELAGABALUS

## THE LIFE AND LEGACY OF ROME'S
## DECADENT BOY EMPEROR

MARTIJN ICKS

I.B. TAURIS

LONDON · NEW YORK

Published in 2011 by I.B.Tauris & Co. Ltd
6 Salem Road, London W2 4BU
175 Fifth Avenue, New York NY 10010
www.ibtauris.com

ISBN: 978 1 84885 362 1

Typeset in Calisto by Dexter Haven Associates Ltd, London
Printed and bound in Great Britain by T.J. International, Padstow, Cornwall

# CONTENTS

# LIST OF ILLUSTRATIONS

11. Reconstruction of the Elagabal temple on the Palatine, seen from above. Y. Thébert et al., 'Il santuario di *Elagabalus*', p. 84.

12. Reconstruction of the Elagabal temple on the Palatine, drawing. Y. Thébert et al., 'Il santuario di *Elagabalus*', p. 85.

13. Capital with the betyl of Elagabal, flanked by two female deities. F. Studniczka, 'Ein Pfeilercapitell', Pl. XII.

14. Simeon Solomon, *Heliogabalus, High Priest of the Sun* (1866). Private collection.

15. Lawrence Alma-Tadema, *The Roses of Heliogabalus* (1888). Private collection.

16. Gustav-Adolf Mossa, *Lui* (1906). Musée des Beaux-Arts, Nice.

17. An Italian designer-clothing store called Eliogabalo. Appropriately for an emperor who worshipped the sun, there is a tanning salon above.

# ACKNOWLEDGEMENTS

It is an interesting thought that Elagabalus ruled the Roman world for about the same time as it took me to write this book. Naturally, the problems and challenges faced by the average scholar of ancient history shrink into insignificance when measured against the worries of a Roman emperor – especially if that emperor happens to be Elagabalus, who had so much to worry about. Nevertheless, the road I have travelled for the past four years has not been without its bumps and pitfalls. Many guides have helped me to find my path. Here, I want to give them a well-earned moment in the sun.

Luuk de Blois has played a key role from the very start, supporting me through the writing of this book with an endless supply of valuable comments and good cheer. I admire him for his encyclopaedic knowledge and his unwavering devotion to the people working under his guidance. Eric Moormann has proved an excellent guide in the worlds of art and archaeology. His extensive remarks on my drafts bespoke a sharp eye for even the smallest detail, from which I have benefited greatly. Last but not least, Sophie Levie was a welcome contributor to the team. As an expert in the field of modern literature, she prevented me from making many mistakes and corrected many more.

I very much enjoyed my year at Brasenose College, Oxford, where I had stimulating discussions with many outstanding scholars. I am much indebted to Alan Bowman, who commented on the drafts of my first three chapters. Ted Kaizer made time for me on several occasions, helping me to understand the Roman Near East. I also have fond memories of my meetings with Ittai Gradel, who was always happy to discuss the 'naughty boy' Elagabalus while treating me to several cups of coffee. A year later, when I went to Paris, Ségolène Demougin was kind enough to receive me as a guest at the École Pratique des Hautes Études. The three months I spent researching in the Bibliothèque Nationale were of great value for writing the sixth chapter.

Still, most of the work was done at Nijmegen, where I had the good fortune of sharing an office with Marloes Hülsken and Erika Manders. Their pleasant company made my time on the tenth floor of the Erasmus building a lot more *gezellig*. The same goes for all those other wonderful people at the History department, in particular my fellow ancient historians. Luuk and Erika have already been mentioned; I want to add Lien Foubert, Janneke de Jong, Nathalie de Haan, Olivier Hekster, Gerda de Kleijn, Inge Mennen, Jasper Oorthuys, Sanne van Poppel, Rob Salomons, and Daniëlle Slootjes to the list. Nobody could wish for a better team of colleagues, and indeed I never have.

Without Vincent Hunink, this thesis would probably not have been written at all. He may not be aware of the vital role he played, but it was his Dutch translation of the *Vita Heliogabali* which first set me on the trail of this weird and fascinating emperor. I hope he will enjoy my book as much as I enjoyed his.

Jason Hartford performed the tedious task of correcting my English, which he has done with much accuracy and humour. His witty remarks in the margin never failed to put a smile on my face. For that, and for everything else, I thank him.

My parents were always there in the background to support me, even if the object of my research must have seemed a tad obscure to them. I owe them more than I can express in this short paragraph. Whenever I got too carried away by my findings, my brother Remco was sure to put things into perspective, reminding me that the study of history is nothing but 'dragging up old cows' in the end.

Many others deserve to be mentioned. A mere list of names does no justice to all the people who have been so kind, providing me with suggestions, criticism and references, but for practical reasons I will keep it short. Many thanks are due to Nicole Belayche, Stéphane Benoist, Anthony Birley, Pierre Cosme, Jaś Elsner, Christophe Fricker, Willem Frijhoff, Sky Gilbert, André Hanou, Jan Hartman, Johan van Heesch, Chris Howgego, Willy Jansen, Ellen Kraft, Andreas Kropp, Inger Leemans, Barbara Levick, Marco Mattheis, Michael Meckler, Fergus Millar, Stephan Mols, Frits Naerebout, Marc van der Poel, Leonardo de Arrizabalaga y Prado, Bert Smith, Natascha Veldhorst, Jessica Walker, Jan Waszink, Ryan Wei, Caroline de Westenholz, Christiaan Willemsen, and anybody else whom I may have inadvertently forgotten, but who made a valuable contribution to my study of the priest-emperor in one way or another.

This project would not have been possible without the support of the Radboud University of Nijmegen, which provided the necessary funds, working space and all the facilities I needed to carry out my research. In addition, I have received grants from the VSB Foundation and Dr Hendrik Muller's Vaderlandsch Fonds, allowing me to spend valuable research time in Oxford and Paris.

The author of this work claims sole responsibility for any remaining mistakes. Should this study be hacked to pieces by the critics and suffer damnatio memoriae, the blame is mine for not paying enough heed to the wise words of many advisers.

# INTRODUCTION

From Nero to Caligula, the Roman Empire is credited with many colourful, eccentric and notorious emperors. Among these, Elagabalus (also known as Heliogabalus) occupies a prominent place. Infamous anecdotes about this remarkable ruler abound, from his devotion to an exotic god, his conduct of human sacrifices and his insatiable sexual appetite, to such noteworthy feats as the institution of a women's senate and the building of a suicide tower. Even if only a fraction of these tales is true, Elagabalus must have been one of the most intriguing and unusual characters ever to sit on the Roman throne.

Officially called Marcus Aurelius Antoninus, the emperor got his name from Elagabal, the sun god of the Syrian town of Emesa, from where his family hailed.[1] Before his rise to power, Elagabalus acted as Elagabal's high priest, performing ritual dances for the god. Because of his good looks and distinguished lineage, he attracted the attention of soldiers from a Roman legion stationed near Emesa. On 16 May 218 CE, they proclaimed him emperor on the pretence that he was a bastard son of the deceased emperor Caracalla. Elagabalus, who was just 14 years old at the time, emerged victorious from the ensuing civil war and gained the recognition of the senate. He travelled to Rome and took Elagabal – represented by a conical black stone – with him.

Elagabalus's reign was short, but certainly not short on interesting events. In a shocking and unprecedented move, the emperor put Elagabal at the head of the Roman pantheon, usurping Jupiter's supreme position. He styled himself as Elagabal's 'most elevated priest' and propagated this priesthood on coins, in inscriptions and papyri. In addition, he married a vestal virgin, one of Rome's most august priestesses, while marrying Elagabal to Urania, a deity from the African city of Carthage. In March 222 CE, less than four years after he had gained the throne, the emperor was

1

killed by rebellious praetorians, soldiers of the imperial guard. His body was dragged through the streets and dumped in the Tiber, his memory cursed by the senate, the black stone sent back to its temple in Emesa. Thus the reign of the priest-emperor ended as suddenly and violently as it had begun.

Although Elagabalus is not as widely known as Caligula or Nero, his reputation for luxury, licentiousness and insanity is just as extreme, if not more so. The three main ancient authors who have described his reign – Cassius Dio, Herodian and the unknown author of the *Vita Antonini Heliogabali* – portray him as one of Rome's notorious 'bad emperors'. Their hostile accounts set the tone for later historians. The eighteenth-century scholar Edward Gibbon had nothing but disdain for the infamous ruler, remarking,

> It may seem probable, the vices and follies of Elagabalus have been adorned by fancy, and blackened by prejudice. Yet confining ourselves to the public scenes displayed before the Roman people, and attested by grave and contemporary historians, their inexpressible infamy surpasses that of any other age or country.[2]

Despite these condemning words – or perhaps in part because of them – the legacy of Elagabalus has endured. Ever since the Renaissance, but especially during the last two hundred years, many novelists, poets, playwrights and painters have been inspired by the emperor. The list includes several famous names, such as Francesco Cavalli, Lawrence Alma-Tadema, Stefan George and Antonin Artaud, but also obscure authors like the eighteenth-century Dutch playwright Gysbert Tysens. From the novels, poems, plays, paintings and, more recently, movies, comic books and pop songs of these authors and artists, Elagabalus emerges in many different guises: from evil tyrant to devoted anarchist, from mystical androgyne to modern gay teenager, from Decadent sensualist to ancient pop star.

## IN THE HANDS OF HISTORIANS

Historians, too, have been fascinated by Elagabalus. In the twentieth and twenty-first centuries, several academic works have been devoted to the emperor and his sun god. The ball was set rolling by Georges Duviquet, who edited *Héliogabale raconté par les historiens grecs et latins*

(1903), a collection of ancient texts (and some other sources, such as coins and inscriptions) on Elagabalus. These literary sources play a central role in subsequent studies on the person and reign of Elagabalus. Often, this occurs at the expense of taking into account coins, inscriptions, papyri, busts and archaeological remains. As a result, the portrayals of the emperor in modern academic literature are often one-sided and unbalanced.

John Stuart Hay, the author of *The Amazing Emperor Heliogabalus* (1911), attempted to delve into Elagabalus's psyche. He criticises the literary accounts, stating that they have slandered the young ruler, but his own, remarkably positive take on Elagabalus is not founded on any evidence or plausible reasoning. Another attempt at psychoanalysis was made by Roland Villeneuve, whose *Héliogabale, le César fou* (1957) is less positive about the emperor than Hay's study, but equally unconvincing.

Other scholars have not fared much better. G.R. Thompson's unpublished PhD thesis 'Elagabalus: Priest-Emperor of Rome' (1972) has the merit that it makes extensive use of non-literary sources and references them meticulously, but its critical attitude still leaves much to be desired. The latter is also true for Robert Turcan's *Héliogabale et le sacre du soleil* (1985), which mostly seems to take the ancient accounts at face value and does not trouble itself with references. A recent study by Saverio Gualerzi, *Né uomo, né donna, né dio, né dea* (2005), concentrates on Elagabalus's sociopolitical, sexual and religious roles to make sense of his reign. Although the author makes extensive use of both ancient and modern literature, he largely ignores the non-literary sources. His conclusions are highly speculative and do not fit well with the available evidence.

Finally, two monographs have concentrated on the cult of Elagabal, the Emesene sun god. The first of these is Gaston Halsberghe's misguided *The Cult of Sol Invictus* (1972), in which the author presents Elagabalus as a monotheist who aimed to unify the empire under a universal religion.[3] We also encounter this view in the works of Hay and Thompson, who likewise regard Elagabal as a monotheistic god.[4] The notion is resolutely dismissed by Martin Frey, the author of the excellent work *Untersuchungen zur Religion und zur Religionspolitik des Kaisers Elagabal.*[5] Frey gives valuable information about Elagabal and the other gods worshipped in Emesa, which he subsequently applies to reconstruct and interpret Elagabalus's religious reforms in Rome.

Although some valuable contributions have been made by the authors mentioned above, a plausible reconstruction of the reign of Elagabalus, encompassing not only religious, but also political, economic and other aspects, is still lacking.[6] Moreover, most of the aforementioned authors are primarily concerned with the (alleged) *reality* of the emperor's reign, i.e. what happened, and why. While these are legitimate and interesting questions, much can be learned about the life and legacy of Elagabalus through the *images* of him that have been constructed throughout history. The term is used in a broad sense here, including not only statues, reliefs and paintings, which provide us with images in the literal sense of the word, but also literary representations. Hence, the portrayal of the emperor Tiberius as a sinister tyrant in the writings of Tacitus also constitutes an 'image', as does the favourable description of the emperor Trajan in Pliny's *Panegyricus*.

When looking at images of emperors, we can distinguish between the positive images sent out by the imperial administration – what we may term imperial propaganda – and the varied images constructed by contemporaries and people from later historical periods. For instance, the emperor Commodus presented himself to his subjects as Hercules and gladiator to boost his prestige, but was portrayed as a mad tyrant by Roman historians[7] – a reputation he has kept to this day, as testified by the Hollywood blockbuster *Gladiator*. The infamous Nero was likewise condemned by ancient authors, leading to many representations in modern popular culture – mostly as a bloodthirsty monster.[8]

Images of Elagabalus abound. There is the imperial propaganda, spread during the emperor's reign; the negative portrayals by ancient authors; and the many different representations of the young ruler in modern historiography, art and literature. To a greater or lesser extent, all these images, whether visual or literary, all derive from a historical core: the 'real' Elagabalus who, at least in name, ruled the Roman world from 218 to 222.

Why has this particular emperor, whose reign lasted only four years during one of the lesser-known eras of Roman history, inspired so many diverse and colourful incarnations? How has he been constructed as one of Rome's notorious 'bad emperors' in ancient literature, and how did his negative reputation evolve in later times, both in the learned books of scholars and in the plays, novels and paintings of artists? Which elements of Elagabalus's personality and reign have been highlighted, exaggerated or distorted by those portraying him? Which elements have been downplayed or ignored? Which values and notions can be discerned in the different depictions and evaluations of the emperor?

These are all intriguing questions, since the answers will not only tell us about how Elagabalus has been perceived and reinvented throughout the ages, but also shed light on the ways history is constantly being reimagined by scholars, writers and artists to reflect contemporary values, ideas and preoccupations. For a Christian author, Elagabalus may be first and foremost a heathen; for a staunch republican, he may represent the vices of absolute monarchy; for a modern gay man, he may be a congener to sympathise with. The modest size and diverse nature of the priest-emperor's fictional afterlife – or *Nachleben*, as the Germans call it – make him a suitable case study to examine this phenomenon.

EXAMINING THE EMPEROR

This book aims to do two things. The first is to reconstruct and interpret events and developments during the reign of Elagabalus, making use of ancient sources as well as modern academic literature. The second is to describe and interpret Elagabalus's fictional legacy, and the myriad layers of ancient and modern images which have formed around the historical core. Of course, these two pursuits are very much intertwined. One cannot properly examine a subject's *Nachleben* without some notion of the historical core from which it is ultimately derived. At the same time, one cannot plausibly reconstruct a historical person or period without taking later distortions and interpretations into account. This paradox is fundamental to all historical research and cannot be completely solved; but sound reasoning and the adequate use of non-literary sources and parallel examples can get us a long way towards a view of the life and legacy of this infamous emperor.

THE ANCIENT SOURCES

Before we turn our attention to Elagabalus, we should take a quick look at the source material. As has been mentioned, there are three ancient authors who deal extensively with the reign of the priest-emperor. The first is Cassius Dio, a senator from Bithynia (northern Turkey) who lived from c.164 to sometime after 229 CE. His *Historia Romana*, written in Greek and encompassing 80 books, describes events from the foundation of Rome (traditionally dated to 753 BCE) to the year 229 CE. Large parts of Dio's work have survived only as epitomes by the Byzantine scholars Xiphilinus and Zonaras. However, the second half of book LXXIX and the first half of book LXXX, including most of the description of Elagabalus's reign, have come to us unabridged, with only a few *lacunae*.

As a Greek-speaking senator, Dio displays a clear affinity with Greek culture, as well as subscribing to the conservatism of the Roman elite. He wants the senate to have as much prestige and power as possible, while being hostile towards all influences which he deems alien to Greek and Roman culture.[9] Although a contemporary of Elagabalus, Dio had no personal experience of the emperor, since he was not present in Rome during the latter's reign. It seems likely that Dio based his account of this period mainly on the rumours which reached him in Asia Minor, where he lived at the time, and on the oral information he collected after his return to the capital.

The second author is Herodian, in all likelihood (the son of) an imperial freedman, a released slave who had worked in the imperial administration. He was probably from the west of Asia Minor and lived from c.175 to c.255 CE.[10] Herodian's *Ab excessu divi Marci*, comprising eight books and written in Greek, describes events from the death of Marcus Aurelius (180 CE) to Gordian III's ascension to the throne (238 CE). The work has survived intact and unabridged.

Like Dio, Herodian displays affinity with Greek culture and Roman traditions, although he is less concerned with the senate's prestige than his fellow historian. His audience appears to have been the same as Dio's, namely the Greek-speaking elite of the empire. However, he is much sloppier than his predecessor, especially where dates and years are concerned, and has a tendency to sacrifice factual correctness to the demands of dramatic narrative.[11] According to a careful comparison by Andrea Scheithauer, Herodian's description of the period 218–22 CE relies directly on Dio in many places.[12] Still, the former provides many details which are not mentioned by the latter. Whether Herodian witnessed the events he describes personally remains uncertain.

Thirdly, there is the *Vita Antonini Heliogabali*, allegedly written by one Aelius Lampridius and dedicated to the emperor Constantine. The *Vita* is part of the *Historia Augusta*, a series of imperial biographies describing the emperors from Hadrian (117–38 CE) to Numerian (283–84 CE). The work, which is composed in Latin, claims to be the product of six different authors, writing during the reigns of Diocletian and Constantine. In reality, as Ronald Syme has demonstrated, it must have been the work of one man, who probably lived around the end of the fourth century CE.[13] Not much is known about the author, except that his sentiments indicate he was a pagan.

In writing the *Vita Heliogabali*, 'Lampridius' used both Dio and Herodian as sources (the former perhaps through an intermediary work). Like many of the later lives in the *Historia Augusta*, the *Vita* largely consists of wild inventions and fantastic anecdotes. However, it does appear to contain some reliable passages with regard to Elagabalus's downfall. According to Syme, any factual information is probably based primarily on the account of the senator Marius Maximus, a contemporary of Elagabalus whose work has been lost.[14] In general, though, the *Vita Heliogabali* is more interesting as a work of fiction than as a source for reconstructing the priest-emperor's reign.

The accounts of Dio, Herodian and the author of the *Vita Heliogabali* are complemented by several other ancient and Byzantine authors. Most of these do not devote much attention to the period 218–22 CE and add little of interest. We do, however, have many coins and inscriptions from the reign of Elagabalus, as well as some papyrus texts, imperial busts and archaeological remains.

### THE MODERN SOURCES

Tracing Elagabalus's legacy in Western art and literature over a period of many centuries is not an easy task. Along with Internet searches on variations of his name, I have searched on title and subject in the catalogues of several great libraries, such as the British Library and the Bibliothèque Nationale de France. My fellow scholar Leonardo de Arrizabalaga y Prado, who shares my interest in the *Nachleben* of Elagabalus, has kindly provided me with his findings, which represent the fruits of ten years of research. Lastly, I have made grateful use of the scattered references in scholarly and artistic works, most notably Marie-France David's study *Antiquité latine et Décadence*.

# 1

# THE BOY ON THE THRONE

In his four years as emperor [...] Heliogabolus did lots of interesting things. Not nice things; but nonetheless interesting.

Neil Gaiman, *Being an Account of the Life and Death of the Emperor Heliogabolus* (1991–92)

When Elagabalus gained the throne in 218 CE, he was the youngest sole-ruling emperor the empire had ever seen. Being only 14 years of age and without any political or military experience, he seems an unlikely candidate for the imperial purple. How did a 14-year-old boy, living in the Syrian town of Emesa, become the ruler of the Roman world? How much power did he actually have during the four years in which he held the principate? It is difficult to answer these questions accurately, because they require a detailed insight into the political and military dynamics of the time – a reality which was probably much more complex than the ancient writers would have us believe.

Analysing 'what happened' under Elagabalus becomes even more difficult when we take the religious reforms of this period into account. Given their controversial and unprecedented nature, they not only complicate the issue of power balance within the imperial administration, but provoke the question of what exactly Elagabalus and his supporters were trying to achieve – and to what extent the religious innovations contributed to the downfall of the infamous 'priest-emperor'. This chapter will give a chronological survey of the period 218–22, addressing all of these questions.

GAINING THE THRONE

On 8 April 217, the emperor Caracalla met with a sudden and violent end. The 29-year-old ruler – son of Septimius Severus, who had founded the Severan dynasty – had spent the last years of his reign in the East, waging war on the Parthians, and was on his way from Edessa to Carrhae when he was attacked by one of his own men. The blow he received was not immediately fatal, but the onrushing guards grasped the opportunity to kill the emperor themselves. According to both Dio and Herodian, the murder had been plotted by Macrinus, one of Caracalla's praetorian prefects (commanders of the imperial guard). Whether this is true or not, Macrinus was certainly the person who gained most from the emperor's untimely death, since the soldiers proclaimed him Caracalla's successor. The senate could do little but accept the choice of the army, despite the fact that Macrinus was only of equestrian rank and therefore in principle not a qualified candidate for the imperial purple.

However, Rome would never lay eyes on this new emperor. There were matters in the East which had to be dealt with first, most of all the war with the Parthians. Unwilling to continue Caracalla's campaign, Macrinus bought a truce with the enemy, an act which did not make a good impression on the soldiers. Moreover, he decided to reduce the army's pay and to withhold the privileges that new recruits had been granted by Caracalla, denying them prizes and exemption from military duties. This further reduced his popularity with the soldiers. As Herodian remarks, 'it was obviously inevitable that Macrinus would lose the empire, and his life too, whenever chance provided a small, trivial excuse for the soldiers to have their way.'[1]

After the death of Caracalla, it had seemed the days of the Severan dynasty were over. The emperor had left no legitimate children and had murdered his brother and co-ruler Geta several years earlier. Caracalla's mother Julia Domna had committed suicide – perhaps at the instigation of Macrinus, who may have perceived her as a threat. Her elder sister Julia Maesa, who had been living with her, had returned to her home town Emesa. It is quite likely that she was forced to go there by the new emperor, as Herodian claims. After all, Maesa was a very rich and probably quite influential woman. Now, she and her family would be the axis of a military revolt against the unpopular Macrinus.

Julia Maesa had two grandsons by two daughters, the 14-year-old Varius Avitus and the nine-year-old Alexianus, who were both dedicated to the service of the local sun god Elagabal. The elder boy, Elagabalus, served as Elagabal's high priest. In this role, he attracted the attention of the soldiers of Legio III Gallica, a large garrison stationed not far from Emesa. Herodian describes:

> As Bassianus [Elagabalus] performed his priestly duties, dancing at the altars to the music of flutes and pipes and all kinds of instruments in the barbarian fashion, everyone, especially the soldiers, viewed him with fairly close interest because they knew he was a member of the imperial family (apart from the fact that his beautiful appearance attracted everyone's attention).[2]

According to Herodian, Julia Maesa told the soldiers that Caracalla had slept with both her daughters and that Elagabalus was actually Caracalla's bastard son. A rumour spread that the old lady was willing to distribute her immense wealth to the soldiers if they restored her family to power. Maesa and her family were invited to come to the camp at night, where Elagabalus was immediately acknowledged as emperor and clad in imperial purple.

Cassius Dio gives a rather different account of the events, making no mention of Elagabalus's priesthood of Elagabal and naming a certain Gannys as the main instigator of the revolt. This person, who is not mentioned in any other source, plays an important part in Dio's account of Elagabalus's rise to power. According to Dio, Gannys was a youth who 'had not as yet fully reached manhood'.[3] He had been raised by Julia Maesa and was the lover of Elagabalus's mother Julia Soaemias. Since Soaemias's husband was no longer alive, Gannys acted as the boy's protector and foster father. He allegedly dressed Elagabalus up in clothes which had been worn by Caracalla as a child, pretending that his young protégé was the murdered emperor's son, and smuggled him to the army camp at night without telling either Maesa or Soaemias. On the morning of 16 May 218, he persuaded the soldiers to revolt.

It is hard to believe that Julia Maesa, who had so much to gain if her grandson were to become emperor, was completely uninvolved in hatching the plot. On the other hand, it seems equally improbable that she acted completely on her own, as Herodian apparently suggests. Dio mentions that Gannys was supported by a few freedmen (former slaves) and soldiers, but also by some (unspecified) equestrians and senators of Emesa. This indicates that the initiative for the rebellion was taken not only by Maesa and her family, but also by part of the ruling elite of the Syrian town. Despite Dio's assurance to the contrary, we might wonder if any Roman senators or equestrians were in on the plan as well. Although it is impossible to establish how many conspirators were in on the coup, the involvement of powerful figures from Rome is certainly not beyond reasonable imagination.

Another detail is also of interest. Different though Dio's and Herodian's accounts may be, they both make mention of the story that Elagabalus was Caracalla's bastard son. Although almost certainly not true, this story would be of prime importance for Elagabalus's legitimation, as is apparent from the imperial name he took: Marcus Aurelius Antoninus, which had also been the official name of his 'father', Caracalla. The emperor even made his invented ancestry explicit by styling himself 'son of the divine Antoninus, grandson of the divine Severus'.[4] The implicit ideals of imperial succession were regarded in this way: the new Antoninus was not a usurper, but could claim the throne by rights of his blood. At the same time, the name held the promise of a continuation of Caracalla's military policy, which must have appealed greatly to the army.

Emperor Macrinus was staying in Antioch when word reached him of the rebellion at Emesa. According to Herodian, he did not take the threat too seriously, and sent his prefect Julianus to deal with it, but Dio records that Julianus was already in the vicinity of Emesa and acted on his own initiative. The prefect killed a daughter and son-in-law of Marcianus, the husband of Elagabalus's aunt Julia Mammaea. The passage does not mention Marcianus's own death, but it is highly likely that he was also killed sometime during the power struggle, since he is no longer mentioned in any source afterwards.

Julianus proceeded to lay siege to the camp in which Elagabalus, his family and the revolting legion were gathered. However, the besieged rebels made tempting promises to the attacking soldiers: namely, that they would receive the posts and possessions of their officers if they killed them; that Elagabalus would give back possessions and civil status to deserters; that he would pardon those who had been exiled; and (emphasised by Herodian) that riches would be distributed to those who joined the other side. As a result, the soldiers revolted and killed their officers.

According to Herodian, Julianus was beheaded on the spot, and his head sent to Macrinus in Antioch. The emperor then decided to pick up the sword himself. Dio gives a more elaborate version of the events. He records that Julianus managed to escape initially. Macrinus, on learning that his prefect had been beaten, hastened to Legio II Parthica, the Roman legion which was stationed at Apamea. There, he granted his ten-year-old son Diadumenianus, who up until that point had only held the honorary title of Caesar, the title of Augustus, making him his official co-ruler. This may be regarded as a last attempt at dynastic legitimation, especially since Diadumenianus bore the name Antoninus. However, Dio regards the act as no more than an excuse to load gifts and promises upon the troops and the people of Apamea. Whatever Macrinus's reasons, he failed to win the favour of Legio II Parthica. A soldier handed him a sack which turned out to contain the head of the prefect Julianus, who had apparently been captured after his initial escape.

The emperor, realising that his cause was lost with this legion, returned to Antioch and tried to gather an army there. Given the distance he had to travel, it is unlikely that he reached the Syrian capital before 27 May. Since the decisive battle took place on 8 June, Macrinus had less than two weeks to gather his forces. The nearest legion, IV Scythica, was stationed at Zeugma, more than 120 miles from Antioch; Legio XVI Flavia was even further away, at Samosata. Dio records that Elagabalus also sent messengers to these legions to win them for his cause, so we do not even know for certain that they fought entirely on Macrinus's side. However, the messengers sent by the usurper to Basilianus, prefect of Egypt and since the death of Julianus also praetorian prefect, and Marius Secundus, governor of Syria Phoenice, were put to death by these men.

Meanwhile, more and more troops were joining the ranks of Elagabalus. The whole of Legio II Parthica went over to the youthful pretender. As Hans-Georg Pflaum has argued, the commander of this legion was probably P. Valerius Comazon, who would play an important role during Elagabalus's reign.[5] With the support of a second legion, Elagabalus's chances of winning the throne increased significantly. According to Dio, the rebel troops marched on Antioch quickly, undoubtedly to give Macrinus as little time as possible to prepare himself. On 8 June, barely more than three weeks after Elagabalus had first been proclaimed emperor, the decisive battle took place at a small village near Antioch. Allegedly, it was Gannys who led Elagabalus's troops, despite his youth and the fact that he did not have any military experience. Macrinus seemed to be winning at first, but the tide turned when Maesa and Soaemias started encouraging the fleeing men and Elagabalus himself stormed forward on a horse with unsheathed sword. This terrified Macrinus, and he fled the battlefield, leaving victory to the young priest.

Although Elagabalus's uncharacteristically heroic role in the battle leaves room for doubt, Dio's account seems more likely than that of Herodian, who records that Macrinus took the initiative in the conflict and marched towards Emesa to defeat his rival. Elagabalus met the emperor at the border of Syria Phoenice and Syria Coele. Battle ensued, but when Macrinus saw many of his soldiers defecting to the other side, he fled the field. His remaining followers surrendered and joined the army of Elagabalus. In view of the lack of loyal troops Macrinus had at his disposal, it is hard to believe that he would have chosen to challenge the pretender so quickly, although he may have decided that this threat should be eliminated as soon as possible.

Whichever account comes closest to the truth, both Dio and Herodian agree that Macrinus met with a sorry end. The defeated emperor was arrested and killed when he tried to travel to Rome incognito. His son Diadumenianus, who had been Augustus for just a few weeks, met a similar fate.

Elagabalus entered Antioch as the new ruler, promising the soldiers 2000 sesterces apiece if they refrained from sacking the city. According to Dio, the victorious boy sent a message to the senate and the people of Rome, styling himself 'emperor and Caesar, the son of Antoninus, the grandson of Severus, Pius, Felix, Augustus, proconsul, and holder of the tribunician power' before these titles had been officially granted to him.[6] Once again, the senate was confronted with a *de facto* emperor whom it had no choice but to recognise. The 'dies imperii', the anniversary of Elagabalus's ascent to the throne, may have been 14 July, since that was the day on which the boy became a member of two important Roman priestly colleges, the arval brothers and the 'sodales Antoniniani'.[7] Just a few weeks earlier, the senate had declared war on him and his family at the instigation of Macrinus. Now the tables were turned and Macrinus was declared an enemy of the state. Elagabalus took over his predecessor's consulate for the remainder of the year, allowing the other consul, Oclatinius Adventus, to keep his post.

Yet even with the official approval of the senate, the position of the new emperor was by no means secure. Cassius Dio describes how several pretenders made their own bid for the purple now that Macrinus was out of the way. Ironically, one of them was Verus, the commander of Legio III Gallica, the legion which had first proclaimed Elagabalus emperor. Strict measures were taken against the pretenders: Verus was executed and the legion temporarily disbanded.[8] Gellius Maximus, the commander of Legio

IV Scythica, met with the same fate when he too rebelled. According to Dio, many others tried to seize power, including a worker in wool and a private citizen. It is highly likely that these stories tell us less about the reality than about Dio's opinion that if Elagabalus could become emperor, anybody could. Even so, the many imperial coins with legends like 'FIDES EXERCITVS' or 'CONCORDIA MILIT(VM)' suggest that the loyalty and unity of the army were certainly not taken for granted by the members of the recently restored dynasty and their supporters.[9]

The new Severan ruler and his family spent about a year in the East to consolidate their power, first in Antioch and later in Nicomedia, where they were forced to spend the winter. According to Herodian, Elagabalus immediately dressed in luxurious garb and began to practice the rites of his cult. His grandmother and advisers were left to deal with affairs. Dio records that Gannys was probably frequently employed as the emperor's associate in government. However, he allegedly soon lost imperial favour:

> To be sure, Gannys was living rather luxuriously and was fond of accepting bribes, but for all that he did no one any harm and bestowed many benefits upon many people. Most of all, he showed great zeal for the emperor and was thoroughly satisfactory to Maesa and Soaemias, to the former because he had been reared by her, and to the latter because he was virtually her husband. But it was not at all because of this that the emperor put him out of the way, inasmuch as he had wished to give him a marriage contract and appoint him Caesar; it was rather because he was forced by Gannys to live temperately and prudently. And he himself was the first to give Gannys a mortal blow with his own hand, since no one of the soldiers had the hardihood to take the lead in murdering him.[10]

The story sounds too much like a topos, a literary commonplace, meant to make Elagabalus look bad, to be credible – especially when we consider the comment on Gannys's own lifestyle. If we take Dio's word for it, Gannys himself made no effort to live up to the high moral standards he set for his pupil. We can only speculate about alternative explanations for the man's death, but perhaps his favoured position with the emperor made others, like Maesa and Comazon, decide that he was becoming too influential and had to be removed. Even if that was the case, however, it is anyone's guess who was responsible for his death.

Gannys was by no means the only person who perished. During the first year of Elagabalus's reign, many men who had supported Macrinus or were deemed untrustworthy for other reasons were executed. The list includes Fabius Agrippinus, governor of Syria Coele; Pica Caerianus, governor of Arabia; Aelius Triccianus, governor of Pannonia Inferior; and M. Munatius Sulla Cerialis, former governor of Cappadocia. The proconsul of Cyprus, L. Claudius Attalus, was allegedly killed because he had once sent Elagabalus's ally Comazon to the galleys as punishment for some unspecified crime. Julius Basilianus, prefect of Egypt and one of Macrinus's praetorian prefects, who had fled after the defeat of his master, was arrested and executed. Macrinus's other praetorian prefect, Julianus Nestor, was killed as well. Governors of the western part of the empire were apparently spared, perhaps because they had not been involved in the civil war.

According to Dio, Elagabalus's only praiseworthy act as emperor was that he refrained from punishing knights and senators who had insulted him or his 'father' Caracalla before he came to power. However, several senators lost their lives for other reasons. Seius Carus and Paetus Valerianus Galata were killed on the charge that they were plotting a rebellion to overthrow the emperor. Silius Messalla and Pomponius Bassus were condemned to death by the senate on the instigation of Elagabalus, officially because they were criticising imperial policy. According to Dio, that was not the real reason: Messalla had related many compromising (but unfortunately unspecified) facts to the senate, while Bassus had a wife the emperor wished to marry. In fact, these men had already been executed before they were condemned, reducing the judgement of the senate to a mere formality.

Others were rewarded for the support they had given to Elagabalus and his family during the revolt against Macrinus. Comazon, who had probably commanded Legio II Parthica, became praetorian prefect and shared the consulate with the emperor in 220. In addition, he became urban prefect of Rome three times. Legio II Parthica was rewarded as well, being granted the title 'pia felix fidelis aeterna', 'eternally dedicated, fortunate and loyal'.[11] Claudius Aelius Pollio, a centurion from an unspecified legion, received the rank of ex-consul and was made governor of Germania Superior because he had captured Diadumenianus and had subdued Bithynia for the new emperor. A certain '…atus', whose full name has not been preserved, was allowed to call himself the emperor's 'comes' and 'amicus fidissimus', 'companion' and 'most loyal friend'. We do not know which services he provided for Elagabalus, but he may have been the commander of Legio XVI Flavia Firma during the time of the revolt. Obviously, he managed to prove his loyalty to the new emperor, because he was made prefect of the grain supply, 'pontifex minor' (a priestly office) and eventually praetorian prefect. Perhaps he was rewarded for not joining in the rebellions of the commanders Verus and Gellius Maximus.[12]

After spending the winter of 218–19 in Nicomedia, Elagabalus and his family set off for Rome. Before they did so, the emperor allegedly made a remarkable decision. Herodian describes how Julia Maesa urged her grandson to wear Roman clothes when he entered the capital, but Elagabalus had different ideas:

> However, he was anxious that the senate and people of Rome should get used to seeing his dress, and to test out their reactions to the sight before he arrived. So an enormous picture was painted of him as he appeared in public performing as a priest. Also in the picture was a portrait of the Emesene god, to whom he was represented making a favourable sacrifice. The picture was sent to Rome with orders that it should hang right in the middle of the senate house, very high up over the head of the statue of Victory. This was where all the members, on arrival for meetings at the house, burn an offering of incense and make a libation of wine. Instructions were also issued to every Roman magistrate or person conducting public sacrifices that the new god Elagabal's name should precede any of the others invoked by the officiating priests.[13]

Although this story is not mentioned by Cassius Dio or any other ancient author, it touches on an interesting question: to what extent did the priesthood of Elagabal already interfere with Elagabalus's emperorship in this early stage of his reign?

Hans Baldus has pointed out a peculiar 'antoninianus' coin which must have been minted in Rome in 219 (see Fig. 6). It shows Elagabalus sacrificing at an altar in front of a chariot which carries the black stone of Emesa, the earthly representation of the god Elagabal. Since the portrait mentioned by Herodian was also said to portray both the sacrificing emperor and his god, Baldus believes the image on the coin was based on the painting.[14] If this painting indeed existed, Baldus may well be right. At the very least, the coin indicates that Elagabalus did not shy away from showing the sacred stone to the Roman public as soon as he arrived in the capital. The particular antoninianus even presents the stone as 'CONSERVATOR AVG(VSTI)', 'divine protector of the emperor'. Normally, this role was assigned to Jupiter. Some of Elagabalus's coins do indeed show Jupiter as conservator Augusti, although none of these can be dated later than 219 with certainty. It seems, therefore, that both Jupiter and Elagabal appeared as the emperor's protector during the first years of the reign. The Emesene deity played a subdued role on the coins which were minted in Rome in 218–19, but he was emphasised much more strongly on coins from the imperial mints in the East.[15]

The impression we get from all this is that Elagabal was brought to the attention of the Romans, but not without some caution. The portrait may have been sent ahead to test how the senate and people of Rome would react to it. Herodian's claim that the emperor commanded Elagabal to be invoked before all other gods – which basically meant that he was henceforth to be regarded as the supreme Roman deity – is almost certainly based on fact, but the command was probably not issued in Nicomedia. The historian, whose chronology is often inaccurate, may well have made this assumption, but the fact that Elagabal does not feature prominently on Roman coins in the first years of Elagabalus's reign pleads against it. Both epigraphic and numismatic evidence suggests that Elagabal replaced Jupiter as chief Roman god only at the end of 220, as we will see.

Setting out from Nicomedia, Elagabalus and his family travelled through Thrace, Moesia and both the Pannonian provinces, finally reaching Rome in the summer of 219. The exact date of their arrival is unknown, but Eutropius remarks that the emperor ruled in Rome for two years and eight months, which would place the imperial arrival in July.[16] Considering the emperor's slow progress and his devotion to Elagabal, it seems likely that the black stone travelled with him and entered the city together with its high priest. The aforementioned antoninianus from 219, showing both the emperor and his god, could be taken as support for this hypothesis.

Presumably not long after his arrival in the capital, Elagabalus married Julia Cornelia Paula, described by Herodian as 'a woman from the most aristocratic family in Rome'.[17] It seems an effort was made to make the emperor 'fit' into Roman high society. On coins, promises were made with regard to a steady grain supply ('ANNONA AVGVSTI') for the common people, while the elite were assured of civil liberty and legal security ('LIBERTAS').[18] To celebrate Elagabalus's arrival, and to boost his popularity, many lavish spectacles were organised and a cash bonus was paid to the people. For the first time in years, Rome could look upon the face of an emperor again.


EMPEROR OF ROME


To what extent was the reign of Elagabalus actually the reign of Elagabalus himself? After all, the emperor was only 14 years old when he gained the throne, and had no political experience whatsoever. Not surprisingly, the accounts of his rise to power all strongly suggest that he was mostly a tool for the ambition of others. But which others? The most obvious answer, commonly given by both ancient and modern historians, seems to be the clan from Emesa, led by Julia Maesa. After the murder of Caracalla had temporarily turned the fortune of this wealthy and influential family, it once again managed to rise to the centre of power by means of Elagabalus's dynastic claim.

Both Julia Maesa and Julia Soaemias feature prominently in the literary accounts of Elagabalus's reign, and are credited with much influence. According to the *Historia Augusta*, Julia Soaemias was allowed to attend meetings of the senate, and even took charge of a 'senaculum' or 'women's senate', deciding on matters of fashion and protocol. The story is probably the product of the author's characteristic exaggeration, but there may be a grain of truth in it. In several inscriptions dedicated to Elagabalus, Julia Maesa and Julia Soaemias are also mentioned. Julia Maesa is honoured with the titles 'Augusta, mater castrorum et senatus' ('mother of the army camps and the senate') and 'avia Augusti' ('grandmother of the emperor'), while Julia Soaemias is called 'Augusta, mater Augusti' ('mother of the emperor') and in one instance even 'mater castrorum et senatus et totius domus divinae' ('mother of the army camps and the senate and the whole divine house').[19] Both women were often portrayed on imperial coins with the honorary title 'AVGVSTA', strengthening the impression that they were the ones really in charge while the young and inexperienced Elagabalus sat on the Roman throne.

However, several other factors need to be taken into account. Firstly, Julia Maesa and Julia Soaemias were not the only women thus honoured by the emperor. His successive wives Julia Paula, Aquilia Severa and Annia Faustina likewise appeared on coins and bore the title 'AVGVSTA'. Secondly, Septimius Severus had already focused on his wife Julia Domna by giving her a prominent place on his coinage and granting her the titles 'AVGVSTA', 'MATER CASTRORVM' and 'MATER DEVM'. In doing so, he stressed the idea that the principate was connected not just to him personally, but to his whole family. His house was a 'domus divina', a 'divine house', destined to rule the empire. Elagabalus and his advisers probably had the same intention when they issued coins of the emperor's wives and family members. Notably, the title 'mater castrorum' does not feature on Elagabalus's coinage, whereas 'mater deum' ('mother of the gods') appears only on two types of Julia Soaemias coinage.[20] The other women just bear the title 'Augusta'. It does not necessarily follow that Julia Maesa and Julia Soaemias were without power during Elagabalus's reign, but we can only guess how far their influence actually extended. It seems a bit hasty to conclude that 'the greater part of the civilised world was ruled by women', as Michael Grant does.[21]

Two people who appear to have had considerable influence in the period 218–22 were P. Valerius Comazon and … atus. As has already been discussed, Comazon was probably the commander of Legio II Parthica. Elagabalus promoted him to the post of praetorian prefect and shared the consulate with him in 220. Since inscriptions mention Comazon as consul 'iterum' (for the second time) he must have been elevated to the rank of consul earlier, probably when the imperial company was still in Syria.[22] Dio mentions that Comazon became city prefect three times, the last of which was under Severus Alexander: 'for just as a mask used to be carried into the theatres to occupy the stage during the intervals in the acting, when it was left vacant by the comic actors, so Comazon was put in the vacant place of the men who had been city prefects in his day.'[23] Although the remark implies that Comazon was no more than a puppet used by his superiors whenever they deemed it convenient, the impressive number of important posts held by this man between 218 and 222 suggests otherwise. The same goes for the elusive … atus, who does not appear to be mentioned by name in the literary sources, but was granted the titles 'comes' and 'amicus fidissimus' of the emperor, became prefect of the grain supply, 'pontifex minor' and eventually praetorian prefect.

Since both Comazon and … atus came from a military background, their powerful positions may indicate the army's influence during the reign of Elagabalus. However, after the emperor had arrived in Rome and his position was relatively secure, there is nothing to suggest that military matters played a major role in the imperial administration. No wars were waged by Elagabalus, nor was the army much emphasised on imperial coins after 219. Perhaps another group benefited more from the restoration of the Severan dynasty. A survey of the men who were certainly or probably of senatorial status in the period 218–22 makes it clear that there was much continuity with earlier and later reigns.[24] Many senators who had held administrative posts under Septimius Severus and/or Caracalla continued to do so under Elagabalus. Likewise, many senators who had a hand in governing the empire under Elagabalus continued their career in the reign of Severus Alexander.

In all likelihood, some of these men had strong ties to the Severan house. A good example may be M. Aufidius Fronto, who had been consul under Septimius Severus in 199 and was made proconsul of Asia by Elagabalus; or C. Vettius Gratus Sabinianus, who held the consulate in

221 and was a member of a family which had probably achieved patrician status by the end of the second century.[25] The pro-Severan segment of the senate probably approved of Elagabalus's rise to power, and may even have had a hand in starting the revolt against Macrinus. It is certainly not inconceivable, and perhaps even likely, that some of these supporting senators were a major political influence during the reigns of Elagabalus and his equally young and inexperienced successor, Severus Alexander.

In the end, it is impossible to tell for certain which people or groups of people wielded the most power during the reign of Elagabalus. The members of the Emesene family were certainly not the only ones who benefited from the restoration of the Severan dynasty. It may have been in the interests of many political players to keep an 'heir of Caracalla' on the Roman throne. These could include senators who were closely affiliated with the Severan family, knights who had held important posts under Caracalla, and jurists who had been influential in the emperor's personal council.

Apart from religious matters, the reign of Elagabalus does not appear to have been very remarkable or innovative. After the defeat of Macrinus, no wars were waged, nor were there any important political or economic reforms. Nevertheless, ancient writers heavily criticise the way Elagabalus allegedly governed the empire. The most common accusation, uttered by all the major sources, concerns the appointment of unworthy and unqualified favourites in important administrative posts. According to Herodian, 'the emperor was driven to such extremes of lunacy that he took men from the stage and the public theatres and put them in charge of most important imperial business.'[26] The *Historia Augusta* records that candidates for honorary functions were selected for the size of their private parts. Honours, distinctions and positions of power were sold or given to chariot-drivers, dancers and mule-drivers, who now became governors, consuls and generals. Dio is less elaborate on the subject, but sums it all up by stating that Elagabalus favoured those who had supported him in his uprising or committed adultery with him.

Most of the names mentioned in the literary sources as the emperor's scandalous appointees cannot be traced back to inscriptions or papyri. The one possible exception is Aurelius Zoticus, who, according to Dio, was the son of a cook and became Elagabalus's lover. The emperor allegedly made him 'cubicularius' (chamberlord) because of his huge member, but banned him from the palace when he could not produce an erection. The *Historia Augusta* also mentions Zoticus and credits him with much influence during the young emperor's reign. An inscription from the reign of Severus Alexander mentions one Zoticus as 'nomenclator a censibus'.[27] We cannot exclude the possibility that this is the same person, who may have returned after the death of the emperor who had banned him. Even so, Zoticus is only said to have become 'cubicularius': a potentially influential post, perhaps, but a far cry from general or consul.

No evidence can be found for the existence of Hierocles, the beautiful chariot-driver with whom Elagabalus supposedly fell in love. This does not necessarily mean that there was no such person, but renders it quite doubtful that Hierocles had more power than the emperor himself, as Dio claims, let alone that Elagabalus planned to make him Caesar. Likewise, the numerous actors and dancers who supposedly ruled the empire between 218 and 222 have left no discernable traces. The only 'unworthy' governors of whom we have any knowledge are two equestrians who were put in charge of provinces which were traditionally governed by senators: Ulpius Victor in Dacia Porolissensis and M. Aedinius Julianus in Gallia Aquitania and Lugdunensis.[28] However, the practice of appointing equestrians to senatorial posts had already started under Septimius Severus. The policy was probably adopted to reduce the risk of rebellions in the provinces, and was by no means an innovation of the Syrian clan.

On the other hand, Dio is right in stating that Elagabalus favoured those who had supported him in his uprising. The most obvious example of this is undoubtedly Comazon, who joined forces with the pretender from Emesa and may have played a crucial role in the defeat of Macrinus. Figures like Claudius Aelius Pollio and ... atus also benefited from their services to the new ruler, although ... atus probably fought for Macrinus in the battle of 8 June 218, and proved his loyalty only later. Dio also mentions a certain Aurelius Eubulus, a native Emesene who was made head of the *fiscus* and apparently invoked universal hatred by his depraved lifestyle and his many confiscations of property. Perhaps Eubulus was one of the Emesene senators involved in the plot to put Elagabalus on the throne.

Not everybody prospered. According to the *Vita Heliogabali* and Aurelius Victor respectively, Elagabalus banished the famous jurists Paul and Ulpian from Rome.[29] No clear reason is given for the misfortune of these men. Tony Honoré speculates that both Paul and Ulpian may have held important posts before they fell out of favour with Elagabalus, the former as praefectus praetorio and the latter as praefectus annonae.[30] However, there is no evidence to support this hypothesis.

The list of consuls from the period 218–22 is a mixture of traditionally acceptable candidates and favourite 'homines novi', 'new men'. With the exception of 221, Elagabalus was consul in each year of his reign. In 218, his opposite number in this post was M. Oclatinius Adventus, who had been appointed by Macrinus and was allowed to remain in office. Q. Tineius Sacerdos, who shared the consulate with the emperor in 219, was an Italian of noble ancestry and had already been consul 'suffectus' in 192.[31] The traditional Roman elite probably considered him a worthy candidate for the office. That would hardly have been true in the case of the upstart Comazon, who had already been granted the 'ornamenta consularia' (the honorary status of a consul without actually holding the office) and became consul 'iterum' in 220. In 221, the consulate was held by C. Vettius Gratus Sabinianus and M. Flavius Vitellius Seleucus. The former was a senator from a respectable family; the latter's ancestry is unknown to us. He was probably a Syrian, which may or may not have something to do with the fact that he was appointed consul.[32] Severus Alexander, who shared the consulate with Elagabalus in 222, obtained the office because he was a member of the imperial family and – since the summer of 221 – the emperor's adopted son and heir.

All in all, the stories about Elagabalus's excessive favouritism seem little more than negative rhetoric, meant further to discredit an emperor of whom the ancient authors did not think much in the first place. The appointment of some loyal allies into powerful positions seems hardly any justification for the outrageous comments in the literary sources. As has been remarked before, both the structure of the senate and the appointment of government officials in 218–22 show much continuity with the reigns of Caracalla and Severus Alexander. Accusations of mismanagement in this field cannot be substantiated.

The financial policy under Elagabalus was in many respects a continuation of the financial policy of Caracalla. The production of the antoninianus, the new coin which this emperor had introduced, had ceased under Macrinus. Elagabalus minted antoniniani again, but only until 219. He also continued the trend of coin debasement. During the reign of Caracalla, 192 denarii had been minted out of one pound of silver; under Elagabalus, this number rose to 228. The median of the purity of silver coinage fell from 51 per cent under Caracalla to 45.5 under Elagabalus. Gold coins stayed roughly stable at 99 per cent, a purity which they had already had in the days of Augustus. The number of aurei minted from one pound of gold had risen from 41 to 50 between Augustus and Caracalla, but hardly changed between Caracalla and Elagabalus.[33]

The *Historia Augusta* in particular accuses Elagabalus of squandering huge amounts of money and goods. If the author of the *Vita Heliogabali* is to be believed, the emperor built many baths, houses, palaces and summer dwellings in Rome. However, few remains have been found of this supposedly outrageous building programme. Apart from a circus and two temples for Elagabal, which shall be discussed later in this chapter, Elagabalus's main building activities in Rome seem to have consisted of putting up columns around the Baths of Caracalla and making repairs to the Colosseum, which had been struck by lightning in 217.[34] In the provinces, several inscriptions are devoted to Elagabalus for erecting or restoring buildings. The emperor's name also occurs on some milestones.[35] This indicates that the imperial administration made an effort to maintain buildings and infrastructure outside Rome, despite a comment in the *Vita Heliogabali* that Elagabalus completely neglected the provinces after his arrival in the capital.

Accusations of squandering money may be more justified with regard to the 'congiaria' (money grants to the people) in the period 218–22. Coins show that no less than four gifts were distributed during the short reign of Elagabalus. As Richard Duncan-Jones has indicated, this was the highest number of congiaria per year in the principate until the reign of Maximinus Thrax (235–38). Roughly estimated, Elagabalus spent about 630 sesterces per person per year on gifts – 2400 sesterces per person for the whole of his reign, or 113 million sesterces per year.[36] Herodian also mentions that the emperor instituted many festivals and constructed circuses and theatres, 'imagining that, if he provided chariot races and all kinds of spectacles and entertainments, and if he feasted the people all night long, he would be popular'. Indeed, the remains of a circus built in the Horti Spei Veteris are attributed to Elagabalus, suggesting that although Herodian's account is probably exaggerated, it may have a grain of truth to it.[37]

The money which Elagabalus spent on gifts and entertainment for his subjects may partially account for the high taxes which, according to the author of the *Historia Augusta*, existed under the young ruler. When Severus Alexander ascended the throne, the cities of the empire were apparently so financially strained that he refrained from demanding the traditional coronation tax, the 'aurum coronarium', due from them.[38] Still, we need to bear in mind that the state had also been confronted with big expenditures by Elagabalus's immediate predecessors, such as Caracalla's military campaigns, which may still have pressed on the imperial budget. In contrast, the new emperor did not wage any expensive wars. If taxes were indeed as high as the *Historia Augusta* claims, the administration of Elagabalus cannot be held solely responsible for this.

RELIGIOUS REFORMS

Elagabalus's religious reforms are without doubt the most striking and notorious feature of his reign. Dethroning Jupiter as the chief Roman god in favour of an exotic, unknown deity was a measure without precedent, defying many centuries of Roman tradition. What did Elagabalus hope to achieve by reorganising the state religion? Which new religious order did he have in mind? Whatever the answers to these questions are, there can be little doubt that the emperor's radical reforms must have gravely offended everyone who was attached to traditional Roman religion. Therefore, it seems highly unlikely that the initiative for these reforms was taken by Elagabalus's political allies, who supported him in order to gain or maintain political power.

It must have been the emperor himself, high priest of Elagabal since his days in Emesa, who wanted to promote his local god. Zosimus mentions that Elagabalus spent his time with 'mages and charlatans'.[39] Considering that both the high priest and the black stone of Elagabal had gone to Rome, they were probably accompanied by many other priests and servants of the sun god. If that was indeed the case, it seems likely that they wielded great influence over the young, devout emperor.

Elagabalus may have listened to his Syrian priests, but he seems to have been outside the control of his other advisers. If we accept that the boy was put on the throne mainly as a puppet, meant to serve the interests of others, it is obvious that the scheme backfired. The young emperor may not have taken much interest in the business of governing the empire, but he had very strong views on religious matters and did not hesitate to act on them. To some extent, Elagabalus's reforms may have been supported by the members of his family, who probably likewise worshipped Elagabal. However, a quick glance at the reign of Severus Alexander is enough to establish that at least some members of the Emesene clan were willing to distance themselves from the invincible sun god if it seemed politically opportune. The same cannot be said of Elagabalus, the 'priest-emperor', who would persist in his devotion to Sol Invictus Elagabal until his death.

Cassius Dio records that Elagabalus let himself be voted priest of Elagabal in Rome. Frey points out that the senator makes use of the word 'ψηφισθῆναι', which he uses in other instances to indicate that the senate voted to honour somebody with the imperial titles. Apparently, Elagabalus instructed the senate to include his priesthood of Elagabal in his official titles as Roman emperor. Some inscriptions mention him not only as 'pontifex maximus', but also as 'sacerdos amplissimus dei invicti Solis Elagabali', 'most elevated priest of the invincible sun god Elagabal'.[40] Imperial coins bear the legends 'SACERD(OS) DEI SOLIS ELAGAB(ALI)', 'SVMMVS SACERDOS AVG(VSTVS)' and 'INVICTVS SACERDOS AVG(VSTVS)'; 'priest of the sun god Elagabal', 'highest priest-emperor' and 'invincible priest-emperor'.[41] As far as the coins can be dated exactly, these legends occur only in the period 220–22. The inscriptions with the 'sacerdos' title can all be dated to 221 or 222, with one exception from 220. Therefore, we can assume that the senate voted Elagabalus high priest of Elagabal at the end of 220.

When he mentions that Elagabalus was voted priest of Elagabal, Dio remarks in the same sentence that the Emesene deity was elevated above all other gods, including Jupiter. Although Herodian claims that the emperor had already ordered Elagabal to be invoked before all other gods while he was in Nicomedia during the winter of 218–19, it seems likely that the elevation of Elagabal to chief Roman deity occurred at the same time as the senate acknowledged the emperor as Elagabal's high priest. Some coin types already mention the black stone as 'CONSERVATOR AVGVSTI' before 220, but Jupiter was honoured as 'IOVI CONSERVATORI' until at least 219, possibly longer. Only after 220 does the traditional chief Roman god disappear completely from Elagabalus's coinage. From then on, only Elagabal served as the emperor's divine protector.[42]

As becomes clear from inscriptions, the Emesene deity was looked after by at least one sun priest, called 'sacerdos Solis Elagabali', although there were probably more. Interestingly enough, this man – Titus Julius Balbillus – had already been sacerdos Solis during the reigns of Septimius Severus and Caracalla.[43] Although the inscriptions mentioning Elagabal in the priestly title cannot be dated, it seems likely that this specification was added only during the reign of Elagabalus. Alternatively, Balbillus may already have been appointed priest of Elagabal in Rome on the instigation of Julia Domna, but if that was the case, the god does not seem to have played a prominent role in the religious life of Rome before the arrival of its high priest and cult object in 219.

The obvious question is what sparked these remarkable reforms halfway through Elagabalus's reign? Before 220, Elagabal had featured prominently only on the imperial coins minted in the East. If the coinage can be taken as any indication of imperial attitude, Roman religious traditions must have been largely respected in this early period. Why did that change at the end of 220? As far as we can tell, no particular incident occurred which may have caused the unprecedented measures described. Possibly, they were simply the consequence of Elagabalus's increasing power within his own court. After all, the emperor was no longer a 14-year-old boy at this point. He must have been 16 or even 17 years old at the end of 220, an age at which he could well be expected to take initiatives of his own and act against the will of those who disagreed with his point of view. In short, the boy on the throne was growing into a man – a man with strong religious convictions.

An alternative explanation may be that the years 218–20 should be interpreted as a period of 'preparation' for the Roman people, intended to acquaint them with the cult of their new ruler before Elagabalus's religious programme was unfolded in all its exotic glory. This would explain why Elagabal already played a subdued role on imperial coinage in these early years: the black stone did not just appear on coins minted in the East (see Fig. 5), but also on at least one (rare) type of antoninianus, minted in Rome in 219 (Fig. 6). Several Roman coins showing an anthropomorphic Sol were issued. Since the image was not accompanied by a legend identifying the god as Sol Elagabal, it may have been left deliberately vague whether or not the god was supposed to be the Emesene deity.[44] Additionally, there is Herodian's story about the portrait which the emperor sent from Nicomedia to Rome. If true, this would have been the city's first official introduction to the black stone and its high priest, months before the two would actually enter the capital.

Another indication that the religious reforms may have involved some planning in advance is the building of an 'enormous and magnificent' temple for Elagabal. According to the *Historia Augusta*, this temple should be located on the Palatine. Allegedly, it was located on the spot where the temple of Orcus ('aedes Orci') had been before. Since no such building is known to us, several alternative readings have been proposed, such as 'Adonidis horti' or 'Adonaea horti'.[45] Excavations by the École française de Rome on the Palatine have provided an answer to the riddle. Archaeologists have identified foundations on the site of the Vigna Barberini, next to the palace, as belonging to the Elagabal temple. In its entirety, the complex covered an area of 160 by 110 metres (see Figs 11 and 12).[46]

The sixth-century chronicler Cassiodorus mentions that the temple was completed in 221. Hieronymus, who wrote his chronicle in the fourth century CE, dates the completion of the temple even earlier, to 220.[47] Because it mentions the names of the consuls, Cassiodorus's date may be more accurate, but that still means that the temple of Elagabal was finished – or at least ready to be used – within one year of the religious reforms at most. Moreover, Herodian also mentions a second temple, built in the suburbs. Since this temple is described in words similar to those used for the temple on the Palatine, and is not mentioned in any other source, its existence could be doubted, but Herodian adds that the black stone was moved from the Palatine to the suburb temple each year at midsummer. He gives a very detailed description of the ceremonial procession accompanying the god, which makes the notion of a second temple credible. The second sanctuary may have been situated on the site of the Vigna Bonelli, in Trastevere.[48]

How did Elagabalus manage to build two temples within a year of the elevation of Elagabal to chief deity of the empire? One possible answer would be that the construction of the temples started early in the reign, right after, or even before, the emperor's arrival in Rome. However, it is also possible that existing temples were rededicated to the sun god. In Trastevere, a quarter where many gods from the Near East were worshipped, inscriptions record the existence of a temple for the Palmyrene god Bel. It seems plausible that Elagabalus devoted this sanctuary to Elagabal, as François Chausson argues.[49] At the same time, Balbillus, who was active in the area as sacerdos Solis, as inscriptions attest, may have been promoted to sacerdos Solis Elagabali.

It has been suggested that Elagabal's temple on the Palatine had originally been the temple of Jupiter Victor. This building, depicted on a coin from Trajan's reign, supposedly looks remarkably like Elagabal's temple on a medallion from the reign of Elagabalus.[50] However, the differences between the two sanctuaries are too great to justify the conclusion that they are the same building. Arguing from archaeological evidence, Henri Broise and Yvon Thébert state that the temple was basically a creation *ex nihilo*, built on an already existing terrace.[51] However, it would not necessarily take years to erect such a building. Besides, even if the emperor started construction right after his arrival in Rome, that only indicates the intention to grant Elagabal an important place in the capital. The temple occupied a prominent location in the urban landscape, but we should keep in mind that it was erected on the grounds of the palace – that is, on private property. Therefore, it does not necessarily follow that Elagabalus already intended to elevate the Emesene deity to the head of the Roman pantheon at this early stage.

One important event seems to argue against the notion that Elagabalus's religious reforms were planned years in advance. This is the marriage of the emperor to the vestal virgin Aquilia Severa, to be discussed in more detail shortly. Obviously, this union of priest and priestess must have had some religious significance. Yet if Elagabalus had meant to marry Severa from the start, why then did he first take Julia Paula as his bride? According to Dio, Julia Paula was dismissed because she had a blemish on her body. Frey interprets this as meaning that she was deemed unfit for an upcoming religious ceremony, namely a symbolic marriage with the emperor to mirror the marriage of the god Elagabal to the goddess Urania.[52] However, blemish or no blemish, Elagabalus marrying Julia Paula could never have had the same religious connotations as him marrying Aquilia Severa, since Julia Paula was not a priestess, let alone a vestal. Therefore, the idea of the priest-emperor marrying a Roman priestess must have been conceived only after Julia Paula had already become Elagabalus's wife. At the very least, this suggests that the religious course which Elagabalus and his supporters were pursuing left some room for changes of plan.

Rather than presuming a carefully planned and prepared reorganisation of state religion, we should probably see the growing role of Elagabal during Elagabalus's reign as the consequence of a number of more or less spontaneous decisions. The emperor, whose influence probably increased when he became older, went ever further in glorifying and promoting his personal god. In all likelihood, it was left to his subordinates to 'sell' his actions to an increasingly bemused and disgruntled public.

From 220 onwards, and to some extent perhaps also before that time, the people of Rome were frequently confronted with unfamiliar religious events. Dio and Herodian both mention that Elagabalus appeared publicly in his 'Oriental' priestly garb, which according to Dio earned him the nickname 'the Assyrian'. The story is confirmed by coins which show Elagabalus sacrificing, wearing a pair of Parthian trousers and a long cloak (see Figs 8 and 9).[53] Considering that he now styled himself 'sacerdos amplissimus' of Elagabal, it is hardly surprising that the emperor would dress according to his priestly office. Herodian gives us the impression that Elagabalus wore the priestly garb all the time, but Dio contradicts this by stating that he appeared in it 'frequently'.[54] If this is true, it indicates that the young ruler acknowledged that he had other tasks apart from being Elagabal's high priest. Nevertheless, serving Elagabal was probably Elagabalus's main concern. Herodian describes how the emperor made huge, public sacrifices to his god on a daily basis:

> Each day at dawn he came out and slaughtered a hecatomb of cattle and a large number of sheep which were placed upon the altars and loaded with every variety of spices. In front of the altars many jars of the finest and oldest wines were poured out, so that streams of blood and wine flowed together. Around the altars he and some Phoenician women danced to the sounds of many different instruments, circling the altars with cymbals and drums in their hands. The entire senate and the equestrian order stood round them in the order they sat in the theatre. The entrails of the sacrificial victims and spices were carried in golden bowls, not on the heads of household servants or lower-class people, but by military prefects and important officials wearing long tunics in the Phoenician style down to their feet, with long sleeves and a single purple stripe in the middle. They also wore linen shoes of the kind used by local oracle priests in Phoenicia. It was considered a great honour had been done to anyone given a part in the sacrifice.[55]

Cassius Dio confirms that the emperor danced while making sacrifices, but does not record that all senators and knights were obliged to attend these daily rituals, let alone that they had to take part in them. This could be explained by the sloppy, badly organised nature of Dio's account of the reign, although one would not expect him to keep silent about such an affront to Roman tradition and senatorial dignity. Although Herodian's account is too detailed to be dismissed completely, it is possible that he is exaggerating about the frequency of the ritual and the number of people who had to attend. Nevertheless, the mandatory presence of senators and knights at public sacrifices to Elagabal seems to fit well within the new religious order Elagabalus was trying to establish. After all, the Emesene sun god was now the chief deity of Roman state religion. When Elagabalus was sacrificing as its high priest, he was acting as a state magistrate.

Another event which Herodian describes in detail is the procession of the black stone from the Palatine temple to its suburban sanctuary. According to Herodian, the god made this journey each year at midsummer. It is not clear why the stone should have been moved from one temple to the other, but it must have been quite a spectacular sight:

> The god was set up in a chariot studded with gold and precious stones and driven from the city to the suburb. The chariot was drawn by a team

of six large, pure white horses which had been decorated with lots of gold and ornamented discs. No human person ever sat in the chariot or held the reins, which were fastened to the god as though he were driving himself. Antoninus [the emperor] ran along in front of the chariot, but facing backwards as he ran looking at the god and holding the bridles of the horses. He ran the whole way backwards like this looking up at the front of the god. But to stop him tripping and falling while he was not looking where he was going, lots of sand gleaming like gold was put down, and his bodyguard supported him on either side to make sure he was safe as he ran like this. Along both sides of the route the people ran with a great array of torches, showering wreaths and flowers on him. In the procession, in front of the god, went images of all the other gods and valuable or precious temple dedications and all the imperial standards or costly heirlooms. Also the cavalry and all the army joined in.[56]

Afterwards, Elagabalus made sacrifices to Elagabal and then climbed on to a high tower, from which he threw down presents to the crowd: gold and silver cups, all kinds of clothes, fine linen and even domestic animals. This last category may be inspired by Lucian's *De Dea Syria*, in which the author mentions that animals were thrown from the temple of Atargatis in Hierapolis.[57] On the other hand, it could also indicate that a similar custom existed in Emesa. According to Herodian, the gift-giving resulted in a scramble, in which many people were trampled to death or impaled on the soldiers' spears.

One of the most remarkable stories about Elagabalus is that he married a vestal virgin. At first, this may seem like no more than a topos, made up to illustrate how bad a tyrant the emperor was. The worship of Vesta was one of the most important cults in Rome; marrying a vestal virgin would mean nothing less than an outright insult to Roman religion. However, given the violations of tradition he had already committed, there seems no reason to assume that such a deed would be beyond Elagabalus. Indeed, several clues indicate that the marriage actually took place. Firstly, the affair is recorded by all three major literary sources, although Herodian is the only one explicitly stating that the pair got married. Secondly, Dio provides us with the name of the emperor's priestly spouse: Aquilia Severa. According to Dio, she was not just any vestal virgin, but Vesta's high priestess. Her name is mentioned on imperial coins, accompanied by the epithet 'AVG(VSTA)'. The reverse of one coin type shows Elagabalus and Severa clasping hands; another bears the legend 'VESTA'.[58] Although the latter probably does not mean much – some coins of Julia Paula, Julia Soaemias and Julia Maesa bear the same legend – the evidence seems to be in favour of the story of this remarkable union between the emperor and Vesta's high priestess.

An exact date for the marriage cannot be given. By looking at Alexandrian and Syrian coins, Joseph Vogt has concluded that Elagabalus probably married Aquilia Severa at the beginning of 221. There are plenty of Alexandrian coins with Julia Paula from the fourth year of Elagabalus's reign, which, according to the Alexandrian count, started on 29 August 220. Moreover, several Syrian coins attest that Julia Paula was still empress in the autumn of 220.[59] Frey dates a bronze medallion showing Elagabalus and Severa on the obverse before the start of 221, a date he derives from the fact that the emperor is still portrayed completely beardless.[60] This would place the marriage sometime at the end of 220 – around the same time as the elevation of Elagabal to chief Roman deity.

Why did Elagabalus take such an extraordinary step, violating one of Rome's most important and revered cults? According to Dio, the emperor was quite clear on his motivation: 'Indeed, he had the boldness to say: "I did it in order that godlike children might spring from me, the high priest, and from her, the high priestess."'[61] This seems plausible enough. By marrying Aquilia Severa, Elagabalus could found a priestly, 'godlike' dynasty to rule Rome after him. At the same time, the marriage forged a personal bond between the traditional state religion of Rome, represented by its most important priestess, and the cult of the new chief god Elagabal, represented by the emperor as sacerdos amplissimus. Ironically, therefore, this highly controversial act may well have been intended to bring the religions of Rome and Emesa closer together.

Herodian records that it was not just the emperor who got married, but Elagabal as well. Apparently, the god's first bride was the goddess Athena, symbolised by her cult object, the Palladium. However, this goddess was too warlike for the tastes of Elagabal, so the union was dissolved and new arrangements were made. The statue of the Punic goddess Urania was brought from Carthage to Rome, accompanied by all the gold from her temple. Not just Rome, but the whole of Italy was instructed to celebrate the divine marriage. Dio makes no mention of Elagabal marrying Athena, but confirms that the sun god took Urania as his bride. He adds that she brought two golden lions as a dowry, while the emperor collected wedding gifts from his subjects.[62]

An inscription which was found in the Spanish city of Córdoba (Corduba in antiquity) mentions Elagabal together with two goddesses.

One of these is Athena Allath, whose name immediately brings the alleged marriage between the sun god and Athena to mind. The name of the other is damaged, but has been reconstructed as Kypris Charinazaia. Kypris was a Cyprian love goddess of Phoenician origin. Frey argues that she was brought from Cyprus to Carthage, where she was connected to the moon and became known as Urania – Elagabal's divine bride, according to Dio and Herodian.[63]

The question remains why Elagabalus chose to import a goddess from Carthage as a bride for his god, instead of picking a deity from Rome or Syria. Perhaps the Punic cult object was chosen simply because it was famous and highly venerated, or because of the mythical bonds between Rome and Carthage, the latter being the city where Aeneas sailed from to find a new home in Italy. Moreover, Urania was a moon goddess, so that a marriage between her and the sun god Elagabal could be interpreted as a symbol of cosmic harmony. Herodian indicates as much by stating that the emperor deemed a marriage between the sun and the moon to be 'very appropriate'.[64]

Dio and Herodian do not connect the marriage(s) of Elagabal with the marriages of the emperor. Nevertheless, some modern historians have tried to relate these unions to each other. Halsberghe thinks that Elagabalus married Aquilia Severa to establish a link between the cult of Elagabal and the cult of Vesta, thereby attempting to make the Emesene deity more popular with the Romans. For the same reason, the emperor supposedly intended to marry Elagabal to Vesta. That he married the god to Athena instead should be seen as a mistake: according to Halsberghe, Elagabalus mistook the Palladium for a representation of Vesta because it was kept in Vesta's temple. The modern historian presumes that both the imperial and the divine marriages caused so much consternation that Julia Maesa managed to persuade her grandson to dissolve them. Elagabalus then married Annia Faustina, while Elagabal got Urania as his new bride. Halsberghe concludes, 'This choice gave evidence of greater wisdom and caution, and also satisfied the requirements of the situation completely, so that with it Elagabalus crowned his work of reform.'[65]

The notion that the emperor would mistake the Palladium for a representation of Vesta seems hard to believe. Frey dismisses the whole marriage between Elagabal and Athena as false, a fantasy sprouting from Herodian's misunderstanding of what actually happened. He points at a capital found at the Forum Romanum, which was in all likelihood part of the great Elagabal temple on the Palatine. It shows the black stone of Elagabal, a conical stone with an eagle in front of it, flanked by two damaged figures who probably represent Athena Allath and Kypris Charinazaia, or Athena and Urania (Fig. 13).[66] If Elagabal exchanged one wife for another, one would not expect Athena and Urania to appear together. Therefore, Frey argues that both female deities formed a *trias* with Elagabal, a standard couple of three in which Urania was the sun god's wife and Athena perhaps their daughter.[67] Although this theory sounds plausible, we should also allow for the possibility that Elagabal took Urania as his second wife, without divorcing Athena. That way, Herodian could be right after all in claiming that there were two divine marriages.

Frey connects the marriage of Elagabal to Urania with the marriage of Elagabalus to Aquilia Severa. He points out that, in Semitic religions, a marriage of the gods was often mirrored on earth by a symbolic marriage between the king and the queen or a priestess. These marriages were celebrated at the beginning of a new year, which in Syria and Phoenicia started in the autumn.[68] Could it be that the emperor married the high priestess of the vestal virgins to mirror the marriage of his god to Urania? The theory does not seem to fit the literary accounts very well. After all, if the union of Elagabalus and Severa had been symbolical of the union of Elagabal and Urania, then one would have expected Elagabalus to marry a priestess of Urania or Venus, not one of Vesta – or, vice versa, to marry Elagabal to Vesta instead of Urania.

Pietrzykowski, who agrees with Frey that Elagabal married only once, suggests that the marriage of the Emesene deity to Urania was a means to introduce Elagabal, Kypris Charinazaia and Athena Allath as the new triad of Rome, taking the places of the traditional Jupiter, Juno and Minerva.[69] This seems like a plausible theory, even if we take into account the possibility that Elagabal did not just marry Urania/Kypris, but took Athena (Allath) as his wife as well. However, evidence is scarce. Juno appears on the reverse of a coin of Julia Paula as 'IVNO CONSERVATRIX', but is absent from the coins of Aquilia Severa and Annia Faustina. Also, coins of Julia Soaemias bear both the legends 'IVNO REGINA' and 'VENVS CAELESTIS' on the reverse.[70] Possibly, the former have been struck before the introduction of the new triad and the latter afterwards, but since the coins cannot be dated exactly, this is mere speculation. In the end, the emperor's motivations for the divine marriage(s) of Elagabal remain a puzzle without any evident solution.

The *Historia Augusta* mentions another important measure which was allegedly taken by the priest-emperor. According to the author of the *Vita Heliogabali*, the young ruler intended to collect all the city's cult objects in the Palatine temple:

> He also built him [Elagabal] a temple, to which he desired to transfer the emblem of the Great Mother, the fire of Vesta, the Palladium, the shields of the Salii, and all that the Romans held sacred, purposing that no god might be worshipped at Rome save only Elagabal. He declared, furthermore, that the religions of the Jews and the Samaritans and the rites of the Christians must also be transferred to this place, in order that the priesthood of Elagabal might include the mysteries of every form of worship.[71]

Herodian confirms that Elagabalus abducted the Palladium, but claims that this happened because of the planned marriage between Elagabal and Athena. He also records that the statues of other gods and temple treasures took part in the procession of 221. Moreover, although he does not explicitly state that Elagabalus gathered all cult objects in the temple of Elagabal, he mentions that they were returned to their original places after the emperor's death. This casual reference adds an air of credibility to the story in the *Historia Augusta*, despite the fact that Dio is silent on the subject.

The question which lies at the base of this matter is what exactly the elevation of Elagabal to supreme Roman deity meant. The author of the *Historia Augusta* seems unable to make up his mind about this. On the one hand, he gives us the impression that the emperor intended to subdue all other gods to Elagabal: 'In fact, he asserted that all gods were merely the servants of his god, calling some its chamberlains, others its slaves, and others its attendants for diverse purposes.' On the other hand, it is suggested that Elagabalus wanted to destroy all other religions: 'In fact, it was his desire to abolish not only the religious ceremonies of the Romans but also those of the whole world, his sole wish being that the god Elagabal should be worshipped everywhere.'[72] Apparently, this did not stop the emperor from dressing up as Venus and holding a procession for the goddess Salambo. Dio mentions only that Elagabal was placed above Jupiter; Herodian writes that the Emesene god had to be invoked before all other gods by magistrates and at public ceremonies.

Evidently, Elagabalus did not intend to establish a monotheistic state religion. There was no monotheistic tradition in Emesa, as shall be discussed in the next chapter; nor does any source besides the *Historia Augusta* suggest that the emperor tried to make Elagabal into the only god. After 220, Jupiter and Mars are no longer mentioned on imperial coins, but Venus Caelestis and/or Juno Regina still appear, as well as such personifications as Providentia and Victoria.[73] State cults and priesthoods like the 'sodales', the 'pontifices' and the arval brothers continued to exist.[74] As may be indicated by the marriage of the emperor to the high priestess of Vesta and the marriage of Elagabal to Urania (and perhaps Athena), Elagabalus sought to merge the religion of Emesa with Roman state religion. Elagabal was the new head of the pantheon, but that did not mean that Jupiter, Juno and the other traditional Roman deities were completely abandoned. They were still called upon by magistrates and were still a part of public ceremonies, as Herodian implies by stating that Elagabal now had to be invoked before them. It may well be true that all cult objects had to be gathered in the Palatine temple; but that only indicates that Elagabal ruled supreme, not that it was forbidden to worship any other gods. The hierarchy of the Roman pantheon had been changed, but it remained a pantheon nevertheless.

It is hard to estimate how much impact the reforms of the priest-emperor had outside Rome. Apart from Herodian's remark that the whole of Italy was instructed to celebrate the marriage of Elagabal and Urania, the literary sources do not tell us how much effort was made to export the worship of Elagabal beyond the capital. Of course, coins showing either Elagabal or the emperor sacrificing to him circulated throughout the empire, but that may have been the only way the sun god was actively promoted in the provinces. Rudolf Haensch has pointed out that, from some time during the first half of the third century CE onwards, Roman legions were accompanied by official army priests. He speculates that these priests had originally been instated by Elagabalus, since they are sometimes referred to as 'sacerdotes' in inscriptions and papyrus texts, which is reminiscent of the emperor's title, sacerdos amplissimus.[75] If Haensch is right, Elagabalus bestowed a priest for Elagabal on each army unit. Although this is a plausible theory, sacerdos seems too common a title to justify any definite conclusions. Moreover, there is no other evidence suggesting that the emperor made efforts to have all the soldiers in the empire worship Elagabal.

As will be discussed in the third chapter, some provincial coins show the black stone of Emesa, and at least one case is known of a city celebrating Elagabalia, but since evidence is lacking from many other cities we should see these cases as cities paying respect to the emperor's god of their own initiative, rather than complying with orders issued from Rome. There is no reason to assume that the worship of Elagabal was imposed on the empire as Christianity would be in the fourth century CE.

### DOWNFALL

As the negative tone of Cassius Dio's and Herodian's accounts indicate, the Roman imperial elite did not approve of Elagabalus's religious reforms. The priest-emperor was also unpopular with the praetorians. According to the ancient authors, this was due to his revolting behaviour and the power he gave to his favourites, especially Hierocles. It seems plausible to assume that the praetorian soldiers could no longer identify with an emperor who seemed to focus entirely on a strange, exotic cult and acted in such an 'un-Roman', fanatical fashion, while failing to do anything that commanded their respect. Considering how crucial their support was for any Roman ruler to survive, this was a dangerous development.

Herodian records that Julia Maesa took measures to prevent things from getting out of hand. The old lady persuaded Elagabalus to adopt his cousin Alexianus as Caesar with the argument that this would leave him more time to devote himself to religious matters. In Dio's version, the emperor claimed that Elagabal had commanded him to do so. Some time during the summer of 221, probably on 26 June, Elagabalus adopted the 12-year-old Alexianus as his son and heir.[76] The new Caesar took the name Marcus Aurelius Alexander, which referred not only to his 'father' Elagabalus, but also to Caracalla, who had striven to become a second Alexander the Great. Interestingly, Herodian mentions that Severus Alexander's dynastic claim was strengthened by the rumour that he, too, was in reality a bastard son of Caracalla. As long as Elagabalus was still emperor, this claim was never made official: inscriptions from 221 and the first quarter of 222 mention Alexander as the son of Elagabalus and the grandson of Caracalla. Only during Alexander's sole rule would Caracalla be mentioned as the boy's father, while Elagabalus would be left out of the ancestral line completely.[77]

Whether framed by Julia Maesa or not, the adoption of Alexianus as Caesar marks a strategic shift by the group which had initially supported Elagabalus. It seems that at least some of these supporters felt it was no longer wise to tie their fate too closely to that of the priest-emperor, who stirred up many controversies and was probably difficult to control. Alexianus provided them with an alternative; a potential successor of the same house who could be put forward if anything happened to Elagabalus. In a military diploma of 7 January 222, the young prince is mentioned as 'nobilissimus Caesar imperi et sacerdotis [sic]', 'most noble Caesar of the empire and the priesthood', a title which no other Caesar before or after ever held.[78] Does it indicate that he had special powers? Slobodan Dušanić argues that Alexander did not have 'tribunicia potestas', the power of a tribune of the plebs, or the authority of a pro-consul, but did share in the emperor's legislative power.[79] This is proven not only by two military diplomas which mention both Elagabalus and Alexander, but also by several edicts in the Codex Iustinianus.[80] However, the title Caesar makes it clear that Alexander was still subordinate to Elagabalus. To what extent he could and did indeed act independently of the Augustus can only be guessed.

Besides establishing a 'back-up emperor', Elagabalus's allies made an effort to turn the rising tide of his unpopularity. Around the same time as he adopted Alexianus, the emperor divorced Aquilia Severa and married Annia Faustina instead, a descendant of Marcus Aurelius and Claudius Severus. Although Dio and Herodian present this as another typical example of Elagabalus's whimsical and irresponsible nature, the measure may well have been taken on the advice of the boy's supporters, with the intention of making him less controversial to the elite and the soldiers. After all, Annia Faustina's ancestry did not just make her a much more respectable empress than a vestal virgin could ever be; it also meant that any children she and Elagabalus produced would be of the line of the beloved second-century emperor Marcus Aurelius and would have a very strong dynastic claim on the Roman throne.

The coincidence of Alexianus's adoption and the change of wives supports the notion that both measures represent a conscious change of course by the imperial administration and its supporters, whose interests were best served with the continuation of the Severan dynasty. However, there is nothing to suggest that the emperor's religious reforms were also reversed at this time. As far as we can deduce from coins and inscriptions, Elagabal remained the chief deity of the Roman Empire and Elagabalus continued to serve as his high priest.

If there ever was harmony and mutual goodwill between the Augustus and his Caesar, it did not last long. Alexander seems to have been deliberately kept away from everything which had to do with the cult of

Elagabal. Many coins bearing the young prince's portrait have the legend 'PIETAS AVG(VSTI)', 'the piety of the emperor', on the reverse, but instead of depicting something which clearly relates to the new chief god Elagabal, they show priestly emblems which were associated with the traditional Roman state cult: a patera (libation dish), a lituus (curved augural staff) and a simpulum (long-handled ladle).[81] Although these emblems are not uncommon on coins of Caesares, they form a strong contrast to the pictures on the reverse of Elagabalus's coins, which usually show the emperor sacrificing in 'Oriental' dress. Apparently Alexander was presented to the public as a traditional Roman boy, not to be associated with the exotic weirdness of his superior. This notion is echoed in a story told by Herodian:

> After Alexander's appointment as Caesar, Antoninus wanted him to be trained in his own pursuits of leaping and dancing, and to share in his priesthood by wearing the same dress and following the same practices. But his mother, Mammaea [mother of Alexander], removed him from contact with such activities which were shameful and unbecoming for emperors. In private she summoned teachers of all the arts, and trained him in the exercise of self-control, introducing him to the wrestling schools and manly exercises, and gave him both a Latin and a Greek education.[82]

The emperor, Herodian continues, was not pleased by this rejection: he exiled or executed all of Alexander's teachers and regretted adopting the boy. Annia Faustina was obviously not to his liking either: before the end of the year, Elagabalus divorced her and restored Aquilia Severa as his wife and Augusta.

Inevitably, tensions between Elagabalus and Alexander were rising. According to Herodian, the soldiers were revolted by the effeminate appearance of the priest-emperor, and looked ever more favourably upon the young Caesar. Nothing could be done to reverse this trend. Dio records how Elagabalus complained that he could not satisfy the praetorians, regardless how much he gave them. It sounds quite plausible that the imperial administration spent large amounts of money on the legions in Rome in an effort to keep them loyal to Elagabalus, but if that was indeed the case, money alone was obviously not enough. The emperor's base of power grew weaker every day. As Dio perceived, he was safe only as long as he continued to love his more popular cousin.

The growing rivalry between Julia Maesa's grandsons divided the imperial family – and probably its allies and supporters as well. Julia Soaemias and Julia Mammaea both chose the sides of their respective sons. According to Herodian, Mammaea even gave money to the soldiers to gain their support for Alexander. Julia Maesa also seems to have allied herself with the young Caesar, probably well aware that he was the 'safer bet'.

The power struggle within the imperial court is perhaps also reflected in the career of Comazon. Since this man shared the consulate with the emperor in 220, he was clearly still in Elagabalus's favour at that time. Dio records that Comazon became not only praetorian prefect, but also city prefect three times. Supposedly he was both the successor and the predecessor of Fulvius, the man who was city prefect when Elagabalus was murdered. In all probability, Comazon was therefore removed from this post in 221. Dio mentions that both Fulvius and the prefects (presumably the praetorian prefects) were murdered together with the emperor.

Since Comazon would once again hold the function of city prefect under Severus Alexander, it follows that he was not one of the unlucky praetorian prefects who died in the final revolt against Elagabalus. Why had this influential man lost both the city prefecture and the praetorian prefecture, perhaps around the same time? The only likely explanation seems to be that Comazon chose the side of Mammaea and her son in the conflict between Elagabalus and Alexander. This lost him the favour of the reigning ruler, but paid off when his successor ascended the throne. The same may be true for the jurist Ulpian, who was allegedly banished by Elagabalus, but became an important figure at the court of Alexander.[83]

During the final months of his reign, Elagabalus made several attempts to kill his adopted son. However, Alexander was heavily guarded by soldiers. When they found out that the emperor had tried to harm their charge, they grew angry. According to Dio, the unrest was so serious that Elagabalus was forced to come to the praetorian camp with his cousin and had to beg the soldiers to forgive him. He managed to calm them down and secure their loyalty a bit longer, but only by promising to get rid of all his 'companions in lewdness', with the exception of Hierocles.

The *Historia Augusta* gives a different version of events, in which the emperor was waiting for the message of his cousin's death in the gardens of his suburban villa. Some angry praetorians came to the villa, but were calmed down by the prefect Antiochianus. The soldiers who had remained in the camp, however, only wanted to spare the emperor if he got rid of all his licentious companions, charioteers and actors – including Hierocles – and started leading a decent life again. Despite the difference in details, both accounts signify the same thing: by now, Elagabalus's fate was hanging by a thread.

Another incident occurred on 1 January 222, when Elagabalus and Alexander were supposed to open the consular year together. The emperor did not want to appear in public with his cousin, and refused to go to the Capitol to make the customary promises and sacrifices. Imperial coins which probably refer to the consular procession picture both Elagabalus and Alexander, but only separately, not together.[84] Cassius Dio quotes the emperor as having said – when some senators congratulated him on being consul with his son – 'I shall be more fortunate next year; for then I am going to be consul with a real son.'[85] This slightly puzzling remark may indicate that the emperor still intended to start a dynasty of 'godlike children' with Aquilia Severa.

According to the *Historia Augusta*, Elagabalus at one point commanded all the senators to leave the city. Supposedly he did this to prevent meeting with senatorial opposition after he had killed Alexander. The story, which is mentioned neither by Cassius Dio nor by Herodian, does not ring true. After all, the praetorians, not the senators, were the most immediate threat to the emperor's life and power. Herodian records that Elagabalus gave up all attempts to kill his cousin, since he failed time and time again. Instead, he did not let Alexander appear in public any more and tried to take the title of 'Caesar' away from him. The former is not mentioned in other sources and might be a generalisation of the events of 1 January. The second is also attested by the *Historia Augusta*, although the author of this work claims that the attempts to deprive Alexander of his title preceded the attempts at murdering him. Allegedly, Elagabalus resorted to this desperate measure because the senate refused to take Alexander's title away from him. If this is true, it shows how little actual power the emperor had left.

Inscriptions from the first quarter of 222 still mention Elagabalus and Alexander together, maintaining the fiction of unity and harmony within the imperial house.[86] However, the uneasy alliance would soon come to an end.

In all probability, the murder of Elagabalus occurred on 13 March 222. One day later, the senate recognised Alexander as the new emperor.[87] Our three major literary sources all give a detailed account of the emperor's death. Dio records that the praetorians lost their patience again after Elagabalus made another attempt to kill his cousin. The emperor took Alexander with him to the praetorian camp to calm the soldiers down. However, that turned out to be a mistake:

But he [Elagabalus] then became aware that he was under guard and awaiting execution, as the mothers of the two youths, being more openly at variance with each other than before, were inflaming the spirits of the soldiers; so he made an attempt to flee, and would have got away somewhere by being placed in a chest, had he not been discovered and slain, at the age of eighteen. His mother, who embraced him and clung tightly to him, perished with him; their heads were cut off and their bodies, after being stripped naked, were first dragged all over the city, and then the mother's body was cast aside somewhere or other, while his was thrown into the river.[88]

According to Dio, several others were killed together with Elagabalus and Julia Soaemias: the emperor's lover Hierocles, both praetorian prefects, Aurelius Eubulus, who was in charge of the fiscus, and Fulvius, the city prefect. The god Elagabal was banished from Rome; Alexander was proclaimed as the new emperor.

Herodian tells us roughly the same story. He confirms that Elagabalus went to the praetorian camp with Alexander, but gives a different reason for their visit. Supposedly, the emperor had spread the rumour that his heir was dying. The soldiers were very upset at this news and refused to guard the emperor, undoubtedly suspecting that he was to blame for his cousin's illness, until Alexander showed himself in the camp shrine. On arrival in the camp, the soldiers greeted Alexander enthusiastically, but completely ignored his imperial companion. Elagabalus grew angry and shouted at them all night long. He intended to arrest the men whom he suspected of causing riots or even greeting Alexander as emperor openly. For the praetorians, this was the final straw. Herodian's account ends in much the same way as Dio's: the emperor, his mother and his followers were killed, the bodies of Elagabalus and Julia Soaemias dragged through the streets and finally thrown into the sewer. Then the soldiers proclaimed Alexander emperor and carried him to the palace. Unlike Dio, Herodian does not tell us what became of Elagabal.

According to the *Historia Augusta*, the murder of Elagabalus did not happen spontaneously, but was actually planned by the praetorians. The author records how, after the senators had been commanded to leave the city, the soldiers decided to get rid of the emperor before he could harm Alexander. They slaughtered Elagabalus's minions first, tearing out their vital organs or piercing their anuses, and then fell upon the boy himself, who had taken refuge in a latrine. Elagabalus was killed, his body dragged through the streets. Since the sewer turned out to be too small to dump his corpse, it was finally plunged from the Aemilian Bridge into the Tiber, with a weight attached to it to make sure it would sink. As the author smugly remarks, 'those who do not win the love of the senate, the people, and the soldiers do not win the right of burial.'[89]

It seems implausible that Elagabalus's murder was indeed planned in advance by the praetorians. Although this part of the *Vita Heliogabali* has been classified as 'a coherent piece of clear and accurate narration' by Syme,[90] both contemporary writers claim that the murder took place in the army camp, where the emperor had come of his own free will. If we accept this reading of events, a planned murder does not make much sense. The accounts of Dio and Herodian unmistakably give us the impression that Elagabalus was killed on the spur of the moment, regardless of how much the priest-emperor's death benefited Alexander and his supporters.

After his death, the senate condemned Elagabalus's memory, leading to the destruction of the young man's portraits. His name was erased from inscriptions and papyri, as the *Historia Augusta* confirms. From now on, Alexander was mentioned as the son of Caracalla, instead of as the son of Elagabalus. Moreover, the damned monarch's name would no longer be mentioned in documents referring to his reign. The honours which he had bestowed on certain cities, like an additional neocory (an honour connected with the right to erect a temple to the emperor) for Sardes and Nicomedia, were withdrawn.[91] No objections to this condemnation were made by the surviving members of the imperial house. Instead, the new government tried to distance itself from the priest-emperor as much as possible. According to Herodian, Alexander's wise and modest rule broke rigorously with the past. Civil, legal and military posts were once again bestowed on able, qualified men, after appointments which were deemed unjust had been annulled.

Above all, Elagabalus's religious reforms were reversed. The robbed statues of the gods were returned to their original shrines. Interestingly, this was also true for the stone of Elagabal, which was not destroyed, but sent back to Emesa – perhaps because the Syrian clan still held it in reverence. Jupiter once again took his place as the chief god of the Roman pantheon. Elagabal's temple on the Palatine was probably rededicated to Jupiter Ultor – the Avenger.[92] The message could not have been clearer. For both Elagabalus and Elagabal, their rule of Rome had come to an end.

# 2

# THE CHILD PRIEST
# FROM EMESA

L'Empereur, c'est l'Asie, et Rome est sa sujette.

Auguste Villeroy, Héliogabale (1902)

It is tempting to see the reign of Elagabalus as a clash between the Syrian 'East' and the Roman 'West', with the emperor's downfall as the inevitable result – and indeed many scholars have adopted such a view.[1] It is beyond dispute that the young emperor's reign contains many elements which bear a strikingly un-Roman, 'Oriental' character. This is not only attested by the works of the contemporary historians Cassius Dio and Herodian, but also by many imperial coins and inscriptions dating from the priest-emperor's reign. The god Elagabal, depicted as a black stone on some of Elagabalus's coins, was a distinctively Emesene god. The emperor styled himself as Elagabal's high priest and used this title, including the god's name, in inscriptions and on coins. In the words of Fergus Millar, 'any discussion should take into account the clear evidence that the representation of the cult [of Elagabal] was accompanied by features which deliberately accentuated its "Oriental", "Syrian" or "Phoenician" features.'[2] With this in mind, it seems justified to put some emphasis on Elagabalus's Syrian background. Knowledge of the Syrian town of Emesa, Emesene religion, and the Emesene family into which the future emperor was born might help us to gain some insight into the seemingly strange events of the period 218–22.

However, we should be hesitant in simply labelling Elagabalus 'Oriental' or 'Syrian'. When applied to culture or religion, these terms cause many interpretative problems. It is also important to realise that, even before the revolt which would bring him to the Roman throne, the boy and his family had very close ties to the imperial house. The men of the Emesene family had been Roman citizens for two centuries. Could Elagabalus really have been a total stranger to Roman culture, as he has often been depicted by both ancient and modern historians? It is a question well worth exploring, and this chapter will not only discuss to what extent Elagabalus could be considered 'Syrian' or 'Oriental', but also to what extent he might be seen as 'Roman'.

EMESA AND ITS HISTORY

Relatively little is known of Emesa (modern-day Homs), the Syrian city which would provide the Roman world with two emperors in the third century CE. It was located in the province of Syria Phoenice, on the bank of the river Orontes, on the edge of the Syrian–Arabian desert. Emesa was probably not big, but could still be regarded as a notable city. It is not certain what its economic basis was. Both Emesa and Palmyra, a city located to the east, seem to have shared a similar fate of a rise in the first century BCE and decline in the fourth century CE. It is possible that a trade route existed between these cities, on which Emesa was economically dependent. While in Phoenicia, the second-century physician Galen claimed to have purchased some Indian herbs which had been brought there by camels.[3] This would imply that the herbs came to the Phoenician coast overland, in which case they might well have travelled through Palmyra and Emesa. The Emesene necropolis offers more clues. Two objects which have been found in one of the graves probably came from Iran and Central Asia. This makes it likely that there was indeed a long-distance trade route connecting Phoenicia, Emesa and Palmyra to far-away eastern lands.[4]

Perhaps some trade was carried along the river Orontes. Small boats might have been able to get as far upstream as Emesa, providing a direct connection between the city and the Mediterranean. However, since the river was not deep enough for bigger boats to reach Emesa, the possibilities for river trade must have been limited. More important for the city's life support was undoubtedly the damming of a nearby lake, which perhaps occurred in the first century CE. By means of this dam, much water could be gained to irrigate the lands surrounding the city.

To which culture(s) did the inhabitants of Emesa belong? In a region as culturally diverse and mixed as Roman Syria, probably no unambiguous answer can be given to this question. Possible Roman structures have been noted during excavations on the tell in the south-west of the old city.[5] Several objects which have been found in the Emesene necropolis depict figures from Greek mythology, for example Apollo and Medusa. Although most objects seem to be of Syrian origin, they do not depict any particular Syrian deities. A golden ring, probably from around the beginning of the Christian era, shows a relief bust in Hellenistic style. The bust is presumably that of an Emesene monarch.[6] The portrait is highly reminiscent of the portraits of the Julio-Claudian emperors, except for one detail: the earring, which is a typical feature of Parthian and, later, Persian kings. The custom of wearing earrings was probably widespread throughout the Near East. Apparently, the depicted monarch wanted to display his adherence to Greco-Roman culture, but at the same time wanted to stress his identity as a Syrian aristocrat. Emesene inscriptions are all in Greek, but Semitic names were common in the area where the city was located.

Herodian describes Elagabalus's grandmother, Julia Maesa, as 'a Phoenician by race, from the city called Emesa in Phoenicia'.[7] The historian deems the name of the Emesene sun god, called ''Ελαιαγάβαλος' in his work, to be Phoenician as well. This could be taken as evidence that Phoenician language and culture had spread further inland from the coastal region. However, it is more likely that the institution of the province Syria Phoenice by Septimius Severus had given rise to a sort of pseudo-ethnic identity. Some Emesenes, at least, claimed to be Phoenician: in his Greek novel, *Aithiopica*, the novelist Heliodorus describes himself as 'a Phoenician man, an Emesene'.[8]

The history of Emesa sheds further light on the question of which cultures influenced it. There is a reference to 'the people of the Emesenes' in Strabo's *Geographica*. Around the middle of the first century BC, they were governed by Sampsigeramus and his son, Iamblichus, who also ruled the city of Arethusa. Strabo names Arethusa as an example of his observation that peoples are more civilised and have a better-organised government in proportion to their proximity to the Syrians (as opposed to the more barbaric, less organised 'Arabians and Scenitae'). Yet Iamblichus is described as an 'Arabian phylarch' by Cicero and as 'the king of some Arabs' by Dio.[9] This seems to imply that the Emesenes were originally a nomadic tribe from the Arabian desert. However, what the ancients meant by the term 'Arab' is at present indefinable. Arabs could indeed originate from the Arabian desert or lead a nomadic life, but certainly not all of them did. Therefore, we cannot make any definite statements about the origins of Sampsigeramus and his people.

The name Emesa is first mentioned in connection with Sampsigeramus II, 'king of Emesa', who ruled in the middle of the first century CE.[10] We have several mentions of Emesene rulers in the first centuries BCE and CE, who probably all descended from the original Sampsigeramus. When Roman influence in the Near East grew in the first century BCE, they became Roman allies. Cicero speaks approvingly of Iamblichus, 'whom men consider to be [...] a friend of our state', because the latter warned him of a threatening Parthian invasion in 51 BCE.[11] This friendship with Rome allowed the Emesene monarchy to prosper well into imperial times. Judging from the many costly objects which have been found in the necropolis, the dynasty was quite wealthy. It forged strong ties with other royal families by means of marriages, especially with the royal family of Judaea. The Emesene rulers could also muster considerable forces to give military aid to the Romans, and did so on several occasions.

Emesa must have played its role as a client-kingdom well, because in 54 CE, Nero added the district of Sophene to the lands of the Emesene king Sohaemus. Despite this apparent good fortune, Sohaemus is the last Emesene king known to us. He is mentioned as 'great king, friend of Caesar and friend of the Romans' in an inscription on the pedestal of a bronze statue found in Baalbek (the former Heliopolis).[12] From this inscription, we also learn that Sohaemus had been granted the 'ornamenta consularia' by the Romans and was the city patron of Heliopolis. His family must have achieved Roman citizenship some time during the Julio-Claudian era, since he bears the name Julius. This probably occurred when Augustus made Iamblichus II his client king in 20 BCE.

It is likely that Sohaemus or his immediate successor fell victim to the policy of consolidation of the Near East of the Flavian dynasty (69–96 CE), in which client kings were removed and the emperor established a direct rule over the area. A sepulchral monument at Emesa bears an inscription, dated in 78/79 CE, naming a Julius Sampsigeramus.[13] Although the name suggests that this person was a member of the Emesene royal family, no royal titles or royal relatives are mentioned. Presumably the kings of Emesa had been deprived of their power by this time.

In the second century CE, grave inscriptions from Emesa provide us with several other names which seem to suggest that their bearers descended from the Emesene rulers of the first centuries BCE and CE. While this may have been the case, however, they did not play such important roles on the political stage of the Near East as their (possible) royal ancestors. Emesa seems to have dwindled into political insignificance after the days of Sohaemus. Only by the time of the Severans, more than a century later, would the city once again make it into Roman history books.

## THE CULT OF ELAGABAL

One of the few things we know about religious life in Emesa is that Elagabal was worshipped there. The name of the god is attested by both Cassius Dio and Herodian, who call him ''Ελεγάβαλος' and ''Ελαιαγάβαλος' respectively. Inscriptions from the period before 218 CE give the deity the name Elagabalus, Aelagabalus, or Helagabalus, while imperial coins and inscriptions from the reign of Elagabalus consistently name him Elagabal.

It has long been debated what the origin of the god's name might have been. In 1976, new light was shed on this question by the publication of a relief found 80km south-east of Emesa (see Fig. 2).[14] The relief, probably made in the first century CE, shows two deities, labelled with Aramaic names in Palmyrene letters. The one on the left is portrayed as an armed man, called ''RSW' ('Arsu'). The one on the right does not have an anthropomorphic shape, but is depicted as a conical stone or mountain with an eagle perched on top. It is labelled ''LH'GBL', which Jean Starcky reads as 'Ilâhâ Gabal' or 'God Mountain'.[15] Although there are no mountains in the immediate vicinity of Emesa, this reading has been accepted by most scholars.

Mountain gods were worshipped mainly in Anatolia and the northern parts of Syria, in some cases up until imperial times. They were of a powerful, celestial nature, and were often likened to Zeus/Jupiter, like Jupiter Turmasgades and Jupiter Dolichenus in the area around Doliche in the region of Commagene. From well before the period of Greek civilisation, many mountain gods were symbolised by an eagle. The god of Mount Argaios, which features on coins from Caesarea (Cappadocia), is sometimes depicted as a stone or mountain with an eagle on top. Several Emesene coins depict Elagabal in a similar manner. Others show a big, conical stone and eagle in a temple.[16]

Clearly, what we are seeing here is a 'betyl', an abstract object of worship. The word is probably derived from the Semitic 'bethel' ('BT'L'), which means 'house of god'. Betyls are quite common in Semitic religions. Often, they come in the form of large stones. This was also the case with the betyl of Elagabal, which is described by Herodian: 'There was no actual man-made statue of the god, the sort Greeks and Romans put up; but there was an enormous stone, rounded at the base and coming to a point at the top, conical in shape and black.'[17] A large stone seems like an appropriate home for a mountain god. However, both Dio and Herodian make it clear that Elagabal, at least by the third century CE, was a sun god. Herodian records that some small projecting pieces and markings on the stone were believed to be a rough picture of the sun. The stone itself was said to have fallen from heaven. Perhaps it was believed to come from the sun. When Elagabalus brought Elagabal to Rome, the deity was exclusively represented as a sun god. Several of Elagabalus's coins bear the legend 'SANCT(O) DEO SOLI ELAGABAL(O)' and the emperor styled himself 'sacerdos amplissimus dei invicti Solis Elagabali'.

When did this transformation from mountain god to sun god occur? It certainly predates the reign of Elagabalus, since an inscription from the period 198–209 CE, erected by Emesene soldiers, is devoted to 'Deo Soli Aelagabalo'.[18] Emesene coins from the reign of Antoninus Pius show the radiate head of a sun god. The only other god attested on Emesene coins is Elagabal, represented by his betyl. It might go too far to identify the anthropomorphic sun god with Elagabal, but at least these coins show that by the middle of the second century CE, the worship of the sun had gained an important place in the religious life of Emesa.

Perhaps Elagabal was worshipped as a mountain god by the original inhabitants of the Emesene region and became a sun god after Sampsigeramus had established his rule there. The name Sampsigeramus contains the name of the Arab sun god Shamash, and means 'the Sun has decided'. The word 'phylarch', used by Cicero to describe Iamblichus, was also used in the Septuagint (1 Esdras 7/8), where it may designate a 'chief priest of a tribe among the Jews'. Moreover, the inscription from Baalbek mentioned earlier shows that Iamblichus's descendant Sohaemus at least had some honorific religious function in Heliopolis.

As far as we can see, Elagabal was first and foremost a local deity. Nevertheless, Herodian asserts, he attracted many worshippers from outside Emesa as well. According to the historian, the city functioned as a regional religious centre: 'There was a huge temple built there, richly ornamented with gold and silver and valuable stones. The cult extended not just to the local inhabitants either. Satraps of all the adjacent territories and barbarian princes tried to outdo each other in sending costly dedications to the god every year.'[19] Unfortunately, no archaeological remains of this splendid temple have been found. It is depicted on some Emesene coins, however, showing an elevated building with stairs leading up to a six-column façade, supporting a tympanon. Between the columns, the betyl of Elagabal is visible. In Avienus's fourth-century work *Descriptio orbis terrae*, it is mentioned that the people of Emesa devotedly worshipped the sun and had a temple (presumably for the sun) which competed with the Lebanon mountains in height.[20]

All in all, there seems to be enough evidence to confirm the existence of a big, impressive temple for Elagabal in Emesa, which attracted worshippers from outside the city. Nevertheless, we should be careful not to overestimate the importance of Elagabal outside the immediate vicinity of Emesa. There are only four inscriptions calling the god by name which undoubtedly date back before 218 CE.[21] Three of those were certainly erected by people from Emesa. We are not dealing with a god who was well known throughout the empire before the rise of Elagabalus.

The cult of Elagabal was led by a high priest, whose position might have been hereditary. In the *Epitome de Caesaribus*, we can read that Elagabalus was not the first one in his family to hold this high office. The function had earlier been performed by his great-grandfather, Bassianus.[22] Of course, the fact that members of a prominent local family attain a prestigious position in successive generations does not mean that that position is hereditary. But Anthony Birley suggests that the name Bassianus is the Latinised form of the Phoenician word 'basus', which means 'priest'.[23] If so, there would be a clear link between the priesthood of Elagabal and the family of Elagabalus. Several of the boy's family members – including his great-uncle Caracalla – bore the name Bassianus or Bassiana. According to Herodian, Elagabalus's original name was Bassianus as well.

In his account of Elagabalus's acts as high priest in Emesa, Herodian gives a detailed description of the ceremonial dress the boy wore:

> He used to appear in public in barbarian clothes, wearing a long-sleeved 'chiton' that hung to his feet and was gold and purple. His legs from the waist down to the tips of his toes were completely covered similarly with garments ornamented with gold and purple. On his head he wore a crown of precious stones glowing with different colours.[24]

Later, while performing rites for Elagabal in Nicomedia, the young emperor reportedly wore purple and gold as well. He had adorned himself with necklaces, bangles and a precious tiara-shaped crown. 'The effect was something between the sacred garb of the Phoenicians and the luxurious apparel of the Medes,' Herodian states.[25] In fact, the outfit he describes most closely resembles the so-called 'Iranian' dress of some Syrian priests, which is attested in Palmyra and some places near the Mediterranean coast.

As has been discussed in the previous chapter, Herodian also tells us about the rites which the high priest of Elagabal had to perform to honour his god. He describes how Elagabalus danced around the altars to the music of flutes, pipes and other instruments. Several women joined him in his dance. Many bulls and sheep were sacrificed, and wine was poured in front of the altars, so that it mixed with the blood. There are several imperial coins showing Elagabalus standing next to an altar with a 'patera', a dish for pouring libations, in his hand. Sometimes, a small bull is depicted next to the altar. The twig the emperor is holding in his left hand may have been a Syrian fertility symbol.[26]

Both Cassius Dio and the *Historia Augusta* claim that the emperor sacrificed not only animals, but children as well. It seems unlikely that human sacrifice was still practised in Semitic religions in the third century CE. Tertullian mentions human sacrifices to Saturn in African cities in his *Apologeticus*, written in 197 CE.[27] Although many urns containing the ashes of young children have been found in North Africa, Sardinia and Sicily, there is still no consensus on whether children were sacrificed here in imperial times or not. Even if they were, however, we do not have any contemporary Syrian parallels for the practice of human sacrifice. It has been thought that Lucian, in his second-century work *De Dea Syria*, mentions children being thrown to their deaths from the temple of Atargatis in Hierapolis, but Jane Lightfoot points out that 'they lower them down by hand' is a much more likely translation of the words in question.[28] Moreover, according to the *Historia Augusta*, Elagabalus examined his victim's vitals: a typically Etruscan and Roman ritual, which has nothing to do with Semitic religions whatsoever. This makes the claim that Elagabalus practised human sacrifice even more unlikely.

Cassius Dio mentions many other acts of Elagabalus, whether fictional or not, which could be connected to the boy's religious convictions. According to Dio, Elagabalus abstained from eating swine flesh and circumcised himself. These details are striking, not only because they are reminiscent of Judaism, but also because they do not appear to be of a scandalous character, which lends them an air of credibility. Perhaps Emesene religion had, to some extent, been influenced by Judaism, although there are no other clues pointing in this direction. Dio also mentions that Elagabalus planned to cut off his genitals altogether, as the 'galli' of Cybele and Atargatis did, though he assures us that this desire was prompted solely by the emperor's effeminacy. Furthermore, the historian relates how Elagabalus wore many amulets and locked up a lion, a monkey and a snake together in the temple of Elagabal, throwing human genitals in among the animals.[29] Of course, we should keep in mind that Dio was probably more interested in portraying the emperor's religion as 'weird' than descriptive accuracy, which calls his remarks into question.

It would be going too far to discuss all these stories and their likelihood extensively. Even if we did, it is unlikely that a coherent, meaningful picture of the cult of Elagabal and its rites would emerge. Elagabal had evolved from a mountain god to a sun god, but had maintained the name and the betyl of his original identity. The meaning of other aspects of his cult were probably likewise blurred. There are no traces of a deep, philosophical theology. As far as we can see, the cult of Elagabal was mainly about worshipping Elagabal.

OTHER GODS IN EMESA

The cult of Elagabal has sometimes been perceived as a form of monotheism.[30] However, other gods could be worshipped together with Elagabal, as the first-century relief depicting Elagabal and Arsu demonstrates. In the previous chapter, we have discussed a Spanish inscription honouring Elagabal, Athena Allath and (probably) Kypris Charinazaia. Both these goddesses were connected to Syria. Allath, who is usually depicted as a companion of the sun god Shamash, was worshipped by the Nabataeans, in Emesa and in Palmyra. Because she bore weapons, she was identified with the Greek warrior goddess Athena. Kypris Charinazaia was a Cyprian love goddess who was probably exported to Carthage, where she became the moon goddess Urania. According to Herodian, the Phoenicians saw Urania as the moon goddess Astroarche.[31] This goddess, also known as Astarte or Atargatis, can be equated with Lucian's 'Syrian Goddess', and was one of the major deities in Semitic religions. To what extent Elagabal, Urania and

Athena Allath should be considered a standard Emesene triad is impossible to tell.

Two other gods who were worshipped in Emesa are Azizos and Monimos, a divine pair representing Venus as the Morning and Evening Star. They originate from Arabia and were originally worshipped in the form of a singular male deity. In the works of the fourth-century emperor Julian, we can read that Azizos was associated with Ares and Monimos with Hermes.[32] This probably refers to the deities' militant qualities on the one hand, most prominent in Azizos, and their guiding or shepherding qualities on the other, especially associated with Monimos. They were both escorts and protectors of the sun in its daily course, but also of caravans and travellers in the desert, and were thought to be the channel for many blessings. An altar dedicated to Azizos has been found at Emesa.[33] Apparently, the gods were not always worshipped together, and should not be seen as inseparable twins. Both Azizos and Monimos occur frequently as personal names in inscriptions from the region. An Emesene king of the first century CE was named after Azizos as well.

One inscription which has been found in Emesa is dedicated to 'the lady Semea'.[34] It is hard to discern anything about her identity. Like other forms attested in inscriptions from the Greek East – Semia, Seimios – the name is probably derived from the Greek 'σημήϊον', or a close variant of this word. According to Lucian, the 'σημήϊον' was a divine standard in the temple of Atargatis in Hierapolis. He records that 'it is called "the standard" by the Assyrians themselves, who have not given it a name of its own, nor have they anything to say about its place of origin or form.'[35] On coins from Hierapolis, it is depicted as a pole hung with four rings, surrounded by a structure with a pedimented top and side-pieces descending as far as the lowest ring. On top is a dove. Many different shapes and forms exist elsewhere throughout Roman Syria, often more or less resembling a Roman standard. According to Lightfoot, the standard came from an ancient Syrian tradition and should not be seen as the reflection of a deity 'Simios', 'Simia' or 'Simi'.[36] However, since the Emesene inscription specifically speaks of a 'lady Semea', it seems likely that the standard was in fact interpreted as the reflection of a goddess by the people of Emesa, even if this may not have been the case elsewhere.

While several gods were worshipped in Emesa, we should be wary of simply grouping them together as the 'Emesene pantheon'. Since virtually nothing is known of the myths which existed about these gods, it is hard to tell if they were all involved in a cohesive mythology, like the Olympian pantheon of Greece. The fact that several gods could appear together in an image or inscription does not necessarily imply that they had a well established, generally recognised relation to each other, like for instance Zeus, Hera and Ares. There seems no reason to doubt that Elagabal was the supreme deity of the city, but apart from that, it might be best not to make too many assumptions.

THE FAMILY OF ELAGABALUS

Although no record of it has been preserved, it is likely that Emesa received a remarkable visitor in the early 180s CE. The future emperor Septimius Severus, at that point legate of the Syrian Legion IV Scythica, probably came to visit the city and met Julius Bassianus, high priest of Elagabal, and his youngest daughter, Julia Domna. A few years later, when he was governor of Gallia Lugdunensis, Severus's wife died. The widowed governor wrote to Julius Bassianus and asked for the hand of Julia Domna, presumably because her horoscope predicted that she would be married to a king.

In 187 CE, Septimius Severus and Julia Domna married. The event would prove to be very significant, not just for Julia Domna, but for her Emesene family as well. Six years later, after the murder of emperor Pertinax in 193 CE, Severus marched to Rome with several legions and successfully claimed the imperial throne. He defeated the other pretenders and styled himself the adopted son of Marcus Aurelius and the brother of Commodus, although his adoption took place 15 years after Aurelius's death. Julia Domna became empress of the Roman world. Suddenly, the relatively insignificant city of Emesa had very close ties to the imperial house.

Even before Julia Domna became empress, her family was of high status and wielded considerable power in Emesa. The name Julia, borne by several family members, indicates that the family had probably received Roman citizenship before the reign of Claudius (41–54 CE). It is not unlikely that they had descended from the Emesene kings of the first centuries BCE and CE. After all, several grave inscriptions indicate that the descendants of the dynasty might still have been around in the second century. The name Soaemias, as a niece of Julia Domna was called, is strongly reminiscent of the name Sohaemus, born by the Emesene king of the first century CE. The evidence is far from conclusive, but is tantalising nevertheless. If the Emesene kings indeed functioned as high priests of the sun god, as has been suggested above, it becomes even more compelling to link them to the high priest Bassianus and his descendants. But we cannot be sure, and should remain cautious of raising possibilities, even likely ones, to the level of certainties.

Whether Julia Domna had royal ancestors or not, her children were destined to become emperors. In 188, on 4 April, she gave birth to Lucius Septimius Bassianus. The next year a second child, Publius Septimius Geta, was born. Two years after Severus had become emperor in 193 CE, he granted his oldest son the title 'Caesar'. The boy was renamed Marcus Aurelius Antoninus, to put further stress on the claim that Severus was Marcus Aurelius's adopted son. However, the young Antoninus would also become known as Caracalla, nicknamed after the soldier's mantle or 'caracallus' he liked to wear. In 198, his father granted him the title of 'Augustus'. Imperial power still lay in the hands of Severus, but the emperor had made it clear who his successor was going to be. Geta, the younger son, had received the title 'Caesar' in 198, when his brother was made 'Augustus'. However, for reasons unknown to us, in 209 Severus decided to grant Geta the title 'Augustus' as well. The old emperor wanted his sons to rule together. On his deathbed in 211, he urged them not to fight each other.

Caracalla and Geta did not pay much heed to this fatherly advice. After a short period of joint rule and mutual suspicion, Geta was murdered by his brother. He suffered 'damnatio memoriae', which meant that his name and image were erased from papyri, inscriptions, wall paintings and buildings. Caracalla's sole rule lasted until 217. He was murdered by his guards while on a military expedition against the Parthians. Just as suddenly as it had arisen, the Severan dynasty seemed to have come to an end. The emperor had left no sons, and power fell to Macrinus, one of the praetorian prefects. Julia Domna, who according to Dio suffered from breast cancer, despaired at these misfortunes and committed suicide.

Julia Domna's elder sister, Julia Maesa, had not married a future emperor, nor did she give birth to any. Both her grandchildren, however, would gain the imperial purple. According to Cassius Dio, Julia Maesa had been born in Apamea, but even if this is true, she probably spent her youth in Emesa, where her father was high priest. She married C. Julius Avitus Alexianus, whose impressive career is known to us from two inscriptions.[37] Julius Avitus held the equestrian post of 'procurator annonae' around 193, was then promoted to senatorial rank by Septimius Severus, became a priest of Apollo, served as 'praetor' in 194 and was afterwards sent to command a legion, probably IV Flavia. He became governor of Raetia in 196 or 197 and held the consulate sometime between the years 198–200. After this prestigious post, he did not gain any offices for several years, perhaps due to the influence of Severus's praetorian prefect, Plautianus, who may have seen him as a potential threat to his own position.[38] During the period 208–11, Julius Avitus accompanied Severus and his sons to Britannia as 'comes', official companion. He held the prefecture of the grain supply twice, was 'comes' to Caracalla on the emperor's Germanic expedition in 213, became governor of Dalmatia for a short time, and, in 215–16, proconsul of Asia. In 216–17, he was 'comes' for the third time, accompanying Caracalla to Parthia. Lastly, the emperor sent him to Cyprus to advise the resident governor in 217.[39] It was probably there that Julius Avitus died 'of old age and sickness', some time before his grandson became emperor.[40]

Julia Maesa did not accompany her husband on his journeys. Cassius Dio, Herodian and the *Historia Augusta* all state that she lived at the imperial court with her sister Domna. After Caracalla's reign had ended and Julia Domna had committed suicide, Maesa returned to Emesa. According to Dio, she went back because her husband had died as well, but Herodian says she was forced to go by Macrinus. If the latter is the case, the emperor probably regretted his decision before long.

Julia Maesa and Julius Avitus Alexianus had two daughters, Julia Soaemias Bassiana and Julia Mammaea. Julia Soaemias was the elder of the two and was probably born before 180. An inscription tells us she was in Rome 'among the equestrian wives' at the secular games of 204, indicating that she must have been married by that time.[41] Her husband was Sextus Varius Marcellus, whose sarcophagus has been found in the Italian town of Velletri (ancient Velitrae). The inscription on the sarcophagus, which is both in Latin and in Greek, mentions Soaemias with the honorific 'clarissima femina', woman of senatorial rank.[42] She dedicated the inscription 'cum filis' (*sic*), 'with her children'. The plural is intriguing. It indicates that Elagabalus was not an only child, but had at least one brother or sister. Unfortunately, none of the literary sources mention any other children. We can only assume they had already died when their brother came to power.

Sextus Varius Marcellus, in all likelihood Elagabalus's father, came from the Greek city of Apamea, not far from Emesa. An inscription on a lead pipe from Rome confirms that he had indeed been 'procurator aquarum', in charge of the water supply, in the capital. Since the inscription gives both Severus and Caracalla the title 'Augustus' and mentions Geta only as 'Caesar', it must be dated between 198 and 209.[43] Julia Soaemias was still an equestrian wife during the secular games, so Marcellus cannot have become a senator before 204. He must have died before 218, because Elagabalus is not even mentioned by name in his funerary inscription, which would be unthinkable if he had been emperor at the time. However, apart from these, we do not have any points of reference for Marcellus's career, which makes it hard to reconstruct its exact timeline.

Several attempts have been made to link the magistracies which are mentioned in the sarcophagus inscription to particular years. Both Pflaum and Birley assume that Marcellus could only have served as acting city prefect and acting praetorian prefect when the regular prefects were accompanying the emperor outside Rome.[44] This notion is rejected by Halfmann, who argues that the post of city prefect did not allow its occupant to be absent from Rome for a long time. Halfmann thinks that Marcellus held the two prefectures in extraordinary political circumstances, namely the period just before or just after the murder of Geta, when Caracalla dismissed both the city prefect and the praetorian prefect. Because he was a trusted ally of Severus's oldest son, Marcellus supposedly got both jobs. As a reward for his loyal service, he was made a senator afterwards. Consequently, Marcellus served as 'praefectus aerarii' (prefect of the treasury) and was sent as governor to Numidia, perhaps in 213. He probably died while holding this post, since he did not hold the consulate which always followed it.[45] Halfmann's reconstruction of Marcellus's career sounds likely enough, but even if we were to reject it, the posts which this man held at various times make it clear that he must have been a trusted ally of Caracalla. It seems reasonable to assume that Marcellus received so much trust because he had married into Julia Domna's family.

Julia Mammaea, the youngest daughter of Julia Maesa and Julius Avitus Alexianus, married twice in her life. We do not know the name of her first husband, but he must have been consul, since Caracalla allowed Mammaea to keep the rank of consul's wife after her second marriage.[46] Her second husband, Gessius Marcianus, came from the Syrian city of Arca. He held several posts as a procurator, which marks him as a man from the equestrian order.[47] Dio mentions that Marcianus had a daughter, but does not say if she was Mammaea's daughter as well or a child from an earlier marriage. The historian does identify Gessius Marcianus as the father of Mammaea's son, the later emperor Severus Alexander. According to Dio, the boy's original name was Bassianus, but Herodian names him Alexianus. As far as we can tell, they may both be right.

Alexianus Bassianus was born on 1 October, but it is uncertain in which year. Herodian says the boy had just turned nine when Julia Maesa returned to Emesa. Since the old lady's return must have occurred between 11 April 217 and 16 May 218 (the respective days on which Macrinus and Elagabalus were proclaimed emperor), this would mean that Alexianus turned nine in 217 and must have been born on 1 October 208. Later, Herodian contradicts himself and says Alexianus was 'in his twelfth year' – and thus 11 years old – when he was adopted as son and heir by Elagabalus, an event which occurred on or around 26 June 221.[48] Since the age he gives for Elagabalus in this passage does not correspond with the age he gave for the boy earlier either, and since the earlier given age for Elagabalus is confirmed by Dio, we can assume that the second passage is erroneous and Alexianus was indeed born in 208.

This leads to an interesting implication. Since Caracalla was the emperor who decreed that Julia Mammaea could keep her rank as consul's wife, Mammaea's marriage to Marcianus cannot have occurred before 212, when Caracalla became sole ruler. Alexianus was born at least a few years earlier and was therefore probably the child of Julia Mammaea and her first husband. Dio might not have known of Mammaea's former marriage, and could have erroneously assumed that Alexianus was Marcianus's son.

When we look at the Emesene family as a whole, including the men who married into it, we get the impression of a local elite which benefited from its newly forged ties to the imperial house. Emesa was granted the status of a Roman colony by Caracalla. The family of Julia Domna was likewise favoured. Around 200, the husbands of Julia Maesa, Julia Soaemias and Julia Mammaea were quite active in the ruling of the empire and held posts as governors and consuls. Both Julia Maesa's husband, Julius Avitus Alexianus, and Julia Soaemias's husband, Sextus Varius Marcellus, rose from equestrian to senatorial rank. Yet the family did not disregard its Syrian roots. Julia Soaemias and Julia Mammaea both married men of Syrian origin. While acting as governor of Raetia, Julius Avitus Alexianus dedicated an altar to 'Deus patrius Sol Elagabalus'.[49] And, of course, one of Julius Bassianus's great-grandchildren would follow in his ancestor's footsteps and would become Elagabal's high priest.

## ELAGABALUS

The later emperor Elagabalus was neither born under that name, nor under the name of Marcus Aurelius Antoninus, as he would style himself as emperor. According to Cassius Dio, the boy was originally called Avitus; Herodian gives him the name Bassianus. The *Historia Augusta* uses many variants, among which are Elagabalus, Elagabalus Bassianus Varius and Varius Elagabalus. The *Epitome de Caesaribus* confirms the name Varius. The most likely name we can make out of this is Varius Avitus Bassianus, with Varius referring to the boy's father, Sextus Varius Marcellus; Avitus to his maternal grandfather, Julius Avitus Alexianus; and Bassianus being the 'cognomen' of the Emesene family. When he became emperor, Elagabalus would claim to be the bastard son of Caracalla. While theoretically possible, the story seems too good to be true, especially since a similar claim would later be made about Severus Alexander. There seems to be no good reason to doubt Dio's assertion that Marcellus was Elagabalus's father.

We have no exact date of birth for Varius Avitus Bassianus, but a rough indication can be given. According to Dio, Elagabalus defeated Macrinus on 8 June 218 and reigned for three years, nine months and four days, counting from that day, which means he perished on 13 March 222. The historian mentions that the emperor was 18 years old at the time of his death. This corresponds with Herodian's remark that the boy was about 14 when Julia Maesa returned to Emesa, and places his birth somewhere between 14 March 203 and 13 March 204.

It is an intriguing question where the future emperor grew up. Herodian mentions that both the young Elagabalus and his cousin Alexianus were raised by their mothers and grandmother. Since Julia Maesa lived with her sister during the reigns of Septimius Severus and Caracalla, this would imply that they spent their youth at the imperial court (at Rome or elsewhere). Cassius Dio neither confirms nor contradicts this notion. However, it is supported by Aurelius Victor and the author of the *Historia Augusta*, who both state that Elagabalus went to Emesa only after the death of Caracalla.[50] The sarcophagus of Sextus Varius Marcellus, bearing an inscription dedicated by Julia Soaemias and her children, was found in the Italian city of Velletri. This indicates that Elagabalus and his mother spent at least some time living outside Emesa before 217.

An inscription from Thyatira, Asia Minor, indicates that Caracalla and the young Elagabalus were there together, probably in 214, or else a year later.[51] It is possible that the future emperor and his mother were on their way to Emesa after Marcellus's death. Alternatively, they may have spent the following years with Julia Domna in Antioch, or even have returned to Rome. Whatever the case may be, it confirms that Elagabalus spent at least part of his childhood at Caracalla's court. This means that he must have come into contact with the traditional Roman ways of thinking and acting at a young age. When the boy was proclaimed emperor in Emesa in 218, he had already visited Asia Minor and Italy. He may even have lived in these places for the majority of his life. Only during the reign of Macrinus do we know for certain that he was staying at Emesa.

Nevertheless, the profoundly 'Syrian', 'un-Roman' character of some aspects of Elagabalus's reign cannot be denied. This may partially be due to the influence of Syrian advisers, who held the emperor in their sway. Yet their influence could hardly have been so great if Elagabalus had not agreed with them. Why did a boy who, at least to some extent, must have been aware of Roman thought and customs, choose to act in a way which not only alienated him from his subjects, but also provoked many of them?

Perhaps we should seek the explanation in the fact that most of Elagabalus's 'un-Roman' acts – all of them, if we put the biased accounts of ancient historians aside and concentrate on epigraphic and numismatic evidence – were to do with the cult of Elagabal. Whether he had been brought up honouring the sun god, or whether he was a recent convert, the religious zeal which the emperor showed in honouring the deity cannot be interpreted as anything other than genuine. It is inconceivable that any ruler would impose such an 'Oriental', 'un-Roman' god as the Emesene Elagabal on the Romans for purely political reasons. Elagabalus was probably at least dimly aware of Roman culture and the boundaries it set even for emperors, but his acts were in the first place regulated by his desire to glorify and promote the supreme deity of the cult which he led. More than anything else, it was Elagabal who determined the thinking and acting of the priest from Emesa.

# 3

# THE INVINCIBLE
# PRIEST-EMPEROR

When this age will cherish the fame and glory I give it with my life, it will even surpass the Golden Century.

Aurelio Aureli and Francesco Cavalli, *Eliogabalo* (1667)

Elagabalus had gained the throne with the support of several legions, but his swift victory over Macrinus was not enough to secure his position as Roman ruler. Like all emperors, he had to win and maintain the support of his subjects: not just the soldiers, but also the elite and the populace of Rome. A key step in achieving this was to present them with a sound ideological basis to legitimise his powerful position. Elagabalus had to convince his subjects that he was both the rightful heir to the throne and the fittest candidate to rule the empire. As Jaś Elsner has remarked, 'Power is, then, a far more complex and mysterious quality than any apparently simple manifestation of it would appear. It is as much a matter of impression, of theatre, of persuading those over whom authority is wielded to collude in their subjugation.'[1]

No means of persuasion was probably more effective than the image – whether it was a statue or bust of the emperor, a relief on some public building, or the images engraved on imperial coins. 'In the propagation of the imperial office, at any rate,' Elsner remarks, 'art was power.' However, other means of representation, such as coin legends and imperial titles, should be taken into account as well.

We do not know who was responsible for the construction and distribution of imperial images. While it is plausible to assume that no

61

messages were sent out which went against the explicit wishes of the emperor, it does not seem likely that Elagabalus determined every image and coin legend himself. In all likelihood, he had subordinates to take care of such things. Still, coins minted in Rome were official expressions of the emperor's regime. The same is true for imperial busts and the titles which Elagabalus used. Therefore, when I mention 'the emperor' presenting himself in a certain way, this should be taken as convenient shorthand for the imperial administration, which acted in the emperor's name. In the eyes of the public, the two were probably identical.

In which ways did Elagabalus's advisers try to present the young emperor to the soldiers, the Roman elite and the Roman populace? Did they send different messages to different groups? To what extent were these messages intended to form a coherent ideological programme? And how was the imperial image affected by the religious reforms of the end of 220? These are the questions which will be addressed in this chapter. In addition, I will try to establish how contemporaries reacted to the representation of the boy on the throne – both during his reign and immediately after his death. This may shed some light on the question why Elagabalus ultimately failed to persuade his subjects. Lastly, I will briefly place the emperor in the wider context of Roman imperial history.

THE BENIGN PRINCE

Due to the peculiar nature of the principate, which had been set up by Augustus under the guise of restoring the republic, an emperor was supposed to present himself as 'princeps', the first among his 'equals' in the senate. Although divine connotations certainly played a role in the imperial representation and legitimation, the concept of the emperor as a god was basically at odds with these cherished republican ideals. Therefore, most of the rulers during the principate were somewhat reluctant openly to claim divinity, putting more emphasis on their ancestry, their virtues and their achievements. This is definitely true for the first years of Elagabalus's reign. In 218, the boy was presented to the troops as the son of Caracalla, a suggestion which was strengthened by dressing him up in clothes which the murdered emperor had supposedly worn as a child. Herodian remarks that the soldiers perceived a strong resemblance between the 'father' and his 'son'.[2] This may indicate that the scheme indeed had the desired effect.

Busts of Elagabalus stress the notion that he was Caracalla's son. The so-called 'type 1' shows a youth with a symmetrical face, a bright expression and a short military haircut, chiselled according to the 'penna' technique (see Fig. 3). This type, of which probably four specimens are known, has convincingly been identified as Elagabalus by Klaus Fittschen and Paul Zanker.[3] As they remark, the form of the head, the forehead and the mouth are reminiscent of the later bust types of Caracalla. The same can be said about the military haircut, which was worn by Caracalla as well. Elagabalus's portrait on the obverses of his early coins was based on bust type 1, as the hair in particular shows. The dynastic message conveyed by these busts and coins was probably directed primarily at the army. Elagabalus had been proclaimed emperor by the soldiers because he claimed to be Caracalla's son, probably leading them to expect he would continue his 'father's' military policy. The imperial administration may have deliberately strengthened this impression by presenting the emperor with a military haircut, which not only enhanced his physical resemblance to Caracalla, but also expressed his affinity with the troops.

It was not only by means of images that Elagabalus was presented as the son of Caracalla. By styling himself Marcus Aurelius Antoninus, which had also been Caracalla's official name, the new emperor referred to his invented ancestry on coin legends and in inscriptions. In the case of the latter, the dynastic claim was made explicit by adding the words 'divi Magni Antonini Pii filius, divi Severi Pii nepos', 'son of the divine Great Antoninus Pius, grandson of the divine Severus Pius', or a variant thereof, to the imperial titles.[4] The deification of Caracalla was another means by which Elagabalus emphasised his connections with the earlier Severans. Both the former emperor and his mother, Julia Domna, were deified by the new Antoninus, who minted coins with the legend 'CONSECRATIO' to commemorate the occasion.[5]

The name Marcus Aurelius Antoninus did not just express Elagabalus's affiliation with Caracalla. It also put him forward as a member of the Antonine dynasty and invoked memories of the 'good emperors' Antoninus Pius and Marcus Aurelius. Septimius Severus had adopted himself into the dynasty of these beloved predecessors, renaming his oldest son Marcus Aurelius Antoninus and styling himself 'divi Marci filius, divi Commodi frater', 'son of the divine Marcus, brother of the divine Commodus'. The name Antoninus seems almost to have achieved the status of a title under the Severi. It was borne by both Caracalla and Elagabalus, and may have been offered by the senate to Severus Alexander, who supposedly rejected it because, among other things, he was afraid he would be unable to live up to the high expectations connected with it. In reality, it seems more likely that Alexander wanted to avoid associations with his condemned predecessor. The highly respected name Antoninus may well have become tainted by the bad reputation of Elagabalus, as the author of the *Historia Augusta* suggests.[6] No emperor would bear it after 222.

Both Septimius and Caracalla explicitly traced their ancestry back to the first-century CE emperor Nerva (96–98) in some of their inscriptions.[7] Although none of the known inscriptions erected *by* Elagabalus show him doing the same, several inscriptions devoted *to* the young emperor mention both the earlier Severans and Antonines as his ancestors, as well as Hadrian, Trajan and Nerva.[8] It is therefore not unthinkable, and perhaps even likely, that Elagabalus, too, explicitly made this dynastic claim in some of his inscriptions. The name Marcus Aurelius Antoninus certainly suggested that he descended from the Antonines. Thus, like his 'father' and 'grandfather' before him, the new emperor upheld a myth of dynastic continuity with fondly remembered second-century emperors in order to legitimise his power.

There was another respect in which Elagabalus followed the example of the earlier Severans. Like Septimius Severus and Caracalla, he granted other members of the imperial house an important role in the representation of his reign. As soon as Alexianus became Caesar, the family ties between him and his imperial cousin were tightened: Elagabalus adopted the boy as his son and styled him as such in imperial inscriptions.[9] In this way, he connected the principate to his entire family rather than just to himself. While the notion that the supreme power should be held by members of one specific family dated back to the Julio-Claudians, the importance of the imperial family was stressed more than ever before under the Severans. Septimius had emphasised the notion of a 'domus divina', a 'divine house' that was destined to rule the empire. Elagabalus adopted the same idea. By referring to his Severan ancestors and presenting not just his heir and wives, but also his mother and grandmother to his subjects, he created the impression that the gods had bestowed the ruling of the empire on the Severans, and the Severans alone. In doing so, he strengthened not only the power base of his house, but also his own position as a member of the domus divina.

Elagabalus's ancestry was also emphasised in a more general way. Unlike his immediate predecessor, Macrinus, who had been an 'eques' when he gained the throne, Elagabalus belonged to the senatorial order. Both his real father, Sextus Varius Marcellus, and his alleged father, Caracalla, had been of senatorial rank. In the eyes of the Roman senate, this must have made Elagabalus a more suitable candidate for the throne than Macrinus, who had officially been unqualified for the purple because of his equestrian status. According to Cassius Dio, the boy was well aware of this, for after the victory over his opponent, he is alleged to have sent a dispatch to the people, the soldiers and the senate of Rome, in which he made the following comments with regard to Macrinus: 'This man, to whom it was not permitted even to enter the senate-house after the proclamation debarring all others than senators, dared treacherously to murder the emperor whom he had been trusted to guard, dared to appropriate his office and to become emperor before he had been senator.'[10]

In Rome, denarii (silver coins) were minted with the legend 'NOBILITAS', another reference to Elagabalus's ancestry from the highest social circles.[11] The emperor's marriage to Julia Paula, 'a woman from the most aristocratic family in Rome', can be seen as an attempt to tie him to the Roman aristocracy. The fact that the marriage probably took place soon after Elagabalus's arrival in the capital indicates how important it was deemed to make him fit into Roman high society. After the controversial second marriage to Aquilia Severa, the emperor married Annia Faustina, a descendant of Marcus Aurelius. This marriage had the added advantage that it not only provided Elagabalus with a wife of noble lineage, but also forged a genuine link between the Severans and the Antonines. Any children that Elagabalus and Annia Faustina produced would have descended from Marcus Aurelius and could therefore be regarded as true heirs of the beloved philosopher-emperor.

As was typical of a Roman princeps, Elagabalus did not just boast an impressive ancestry, but also called attention to his own virtues and achievements as emperor. In some instances, this meant referring to specific acts; in others the young monarch prided himself on his general abilities to rule the empire. He strove to present himself to his subjects as a good ruler, worthy of his elevated position. In order to achieve this, it seems that different messages were sent to different groups.

Especially in the first year of his reign, Elagabalus was very dependent on the support of the troops. Therefore, many coins with military themes were minted. Most of these can be dated to the period 218–19 and are made of silver, the metal in which the soldiers were usually paid. This suggests that the messages they bore were primarily aimed at the army. Often, they express the (desired) loyalty of the soldiers to the emperor: 'FIDES EXERCITVS' and 'FIDES MILITVM'. The legend 'CONCORDIA MILIT(VM)' proclaims unity between the legions.[12] These three types almost seem to have a pleading character, trying to prevent treason and discord within the army. Other types strike a more triumphant note, celebrating the victory over Macrinus: 'MARS VICTOR', 'VICTORIA AVG(VSTI)' and 'VICTOR(IA) ANTONINI AVG(vsti)'.[13] These legends probably heightened not only the emperor's prestige, but also that of the troops, which after all had accomplished his victory. They may have functioned as a metaphorical pat on the back, strengthening the ties between emperor and army and helping to ensure military loyalty. The specific reference to the name Antoninus could be seen as an additional attack on Macrinus, implying that the briefly-ruling emperor had been no more than a usurper, defeated by the legitimate heir of the dynasty he had temporarily overthrown.

During the later years of Elagabalus's reign, the army received less attention. Considering that the initial wave of revolts and pretenders seems to have subsided and the emperor was now probably recognised by all legions, the change is understandable. Contrary to Caracalla's approach, Elagabalus did not choose to profile himself in an explicitly militant way. This can clearly be seen from a second type of bust, quite unlike the first (see Fig. 4). 'Type 2', of which at least two specimens have been preserved, shows a somewhat dull-looking young man with a round face, long sideburns and a wispy moustache. The hair, considerably longer than in type 1, consists of lancet-shaped locks which partially cover each other like scales and fall over the forehead in single strands.[14] This haircut is recognisable on coins from 220 onwards. Considering that the new bust type could have been introduced some time earlier, it may first have been issued in 219, perhaps on the occasion of the emperor's arrival in Rome or his marriage to Julia Paula.

Unlike type 1, type 2 does not look like Caracalla at all. It is probably much closer to Elagabalus's actual appearance. Although Fittschen and Zanker mention the 'ethnic features' of this bust, which presumably stressed the emperor's Syrian background and participation in the cult of Elagabal, they fail to specify the details of these alleged features. In fact, there seems to be nothing particularly 'ethnic' about the type 2 portrait.

More plausible are Fittschen's and Zanker's comments about the emperor's hair. As they point out, type 2 moves away from Caracalla's and Geta's military haircut, and seems to refer to older, second-century examples of courtly portraits. The strands of hair falling over the forehead seem to reference portraits of Augustus. This indicates that type 2 was probably aimed primarily at the elite and the people of Rome. Evoking associations with Augustus and the Antonines, it presented Elagabalus as a princeps rather than as a military commander.

According to Dio, Elagabalus claimed to have no desire for titles which had been won by war and bloodshed. However, we can wonder to what extent this was the consequence of a genuine love for peace. After all, military achievements were traditionally one of the key instruments for Roman rulers to legitimise their power. Both Septimius Severus and Caracalla had started wars in order to win renown for their conquests. Perhaps Elagabalus wanted to avoid the huge risks and costs involved in such enterprises. His position on the throne was probably not secure enough to risk the humiliation of a military defeat.

Nevertheless, the young emperor did not completely lose track of his military prestige. During the whole of his reign, he used the title 'imperator', commander of the troops, on all of his coins. This habit had been abandoned by Hadrian in 124 CE. Henceforth, rulers had used the title on coins only during the first year they held the principate, but Macrinus and Elagabalus broke with the tradition. By constantly styling himself 'imperator', Elagabalus emphasised his potential for victory. He let his troops greet him as imperator at least four times, which implied that he had won at least four military victories.[15] However, since he had not waged any wars since the defeat of Macrinus, the imperator-greetings can hardly have been more than hollow phrases, crediting the emperor with a military prestige that he had never won through actual victories. It is possible that the main reason for the greetings was fiscal, because they allowed Elagabalus to collect the 'aurum coronarium' which the cities were obliged to pay him on these occasions.

Some coins from the period 218–19 make reference to Elagabalus's victory over Macrinus, but do not seem to be directed primarily at the army. These coins, most of them minted in Rome, show the cult statue of Roma Aeterna on the reverse, seated and with a small Victory standing in her hand. The image occurs on gold, silver and bronze coinage and seems to imply that it was not just Elagabalus who had triumphed, but Rome. Apart from the possible dynastic implications – namely the suggestion that the usurper had been beaten and the true heir of the empire was victorious – it may also refer to the fact that Macrinus had never been in the capital during his reign. By explicitly making Rome a part of his triumph, Elagabalus showed that he cared more about the city than his predecessor. When he finally reached the capital (about a year after his victory), his arrival was celebrated on coins with the legend 'ADVENTVS AVGVSTI'.[16]

After he had settled in Rome, the emphasis of Elagabalus's representation shifted from military to civic matters. Coin legends testify of the many promises the emperor made to his subjects. Among these, the guarantee of a good grain supply, 'ANNONA AVGVSTI', was one of the most important. The distribution of the proverbial 'bread' was crucial in winning and maintaining the support of the Roman populace. However, it was not the only means by which the emperor proved his generosity. Coins were minted with the legends 'ABVNDANTIA AVG(VSTI)' and 'INDVLGENTIA AVG(VSTI)', 'the abundance of the emperor' and 'the indulgence of the emperor'. No less than four 'liberalitas' gifts (grantings to the people) are known from the short reign of Elagabalus, indicating that the emperor made good on his promises. The new ruler strove to win the favour of the populace, trying to create general joy – 'LAETITIA PVBLICA' – to keep his subjects content.[17] He provided them with lavish games and festivals, banqueting the soldiers and the populace, entertaining them with charioteers, gladiators and wild beasts, and throwing costly goods and animals to the crowd. It seems that Elagabalus took pains to present himself as the great benefactor: not just of Rome, but of the empire at large. He repaired roads and buildings throughout the provinces, erecting inscriptions in which he styled himself 'felicissimus adque invictissimus ac super omnes retro principes indulgentissimus', 'most blessed and most invincible and more indulgent than all previous emperors'.[18]

Imperial promises were not limited to distributing gifts and providing the basic needs for survival. Elagabalus also claimed 'LIBERTAS AVGVSTI'.[19] This legend was sometimes used by rulers who claimed to have freed the Roman people from tyranny. It expressed the promise that the emperor would respect Roman law and would not have any senators arrested and executed without a fair trial – in other words, that he would act as a law-abiding ruler, not as an unchecked tyrant. According to Cassius Dio, Elagabalus had assured the soldiers, the senate and the people of Rome that he would always and in all things emulate the exemplary emperors Augustus and Marcus Aurelius, a promise which had similar implications. His reign was presented as a stable, peaceful time. Coins celebrated the 'SECVRITAS PERPETVA' of an empire which was not under severe pressure of invading barbarians or torn apart by civil war, but could prosper undisturbed under the 'PAX AVGVSTI'.[20]

Next to his ancestry, his virtues and his achievements, there was another aspect to Elagabalus's imperial representation. Even before the religious reforms of late 220, supernatural claims were used to legitimise the boy's reign. Coins proclaimed the emperor's trust in divine providence, the 'PROVIDENTIA DEORVM'.[21] This suggested that Elagabalus was destined to rule the empire. His divine protector was the almighty Jupiter, to whom the legend 'IOVI CONSERVATORI' was dedicated.[22] Moreover, Elagabalus styled himself 'Pius Felix' in inscriptions. These titles, which had been introduced to the imperial formula by Commodus, probably expressed the emperor's new, more elevated religious position. As Pius, he placed himself at the head of traditional religiosity in the empire. As Felix, he claimed divine protection and beneficence. The combination Pius Felix made him into something more than just pontifex maximus of Rome: he became the 'religious champion of all', ensuring the happiness of his subjects by means of his divine felicitas. However, the question can be asked whether Elagabalus was genuinely keen to spread this message to his subjects, or just included the titles because they had become standardised, since few imperial coins have 'P(IVS) F(ELIX)' or 'PIVS FEL(IX)' on their obverse. Only eastern coins from the period 218–19 seem to bear the combination. The title 'PIVS' often appears on its own, both on coins from Rome and from the East. According to Harold Mattingly, we should not regard '*Pius*' just as a reference to Elagabalus's religious devotion, but also as a reference to Caracalla, who had likewise styled himself 'Pius'.[23]

Despite the fact that most coins do not bear the combination 'Pius Felix', several types stress the themes pietas and felicitas separately. Examples of this are coins with the legends 'PIETAS AVG(VSTI)', 'SAECVLI FELICITAS' and 'FELICITAS PUBLICA'.[24] Curiously enough, however, almost none of these types bear a portrait of Elagabalus on the obverse, but one of his grandmother, Julia Maesa. What does this imply? Should we see Julia Maesa, the matriarch of the family, as the personification of the entire imperial house? Do the coins put not just the emperor, but the complete domus divina, at the head of traditional religiosity in the realm? Is it the imperial family as a whole whose felicitas guarantees the prosperity of the empire? If the latter is indeed the case, it underlines the importance of the domus divina in Elagabalus's imperial representation. However, it is important to note that both coins and inscriptions connect the combination 'Pius Felix' exclusively to the emperor himself, establishing him as the ultimate 'religious champion' of the empire.

Not only did imperial coins claim that Elagabalus and his house had the support of the gods, they also suggested that the imperial family, and especially the emperor, had some divine qualities themselves. This point was made rather carefully. In accordance with Roman tradition, only the deceased members of the domus divina, Caracalla and Julia Domna, were actually deified. On the one hand, this allowed Elagabalus to stress that he was a member of the Severan dynasty and could therefore rightfully claim the throne. On the other hand, it also implied that he descended from divine ancestors, whose superhuman status enhanced his own prestige. This suggestion of divinity was emphasised by associating the women from the imperial family with goddesses. 'MATER DEVM' and 'IVNO REGINA' were two of the goddesses who appeared on the reverse of coins of Julia Soaemias; 'IVNO', among others, on the reverse of coins of Julia Maesa; and 'IVNO CONSERVATRIX' and 'VENVS GENETRIX', among others, on the reverse of coins of Julia Paula.[25]

Elagabalus's affinity with the Syrian god Elagabal was no more than a background theme on coins from 218–20, at least as far as the Roman mint was concerned. Although Sol was sometimes depicted on coins, he was not explicitly equated with Sol Elagabal. The ambiguity of the image may well have been deliberate, demonstrating the emperor's devotion to the sun god without presenting him in the unfamiliar guise of the black stone of Emesa. The one or two coin types from this period which do picture the stone style him as 'CONSERVATOR AVGVSTI', an honour also attributed to Jupiter.[26] In some imperial inscriptions, Elagabalus bears the epithet 'invictus', hinting at a connection between himself and Sol Invictus Elagabal.[27] Antoniniani and dupondii show the emperor wearing a radiate crown, but since this is standard for all emperors on coins of 'double value', it does not seem to bear any special significance in Elagabalus's case.

In the East, the Emesene sun god already played a bigger role on the imperial coinage before the end of 220. The black stone appeared on the reverse of some coins with the legend 'SANCT(O) DEO SOLI ELAGABAL(O)', 'to the sacred sun god Elagabal' (Fig. 5).[28] One type is dedicated to 'SOLI PROPVGNATORI', 'Sol the defender', depicted as a naked man wearing a cloak and holding a thunderbolt in his right hand, while his left arm is thrust out before him. Almost exactly the same image occurs on a coin from the reign of Septimius Severus, but this type is not dedicated to Sol, but to 'IOVI PROPVGNATORI'. A coin from the reign of Marcus Aurelius likewise attributes both the lightning bolt and the title 'propugnator' to Jupiter.[29] Did Elagabalus substitute Sol for Jupiter to make a point? It is tempting to regard the 'SOLI PROPVGNATORI' coin as foreshadowing Elagabal's new role as supreme Roman deity from the end of 220 onwards. However, in doing so we may be reading too much into it. The coin may just express the emperor's sentiment that Sol – presumably Sol Invictus Elagabal – was comparable to Jupiter in power and status. It does not necessarily follow that plans already existed to dethrone the latter in order to install the former as the new head of the Roman pantheon.

Quite remarkable is the little star on the reverse of many of Elagabalus's coins (see Figs 7–9). It appears on coins from every year during the period 218–22, although it is more common on coins from the later years of Elagabalus's reign. It can be found on gold, silver and bronze, and appears on imperial coinage from both Rome and the East. Not only do the coins of Elagabalus himself sometimes have a star on the reverse, but also those of Julia Maesa, Julia Soaemias, Julia Paula, Aquilia Severa and Annia Faustina. The only member of the imperial house whose coins are consistently lacking a star is Alexander, but so few coin types of the Caesar have survived that this could well be merely coincidental – especially since the star *does* appear on many of Alexander's coins as Augustus. According to Erika Manders, stars on imperial coinage probably indicate the emperor's special divine status, either as a god or as a man with a special connection to the gods.[30] The star's appearance on the coins of Elagabalus's wives and relatives can be explained by their close connection to the emperor as members of the domus divina.

Elagabalus's representation during the period 218–20 was highly traditional, but it has enough coherence to be regarded as an ideological programme. After an initial phase, in which the emperor relied heavily on the support of the soldiers and put much emphasis on military themes, most messages seem to have been aimed primarily at a civic public. The central image is that of the legitimate heir, descended from Caracalla and the Antonines, restoring the dynasty and heralding an age of peace and prosperity for the empire.

Not all aspects of Elagabalus's representation are equally well worked out and connected with each other. While the dynastic arguments form a consistent whole, some other messages seem less clearly outlined. For instance, although the emperor is styled 'Pius Felix' in inscriptions and on some coins, messages on coins concerning 'pietas' or 'felicitas' are usually not tied to Elagabalus, but to Julia Maesa, as noted before. Jupiter, traditionally the emperor's divine protector, had to share this honour with Elagabalus's personal god Elagabal, probably further muddling the idea of a ruler with a special connection to the divine world. Moreover, the appearance of the black stone of Emesa on several coins, especially on those minted in the East, as well as the appearance of the star, beg the question whether the emperor's representation during the early years of his reign was consciously anticipating the religious reforms of late 220. While this possibility cannot be excluded, the uncompromising nature of the reforms makes it rather unlikely that Elagabalus would allow his subjects a two-and-a-half-year period to get acquainted with their supreme-deity-to-be. It seems more plausible that the idea to put the Emesene sun god at the head of the Roman pantheon was conceived only a short time before it was executed. Up to then, Elagabalus's devotion to Elagabal was probably no more than a curiosity to most of his subjects, a discordant note in the boy's representation as a traditional, moderate and benign Roman princeps.

### PRIEST-EMPEROR OF ELAGABAL

Although Elagabalus expressed his affinity to Sol Invictus Elagabal during the first years of his reign, there is very little evidence that he already emphasised his role as the god's high priest. An interesting exception is the coin type described by Baldus, minted in Rome in 219, showing the emperor sacrificing in front of a quadriga in which the black stone is placed (Fig. 6). Elagabalus is dressed in what appears to be a tunica, rather than in his 'Oriental' priestly garb, but there can be no question that he is depicted as high priest of Elagabal. According to Baldus, the coin had been inspired by the portrait which the emperor allegedly sent to Rome from Nicomedia.[31] It shows him making a sacrifice to Elagabal, who is also in the picture. Herodian records that orders were issued to hang this portrait in the senate house, high up over the statue of Victory, and that all senators had to burn incense and make a libation of wine to it on entering the building.

If this curious story is true, the portrait must have been sent on an imperial whim, as Herodian suggests. Apart from the Baldus-coin, there are no known coins and inscriptions from the period before the religious reforms which attest that Elagabalus was Elagabal's high priest. Even in the East, where the black stone already appeared regularly on imperial coins before the end of 220, the emperor is never presented as its high priest, but only as 'pontifex maximus'. The only coins which show him sacrificing bear the legend 'VOTA PVBLICA', 'public vows'.[32] Since they were minted in the East, they are possibly referring to the consular vows Elagabalus took in Nicomedia at the beginning of 219. Despite Dio's remark that the emperor refused to wear the triumphal dress on this occasion, the coins depict him in the traditional manner: he is wearing a toga, his head is veiled and he is sacrificing out of his open right hand over a lighted tripod or altar, holding a roll in his left hand. Any reference to the cult of Elagabal is absent.

At the end of 220, Elagabalus reformed Roman state religion. He put Elagabal at the head of the Roman pantheon and let himself be voted 'sacerdos amplissimus dei invicti Solis Elagabali' by the senate. Although he still styled himself 'pontifex maximus' as well after 220, inscriptions show that the title 'sacerdos amplissimus' took precedence: the emperor is consistently styled 'sacerdos' first and 'pontifex' second.[33] It is interesting to note that the words 'sacerdos amplissimus' seem like a deliberate allusion to 'pontifex maximus', probably emphasising that the functions described by these titles were very similar. His role as high priest of the empire's new supreme deity put Elagabalus at the head of the new religious order, just as he had been at the head of the old order as 'pontifex maximus'.

Both in Rome and in the East, imperial coins mentioning the emperor as 'pontifex maximus' on the reverse do not add the 'sacerdos amplissimus' title. However, they are often accompanied by an image of Elagabalus sacrificing in 'Oriental' garb (Fig. 8). Similar images are depicted on coin reverses bearing the legends 'INVICTVS SACERDOS AVG(VSTVS)' (Fig. 9), 'SACERD(OS) DEI SOLIS ELAGAB(ALI)' and 'SVMMVS SACERDOS AVGVSTVS'.[34] As Lucinda Dirven has pointed out, the emperor's priestly dress is quite different from the costume described by Herodian. Rather than the ankle-long 'chiton' and tiara-shaped crown the historian mentions, we see the emperor wearing trousers and a long-sleeved short tunic, sometimes with a 'chlamys' (mantle) on top. Instead of a crown or tiara, he wears the conventional imperial diadem.[35]

This outfit, Dirven argues, is not identical with any of the Syrian priestly garments known to us. It probably represents a Roman adjustment of the original costume, if not a complete innovation. She speculates that it may have been designed to appeal to the troops, since long-sleeved tunics, trousers and mantles became common dress for Roman soldiers in the third century CE. Moreover, Dio records that Caracalla wore Germanic dress (consisting of the aforementioned articles of clothing) during his Eastern campaigns.[36] By presenting himself in a similar outfit, Elagabalus may have been attempting to evoke associations with his 'father'. Dirven suggests that his depiction as sacerdos amplissimus could be seen as an appeal to the troops, proclaiming military invincibility. If she is right, Caracalla once again became more central to the representation of Elagabalus. The initial strong association of the emperor with his predecessor had apparently ceased with the introduction of bust type 2 in 219. Now, a year later, the bond may have been tightened again.

What is also striking about the iconography of the coins presenting the emperor as priest of Elagabal is that they present a novel phenomenon in a very traditional way. Elagabalus is depicted standing next to an altar, or, in some cases, a tripod, holding a 'patera' (a ceremonial dish used for libations) in his right hand and a twig in his left hand. Often, there is a prostrate bull next to the altar, and in almost every instance there appears a star. With the exception of the dress, this could have been a coin image of any Roman emperor of the principate, sacrificing as pontifex maximus. Obviously, the images of Elagabalus as sacerdos amplissimus are less outlandish than they may appear to have been on the basis of the extant historiographical records.

A similar point could be made for the coin types depicting the black stone of Emesa as 'CONSERVATOR AVG(VSTI)' (Fig. 7). While the stone itself is obviously not a part of traditional Roman iconography, the quadriga in which it rides is reminiscent of Augustan coins depicting a quadriga with ears of corn in it.[37] The title 'conservator' was usually attributed to Jupiter, but had been granted to other gods as well. By styling Elagabal as such, the emperor's exotic god was, to some extent, incorporated into the familiar territory of Roman tradition. Moreover, according to the *BMC*, there are only two coin types for the period 220–22 showing an image of the black stone. In contrast, no less than 12 coin types depicting an anthropomorphic Sol were struck during this period. Two of these even style the god 'CONSERVATOR AVG(VSTI)', which may indicate that they are referring to Sol Invictus Elagabal.[38] However, the name of the Syrian sun god does not occur on any coins depicting an anthropomorphic Sol, leaving the exact identity of the depicted deity ambiguous – which was probably the intention.

Two noteworthy changes occur in Elagabalus's portraits on the obverses of coins after the religious reforms. Firstly, the emperor grows a beard in 221 (see Figs 8–10). This feat can be explained by his coming of age, although the growth of facial hair may have been exaggerated to underline that the emperor was no longer a boy. In addition, the beard may indicate an attempt to resemble portraits of Caracalla more closely. This could be taken as support for Dirven's theory that the emperor aimed his presentation as sacerdos amplissimus primarily at the troops, with whom Caracalla had been very popular. Secondly, some issues from 221 onwards show Elagabalus with something protruding from his forehead (see Figs 8–10).[39] The object has often been identified as a horn, but on close inspection it does not have the right shape for that. Elke Krengel offers an alternative explanation: she claims the 'horn' is actually the end of a dried bull's penis.[40]

Although this may sound unlikely at first, Krengel's arguments are intriguing. Firstly, when the 'horn' is compared to the end of a dried bull's penis, the similarities in shape are remarkable. Secondly, Krengel gives several parallels of gods and priests wearing a human phallus on their head. Seen in this light, wearing a bull's penis does not seem particularly outrageous. Krengel shows that the 'horn' only appears on coins which show either a sacrificial scene on the reverse or celebrate the appointment of the new consuls – an event at which sacrifices were made as well. This strongly suggests that the significance of the 'horn' was religious. Krengel considers it to have been a symbol of fertility and strength, transferring the power of Elagabal to his high priest. There is at least one ancient parallel for this claim, albeit from a Hethitic, rather than a Syrian, setting.[41] Moreover, the bull was commonly considered to be a strong, energetic and above all virile animal. Some scholars, like Dirven, think that a Roman emperor wearing a bull's penis would have been too outrageous, and reject Krengel's interpretation as a typical example of the notion that everything was possible where 'Oriental' religions are concerned.[42] Still, a more plausible explanation has not been found thus far, so it seems best to keep an open mind.

If the changes on imperial coins and in imperial inscriptions are remarkable, the impact of the religious reforms on the emperor's public appearance must have been even more profound. The pompous, colourful ceremonies conducted in honour of Elagabal, like the public sacrifices and the stone's procession from one temple to the other, must have been exotic events in Roman eyes – amusing perhaps, but undoubtedly alienating and, quite possibly, offensive. Likewise, Elagabalus's marriage to a vestal virgin and his decision to collect all the city's sacred objects in the temple of Elagabal can hardly have been measures on which the Romans looked favourably. While the coins and inscriptions seem to make an effort to fit Elagabalus's religious reforms into a traditionally Roman pattern, using variations on established formulas and iconography, the emperor himself appears to have largely, if not completely, ignored Roman traditions.

How to explain this dichotomy? Does the familiar language used on coins and in inscriptions just indicate that the people responsible for them – whoever they were – tried to come to terms with Elagabalus's reforms within their own cultural framework? Or did they make a deliberate attempt to present the new religious order in ways which were familiar to the Roman viewer?

Although the former explanation is certainly valid, it does not prevent the latter from being true as well. When we look at imperial coins and inscriptions of Elagabalus from the end of 220 onwards, it is clear that the way in which the emperor was represented was drastically redefined. Strikingly, there are far more coins depicting Elagabalus than there are coins depicting his god. The *BMC* lists 31 gold and silver coin types showing Elagabalus as high priest of Elagabal in the categories 220–22, 221 and 222. Twenty-four of these were minted in Rome, seven in the East. In the same categories, we find only ten types showing the sun god, all of which were minted in Rome.[43] Eight of these bear an image of an anthropomorphic Sol, who is not explicitly identified as Elagabal; four present the god as 'conservator Augusti' and are therefore indirectly concerned with the emperor as well. Moreover, bronze coins provide us with a similar picture. In the categories 218–22, 221 and 222, there are no more than four coin types showing the sun god, who is depicted in anthropomorphic shape and is not explicitly identified as Elagabal, while 17 types show Elagabalus sacrificing in his priestly garb.[44] Mattingly correctly concludes, 'The emperor [...] is glorified even more than the god whom he worships.'[45]

The shift in the emperor's numismatic representation was probably orchestrated by members of his court or administration. These people, who had a personal interest in keeping Elagabalus on the throne, must have been aware of his weak position. Unlike his Severan predecessors, Elagabalus had not distinguished himself by fighting foreign enemies or adorning Rome with impressive buildings. He had come to power by pretending to be Caracalla's son – a claim which some of his subjects, at least, knew to be false. Far from being a renowned politician or general, the 'new Antoninus' had gained the throne as a 14-year-old boy without any political or military experience. By dethroning Jupiter as the chief Roman god and marrying a vestal virgin he had displayed grave disrespect for Rome's most sacred traditions. Clearly, the emperor's alleged ancestry, virtues and achievements fell short in providing a solid legitimation for his reign.

Considering these circumstances, it is not surprising that a different strategy was adopted at the end of 220. Elagabalus's subordinates had to find a way to deal with the religious reforms the emperor imposed on Rome. While they could not stop him elevating Elagabal to the position of supreme Roman deity and having his priesthood of the Emesene sun god officially recognised by the senate, they did their best to present these changes in a way which was familiar to the Roman public – and, therefore, hopefully easier to accept. Both the title 'sacerdos amplissimus' and the messages on coins use a language with which the Romans were well acquainted. But the ambitions of the people constructing the messages seem to have gone further than just presenting the religious reforms in an acceptable way. It appears they attempted to use Elagabalus's new priestly role as an alternative ideological foundation for his rule. By emphasising the emperor's special position as sacerdos amplissimus of Elagabal, they tried to make his reputation less dependent on his ancestry and his qualities and achievements as a ruler, instead focusing on supernatural arguments to enhance his withering prestige.

From the end of 220, Elagabalus was portrayed as the faithful servant and priest of a very powerful god: Sol Invictus Elagabal, supreme ruler over the Roman pantheon, who served as the emperor's divine protector. Like the god who watched over him, Elagabalus boasted invincibility: he was the invictus sacerdos Augustus, the invincible priest-emperor. Although the nicknames Elagabalus and Heliogabalus suggest otherwise, there is no reason to assume that the emperor was supposed to be regarded as the earthly incarnation of Elagabal: he is never depicted as Sol and wears a radiate only on coins with 'double value'. There are no contemporary sources calling him Elagabalus or Elagabal: those names are only attributed to the god, whose earthly incarnation was the black stone. Nevertheless, the emperor's close, personal bond with Elagabal may well have suggested a superhuman status. As the supreme mediator between the human and the divine world, Elagabalus occupied a unique and important position. Like a pontifex maximus, the invincible priest-emperor did not make sacrifices on his own behalf, but on behalf of all his subjects, whose well-being depended on the favour of the almighty sun god. Only Elagabalus, high priest of Elagabal, could obtain that divine favour and secure peace and prosperity for the realm.

Elagabalus's new representation as invincible priest-emperor does not seem to have been directed at any specific group. Coins showing the emperor sacrificing to Elagabal were minted both in Rome and in the East and include both silver and bronze issues. Interestingly, Elagabalus is never shown as sacerdos amplissimus on gold coins, although he appears in a more traditional role, standing laureate and togate in a quadriga. The black stone of Emesa is depicted only on two issues in the period 220–22, both of which are aurei.[46] Perhaps this was a way to represent the difference in status between the god and his high priest. In addition, we should keep in mind that aurei only reached a very exclusive group, whereas silver and bronze coins spread among a much wider audience.

In the period 218–19, the black stone was depicted on seven issues, which included both gold and silver coins.[47] Apparently, both the elite and the troops were targeted with this image. The betyl may have gained in status during the later period, but simultaneously seems to have been pushed into the background, confirming that the coins were first and foremost concerned with presenting Elagabalus in his new role as sacerdos amplissimus dei invicti Solis Elagabali.

Despite the changes in the imperial representation, more traditional messages and images did not completely disappear. For instance, traditional Roman figures like Providentia and Victory still appear on coins from 221. A coin of Aquilia Severa mentions 'VESTA' on the reverse. The emperor himself is not only depicted as high priest of Elagabal, but also as dressed in a Roman toga, clasping hands with Aquilia Severa or Annia Faustina, or riding in a quadriga.[48] Imperial inscriptions from 221 and 222 still explicitly claim Elagabalus's descent from Caracalla and Septimius Severus. And while the title 'sacerdos amplissimus' took precedent over that of 'pontifex maximus', the latter was maintained and also continued to appear on the obverses of coins.[49]

Most striking are the coins of Alexander as Caesar. Although the emperor's newly acquired 'son' received the title 'nobilissimus Caesar imperii et sacerdotis', 'most noble Caesar of the empire and the priesthood', presumably not only linking him to the empire but to the cult of Elagabal as well, his coinage makes no reference whatsoever to the sun god from Emesa. On the contrary, several of Alexander's coins bear the reverse legend 'PIETAS AVG(VSTI)' ('piety of the emperor') and depict traditional

Roman priestly emblems: a 'lituus', a knife, a 'patera', a tall jug, a 'simpulum' and a sprinkler. Other issues style the young Caesar 'PONTIFEX CO(N)S(VL)', which seems like a deliberate reference to traditional Roman state religion.[50] Mattingly remarks that the Roman mint under Elagabalus was probably divided into five 'officinae' (divisions), one of which was shared between the imperial women and Alexander. Although this would explain the explicitly traditional messages on Alexander's coins, nothing indicates that such a division in officinae indeed existed. It seems more likely that the presentation of Alexander as a traditional Roman prince was a well-calculated strategy by people in the imperial administration to set the boy up as a potential successor to the controversial Elagabalus. More than anything, perhaps, this shows their awareness that the position of the priest-emperor, whether he was presented as invincible or not, could very well become untenable in the near future.

## RESPONSES OF SUBJECTS

It may well be that the damnatio memoriae which befell Elagabalus after his death has muddled our view of how his subjects perceived him during his reign. The accounts of Cassius Dio and Herodian present the emperor in a very negative way, the former describing him as 'one by whom nothing was done that was not evil and base', the latter as 'an emperor who was a disgrace'.[51] However, we should keep in mind that Dio was closely associated with Severus Alexander, the emperor who had Elagabalus's memory condemned in the first place. It would have been impossible for Dio, who finished his work during Alexander's reign, to show Elagabalus in a positive light. Herodian had no such restrictions, since he wrote after Alexander's death, but based his work partly on Dio's and may therefore have copied many negative stereotypes from his fellow historian.

Even so, it seems unlikely that Dio's and Herodian's real judgement of Elagabalus was much more lenient than the one they presented in their histories. A traditional Roman senator like Dio was probably appalled by the unprecedented violation of sacred Roman traditions which took place during Elagabalus's reign. The historian remarks that the emperor's offence consisted 'not in his introducing a foreign god into Rome or in his exalting him in very strange ways, but in his placing him even before Jupiter himself and causing himself to be voted his priest, also in his circumcising himself and abstaining from swine's flesh, on the ground that his devotion would thereby be purer'. He also condemns the union of Elagabalus and Aquilia Severa, pointing out that the emperor was 'most flagrantly violating the law' by cohabiting with a vestal virgin. The marriage of the god Elagabal to Urania was, in Dio's opinion, an 'extreme absurdity'. All of these seem like genuine sentiments for a man who held Roman traditions in high regard and was displeased to see them treated without respect. It is not unlikely that other members of the Roman elite reacted in a similar fashion to Elagabalus's actions. Herodian certainly agreed with Dio in this respect, since he remarks that 'all that was once held in respect was reduced in this way to a state of dishonour and frenzied madness'.[52]

Both Dio and Herodian use negative stereotypes to characterise Elagabalus, expressing their disapproval of the young emperor whenever possible. We should be hesitant to regard many of these numerous accusations as much more than malicious invention, but there seems at least one other possible reason for Dio to disapprove of Elagabalus. Time and time again, the historian refers to his subject as the 'False Antoninus', indicating that Elagabalus was not the son of Caracalla at all and therefore not the legitimate heir to the throne. He names Sextus Varius Marcellus as Elagabalus's real father. If Dio knew that the emperor was (in all probability) the son of Marcellus, other members of the Roman elite must also have been aware of this.

Interestingly, Herodian does not make up his mind about the matter: he thinks that it 'may or may not have been true' that Elagabalus was Caracalla's son, but does not seem to attach much value to the answer one way or the other.[53] It is also interesting to note that Dio is a lot less vehement about Septimius Severus adopting himself into the Antonine dynasty than he is about Elagabalus pretending to be the son of Caracalla. Perhaps this could be explained by the fact that Severus's position as emperor was already secured when he took this decision, while Elagabalus only managed to gain the purple because of it. Alternatively, it is possible that the name 'False Antoninus' was just another slander against an emperor that Dio already disliked. If the latter is the case, the historian's criticism of Elagabalus's invented ancestry should be regarded as a consequence rather than a cause of his dislike.

We have very little material to answer the question how other members of the Roman elite experienced the reign of Elagabalus, although there is no reason to assume that their perception was much different from Dio's. The *Vita Heliogabali* in the *Historia Augusta* probably used the now-lost historical account of the emperor's contemporary Marius Maximus as an important source. Therefore, the extremely negative tone of the *Vita* could be taken as indication that Maximus likewise disapproved of Elagabalus. Another tantalising clue may be found in the acts of the senatorial priesthood of the arval brothers of 218, the year in which Elagabalus became a member. Contrary to the acts of previous years, this inscription records the rituals of the brothers in a very elaborate and precise manner. The same seems to be the case for the acts of 219, although this inscription is much more damaged. In all likelihood, what remains is only a small fraction. From 220 onwards, the acts are a lot shorter and less specific again.[54] Could it be that the brothers initially feared that Elagabalus would abolish or somehow drastically reform their priesthood? The fact that the emperor joined the brothers himself seems to speak against the former, but not necessarily against the latter. If such a fear did indeed exist, the 'priest-emperor' must have been notorious for his religious zeal from the start. However, we should also allow for the possibility that the elaborate records of the arval rituals during the first two years of Elagabalus's reign are merely coincidental.

According to an anecdote in the work of Flavius Philostratus, the sophist Aelian composed an invective against Elagabalus after the emperor's death, 'because by every sort of wanton wickedness he disgraced the Roman Empire'.[55] When Aelian tells Philostratus of Lemnos about his work, the latter is not impressed, remarking that 'while it takes a real man to try to curb a living tyrant, anyone can trample on him when he is down.' This is a valid point, but even if we put considerations of personal well-being aside, the question remains to what extent Elagabalus's damnatio memoriae influenced Aelian's negative portrayal of the priest-emperor. Was it only out of caution that the sophist waited to write his invective until after Elagabalus's death? Did the official condemnation of Elagabalus by Severus Alexander encourage Aelian to portray him in a more negative way than he would have done otherwise? We can only speculate.

The same can be asked with regard to Flavius Philostratus himself, who, according to Michael Meckler, mocks Elagabalus in one of his love letters.[56] Allegedly, this occurs in the long version of letter number 19, which is addressed to a young male prostitute and probably predates the shorter version, in which a female prostitute is the addressee. Philostratus remarks that the boy should not feel ashamed of putting his body at everybody's disposal, because the sun is a common god, too. The word used for 'common' is 'δημόσιος', which, as Meckler points out, makes reference to the state and thus to state religion. The boy's home is compared to a citadel of beauty, those who enter to priests, those who are garlanded as sacred envoys and their silver to tribute money. The letter concludes, 'Rule graciously over your subjects, and receive what they offer, and, furthermore, accept their adoration.' The image of Elagabalus as a male prostitute can be found in both Dio and the *Historia Augusta*, rendering it not unlikely that Philostratus's letter does indeed refer to the priest-emperor. This hypothesis gains even more plausibility when we take into account that Philostratus probably also criticised Caracalla in one of his love letters.[57]

Considering both the accounts of contemporary historians and other indications of the elite's perception of Elagabalus, the impression is strengthened that dislike of the emperor was genuine among the upper classes and not just the hypocritical by-product of Elagabalus's damnatio memoriae. In fact, it could be argued that the damnatio itself is the most persuasive argument for the emperor's unpopularity with the senate, since Severus Alexander worked in close alliance with this government body and seldom seems to have acted without senatorial consent. Of course, one could argue that Alexander had no choice but to condemn Elagabalus, since his coming to power was the direct result of the revolt against his predecessor. However, the fact remains that Alexander's violent ascension to the throne did no apparent damage to his good reputation and therefore must have met with general approval from the senate. Likewise, it seems beyond reasonable doubt that the reversal of Elagabalus's religious reforms was warmly welcomed by the traditional Roman elite. If there were any knights and senators who mourned the priest-emperor, they have left no traces of their sentiments. In the light of the available evidence, we can assume that the majority, at least, cherished little love or respect for the eldest self-proclaimed son of Caracalla.

Little can be said about Elagabalus's popularity with the people of Rome. Considering the many festivals mentioned in the ancient sources and the many liberalitas gifts of the emperor, it is not unthinkable that the majority of the population held a favourable view of the young monarch, who was the first emperor to spend time in the capital since Caracalla had left for the East. However, more invectives are known for Elagabalus than for any other emperor.[58] Dio alone records 'False Antoninus', 'the Assyrian', 'Sardanapalus' and 'Tiberinus', the last of these referring to the fact that Elagabalus was thrown into the Tiber after his death. Philostratus adds 'Gynnis' ('womanish man', allegedly attributed to the emperor by the philosopher Aelian), and the anonymous author of the *Epitome de Caesaribus* mentions Tiberinus and Tractitius, a reference to the fact that Elagabalus's corpse was dragged through the streets by the soldiers ('trahere', 'to drag').

Have these names merely been made up by hostile writers, or were they actually used during or shortly after the emperor's reign? The *Epitome de Caesaribus* claims that both Tractitius and Tiberinus were names by which the emperor 'was called'.[59] Obviously, this can only have happened after Elagabalus's gruesome death. The other names may already have been used during his lifetime. In general, it seems plausible that reigning emperors received nicknames, whether positive or negative, although the negative names were probably not used to their face. However, even if such invectives as 'False Antoninus' and 'Sardanapalus' were used for Elagabalus during his reign, the question remains who did the name calling. It may well have been the praetorians and the people of Rome, but this is no more than a plausible guess. Ultimately, the sentiments of the Roman populace with regard to the priest-emperor and his peculiar god remain hidden to us.

We are hardly better informed about the opinion of the soldiers. The riots of the praetorians clearly demonstrate that they took a dislike to Elagabalus, probably because they were alienated by his 'un-Roman' behaviour, but it is impossible to discern to what extent the attitude of the praetorian guard reflected that of soldiers in the provinces. To be sure, many troops in Syria supported Elagabalus in the revolt against Macrinus, but that does not tell us anything about their opinion of the boy after he had gained the throne and left for Rome, nor is it clear what soldiers in other parts of the empire thought about Elagabalus. Inscriptions indicate that most soldiers acknowledged the emperor as the son of Caracalla and the grandson of Severus. However, no inscriptions are known in which soldiers use Elagabalus's 'sacerdos amplissimus' title. Only three inscriptions erected by soldiers mention the god Elagabal, all predating Elagabalus's reign.[60] Whether this is merely coincidental or reflects military reluctance to accept the religious reforms of the priest-emperor cannot be decided on the basis of the available evidence.

Civic provincial attitudes towards Elagabalus and his Emesene sun god are better recorded in the surviving sources. Inscriptions by imperial officials, local elites and city populaces mention the emperor as the son of Caracalla and the grandson of Severus. Veterans from the colony of Sitifis in Mauretania Caesariensis (present-day western Algeria) traced Elagabalus's descent all the way back to Nerva, apparently putting pride in the dynastic continuity between the founder of their colony and the current emperor. At least one city, Anazarbos in Cilicia (present-day southern Turkey), celebrated Antoniniana in honour of Elagabalus's victory over Macrinus.[61]

The title 'sacerdos amplissimus' also appears in inscriptions from the period 218–22, although not nearly as often as Elagabalus's alleged descent from Caracalla and Severus. Considering that the priestly office became part of the official imperial titles only at the end of 220, this is perhaps not surprising. However, the 'sacerdos' title is also missing in some inscriptions which certainly date from 221 or 222, which may indicate resistance against it. On the other hand, Elagabalus is addressed as 'sacerdos amplissimus' by Flavius Sossianus, governor of Numidia (eastern Algeria/Tunisia). The title also appears in an official request by representatives of an unknown colony with regard to the water supply. Likewise, the emperor's office as high priest of Elagabal is mentioned by the local senate of Assisi.[62] This shows that, even at a local level, some people were aware of the new priestly title. Moreover, they apparently regarded it as one of Elagabalus's official imperial titles, and seem to have had no reservations in using it.

Some provincial responses went further than simply accepting the changes brought about by the emperor's religious reforms. During the period 218–22, several cities in the empire minted coins with an image of the black stone in a quadriga on the reverse, portrayed either from the front or from the side. Apart from Rome and Emesa, these were Aelia Capitolina, Alexandria, Anazarbos, Hierapolis–Castabala (Cilicia), Juliopolis (Bithynia), Laodicea ad Mare (Syria Phoenice) and Neapolis (Samaria).[63] It is probably no coincidence that three of these cities, Anazarbos, Hierapolis–Castabala and Juliopolis, lie on or relatively near the route from Antioch to Rome which Elagabalus took in 218–19. The emperor seems to have visited at least one of them: Anazarbos, which minted a coin with a reverse showing Elagabalus on horseback with a spear in his hand.[64] This image can probably be interpreted as a variation on the adventus theme, the depiction of an imperial arrival. More surprising, perhaps, is the appearance of Elagabal on coins from Aelia Capitolina, Laodicea and Neapolis. These are all cities where many troops were stationed, which may indicate military approval of the Emesene sun god. On the other hand, the geographical location of these three cities in or near Syria provides an alternative explanation for their readiness to mint coins of a local Syrian deity.

The fact that the black stone appears on the coinage of several cities during Elagabalus's reign is, in itself, not enough to establish that the cult of Elagabal was indeed introduced in these cities. It is possible that local authorities were just following the example of imperial coinage, on which Elagabal was first portrayed in 219. However, in some cases we have definite proof for the introduction of the Emesene sun cult. An inscription from Altava, situated in the province of Mauretania Caesariensis, records that the city's 'possessores' built a temple to Elagabal in 221, paid for with money from collections. In Attaleia (Pamphylia), the city council and the people dedicated an undated inscription to the Emesene deity.[65] Although the name Elagabal has been erased, undoubtedly after the death and condemnation of the priest-emperor, it is still readable.

A coin from Sardes (Lydia), minted during the reign of Elagabalus, records the celebration of 'Elagabalia', a festival not in honour of the emperor, but of the god himself. It was celebrated when one Hermophilos held the office of first archon for the second time. Another Sardes coin, likewise mentioning Hermophilos in this office and therefore minted in the same year, records the celebration of 'Chrysantina', a festival in honour of the fertility goddess Korè. This leads Louis Robert to speculate that the cult of Elagabal was connected to the cult of Korè in Sardes. His claim is strengthened by two other coin types bearing the name of Hermophilos. On one of these, the statue of Korè is carried by a figure in a quadriga, raising his right arm in the traditional greeting gesture of Helios; on the other, the goddess is surrounded by two ears of corn and symbols for the sun and moon.[66] This is reminiscent of the divine marriage between Elagabal and Urania in Rome, since Herodian records that Elagabalus regarded the event as an appropriate union between sun and moon. It seems plausible that something similar happened in Sardes with Elagabal and Korè.

No other instances are known of cities celebrating Elagabalia, although an inscription indicates that the god may also have been honoured with games in Thyatira (Lydia). However, as Robert points out, there do seem to be several other cities in which Elagabal was connected to a female deity. A passage in the *Vita Antonini Caracallae* of the *Historia Augusta* mentions that Elagabalus instituted a shrine in the temple of the divine Faustina in Faustinopolis (Cappadocia), 'either for himself or for the Syrian Jupiter (the matter is uncertain) or for the Sun'. Both on imperial and provincial coinage, Faustina is associated with moon goddesses, which makes it plausible that yet another union between sun and moon took place in Faustinopolis. Likewise, Robert argues that in Hierapolis-Castabala Elagabal was connected to Perasia in Hierapolis-Castabala, a local goddess who could be associated with Selene, Artemis and Aphrodite, and may have been connected to Demeter in Nicomedia, since that city celebrated 'Demetria Antoni(ni)a' during Elagabalus's reign.[67] There is no definite proof for any of these unions, but the evidence gathered by Robert is compelling, especially when one considers the separate cases in relation to each other.

More research on this topic has been done by Ruprecht Ziegler. He has remarked that the holy mountain Zarbos at Anazarbos, which was connected with the deity Zeus Olybreus, is thematised on local coins from the reign of Elagabalus, something which had not happened since Trajan (98–117 CE) and would not happen again after the priest-emperor's death. Perhaps this indicates that Zeus Olybreus was somehow connected to Elagabal, who simultaneously appeared on Anazarbos coins in the form of the black stone. The local deity Aphrodite Kassalitis, a mountain, weather and vegetation goddess who was mainly worshipped on the acropolis, may have been associated with the wife of the Emesene sun god. Ziegler also supposes the introduction of the Elagabal cult in Laodicea and Neapolis, cities which both minted coins showing the black stone as well. In Laodicea, Elagabal may have been associated with a local betyl. This certainly seems to have been the case in Neapolis, which minted coins showing the black stone of Emesa with a representation of the holy mountain Gerizim. As was the case with Mount Zarbos, both the betyl of Laodicea and Mount Gerizim were probably associated with Zeus. They also seem to have had solar aspects, which would have made the association with the Emesene sun god only a small step.[68] However, there are no indications that Elagabal wedded any local deities in these cities.

According to Ziegler, we can assume that the cult of Elagabal was introduced in very many cities, but is only attested in a few because of the shortness of Elagabalus's reign. This seems to indicate that the introduction of the cult did not occur spontaneously, but was the result of an imperial decree, demanding worship from citizens all over the empire. Yet even taking Elagabalus's short reign and damnatio memoriae into account, the available evidence is too scarce to warrant such a far-reaching conclusion. Except for Rome, the only three cities which we know for certain to have adopted the cult of Elagabal are Altava, where the possessores erected a temple for Elagabal; Attaleia, where the city council and the people dedicated an inscription to the Emesene deity; and

Sardes, where Elagabalia were celebrated.[69] The inscription from Attaleia is undated, making it highly likely, but not absolutely certain, that Elagabal was introduced there during Elagabalus's reign.

In addition, many of the cities which certainly, probably or possibly adopted the worship of the invincible sun god from Emesa are situated in Asia Minor, where Elagabalus lingered for several months after his victory over Macrinus. Anazarbos, Attaleia, Faustinopolis, Hierapolis-Castabala, Juliopolis, Sardes and Nicomedia all must have either received a visit from the new ruler, or at least had him pass close by. It is significant that several of these cities managed to secure desirable honours from Elagabalus. Sardes and Nicomedia both received a third neocory, an honour connected with the right to erect a temple to the emperor, while Anazarbos was granted the right to call itself 'πρώτη, μεγίστη' and 'καλλίστη', 'first, biggest and most beautiful' city of Cilicia. Moreover, the emperor honoured the city by accepting the office of demiurge in 221–22.[70] It seems reasonable to assume that these honours were meant as rewards for including Elagabal into the local pantheon. In all likelihood, cities which did so were not submitting to an imperial policy of compulsory worship, but acted on their own initiative. In the eternal rivalry between the poleis of the empire, adopting the cult of the emperor's personal god was just another means of winning imperial favour.

The damnatio memoriae of Elagabalus led to the destruction of his portraits and the deletion of his name from inscriptions and papyri. Sardes and Nicomedia lost the neocories which the emperor had bestowed on them. Anazarbos had to give up its right to the titles 'first, biggest and most beautiful', and ceased to celebrate Antoninia in honour of Elagabalus.[71] Since Severus Alexander re-established Jupiter as the chief god of the Roman pantheon and banished Elagabal from the capital, it is not surprising that the black stone disappeared from civic coinage. Nor are there any inscriptions after 222 which mention temples being erected for Elagabal, or games being held in his honour.

Of course, all these measures may have been no more than formal responses to the damnatio of the priest-emperor, and do not necessarily reflect the sentiments of those involved. Yet there are some indications that the negative images of Elagabalus broadcast by his successor and found in the literary works of the elite influenced the general view of the late emperor. Two papyrus texts from Oxyrhynchus, both written by unknown authors and dated several decades after Elagabalus's death, are very outspoken in their contempt. The first, a horoscope, calls him

'Antoninus the catamite'; the second, a planetary table, refers to him as 'the unholy little Antoninus'.[72] It seems that, by the late third century at least, the alleged vices of the priest-emperor were taken for granted.

It has been remarked that the reign of Elagabalus was 'practically devoid of political interest'.[73] Leaving the matter of the religious reforms aside – for in Rome, religion was as much part of politics as politics were part of religion – this statement may well be true. After Elagabalus had defeated Macrinus in 218 and gained the throne, he seems to have taken no decisions of great importance. No wars were waged during his reign. There were no important economic reforms, nor were there any grand monuments added to the face of the Eternal City, with the exception of one or two big temples to Elagabal. Only the adoption of Alexander in 221 would have significant consequences beyond the emperor's short reign. On the other hand, there were no large-scale famines or epidemics, no civil wars or barbarian invasions. There are no signs of misgovernment: roads and buildings were maintained and the provinces were governed by men who were at least of equestrian rank. Compared to the political and military upheaval which would follow, the years 218–22 can be considered one of the most tranquil and peaceful periods of the third century.

Nevertheless, Elagabalus was violently overthrown by the praetorians and suffered a damnatio memoriae. It seems too easy to explain these events solely, or even primarily, by pointing to the ambitions of Severus Alexander and his supporters. After all, the last Severan emperor was about the same age as his predecessor when he gained the throne, had a similar dynastic claim, and likewise refrained from taking important decisions. However, Alexander managed to stay in power for 13 years and was overthrown only when the empire was facing dire military threats from the Persians and the Germans.

The explanation for Elagabalus's short reign should probably be sought first and foremost in his attempts to reform Roman state religion. The radical changes which the young monarch brought about in this field clashed with traditions which many Romans held sacred. Jupiter had to make room for a new chief deity, whose appearance and cult were distinctly 'un-Roman', while the emperor himself committed the unprecedented crime of marrying a vestal virgin. Both the Roman elite and the praetorian guard probably could not identify themselves with the priest from Emesa, who dishonoured their traditional gods, tried to impose a cult on Rome which many seem to have regarded as typically 'Oriental', and probably did little or nothing to make a positive impression. Where Alexander was careful and reigned in concordance with the senate, Elagabalus provoked.

Yet it would be misleading to look upon the religious reforms of 220 as nothing more than the acts of a religious fanatic. Elagabalus himself may have been primarily, or even exclusively, interested in the elevation of his god to the foremost ranks of the imperial pantheon, but his assistants and advisers, whose positions depended on his survival, had more mundane interests in mind. As has been discussed, the emperor's position as sacerdos amplissimus of Elagabal was used in an attempt to grant him the prestige which could not be derived from his alleged ancestry, personality and worldly achievements. Elagabalus was presented as the 'invincible priest-emperor' who, as the privileged intermediary to the empire's new chief deity, secured the welfare of his subjects.

This supernatural legitimation was not completely new. Commodus (180–92 CE) had already experimented with somewhat similar arguments, presenting himself as a superhuman gladiator and Roman Hercules who personally guarded the empire against any 'monsters' which might attack it. Septimius Severus broadened the personalistic god-emperorship of his predecessor to the whole Severan house, connecting the 'felicitas' ('blessing') of the empire to the imperial household. Both he and his son Caracalla also accentuated their own superhuman status, albeit less emphatically than Commodus had done. Like the last Antonine emperor, they claimed Hercules as their personal god. The Roman Sol also played an important part in their representation. Severus and Caracalla connected their dynasty to the sun god and used solar and astral symbolism to imply that they were destined to rule.[74]

After the death of Severus Alexander in 235, the empire entered a period of turmoil which has become known as the 'crisis of the third century'. Wars with the Persians, invading tribes, famine, pestilence and an endless line of claimants to the imperial title put a heavy strain on the empire. During these troublesome times, other emperors followed on the path which Commodus and the Severans had taken. Like Elagabalus, most of them could not boast any strong dynastic claims or impressive military victories. Since these traditional means of legitimation were no longer practicable, they searched for other ways to justify their power and enhance their prestige. The alarming disintegration of the empire called for a strong, uniting figure, someone with power and charisma surpassing that of mere mortals. More and more, the emperor was elevated above his subjects, transforming from princeps into dominus. His position became sacred, a development which culminated in the reigns of the Christian emperors of the Late Empire, who presented themselves as rulers by the grace of the one, universal God of the Bible.

Elagabalus's role as sacerdos amplissimus of Elagabal may be considered an intermediate stage in this process towards sacred emperorship. However, we should be careful that our knowledge of the outcome does not make us overestimate the young monarch's importance. Elagabalus was but one of many third-century emperors who tried to create a supernatural basis of power, and a shortlived one at that. His representation as 'invincible priest-emperor' was a product of the times, rather than a determinant for them.

Even less plausible is the notion that Elagabalus prepared the way for Christian monotheism, as some historians would have it.[75] Apart from the brevity of his reign and his unfavourable reputation, which destroyed any exemplary value his reforms may have had, Elagabalus never attempted to make Elagabal the empire's sole god. The elevation of Elagabal to chief Roman deity should therefore not be compared to Constantine's acceptance of Christianity, but rather to the religious reforms of Aurelian (270–75 CE). Like his predecessor, this emperor used Sol Invictus to legitimise and strengthen his position. In 274, he instated the sun god at the head of the Roman pantheon. However, in doing so, Aurelian avoided any explicitly un-Roman elements, not identifying the sun as Elagabal or another local deity, but presenting it as a god of a more general nature. A new college of priests, the 'pontifices dei Solis', was put in charge of the worship of the god. Although this college fell under the authority of Aurelian as pontifex maximus, the emperor did not create a new title to present himself as high priest of the sun. Instead of putting himself at the centre of the cult, as Elagabalus had done, he was content to call Sol his 'divine comes' and 'conservator.' Not he, but the sun god was the true lord of the empire, the 'dominus Imperii Romani'. In his worship, the people of the empire should be united.[76]

Although Aurelian was murdered the year after he put through his religious reforms, there are no indications that his downfall was hastened by the elevation of Sol to the head of the Roman pantheon. Unlike Elagabalus, the emperor did not disturb the religious traditions of Rome, and avoided the impression that Jupiter had been overthrown by a 'foreign' god. Arguably, the mental climate in the 270s may have been less hostile towards religious reforms than the period fifty years before; dethroning Jupiter had been unprecedented. Nevertheless, it seems likely that Aurelian would have met with more resistance if he had followed the example of Elagabalus. The priest-emperor from Emesa made the mistake of confronting the Romans with a local cult that proved incompatible with their traditional religion. As we have seen, it was not the claim of a personal god which made Elagabalus exceptional, but the exotic, 'un-Roman' nature of the deity to whom he had connected his fate, as well as the undiplomatic way in which he tried to force his divine champion upon the Romans. The mistake was fatal. Not even the protection of Elagabal proved sufficient to save Elagabalus from his enemies. As it turned out, the 'invincible priest-emperor' was not so invincible after all.

# 4

# THE REJECTED RULER

Nor emperor he, nor Antoninus, nor citizen, nor senator, nor man of noble
blood, nor Roman

*Historia Augusta, Vita Severi Alexandri*

During his reign, Elagabalus had presented himself as a good and
worthy ruler: first as a benevolent monarch in the tradition of the Antonines,
later as the invincible priest-emperor of Elagabal. After he had been
violently overthrown by the praetorians, this positive image was discarded
in favour of another, far less flattering view. To what extent this change
reflected a genuine dislike for the priest-emperor, and to what extent it
merely followed the line of propaganda in favour of Severus Alexander –
who had little choice but to condemn his predecessor – is a question which
remains ultimately unanswerable. However, this chapter will not only
describe the negative images which emerged in Greek and Roman literature
after Elagabalus's death, but offer possible reasons why particular authors
chose to portray the emperor in particular ways. What we are interested in
is the construction of a fictional Elagabalus, an imperial monster who
surpassed Caligula, Nero and Commodus in alleged wickedness and vice.

Starting in the fourth century BCE with Xenophon, who wrote a
panegyric on the Spartan king Agesilaos, many Greek and Roman authors
had defined the boundaries of good and bad rule.[1] A good ruler typically
came from a line of noble and worthy ancestors. He respected the gods,
loved his country and ruled wisely and justly, taking heed of the advice of
good and worthy councillors. Although he was not aggressive, he showed

valour in battle and invoked fear in his enemies. To his subjects, he set an example by means of his modesty and moderate way of life. He was accessible, paid attention to their problems, and earned their enduring love and respect by always placing their interests before his own, acting as a shepherd or a father. A bad ruler, on the contrary, possessed none of these characteristics, and was defined by their exact opposites. He was cruel, foolish, megalomaniac and extravagant, repressed his subjects and was hated and feared by all. Tacitus's Tiberius and Nero are prime examples of bad rulers, as are Tiberius, Caligula, Nero and Domitian in the work of Suetonius.

The negative images of Elagabalus in the works of Cassius Dio, Herodian and the author of the *Vita Heliogabali* can be placed in this tradition. The authors make use of many literary 'topoi' or 'loci communes' ('commonplaces') to cast the emperor in an unfavourable light. These topoi are usually 'not [...] devoid of any connection with reality', as Lukas de Blois has pointed out, but tend to over- or underexpose facts, connections, and actions, place them in a traditional frame of reference or label them.[2] Literary commonplaces are part of an inflated moralising discourse, following rather special rhetorical and sociological principles. I will point out some of these principles as we encounter them.

Following the example of Suetonius, imperial biographers usually broke the emperor's life up into mostly synchronic rubrics, including everything from physiognomy and familial relations through to spectacles, building projects and legislation. Cassius Dio and Herodian combine this approach with Tacitus's annalistic year-by-year structure, whereas the *Historia Augusta* fully adopts the model of Suetonius. In this chapter, I will discuss the works of Dio and Herodian and the *Vita Heliogabali* separately, structuring my account by the many recurring themes and topoi they have in common, such as favouritism, cruelty and sexual excesses. These themes can also be found in the works of other ancient and Byzantine writers, who devote considerably less attention to Elagabalus. Therefore, their works will be grouped together in one section and discussed thematically. This should make any patterns and developments in the manifold image of the priest-emperor obvious.

Finally, the images of Elagabalus in ancient and Byzantine literature will be briefly compared with the conclusions drawn from the first three chapters. Which aspects of the emperor's person and reign are exaggerated, distorted or ignored in the historical and biographical records, and what does this signify?

ELAGABALUS IN THE WORK OF CASSIUS DIO

Cassius Dio was not in Rome during the reign of Elagabalus, and had to base his description of this period on the accounts of others, yet he did not hesitate to condemn the young monarch in the strongest terms. Elagabalus emerges from his work as 'one by whom nothing was done that was not evil and base', and his reign as a period in which 'everything got turned upside down'.[3] It is clear that Dio was not attempting an accurate portrayal of the emperor, but was modelling him on the stereotypical bad ruler of many Greek and Roman works.

For Dio, the paradigm of a good ruler was Augustus. In a key passage of his work, he describes how the young Octavian, after having defeated his political opponents, plans to lay down his arms and restore the republic. When he discusses this intention with his loyal friends Agrippa and Maecenas, Agrippa approves, but Maecenas urges him to stay in power as sole ruler. He gives a long speech on how an emperor should rule, undoubtedly voicing Dio's own opinion. Many elements in this speech confirm the standard of good rule set by previous authors. Octavian is urged to work together with the senate and the knights, avoiding extravagance and waste. He should refrain from treating his subjects as slaves, but should set an example to them, distinguishing himself by means of 'virtus' ('manly virtue') rather than by marks of honour. He should be like a father to his subjects, always using his power to their benefit; successful in war, but striving for peace. Moreover, he should honour the gods and – an interesting addition – abhor and punish those who want to replace old divinities with new ones, since that was not only an insult to the gods, but would also cause conspiracies and intrigues. This last remark is probably anachronistic, inspired by the flourishing of foreign religions in Rome during Dio's own lifetime.[4]

In the funeral speech which Dio has Tiberius make after Augustus's death, it is made clear that the dead emperor has managed to live up to the high standard set by Maecenas. In addition, he is also praised for keeping the soldiers in check – another reference to problems from the Severan age, when the power of the military was rising and could not always be kept under control. This is a notable difference between Augustus and Elagabalus, who gained the purple because of a military uprising and was therefore the product of that same army disobedience which Dio despised. Not coincidentally, the historian keeps stressing that Elagabalus is an illegitimate ruler, calling him the 'False Antoninus' and branding him a usurper. The boy is characterised as an upstart by the remark that Macrinus had not even known his name before the revolt. Even more telling is the passage in which Dio describes how many men of low birth made a bid for the throne after Elagabalus had come to power, 'being encouraged thereto by the fact that many men had entered upon the supreme rule contrary to expectation and to merit'.[5] This comment possibly refers to both Macrinus and Elagabalus.

It is no surprise that Dio portrays the young emperor from Emesa as completely incapable of governing the empire. He mentions that Elagabalus was merely 'a boy' when he was elevated to the throne.[6] From the start, it is obvious that the upstart ruler shows little respect for Roman traditions, granting himself imperial titles before they have been voted; entering his name in the list as consul instead of Macrinus, without having held any office previously; and not wearing the triumphal dress on the Day of Vows. Curiously, Dio regards these as only minor crimes, being of simple character and mostly harmless. Presumably that lenient verdict does not apply to the emperor's religious reforms, which are discussed immediately afterwards.

In Dio's account, few things demonstrate Elagabalus's inability to govern better than his favouritism. The most blatant example of this is the career of Comazon, who was richly rewarded for his support in the revolt against Macrinus. Dio paints a very black picture of this man, accusing him of having a bad character and 'a name derived from mimes and buffoonery'. He counts it as 'one of the greatest violations of precedent' that Comazon, who, with the exception of his command of an army camp, had never been tested in any position of responsibility, became prefect of the praetorian guard, received the rank of consul and later even held that post. On top of that, the man also became city prefect no less than three times, 'for just as a mask used to be carried into the theatres to occupy the stage during the intervals in the acting, when it was left vacant by the comic actors, so Comazon was put in the vacant place of the men who had been city prefects in his day'. This is the second time that Dio associates Comazon with 'buffoonery' and the stage, which underlines the bad opinion the historian had of him. After all, actors had a very low status in Rome and were often perceived, in the words of Catherine Edwards, as 'paradigms of the low'.[7]

Other favourites likewise acquired great power under Elagabalus, some, according to Dio, 'because they had joined in his uprising and others because they committed adultery with him'.[8] Several examples of this are given. Apart from the notorious Comazon, there is Zoticus, who was appointed cubicularius before the emperor had even seen him, for no other reason than that he had a beautiful body and a large member. Elagabalus allegedly also intended to grant his foster father, Gannys, the position of Caesar. Later, he wanted to bestow this extraordinary honour on his 'husband', Hierocles, who had been a charioteer and slave before he gained the emperor's love.

The impression arises that Dio's portrayal of Elagabalus's cronies is a parallel to his criticism of Elagabalus himself. As the latter had gained the throne 'contrary to expectation and to merit', so did men like Comazon, Zoticus, Gannys and Hierocles aspire to, and in many cases attain, positions for which they were both unworthy and unfit. By putting his trust in them, Elagabalus ignored an important guideline, namely that a good ruler should surround himself with capable, trustworthy friends. In the words of Dio Chrysostom,

> For no one, of and by himself, is sufficient for a single one of even his own needs; and the more and greater the responsibilities of a king are, the greater is the number of co-workers that he needs, and the greater the loyalty required of them, since he is forced to entrust his greatest and most important interests to others or else to abandon them. [...] Consequently, it is not a safe policy for him to share his power carelessly with the first men he meets; but the stronger he makes his friends, the stronger he becomes himself.[9]

Augustus, as Cassius Dio makes clear, paid close attention to the advice of his loyal friends and councillors, Maecenas and Agrippa. Many of his successors, however, did not live up to this good example. Some, like the young Commodus, were simply led astray by bad companions; others, like Caracalla, dismissed or killed their tutors and servants for no apparent reason, thus displaying the characteristics of a tyrant. Dio puts Elagabalus in the second category, recounting how the boy kills his foster father Gannys with his own hand, just because the latter tried to force him into living a temperate and prudent life. Clearly, the young emperor did not tolerate anyone who questioned his character and behaviour – which, according to Dio, left much to be desired. Instead, he kept away from virtuous men, preferring the company of those whose standards were as low and despicable as his own.

To what extent does Dio depict Elagabalus as a cruel character? The historian accuses the emperor of drifting into 'the most murderous practices' and gives a detailed account of Elagabalus's 'actions that were tainted with bloodshed', listing all the eminent men who were executed during his reign.[10] However, many of these killings seem to have happened for political reasons, as Dio himself indicates: the victims were often supporters of Macrinus, or men the emperor deemed untrustworthy for other reasons. Sometimes, Dio suggests, the official reason given for an execution was only a pretext; for example, in the case of Pomponius Bassus, who was condemned to death on the charge of being displeased at what the emperor was doing, 'the real motive lay in the fact that he had a wife both fair to look upon and of noble rank.'[11] Yet even in this case, Elagabalus does not display cruelty for cruelty's sake: he stands to gain something, namely Pomponius's wife, and is prepared to kill to get her. Although such calculated ruthlessness is a valid point of criticism in itself, it is still a far cry from the sadism of Tacitus's Nero, who used condemned Christians as torches to illuminate his garden at night, or that of Suetonius's Domitian, who tortured his victims by sticking a glowing poker in their anus and chopping off their hands. Even Dio's off-hand remark that Elagabalus secretly sacrificed boys to his god seems more a slur against the cult of Elagabal than an accusation of cruelty.

It seems that Cassius Dio is actually more concerned about something else: Elagabalus's disrespect for the senate. The relation between the emperor and this traditional body of government was a delicate one. While the emperor was truly in charge, he needed the support of the senate to lend legitimacy to his reign, whereas the prestige of the senate depended on the extent to which the emperor sought its consent in making important decisions. Elagabalus, as Dio indicates, totally failed to appreciate this careful balance. Instead of confiding in the senatorial body – of which Dio, of course, was a member – he executed senators at will, often without even the dignity of a trial by their peers. Dio records that, among others, the governors of Syria, Arabia and Cyprus were put to death by Elagabalus, without any charges against them being communicated to the senate. Silius Messalla and Pomponius Bassus were condemned by their peers, but only after Elagabalus had written the senate a letter, saying, 'The proof of their plots I have not sent you, because it would be useless to read them, as the men are already dead.'[12] The emperor, in short, ruled as a tyrant, abandoning even the illusion of sharing his power with anyone but his favourites.

Not all of Dio's criticism is directed against Elagabalus's illegitimacy and ruthlessness; some is reserved for the ineptitude of his rule. Using the convention that a good ruler ought to set an example to his subjects, he also heavily criticises the flaws in Elagabalus's character. Many of these flaws are linked to the emperor's Syrian descent. The Greeks and Romans considered Syrians foreigners, formally, but not culturally, part of the Roman Empire. Like the Persians, another typically 'Oriental' people, they were associated with extravagance, luxury and a servile mentality, making them more fit to be slaves than warriors. Syrians were not real men, it was thought, but immoral, sexually perverted effeminates who drenched themselves in perfume and were surrounded by eunuchs. Although they possessed a certain cunning and craftiness, which made them notoriously untrustworthy, they were also very superstitious. At best, it could be said that Syrians were generally supposed to be intelligent, but there was little else to be said for them.[13]

Dio may not have credited Elagabalus with much intelligence and craftiness, but apart from that the young monarch is portrayed as a typical 'Syrian' – or, rather, as a typical 'Oriental', for in the Greco-Roman mindset, most 'Oriental' people shared the same basic traits. The emperor is explicitly modelled after Sardanapalus, a mythical Assyrian king by whose name Dio regularly calls him. Sardanapalus, who was credited with having brought about the fall of Assyria, represented all the Greco-Roman stereotypes about 'Oriental' monarchs. His story was first told in detail in Ctesias's *Persica*, which is now lost, except for some fragments preserved in the works of other authors, mainly Diodorus Siculus. The mythical monarch also appears in Athenaeus's *Deipnosophistae*, where he is portrayed as one of the eastern 'female-kings', combining the 'manly' position of king with behaviour and characteristics normally attributed to women.[14]

The similarities between Sardanapalus, as presented by these two authors, and Dio's portrayal of Elagabalus are immediately obvious. Concerning the effeminacy of the Assyrian monarch, Diodorus Siculus remarks that

> [...] he lived the life of a woman, and spending his days in the company of his concubines and spinning purple garments and working the softest of wool, he had assumed the feminine garb and so covered his face and indeed his entire body with whitening cosmetics and the other unguents used by courtesans, that he rendered it more delicate than that of any luxury-loving woman. He also took care to make even his voice to be like a woman's, and at his carousals not only to indulge regularly in those drinks and viands which could offer the greatest pleasure, but also to pursue the delights of

love with men as well as with women; for he practised sexual indulgence of both kinds without restraint, showing not the least concern for the disgrace attending such conduct.[15]

Athenaeus paints a similar picture, but gives a few details which do not occur in the Diodorus account: for instance, he mentions that Sardanapalus painted his eyelids and blackened his eyebrows. He also adds that the king had his beard shaved close.

Dio combines details from both these accounts – or, perhaps more likely, took them from Ctesias's original text – in his description of Elagabalus:

> When trying someone in court he really had more or less the appearance of a man, but everywhere else he showed affectations in his actions and in the quality of his voice. For instance, he used to dance, not only in the orchestra, but also, in a way, even while walking, performing sacrifices, receiving salutations, or delivering a speech. [...] He worked with wool, sometimes wore a hair-net, and painted his eyes, daubing them with white lead and alkanet. Once, indeed, he shaved his chin and held a festival to mark the event; but after that he had the hairs plucked out, so as to look more like a woman.[16]

Except for the dancing, which the Roman elite frowned upon, Elagabalus's behaviour would have been perfectly acceptable for a Roman woman. In fact, working with wool was considered a very appropriate activity for women from the higher classes, to such an extent that it was part of the image of the ideal 'matrona'.[17] Men, however, were not supposed to engage in such domestic chores – least of all kings and emperors, who had kingdoms and empires to rule. Sardanapalus, as Diodorus and Athenaeus make clear, completely neglected this duty, preferring to spend his time with his concubines. According to Diodorus, the king 'was not seen by any man residing outside the palace'.[18] The only time he could be said to take the role of a man was in making love to women.

Interestingly, Cassius Dio's Elagabalus does *not* completely neglect his duties as ruler. Dio grudgingly admits that the emperor had 'more or less the appearance of a man' when he was trying someone in court. However, it seems clear that Elagabalus is not being true to his effeminate, 'Oriental' nature here, but is putting up an act, born of necessity. Although he 'appears both as man and as woman', Dio definitely puts more emphasis on his female side, remarking that 'he [...] could not even be a man.' Thus

Elagabalus, when presented with the well-endowed Zoticus, bends his neck in a feminine pose, treats the man to a melting gaze and says, 'Call me not Lord, for I am a Lady.' He also commits himself to a 'husband', the brute charioteer Hierocles, who beats him up on a regular basis, so that he walks around with black eyes. The reversal of the social order seems complete: the emperor of Rome, consenting to physical abuse by a former slave![19]

Yet Dio finds even more explicit ways to hammer home his point. After he has mentioned that Elagabalus circumcised himself, an act which he links to the cult of Elagabal, he remarks that the emperor 'had planned, indeed, to cut off his genitals altogether', adding, 'but that desire was prompted solely by his effeminacy'. In two inserted passages, it is stated that the young monarch wanted a vagina implanted in his body by means of an incision.[20] These inserted passages are from the works of the Byzantine authors Cedrenus and Zonaras, who summarise Dio's account of the period 218–22. The vagina anecdote may be their addition, but that does not seem likely. For one thing, Cedrenus explicitly states that he got the information from Dio. Moreover, Cedrenus and Zonaras hardly add any other new elements to their summaries of Elagabalus's reign, except for some factual remarks concerning ecclesiastical matters. They certainly do not come up with any other anecdotes as colourful and outrageous as the story about Elagabalus's desire for a vagina. Considering this, and taking into account how well the story fits with other remarks that Dio makes about the emperor's effeminacy (like the plan to castrate himself), it seems safe to assume he is the original author of this anecdote as well.

More parallels can be drawn between Sardanapalus and Dio's Elagabalus in their excessive love for luxury and pleasure, although the similarities are less striking in this area. Diodorus Siculus records that Sardanapalus went to 'such an excess [...] of luxury and the most shameless sensual pleasure' that he composed a funeral dirge for himself, in which he urged readers to enjoy the pleasures of life while they still could.[21] The first lines are,

Knowing full well that thou wert mortal born,
Thy heart lift up, take thy delight in feasts;
When dead no pleasure more is thine.[22]

In addition, both Diodorus and Athenaeus mention the story of Sardanapalus's extraordinary death. According to them, the king decided to take his own life when his kingdom was under attack and he feared falling into enemy hands. He made an enormous pyre in the palace and burned himself with his concubines (and, depending on the author, either his queen or his eunuchs) and all his riches. 'And so,' Athenaeus remarks, 'Sardanapalus, after he had enjoyed pleasure in strange ways, died as nobly as he could.'[23]

Surprisingly, Cassius Dio only hints at Elagabalus's love of luxury. He mentions that a gold statue of the emperor was erected, 'distinguished by its great and varied adornment'.[24] The emperor's marriage to Julia Paula is celebrated with a huge banquet for the soldiers and the populace, and games at which an unprecedented number of 51 tigers are killed. Also, there is Gannys's demand that Elagabalus should live more moderately, which seems an indication that the boy was living excessively.

Much more is made of Elagabalus's licentious behaviour. Dio explicitly connects this flaw to Sardanapalus, remarking:

> But this Sardanapalus [...] lived most licentiously himself from first to last. He married many women, and had intercourse with even more without any legal sanction; yet it was not that he had any need of them himself, but simply that he wanted to get accomplices in his wantonness by associating with them indiscriminately.[25]

The emperor is said to have 'used his body both for doing and allowing many strange things, which no one could endure to hear of'.[26] According to Dio, he visited the taverns of Rome by night, just as Nero had done – but where Nero had gone around in disguise to molest people, Elagabalus played the prostitute. Later, he set up his own brothel in the palace and stood in the doorway naked, awaiting customers. In this, he outdid even Caligula, who had only forced aristocratic women and children to prostitute themselves in the palace, but had not taken up the role of harlot himself. In other things, too, Elagabalus surrendered to pleasures unworthy of an emperor: like several 'bad' emperors before him, he took up chariot driving (although not in public spaces), and even begged gold coins from the senators, knights and imperial freedmen who were watching him.

Finally, there is the aspect of the emperor's religion, the cult of Elagabal. As has already been remarked, Dio expressed his dislike of foreign cults when he has Maecenas warn Octavian about them. According to the councillor, who is speaking on behalf of Dio himself, such cults would insult the gods and cause conspiracies and intrigues. That warning could certainly be applied to Elagabalus, who exalted his foreign god in 'very strange ways', chanting 'barbaric chants' to him, circumcising himself and, for some unclear reason, 'actually shutting up alive in the god's temple a lion, a monkey, and a snake, and throwing human genitals among them'.[27] Dio obviously had no wish to understand the cult of Elagabal, but chose to present it as bizarre and obscene. He dubs the marriage of the sun god to the Punic goddess Urania an 'extreme absurdity', exclaiming 'as if the god had any need of marriage and children!'[28] In his description of Elagabalus's priestly garb, he underlines that the cult of Elagabal is an 'Oriental' religion: 'Furthermore, he was frequently seen even in public clad in the barbaric dress which the Syrian priests use, and this had as much to do as anything with his receiving the nickname of "The Assyrian".'[29]

However, not much attention is devoted to the 'Oriental' character of Elagabalus's religion. Michael Sommer has pointed out that Dio mainly uses the cult of Elagabal to demonstrate that the emperor had no respect for traditional Roman state religion, or even for his own body (referring to his circumcised member and desire for castration). These characteristics define him as a morally objectionable person, suffering from what Sommer calls 'Caesarenwahn', the madness which also plagued emperors like Caligula and Vitellius.[30] Elagabalus possessed this characteristic in great quantities, even going so far as to defile a vestal virgin. Nero had done that as well, but had not dared to lay a finger on the high priestess, as Elagabalus did. 'Thus he plumed himself over an act for which he ought to have been scourged in the Forum, thrown into prison, and then put to death,' Dio remarks, but Elagabalus goes even further: he divorces his newly wed wife, only to take her back later.[31] In an equally shocking insult to Roman religion, the emperor dethrones Jupiter in favour of a foreign god, causing himself to be voted Elagabal's priest. Clearly, Elagabalus's impiety knew no bounds. It is therefore no wonder that the gods arranged for a more suitable successor: Severus Alexander, whose rule was foreshadowed by the appearance of the spirit of Alexander the Great, appearing in Moesia Superior with hundreds of ghostly companions. Like the Persian king Darius, the False Antoninus in Rome would soon be vanquished.

In conclusion, Dio refused to take the reign of Elagabalus seriously, portraying the emperor as negatively as he could. The young priest from Emesa was presented as embodying everything Dio despised. Elagabalus had no right to the throne and came to power only by means of a military uprising. Even worse, he was not a proper Roman, but a foreigner; an intruder who violated Roman traditions and had no respect for the senate, executing senators without trial and giving power to unworthy favourites – in short, ruling as a tyrant. His violation of traditional Roman state religion also fits this pattern. In his character and behaviour, Elagabalus showed traits deemed typical of an 'Oriental': effeminacy and licentiousness. All of these points support Dio's opinion that the rule of Elagabalus was an affront to Roman dignity, a period of unprecedented madness in which 'everything got turned upside down'.[32] Only with the reign of Severus Alexander would the Empire return to a normal state of affairs.

ELAGABALUS IN THE WORK OF HERODIAN

Herodian makes much use of the work of Cassius Dio in his description of Elagabalus's reign. Nevertheless, the inventive historian adds many details to the account of his predecessor – derived from memory, eyewitnesses, his imagination or a combination of the three – and paints a picture of Elagabalus which, although often reminiscent of Dio's portrayal, is distinctly his own.

Like Dio, Herodian has a model emperor to whom all others are compared. His 'optimus princeps' is not the historically distant Augustus, but a ruler from a more recent past: Marcus Aurelius. At the start of the first book, Marcus is dying and summons his advisers and relatives, asking them to keep his adolescent son and successor Commodus on the straight and narrow path of virtue. According to Herodian, the old emperor himself had set the perfect example of good rule, cultivating every sort of virtue. He had been merciful, fair and accessible to his subjects, and had displayed courage, moderation and capability in the fields of politics and warfare. Moreover, he possessed a great love for ancient literature and lived according to his philosophical ideals: that is, in sober and dignified fashion. Of course, Commodus fails to live up to his father's high standards. He gives in to flattery and temptation and ends up as a wicked tyrant, thereby introducing one of the main themes in Herodian's work, namely that the realm suffers when children or young men are put 'in control of absolute, unchecked power without parental authority'.[33]

If Herodian is to be believed, Elagabalus did not fare any better than Commodus. The boy from Emesa is bluntly characterised as 'an emperor who was a disgrace'.[34] However, unlike Dio, Herodian does not connect this harsh verdict to accusations of illegitimacy. He mentions that Julia

Maesa told the soldiers stationed near Emesa that her grandson was the natural son of Caracalla, adding that it was assumed that Elagabalus had a different father. The historian does not confirm or reject Maesa's story, commenting that it 'may or may not have been true' and leaving it at that.[35] Throughout his account, he refers to Elagabalus as Antoninus. Evidently, Herodian was less concerned with matters of legitimacy than Dio. This can probably be explained by the fact that he was not a member of the senatorial elite. Therefore, he had less interest in the preservation of the traditional system of imperial succession, which provided the senate with much of its prestige.

In keeping with his distrust of child emperors, Herodian portrays Elagabalus as an irresponsible brat who abuses the power entrusted to him. After the boy's armies had defeated Macrinus, it is remarked that 'the immediate business in the East was dealt with by his grandmother and his circle of advisers because he was young and without administrative experience or education.'[36] The emperor shows more interest in idle pursuits than in governing the empire, wasting his time with chariot driving, dancing and, of course, the worship of his strange god, which I will discuss in more detail later. He is 'in most matters a thoughtless, silly young man' who can be easily manipulated by those who are older and more politically shrewd, such as his able grandmother.[37] However, there are times when even she is powerless to change his mind, for instance when Elagabalus decides to enter Rome in his 'Oriental' priestly garb.

Ultimately, the young monarch becomes more and more willful and recalcitrant, making it impossible for Julia Maesa to keep him under control. Herodian remarks that Elagabalus 'was driven to such extremes of lunacy that he took men from the stage and the public theatres and put them in charge of most important imperial business'. In all likelihood, this remark was inspired by Dio's comments on Comazon, who attained several high offices and is twice associated with the stage, although Dio never claims he had formerly been an actor. If so, it is a neat example of the way in which Herodian twists the account of his predecessor to enhance the story, rendering historical accuracy subordinate to his desire to entertain and shock his audience. To stress this point further, he adds that Elagabalus 'assigned positions of the highest responsibility in the empire to charioteers and comedy actors and mimes', and appointed slaves and freedmen as governors of consular provinces. Thus, 'all that was once held in respect was reduced [...] to a state of dishonour and frenzied madness.'[38]

To an ever lesser extent than Dio, Herodian presents Elagabalus as a cruel ruler. He records that the emperor 'executed very many distinguished and wealthy men, after information was laid that they disapproved and made fun of his way of life'.[39] The inspiration for this comment is probably Dio's list of executed senators, although Dio does not present the victims as making fun of Elagabalus's way of life. Once again, the accusation seems to be ruthlessness rather than sadism. There are only a few other passages in Herodian's account which could hint at the emperor's cruelty. The most intriguing of these is the scene in which Elagabalus throws presents to the crowd from the tops of high towers, leading to a scramble in which many are trampled to death or impaled on the spears of soldiers. However, Herodian does not state that this unfortunate result was intentional. Since there is no indication that the event should be regarded as anything but a regrettable accident, it seems plausible to interpret it as an example of Elagabalus's carelessness, rather than of his sadism.

Much more is made of the depiction of Elagabalus as an 'Oriental', that is, again, as effeminate and luxury-loving, one who singled himself out as a foreigner through his appearance, behaviour and religion. Unlike Dio, Herodian does not compare the emperor to the Assyrian king Sardanapalus. Nevertheless, he too records that the young ruler went out 'with painted eyes and rouge on his cheeks, spoiling his natural good looks by using disgusting make-up'. The soldiers of the praetorian guard were 'revolted at the sight of the emperor with his face made up more elaborately than a modest woman would have done, and effeminately dressed up in golden necklaces and soft clothes, dancing for everyone to see in this state'. Curiously, Elagabalus's effeminacy is not demonstrated by means of his sexual exploits, except for the vague remark that some of his slaves and freedmen, 'who perhaps excelled in some foul activity', rose to great heights.[40] Hierocles, Zoticus or other male lovers are completely absent from Herodian's tale. In fact, the subject of sex is hardly touched at all, and so the topos of Elagabalus's licentious way of living is not made explicit to the reader. This is typical of Herodian, who shows the same hesitance to discuss sexual matters in his accounts of the reigns of other emperors.

The typical 'Oriental' love for luxury *does* feature in Herodian's account. It mainly manifests itself in Elagabalus's elaborate style of dress, which is explicitly characterised as un-Roman and is associated with the 'East':

He wore the most expensive types of clothes, woven of purple and gold, and adorned himself with necklaces and bangles. On his head he wore a crown in the shape of a tiara glittering with gold and precious stones. The effect was something between the sacred garb of the Phoenicians and the luxurious apparel of the Medes. Any Roman or Greek dress he loathed because, he claimed, it was made out of wool, which is a cheap material. Only seric silk was good enough for him.[41]

The point is stressed further when Herodian records that Elagabalus refused to wear a Roman toga on entering the capital. Instead, the emperor chose to send a portrait of himself ahead, so the citizens could get used to his outlandish appearance.

It is not only Elagabalus who is portrayed as foreign and exotic, but also the cult of Elagabal. Herodian goes into much more detail about the emperor's religion than Cassius Dio, providing – among other things – the information that the god is worshipped in the form of a black stone. He takes pains to describe the rites performed in honour of Elagabal as 'ecstatic and orgiastic'.[42] Although he does not go so far as to accuse Elagabalus of making human sacrifices, there is clearly nothing Roman about his description of the daily slaughtering of cattle for the sun god, accompanied by music, dancing women, spices and wine. To underline how much of an intrusion this sort of extravagant ritual was into traditional Roman religion, Herodian mentions that all senators and equestrians had to be present at these sacrifices, and that military prefects and important officials actually had to partake in it, wearing 'Phoenician style' clothing. The same 'Oriental' splendour can be found in the passage describing the black stone's ritual journey from one temple to the other, seated in a chariot adorned with gold, led by the emperor himself and preceded by a lavish procession of divine images, precious temple dedications, imperial standards and costly heirlooms. On top of that, 'also the cavalry and all the army joined in'.[43] It seems that Herodian is deliberately parodying a military triumph here, suggesting that, under Elagabalus, this was the closest thing to an actual triumph Rome was likely to see.

To counterbalance Elagabalus's 'Oriental' extravagance, the author introduces the virtuous figure of Severus Alexander, whom the emperor is persuaded to adopt as Caesar. Not surprisingly, Elagabalus immediately wants his cousin to be trained in 'his own pursuits of leaping and dancing', wishing him 'to share his priesthood by wearing the same dress and following the same practices'. According to Herodian, both Elagabalus and Alexander had been dedicated to the sun god when the family was still living in Emesa. However, now that Alexander has been made Caesar, his mother keeps him far away from the worship of Elagabal. Instead, she summons teachers to give her son a 'Latin and Greek education', which includes wrestling and 'manly exercises'. Once again, Elagabalus acts as the enemy of all things Roman: he becomes absolutely furious and chases the teachers away, executing some of them and sending others into exile. The charge is that they are 'not allowing him [Alexander] to dance or go into a frenzy, but teaching him moderation and manly arts'.[44] The differences between Greco-Roman and 'Oriental' culture – at least, the differences which Herodian perceived – could hardly be made more obvious.

Sommer has argued that the portrayal of Elagabalus's religious practices in the work of Herodian has a completely different function to corresponding descriptions in the work of Dio. Whereas Dio uses the cult of Elagabal as a means to depict the emperor as a tyrant who disrespects Roman laws and traditions, Herodian uses it to underline the emperor's 'Oriental' nature. However, it should be noted that the 'Oriental' nature of the cult of Elagabal is touched upon by Dio as well, just as Herodian does not completely ignore the violation of traditional Roman state religion.

Sommer continues to argue that Dio's Elagabalus is basically portrayed as yet another mad tyrant, whereas Herodian's version is emphatically presented as a non-Roman, a foreigner.[45] This interpretation fails to take into account that Dio, time and time again, compares Elagabalus to Sardanapalus – a distinctively 'Oriental' monarch who displayed distinctively 'Oriental' traits, such as effeminacy and licentiousness. The polarisation between Greco-Roman and 'Oriental' is therefore certainly present in the work of Dio, although it is arguably more explicit and important in the work of Herodian. The latter, Sommer argues, may have been a Greek living in Syria, in which case he probably distinguished himself from the native population by defining Syrians as non-Greeks. Moreover, being much younger than Dio, Herodian experienced the frequent wars between the Roman Empire and the neighbouring empire of the Persians, which had been re-established in 226. Sommer thinks that Herodian associated Elagabalus with these enemies from the East, turning the emperor into an image of 'the other'. This argument seems far-fetched, considering that Herodian never explicitly associates Elagabalus with the Persians in his work. An additional explanation for the historian's depiction of the emperor as an 'Oriental' may be the fondness for ethnic stereotypes he displays throughout his work.

There are more differences between Dio's and Herodian's images of Elagabalus. As we have seen, Herodian does not show much interest in the legitimacy of the emperor's claim, nor in the many executions of senators. He hardly touches upon the licentious behaviour of the young monarch. However, he agrees with Dio that Elagabalus was completely unfit to rule, appointing the most despicable favourites to govern the empire and reducing everything that was once respected 'to a state of dishonour and frenzied madness'.[46] According to Herodian, Elagabalus was not just an effeminate 'Oriental', but also that which he possibly despised even more: a child emperor who could not be kept under control.

ELAGABALUS IN THE VITA HELIOGABALI

As can be deduced from the text of the *Vita Heliogabali*, the anonymous author used both Cassius Dio and Herodian as sources for this life. However, he seems even less interested in giving an accurate account of the events of the period 218–22 than his predecessors, instead preferring to paint a picture of Elagabalus which defies all credibility. Scheithauer has distinguished three types of emperors in the *Historia Augusta*: the 'princeps bonus', who possesses just about every virtue imaginable, with Marcus Aurelius as the prime example; the 'princeps malus', whose vices are diametrically opposed to the virtues of the princeps bonus; and the 'princeps medius', who combines traits of both types.[47]

Elagabalus is without doubt a princeps malus, 'a man so detestable for his life, his character, and his utter depravity that the senate expunged from the records even his name'.[48] In the introduction to the *Vita*, he is placed in the tradition of Caligula, Nero and Vitellius. Elagabalus is presented as the worst emperor the Roman Empire has ever experienced: his vices will never be surpassed. Indeed, the *Historia Augusta* remarks that 'worse than Commodus is Elagabalus alone', condemning the emperor as 'that filthiest of all creatures, both two-footed and four-footed', who 'in baseness and debauchery outdid a Nero, a Vitellius, a Commodus'.[49] To counterbalance this evil tyrant, Severus Alexander is portrayed as a virtuous and benign prince, whose admirable character and deeds are constantly compared with the vices of his notorious predecessor.

One of the recurring themes in the *Vita Heliogabali* is that Elagabalus styled himself Antoninus without a valid claim to that name. The author remarks that the emperor 'had merely assumed the name Antoninus', although he confirms the story that Symiamira – as he calls Julia Soaemias – had had an affair with Caracalla. The main point of this criticism does not seem to be that Elagabalus had no right to the throne, but that he dragged the noble name of the Antonines through the mud. The author of the *Vita Heliogabali* remarks that Elagabalus was 'a disgrace to the name of Antoninus, on which he had laid violent hands', commenting that 'his life was as false as his claim'.[50] Interestingly, the author also claims that Severus Alexander was more closely related to Caracalla than his predecessor. However, Alexander was too modest to accept the name Antoninus when it was offered to him by the senate. Being virtuous and being an Antonine are thus connected to each other; Elagabalus, of course, was neither.

Like all bad emperors, Elagabalus showed no respect for the senate. He acted as a tyrant, calling the senators his 'slaves in togas', and making fun of them whenever he could. No mention is made of executions, but the topos of favouritism, already present in the works of Cassius Dio and Herodian, receives much attention. According to the *Vita Heliogabali*, the emperor 'made his freedmen governors and legates, consuls and generals, and [...] brought disgrace on all offices of distinction by the appointment of base-born profligates'.[51] The following passage is very interesting:

> As prefect of the guard he appointed a dancer who had been on the stage at Rome, as prefect of the watch a chariot-driver named Cordius, and as prefect of the grain-supply a barber named Claudius, and to the other posts of distinction he advanced men whose sole recommendation was the enormous size of their privates.[52]

Here, the author of the *Vita Heliogabali* takes several elements from the account of Cassius Dio and embellishes them. The prefect of the guard, who is presented as an actor and a dancer, must be based on Comazon, whom Dio associates with the stage. A chariot-driver named Gordius is also mentioned by the third-century historian, although it is never mentioned that he became prefect of the watch. The barber Claudius seems to be an invention of the *Vita Heliogabali*, but the remark that Elagabalus advanced men because they had large members has clearly been inspired by Dio's anecdote about Zoticus, who gained the emperor's favour for exactly that reason. However, the *Historia Augusta* also adds a new element to the details of the emperor's bad appointments: the young monarch is accused of selling positions of power for money.

Most of the time, the *Vita*'s Elagabalus does not seem interested in governing the empire at all. He prefers to spend his days in frivolous and morally dubious activities such as singing, dancing and playing all kinds of instruments. Some of his pastimes are worse, such as his habit of harnessing naked women to a wheelbarrow and driving them about, usually naked himself. Typical is his fondness for practical jokes. Allegedly, Elagabalus loved to frighten his dinner guests by unleashing lions and leopards among them at the end of a meal. Since his guests were not aware that the beasts were tame, their sudden appearance caused an amusing panic.

Many of the emperor's jokes in the *Historia Augusta* have a malicious streak, and some are downright cruel. For instance, Elagabalus is said to have let loose snakes when the populace was assembled for games. Unlike the lions and leopards, these animals were not tame, and caused great injury. Another passage describes Elagabalus binding his dinner guests to a water-wheel and turning it around, plunging them into the water. However, as is the case with the accounts of Dio and Herodian, the topos of cruelty remains underdeveloped – as if it were only added for the sake of completeness. The most noticeable exception is the story that the emperor sacrificed children. This accusation probably originates from a similar remark in the work of Dio. But where the latter primarily seems to be attacking the cult of Elagabal, the author of the *Vita Heliogabali* puts the emphasis on the cruelty of the act (and thus of the emperor): he adds that for his sacrifices, Elagabalus collected beautiful, noble-born children whose parents were both alive, 'intending, I suppose, that the sorrow, if suffered by two parents, should be all the greater'.[53]

It was not just his favouritism and frivolous nature which made Elagabalus unfit to rule – he was also dependent on others and unable to act on his own. Allegedly, the emperor did no public business without the consent of his mother, whom he even invited to come into the senate-chamber to witness the drawing up of a senate decree. As if this violation of precedent was not bad enough, he also established a 'women's senate' on the Quirinal Hill, presided over by Julia Soaemias, to make decisions about matters concerning protocol and etiquette. Apart from demonstrating Elagabalus's contempt for the traditional senate, this anecdote also serves to make another, perhaps even more important, point:

namely, the notion that Rome was actually ruled by women when the boy from Emesa sat on the throne. According to the *Vita Heliogabali*, Elagabalus had to take his grandmother with him whenever he went to the praetorian camp or the senate house, 'in order that through her prestige he might get greater respect – for by himself he got none'.[54] To a Roman, a more blatant form of character assassination was hardly imaginable: any man who needed a woman's help to gain respect could not be much of a man at all.

Indeed, the reversal of gender roles in the *Vita Heliogabali* is also attested in the portrayal of Elagabalus himself. While women were entering the 'manly' domain of government, the emperor displayed many characteristics of a woman. For instance, 'In the public baths he always bathed with the women, and he even treated them himself with a depilatory ointment, which he applied also to his own beard, and shameful though it be to say it, in the same place where the women were treated and at the same hour.'[55]

In addition, Elagabalus dressed up as Venus and wished to wear a jewelled diadem, 'in order that his beauty might be increased and his face look more like a woman's'. He also marries another man, although here his spouse is not Hierocles, as in Dio's account, but Zoticus. Interestingly, the *Vita Heliogabali* does not make an explicit connection between the emperor's effeminacy and his Syrian background. The only remark which could perhaps be interpreted as such is the comment that Elagabalus 'infibulated himself, and did all that the *galli* are wont to do'.[56] The galli were the eunuch-priests of Magna Mater, a deity who had originated in Asia Minor. They were known for their ecstatic singing and dancing, self-chastisement and ritual castration.

Eunuchs, who were associated with the 'East', are mentioned several times in the *Vita Alexandri*, and always in connection with Elagabalus. Allegedly, Alexander removed many eunuchs from important positions, in which they had been installed by his predecessor. The new ruler did not trust these members of the 'third sex', as he regarded them, for they wanted to let emperors live 'in the manner of foreign nations or as the kings of the Persians'.[57] Indeed, it is remarked that Elagabalus 'had begun to receive adoration in the manner of the king of the Persians'. He even dressed as such, bedecking his garments and footwear with jewels. Much of the *Vita Heliogabali* is filled with stories concerning Elagabalus's unrivalled love for luxury and pleasure: the young ruler had urinals made of murra or onyx, held a naval spectacle in canals filled with wine, and made plans for a 'luxurious suicide', which included the building of a 'suicide tower':

And he also built a very high tower from which to thrown himself down, constructed of boards gilded and jewelled in his own presence, for even his death, he declared, should be costly and marked by luxury, in order that it might be said that no one had ever died in this fashion.[58]

Especially noteworthy are the emperor's extravagant banquets, at which such exotic dishes as camels' heels, peacock and nightingale tongues, the heads of parrots, pheasants and peacocks, mullet beards and flamingo brains were served, while even the dogs were fed on goose-livers. Once again, however, this unworthy behaviour is not explicitly connected to Elagabalus's Syrian background. In fact, the emperor himself declares that his role models were the famous cook Apicius and the 'bad' emperors Otho and Vitellius. In addition, there is the anecdote that 'in a banqueting-room with a reversible ceiling he once overwhelmed his parasites with violets and other flowers, so that some of them were actually smothered to death, being unable to crawl out to the top'. The story is clearly inspired by a passage in Suetonius, who, while describing the extravagant decadence of Nero's Golden House, remarks that the ceilings were reversible, so that flowers could be sprinkled through them.[59] Elagabalus is merely outdoing Nero with his avalanche of flowers – there is no indication that there is anything 'Oriental' about his cruel joke.

Likewise, the emperor's licentious behaviour is set in a distinctly Roman tradition. Elagabalus allegedly 'went beyond the perversities of the debauchees of old, and was well acquainted with all the arrangements of Tiberius, Caligula, and Nero'.[60] The author of the *Vita Heliogabali* may very well have been *inspired* by Cassius Dio and Herodian to portray the emperor as a licentious, luxury-loving individual, but he seems to have taken these negative characteristics out of their 'Oriental' context. Curiously, it is only in the *Vita Alexandri* that Elagabalus's 'Oriental' background is stressed. This happens not only by associating him with eunuchs and remarking that he wanted to be honoured in the manner of a Persian king, but also by the repeated remark that his cousin Severus Alexander was ashamed of his Syrian descent and claimed to have Roman ancestors. The fact that he turned out to be a good ruler, although he was a Syrian, is presented as a paradox which needs to be explained. Of course, this reflects on Elagabalus too: apparently, he *did* act as one would have expected of a Syrian. The question remains, though, why this point is made explicit only in the *Vita Alexandri*, and not in the *Vita Heliogabali*.

Only twice in the *Vita Heliogabali* are the emperor's religious acts presented as 'Oriental'. Firstly, it is remarked that Elagabalus adopted the cult of the goddess Magna Mater. Allegedly, he 'would toss his head to and fro among the castrated devotees of the goddess', and infibulated himself, causing the author to compare him to the galli. Secondly, Elagabalus is also said to have celebrated the rite of the Semitic goddess Salambo, which he did 'with all the wailing and the frenzy of the Syrian cult'.[61] Nowhere in the *Vita Heliogabali* – nor in the *Vita Alexandri*, for that matter – is the worship of Elagabal characterised as a stereotypically 'Oriental' religion, or is it even mentioned that the god is of local Syrian origin. Nevertheless, it is made very clear that the cult poses a threat to traditional Roman state religion. As soon as he arrives in Rome, Elagabalus builds a temple for Elagabal on the Palatine, 'to which he desired to transfer the emblem of the Great Mother, the fire of Vesta, the Palladium, the shields of the Salii, and all that the Romans held sacred, purposing that no god might be worshipped at Rome save only Elagabal'. The religions of the Jews, Samaritans and Christians should also be brought together in the Palatine temple, 'in order that the priesthood of Elagabal might include the mysteries of every form of worship'.[62]

The *Vita Heliogabali* ascribes monotheistic tendencies to Elagabalus, but the image is not consistent. At one point, it is stated that the emperor wants to abolish 'not only the religious ceremonies of the Romans but also those of the whole world, his one wish being that the god Elagabal should be worshipped everywhere'.[63] At another point, he is said to regard all other gods as servants of Elagabal. That does not stop him, however, from worshipping Magna Mater and Salambo, or from dressing up as Venus. Moreover, Elagabalus never seems to succeed in destroying other religions. Allegedly, he 'desired' to extinguish the everlasting fire of the Vestals and 'attempted' to take away their holy shrine, but it is never confirmed that he actually achieved the first goal, while a trick of the senior vestal definitely prevented him from achieving the second. In fact, the *Vita* makes it very clear that 'the cult did not suffer at his hands'. However, this remark is undermined by an earlier passage, which states that the emperor 'violated the chastity of a Vestal Virgin, and by removing the holy shrines [...] profaned the sacred rites of the Roman nation'.[64]

Theo Optendrenk speculates that the author of the *Vita Heliogabali* is reluctant to state that Elagabalus managed to lay his hands on the symbols of traditional Roman state religion because he is a pagan himself: by admitting that those symbols have been subject to harm, he would admit that his religion has been damaged.[65] However, as we have seen, the author *does* admit that damage has been done, which means that he is once more inconsistent. The juxtaposition probably derives from the fact that on the one hand he wants to imply that Elagabalus did not manage to weaken the pagan cults of Rome, while on the other he wants to portray the emperor as an intolerant monotheist who does not want any god but his own worshipped in the empire.

It has been speculated that the *Vita Heliogabali* is meant as a pagan attack on the intolerance of Christianity, which had become the dominant religion by the end of the fourth century CE. Supposedly Elagabalus is likened to Constantine, the first Christian emperor. In contrast, the *Vita Alexandri* presents its subject as a paragon of religious tolerance, claiming that Alexander had busts of Orpheus, Abraham, Apollonius of Tyana and Jesus Christ in his personal 'lararium' (shrine), and that he 'respected the privileges of the Jews and allowed the Christians to exist unmolested'. Supposedly, his exemplary behaviour mirrors that of Julian, the last pagan emperor.[66]

Samuel Zinsli has shown that many parallels can be drawn between the *Vita Heliogabali* and Eusebius's biography of Constantine.[67] Although it is not certain that the author of the *Historia Augusta* had read Eusebius's work, Zinsli's analysis makes it seem likely that he knew it in some form. *De vita Constantini* expresses the thought that God punishes wicked rulers with miserable lives and gruesome deaths, while virtuous rulers are rewarded with happy lives and enviable deaths. A similar philosophy – but with the Roman people instead of God as the rewarding or punishing force – occurs in the introduction of the *Vita Heliogabali*, where the author states that good rulers reign long and die of natural causes, while bad rulers are murdered and dragged through the streets. However, some of the given examples are so obviously false – Nero, who ruled for 14 years, is named among the bad emperors, while Titus, who barely ruled for two, is named among the good ones – that they cannot be taken seriously. Therefore, Zinsli argues that we should distinguish between the actual, anonymous author of the *Vita* and his alter ego, Aelius Lampridius, who contradicts himself on several occasions and is deliberately presented as untrustworthy. By using Lampridius as his mouthpiece, the author of the *Vita* manages to criticise Constantine without ever explicitly saying anything negative about him.

While it seems plausible that the *Vita Heliogabali* implicitly likens Elagabalus to Constantine, especially where the matter of religion is concerned, we should not consider it primarily a religious pamphlet. Although the emperor is called by the name of his god, indicating that the author closely links the two, the cult of Elagabal does not play a big role in the *Vita*. In fact, the subject of religious intolerance seems to be only of minor importance, with the bulk of the text describing the emperor's licentiousness and extravagance. Elagabalus's alleged desire to destroy all other gods is but one of the many faults of this tyrant, who is presented as the pinnacle – or, more appropriately, the nadir – of a long tradition of 'bad' emperors. 'Worse than Commodus is Elagabalus alone,' the author states. 'Nor emperor he, nor Antoninus, nor citizen, nor senator, nor man of noble blood, nor Roman.'[68] The eldest self-proclaimed son of Caracalla had nothing going for him – he was the ultimate monster.

## ELAGABALUS IN THE WORKS OF OTHER AUTHORS

Although many Greco-Roman and Byzantine authors have discussed the reign of Elagabalus, Cassius Dio, Herodian and the *Historia Augusta* provide us with the most detailed and complete images of the controversial emperor. Apart from John of Antioch, Xiphilinus and Zonaras, whose accounts of the period 218–22 mostly consist of detailed summaries of Herodian and Cassius Dio respectively, no other author devotes more than a few short paragraphs to the reign of the unfortunate ruler. However, that very brevity makes them interesting, since it requires them to be highly selective in choosing which elements to include in their account, and which to discard. What, according to these authors, were the defining characteristics of Elagabalus? And how do the images of the young monarch develop in late antiquity and the Byzantine period?

One of the elements many authors touch upon is the issue of the emperor's legitimacy. The fourth-century poet Ausonius, who wrote a poem in which he addressed many emperors, sneers at Elagabalus:

> Dost thou also defile the sanctuary of the Augustan palace,
> Falsely bearing the names of the Antonines –
> Thou, than whom no fouler or more filthy monster
> Ever filled the imperial throne of Rome?[69]

The historian Aurelius Victor, who finished his work around 360, paints a picture of Elagabalus which is just as unfavourable, but does not question his right to the throne. Although he used Cassius Dio as a source, and could therefore have been aware of the doubts surrounding Elagabalus's parentage, he unambiguously states that Caracalla was the emperor's father. The same goes for the anonymous author of the *Epitome de Caesaribus*, who wrote about forty years later and may have been familiar with Dio's work as well. However, the *Epitome* puts Elagabalus's parentage in a negative light by remarking that he was 'Caracalla's son from the secret violation of his niece Soemea'.[70]

Other authors are more careful when addressing the topic. The historian Eutropius, who wrote his Roman history some years after Aurelius Victor, states that Elagabalus 'was considered to be the son of Antoninus Caracalla'.[71] Zosimus, whose account of the decline of the empire was written between 498 and 518, merely records that the emperor was related to Caracalla's mother. The Byzantine chronicler Cedrenus, writing after 1057, repeats Dio's slur, 'False Antoninus'. So do Dio's epitomisers, the Byzantine monks Xiphilinus and Zonaras, writing in the eleventh and twelfth centuries respectively. The accusation of illegitimacy thus kept haunting Elagabalus as long as the Roman empire existed in some form, although not all authors took a stance on it, and some even gave credit to the story that he had been sired by Caracalla.

Most authors do not discuss Elagabalus's favouritism or lack of interest in affairs of government. The seventh-century chronicler John of Antioch, whose account of the period 218–22 relies heavily on Herodian, mentions that the emperor appointed actors, slaves and freedmen in important positions, made a dancer military prefect and put a charioteer in charge of the cavalry. Xiphilinus mentions favouritism in general and the career of Comazon in particular, also adding that Elagabalus planned to make his husband Caesar. That last story can also be found in the work of Zonaras, who derived his information at least partially from Xiphilinus.

Elagabalus's alleged cruelty also receives little attention outside the works of Dio, Herodian and the *Historia Augusta*. John of Antioch makes the passing remark that the emperor killed many distinguished men. Syncellus, who wrote in the ninth century, claims that he was 'exceedingly murderous', but does not provide any anecdotes to illustrate his point.[72] Xiphilinus and Zonaras give several examples which derive from Dio, such as the many executions (only Xiphilinus provides names) and the child sacrifices to Elagabal. Neither of them mentions the story that Elagabalus stabbed his own foster father.

1. Map of Roman Syria. Ancient World Mapping Center, University of North Carolina, Chapel Hill, NC.

2. Relief depicting Arsu and Elagabal. J. Starcky, 'Stèle d'Elahagabal', 49 (1975–76) pp. 503–20.

3. Bust of Elagabalus, type 1. Ny Carlsberg Glyptotek, no IN 2073. Picture taken by Ole Haupt.

4. Bust of Elagabalus, type 2. Musei Capitolini, Rome. Picture taken by Ellen Kraft.

5. Coin showing the black stone in a quadriga on the reverse. *RIC* 196a (aureus), Numismatische Bilddatenbank Eichstätt: www. ifaust.de/nbe.

.

6. Coin showing Elagabalus as high priest and the black stone in a quadriga, frontal (antoninianus), not in *RIC*. Kunsthistorisches Museum Wien, Bundesslg. von Münzen, no 43082.

7. Coin showing the black stone in a quadriga on the reverse. *RIC* 61 (aureus), Numismatische Bilddatenbank Eichstätt: www.ifaust.de/nbe.

8. Coin showing Elagabalus as 'sacerdos amplissimus' on the reverse. *RIC* 46 (denarius), Compagnie Générale de Bourse: www.cgb.fr.

9. Coin showing Elagabalus as 'sacerdos amplissimus' on the reverse. *RIC* 88 (denarius), Compagnie Générale de Bourse: www.cgb.fr.

10. Coin showing a bearded Elagabalus on the obverse. *RIC* 68b (aureus), Numismatische Bilddatenbank Eichstätt: www.ifaust.de/nbe.

11. Reconstruction of the Elagabal temple on the Palatine, seen from above. Y. Thébert et al., 'Il santuario di *Elagabalus*', p. 84.

12. Reconstruction of the Elagabal temple on the Palatine, drawing. Y. Thébert et al., 'Il santuario di *Elagabalus*', p. 85.

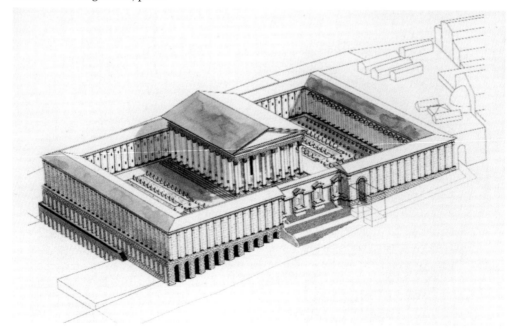

13. Capital with the betyl of Elagabal, flanked by two female deities. F. Studniczka, 'Ein Pfeilercapitell', Pl. XII.

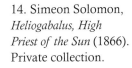

14. Simeon Solomon, *Heliogabalus, High Priest of the Sun* (1866). Private collection.

15. Lawrence Alma-Tadema, *The Roses of Heliogabalus* (1888). Private collection.

16. Gustav-Adolf Mossa, *Lui* (1906). Musée des Beaux-Arts, Nice.

17. An Italian designer-clothing store called Eliogabalo. Appropriately for an emperor who worshipped the sun, there is a tanning salon above.

Better attested is the topos of effeminacy. In the fourth century, the author of the *Epitome* records that Elagabalus 'turned himself into a woman and commanded to be called by the (female) name Bassiana instead of Bassianus'.[73] Quite possibly, this remark has been inspired by Dio, who states that the emperor wanted to be addressed as 'Lady' rather than 'Lord' by Zoticus. John of Antioch repeats Herodian's comment that the emperor spoiled his natural good looks by using make-up. Syncellus calls him 'a thoroughly effeminate man, who had changed to the ways of a woman, adorning himself with and affecting the trappings of females'.[74] Cedrenus remarks that Elagabalus was so effeminate that he married Hierocles. Even worse, he allegedly wanted to be made hermaphrodite by means of an incision – a story which also occurs in Zonaras, but, for unknown reasons, has been omitted by the usually more exhaustive Xiphilinus. Many other examples of the emperor's effeminacy, like the comments that he was termed 'mistress' and 'queen', worked with wool, wore a hairnet and painted his eyes, are recorded by both Byzantine monks.

Extravagance and love of luxury do not feature in most of the images of Elagabalus. Xiphilinus and Zonaras use the name Sardanapalus for the emperor, but we can only speculate how well informed they were about the implications of this name. Apart from that, the only thing which could qualify as an illustration of Elagabalus's luxurious lifestyle is Xiphilinus's description of the lavish festivities surrounding the marriage between Elagabalus and Julia Paula. On the other hand, few authors fail to address the emperor's alleged licentiousness. If Philostratus's love letter number 19 can indeed be read as an attack on the recently deceased emperor, as has been argued in the third chapter, it is telling that Elagabalus is likened to a male prostitute.[75] As we have seen, Ausonius condemns him as the foulest and filthiest emperor of all in his poem, while Aurelius Victor remarks that 'not even the wicked or frivolous women were more indecent'. Eutropius comments that the emperor 'defiled himself with all vices', his life being 'very shameless and depraved'. A few decades later, the *Epitome de Caesaribus* makes a similar comment, stating that Elagabalus 'defiled himself with all vices' after he arrived in Rome.[76]

The topos stayed popular after the fourth century. The Christian author Orosius, who wrote his *Historiae adversus paganos* in 417–18, says that the priest from Emesa 'left no memory of himself except one notorious for its defilements, crimes, and every obscenity'. Zosimus informs us that

Elagabalus 'led a revolting and ignominious life', in which licentiousness prevailed. John of Antioch follows Herodian in steering clear of the topic, even omitting the latter's allusion that the emperor appointed slaves and freedmen 'who perhaps excelled in some foul activity'.[77] However, Cedrenus describes Elagabalus as a licentious individual, a trait he connects to the young man's marriage with Hierocles. Xiphilinus and Zonaras, following Dio, mention the emperor's sexual escapades several times. Both of them give extensive accounts of how Elagabalus prostituted himself and seduced Zoticus, apparently considering these stories important enough to record in detail.

Since most of the authors who are discussed here devote only a few lines or short paragraphs to the reign of Elagabalus, it is hard to discern to what extent they want to portray the emperor as a stereotypical 'Oriental', and to what extent they are merely copying stories about his effeminacy and licentiousness from Dio and Herodian, without any ethnic implications. To Byzantine authors at least, classical Greco-Roman notions of the 'East' and its inhabitants were probably meaningless.

The same is true for the topic of religion. Many authors mention that Elagabalus was a priest of Elagabal – or Heliogabalus, as both god and emperor are often called – but they do not always take care to specify that Elagabal was a Syrian god. Even if they do, however, that information may be neutral in their context. Other authors may not explicitly mention Elagabal and Syria at all, but may still imply that the cult of the sun god possessed typical 'Oriental' traits. This could well be the case with Philostratus's letter number 19, in which he seems to be mocking Elagabalus by comparing him to a boy prostitute. The sophist tells his fictional beloved that his house is 'a citadel of beauty', that those who enter are priests, that those who are garlanded are sacred envoys, and that their silver is tribute money. Moreover, he remarks that 'the sun is a public god'.[78] It is possible to read this letter as a slur against the cult of Elagabal, associating it with prostitution and licentiousness – both aspects which Greeks and Romans often deemed typical of 'Oriental' cults.

Other authors are less subtle. In the *Epitome de Caesaribus*, which claims that Elagabal is a Phoenician sun god, it is mentioned that Elagabalus cut off his genitals and sacrificed to Magna Mater. The anonymous author is also one of the few to refer to the emperor's pairing with a vestal virgin, although he claims they did not actually marry. Aurelius Victor, writing several decades earlier, specifies that Elagabal is a Syrian god, but does not seem to attach any verdict to this information, nor does he present the

THE REJECTED RULER 119

emperor as displaying typically 'Oriental' religious behaviour. Eutropius and Orosius merely mention the god by name, opting to leave out his origins or the characteristics of his cult. Zosimus does not refer to Elagabal at all, but states that the emperor spent his time with magicians and swindlers.

John of Antioch follows Herodian in stressing the foreign character of the cult, for instance remarking that Elagabalus dressed in 'barbarian' clothes as a priest and was accompanied by flutes and drums. However, he leaves out many important details, such as the marriage to Aquilia Severa and the black stone. In fact, it is never specified that Elagabalus worships Elagabal: at one point, it is mentioned that the emperor had 'his gods' – plural – transported to a different temple.[79] Probably, John, as a Christian, was just not interested in the 'clash' between different pagan gods and considered it unnecessary to specify which deity – or deities – Elagabalus worshipped. Syncellus goes even further, omitting both the cult of Elagabal and the emperor's priesthood from his short account. Cedrenus, on the other hand, does mention the Emesene deity, remarking that Elagabalus was circumcised and refused to eat pork. Xiphilinus and Zonaras give the same negative details as Dio, such as the emperor's child sacrifices and his violation of Aquilia Severa (unnamed by Zonaras). They also mention that Elagabalus acquired the nickname 'the Assyrian' by wearing the same clothes as Syrian priests.

On the whole, the authors discussed in this paragraph add little to the images of Elagabalus as he is presented by Cassius Dio and Herodian. Since most accounts are very brief, emphasis is put on a few elements: the emperor's effeminacy, his licentiousness and his devotion to Elagabal, whose cult is on occasion depicted as typically 'Oriental'. All of the images of the priest-emperor are very negative. When the emperor Julian (361–63) describes a banquet to which the gods and all the emperors had been invited, he recounts that Elagabalus was expelled as soon as he tried to enter. In the company of his more dignified colleagues, there was no room for the 'pretty boy from Emesa'.[80]

There is, however, one noticeable exception to all these negative accounts. This is provided by Theodoros Skoutariotes, a thirteenth-century Byzantine chronicler whose work covers history from the birth of Adam to 1261 CE. His Elagabalus is completely unrecognisable, for the emperor is described as 'eloquent, an excellent man, fierce in battle, gentle, wise, swift, conciliating all and justifiably loved by all'.[81] This characterisation of Elagabalus has obviously not been inspired by any previously discussed account of the ruler's character and deeds. Theodoros proceeds to record that the emperor cancelled the debts owed to the treasury, promulgated a law that senators would no longer have to pay for the war expenses of the state – thereby abolishing constitutions dating back to Julius Caesar – and burnt all the relevant documents on the Forum of Hadrian (which never existed; a clear indication of the inaccuracy of the text).

The story is reminiscent of an earlier passage, in which Theodoros records that Antoninus Pius likewise changed a law which Caesar had introduced to extract money from senators, and burnt the relevant documents.[82] This earlier passage appears to be based on a very similar passage in the *Chronographia* of the sixth-century chronicler Malalas, who was one of Theodoros's sources.[83] It seems likely that the same is true for the passage in which Elagabalus cancels senatorial debts, especially since the style and vocabulary Theodoros uses here are reminiscent of Malalas. Unfortunately, the only surviving manuscript of the *Chronographia* has a lacuna between the reigns of Caracalla and Valerian, so no definite conclusions can be drawn.

One wonders whether Malalas (or Theodoros), for whom both Elagabalus and Antoninus Pius must have been figures from a distant past, had somehow mixed them up because they were both called Antoninus. This would explain the remarkably flattering tone of the characterisation quoted above. If so, we have at least one case in which Elagabalus's claim to the name of the Antonines caused him to be associated with this prestigious dynasty. Unfortunately for him, though, other authors did not make the same mistake. Many centuries would pass before the priest-emperor was once again cast in a positive light.

### FACTS AND FICTION

Although we have been dealing with the construction of images in this chapter, these images did not originate in a historical vacuum. A determining factor for the hostile tone of the literary accounts was Elagabalus's *damnatio memoriae*, which left little room to portray the emperor positively. Living memory also provided limitations. Contemporary authors like Dio and Herodian wrote their histories for an audience that, for the most part, had lived through the years 218–22, and may even have experienced Elagabalus and his actions at first hand. These historians could not completely disregard the facts if they wanted to keep their credibility. The author of the *Historia Augusta*, for whom Elagabalus was a long-dead and probably mostly forgotten ruler, was not bound by such restraints. This is clearly reflected in its many fantastical stories.

Several elements in the literary representations of Elagabalus can, to a greater or lesser extent, be linked to concrete events and developments during the priest-emperor's reign. The accusations of illegitimacy are evidently a response to Elagabalus's claim to be the son of Caracalla. As has been pointed out, the way in which the young ruler came to power – inciting Roman soldiers to revolt against their current emperor – robbed the senate of even the pretence that it had any say in the imperial succession. This made Elagabalus's relation with the senatorial elite problematical from the start.

Stories about the emperor's disrespect for the senate, the execution of senators and the promotion of unworthy favourites to important positions can probably also be connected to Elagabalus's military rise to power. It seems likely that the new administration deemed it necessary to remove some of the politicians and commanders who had opposed Elagabalus in his uprising or might form a threat to his weak position, while rewarding men who had played a key role in the revolt against Macrinus. Although the promoted favourites were probably no mimes and charioteers, they did include the likes of Comazon and ...atus, who under Elagabalus rose far above their initial rank and status.

The heavy emphasis on the 'Oriental' character of the emperor and the cult of Elagabal in the literary sources also has some factual basis. Elagabalus's parents were native Syrians, and the boy himself acted as priest of a local Syrian cult. Moreover, coins and inscriptions from the period 218–22 clearly show that the priesthood and cult of Elagabal were not presented in a traditional Roman way, but retained many strikingly Syrian features, such as the emperor's foreign dress as *sacerdos amplissimus*, the name Elagabal and the god's depiction as a black stone. Elagabalus's violations of Roman state religion, such as the elevation of Elagabal to the head of the Roman pantheon and his marriage to a vestal virgin, would only have strengthened the impression that he was a foreigner who knew little about Roman culture and traditions, and cared even less.

Finally, there are the accusations of effeminacy, luxury and licentiousness, which play a large role in the ancient accounts of Elagabalus. As has been pointed out, these were standard topoi to characterise 'bad' emperors. Since they were also applied to 'Oriental' people, Elagabalus seems to have become the victim of two condemning discourses, which merged in the images ancient authors constructed of him. We can only speculate about a possible core of truth. In general, sexual excesses and displays of personal wealth are mostly restricted to the private sphere. Therefore, accusations of misconduct in these matters are easy to make and hard to disprove. In all likelihood, many, if not most, of the stories about Elagabalus's effeminate, luxurious and licentious behaviour have sprouted from the imaginations of ancient authors, or are based on the gossip and jokes of contemporaries. More than any facts, though, they have defined the reputation of the emperor. Real or imaginary, Elagabalus's excesses have never ceased to haunt his memory.

# 5

# THE EVIL TYRANT

What? should I be Emperor, and abide laws myself?
No, it only suits me to give them to others.

Gysbert Tysens, Bassianus Varius Heliogabalus (1720)

While Byzantine historiography came to an end with the fall of Constantinople in 1453, Elagabalus did not vanish into oblivion. As far as we can tell, the young emperor had been largely forgotten by the scholars of medieval Europe, but the Renaissance brought a renewed interest in Roman culture. As ancient texts were rediscovered, copied, translated and studied, Elagabalus was once more brought to the attention of historians. Artists, too, became increasingly familiar with and interested in the ancient Greeks and Romans. As a consequence, Elagabalus made his appearance in several scholarly and literary works. This chapter will concern itself primarily with the *Nachleben* of the emperor from ca. 1350 to ca. 1850 – the period from the start of the Renaissance to the first expressions of the Decadent movement. The line between scholarly and literary works is hard to draw for most of this period, with many works showing characteristics of both genres. I define as 'scholarly' those works which seem primarily concerned with presenting the historical truth, as 'literary' those works which seem primarily intended as fiction.

This chapter will consist of two parts: a general overview of scholarly and literary images of Elagabalus, and an in-depth discussion of selected works. At the start of the first part, a brief overview will be given of the study of ancient history from 1350 to 1810. I have chosen 1810 as an end point here, rather than 1850, because it is the year in which the rise of modern academic scholarship may be said to have begun. I will discuss how scholars from the fourteenth to the nineteenth centuries had access to antiquity, how they perceived it and how they presented it in their works. Special attention will be given to their treatment of Elagabalus. Since historiography was not yet a fully fledged, clearly delineated field for much of this period, I have decided also to include several other scholarly works which mention the emperor (for instance essays on morality and statesmanship).

Next, I will give a brief overview of Elagabalus's *Nachleben* in art and literature from 1350 onwards, focusing on his portrayal as an 'evil tyrant'. I use this term to describe the emperor's image as a malicious antagonist or *exemplum malum*, defined by negative traits such as cruelty, selfishness, gluttony and licentiousness. This theme characterises the *Nachleben* until the middle of the nineteenth century. After this time, the tyrant persona is sharply altered by writers and artists from the Decadent movement, and sometimes abandoned completely in favour of a different image, as we will see in Chapter 6. However, images of Elagabalus as 'evil tyrant' keep emerging in the twentieth and twenty-first centuries. Therefore, we will also devote some attention to the continuation of the evil tyrant theme after 1850.

In the second part of this chapter, we will take a closer look at some of the images of Elagabalus. Three works from the period 1350–1850 will be discussed in detail: the Venetian opera *Eliogabalo*, written by Aurelio Aureli and composed by Francesco Cavalli for the Venetian carnival season of 1667–68; the play *Bassianus Varius Heliogabalus, of de uitterste proef der standvastige liefde* [*Bassianus Varius Heliogabalus, or The Ultimate Test of Persistent Love*] by the Dutch playwright Gysbert Tysens, written in 1720; and the Polish play *Irydjon*, written by Zygmunt Krasiński in 1836. These works have the merit of having been written in three different centuries, by authors of three different nationalities, which allows us to compare the images of Elagabalus in three different cultures.

### THE 'EVIL TYRANT': A GENERAL OVERVIEW

*Elagabalus in scholarly works, 1350–1810*

Although many ancient texts had been lost to medieval Europe and knowledge of ancient Greek had vanished completely in the West, the achievements of the Greeks and Romans had not been completely forgotten. From the ninth century onwards, medieval scholars became increasingly interested in ancient texts. However, they tended to focus on particular subjects, such as grammar, rhetoric, philosophy, law and medicine. Only in the fourteenth century did the interest in classics extend to Roman culture as a whole.

The Italian scholar and poet Petrarch (1304–74) was among the first to shift attention to the ancients' artistic achievements and their way of life. He collected, read and annotated a great number of classical texts, trying to restore them to their original, uncorrupted form. It was not Aristotle who caught his imagination, but Cicero, Virgil and Livy. As 'the father of the Renaissance', Petrarch was no longer satisfied with the biblical values of meekness and humility, which held such a revered place in the minds of many medieval people. Inspired by the ancients, he advocated human worth and dignity, giving man a central place in the grand scheme of things and putting great value on beauty, art and the senses. Many other scholars and artists adopted these humanistic values. Like Petrarch, they rejected the culture of the middle ages – a term first coined by the Humanist Flavio Biondo in the early fifteenth century – and idealised the ancient Roman way of life. Humanist scholars set out to rediscover and restore ancient Latin and (from the fifteenth century onwards) Greek texts, passionately devoting themselves to the study of antiquity.

Images of Elagabalus are scarce in works of this period. Considering the relatively uncritical attitude of early modern scholars towards Greek and Latin texts, it is not surprising that their representations of the emperor stay very close to the ancient sources. In his treatise on famous women, *De claris mulieribus* (1361), the Italian humanist Giovanni Boccaccio dwells on the shameful actions of Julia Soaemias – whom he calls Symiamira – and her 'good-for-nothing son'. Boccaccio reproduces several ancient stories, such as that of the women's senate, and expresses his disapproval of a time 'when enemies of the state and pleasure-seeking young men, foreign and unknown, rule Rome and the world'. We find an equally negative portrayal of Elagabalus in Leonardo Bruni's *Historiae Florentini populi* (1416–42), one of the first works of historiography in early-modern times. Bruni names the young ruler in one breath with Vitellius, Caracalla and Maximinus Thrax, brandishing them as 'monsters [...] who horrified the whole world'.[1]

Many Italian scholars travelled to other parts of western or central Europe, while poets, students and scholars from these parts came to visit Italy. Thus did humanism spread from Italy to other European countries, with Desiderius Erasmus of Rotterdam (1469–1536) as its greatest proponent north of the Alps. The humanistic spirit also affected the educational system. In the course of the sixteenth century, schools and universities throughout Europe gave classical Latin and Greek a central place in the curriculum. From Italy to England and the Low Countries, an increasing number of people became acquainted with the works and ideas of such authors as Cicero, Sallust, Virgil, Homer and Demosthenes.

The preservation and accessibility of classical texts was greatly helped by the art of printing, which had been invented around 1450. Numerous Greek and Latin works appeared in *editiones principes*, first printed editions, reaching a much wider audience than had hitherto been imagined possible. Translations of ancient texts also appeared: not only of Greek texts into Latin, but also of Greek and Latin texts into Italian, French, English, German and other modern languages. These translated works included the three main literary sources on Elagabalus. The *editio princeps* of Cassius Dio's *Historia Romana*, with both the original Greek and a Latin translation, was published in 1548, but included only books XXXVI to LVIII. The *Epitome* of Xiphilinus, which covered (among other things) the reign of Elagabalus, appeared in Greek and Latin in 1551. It was translated into Italian in 1562, into French in 1610, and into English in 1704. Herodian was first published in Latin in 1490, with the original Greek text following 13 years later. Italian, German, French and English editions appeared in the following decades, while the first Dutch version became available in 1614. The *editio princeps* of the *Historia Augusta* was published in 1475, followed by a French translation in 1667 and a German version by the end of the eighteenth century.

Despite these developments, scholarly interest in Elagabalus remained marginal. Niccolò Machiavelli mentions the emperor as a bad example in his famous work on statesmanship, *Il principe* (1532), but only in passing: he remarks that the young ruler was despised, just like Macrinus and Julian, and did not last long.[2] Fifty years later, Elagabalus featured in three of Michel de Montaigne's *Essais* (1580). In 'De juger de la mort d'autruy', about the deaths of famous persons, the emperor's plans for a luxurious suicide (recorded in the *Vita Heliogabali*) are discussed. Montaigne doubts that 'the most effeminate man in the world' would have dared to take his own life. He mentions briefly that Elagabalus was killed on a privy in 'Qu'il faut sobrement se mesler de juger des ordonnances divines', adding that the church father Irenaeus came to a similar end. From this, he argues that we cannot understand God's motives and should refrain from interpreting the fortune or misfortune of individuals as divine reward or retribution: the judgement of our acts occurs in the afterlife, not on earth. Lastly, in 'Des coches', it is noted that Elagabalus impersonated Cybele and Bacchus and drove around in a carriage pulled by stags, dogs or even naked women – another reference to the *Vita Heliogabali*.

Montaigne's essays were widely read, and influenced many other authors. Among these was Johan de Brune, a Dutch statesman and lawyer. De Brune published several works in which he imitated Montaigne's prose, commenting on ethical and moral issues. In one of these works, *Banket-werck van goede gedachten* [*Banquet Work of Good Thoughts*] (1657), he mentions the notorious dining habits of Elagabalus. Being a strict Calvinist, de Brune condemned such indulgence in earthly delights, saying that the emperor and his guests deserved to eat sausages filled with excrement.[3]

For a long time scholars of antiquity set it as their goal to restore the works of the ancients in their original form, but did not research how the texts had come into their present, damaged state. Only with the publication of *De re diplomatica* by the French monk and scholar Jean Mabillon in 1681 was the groundwork laid for the systematic determination of the age and authenticity of ancient Latin documents. A few decades later another learned monk, Bernard de Montfaucon, laid the foundations for Greek palaeography with his *Paleographica Graeca* (1708).

Historiography went through a similar development. Until a more critical attitude developed in the Enlightenment, the authority of ancient texts remained largely unquestioned. The seventeenth-century historian Louis-Sébastien Le Nain de Tillemont, who wrote two large works on early church history and the history of imperial Rome, is a good example of a scholar who excelled through his thorough knowledge of the ancient sources, rather than through his methods of criticism. His description of Elagabalus's reign in *Histoire des empereurs* (1690–1738) is full of ancient biases. For Tillemont, the period 218–22 was nothing but 'a continuous sequence of crimes against decency, against humanity, and against all sorts of laws'.[4]

Edward Gibbon used Tillemont's work extensively, although that did not stop him from making fun of the latter's naivety in accepting some obviously hostile accounts. However, even in Gibbon's own monumental work, *The History of the Decline and Fall of the Roman Empire* (1776–88), we can find many images and anecdotes which come straight from the sources, but are presented to the reader without any caveat or reservation. The author remarks that the 'inexpressible infamy' of Elagabalus's 'vices and follies [...] surpasses that of any other age or country', recording that the emperor, 'corrupted by his youth, his country, and his fortune, abandoned himself to the grossest pleasures with ungoverned fury' and 'lavished away the treasures of his people in the wildest extravagance'. In Gibbon's view, Elagabalus was nothing but an effeminate boy who 'never acted like a man' and came to power through 'a conspiracy of women and eunuchs'.[5] The young ruler's lack of manliness and extravagant lifestyle are explicitly connected to his Syrian background: 'The grave senators confessed with a sigh, that, after having long experienced the stern tyranny of their own countrymen, Rome was at length humbled beneath the effeminate luxury of Oriental despotism.'[6]

Elagabalus's devotion to Elagabal, denigratingly called a 'display of superstitious gratitude', is likewise characterised as typically 'Oriental'. The cult of the sun god is described with all the lavish details provided by Herodian, including 'lascivious dances to the sound of barbarian music', and 'the richest wines, the most extraordinary victims, and the rarest aromatics'. The god Elagabal is said to possess 'the soft delicacy of a Syrian deity', whereas the emperor himself is branded an 'Imperial fanatic' who cares only about 'the triumph of the god of Emesa over all the religions of the earth'. Gibbon does not hide his satisfaction over Elagabalus's miserable end, commenting, 'His memory was branded with eternal infamy by the senate; the justice of whose decree has been ratified by posterity.'[7]

Humanism received a great boost from the famous Johann Winckelmann (1717–68), whose passion for classical Greek art and literature inspired many of his contemporaries, especially in Germany. Winckelmann argued that greatness and immortality could only be achieved by imitating the ancient Greeks. His works ushered in an age of neohellenism, in which Roman culture was made subservient to Greek. As a consequence, Germany experienced a renewal of classical scholarship. Friedrich August Wolf (1759–1824), Winckelmann's most influential disciple, took the lead in employing an analytical, critical method in his study of the classics. He also coined the term for this more methodical way of research: '*Altertumswissenschaft*'.

### The reign of the tyrant, 1350 to the present

Vernacular translations throve to such an extent that a travelled man in the time of William Shakespeare (1564–1616) had almost the whole classical heritage within his grasp, even if he knew only a little Greek and Latin.[8] In fact, it was not even necessary for an interested layman to go back to the sources. He could make use of an increasing body of works of reference, in which famous quotations from ancient figures, historical anecdotes and classical myths had been collected. A prime example is Erasmus's *Adagia*, a collection of thousands of Greek and Latin adages, often accompanied by explanatory notes. Many artists, such as the French comic writer François Rabelais (ca.1494–1553), tried to imitate classical examples, stuffing their works with references to ancient anecdotes, embellishing Greek or Latin ideas and translating Greek or Latin words into the vernacular. Even those who did not go to these lengths, such as Shakespeare, were influenced and inspired by the classics.

Still, few authors before the nineteenth century made more than a passing reference to Elagabalus. One of those who did is the Italian humanist Bruni, already mentioned. Although he barely touched on the emperor in his history of the Florentine people, Bruni wrote a rhetorical oration called *Oratio Heliogabali ad meretrices* (1407–8). Supposedly, this was the speech which Elagabalus gave to the gathered harlots of Rome, as can be read in the *Vita Heliogabali*. Bruni's *Oratio* criticises the (perceived) decadence of Renaissance Rome, which the humanist author associated with imperial times. In the text, which is dripping with irony, Heliogabalus tells his audience that there is too much chastity in the capital. To remedy this unfortunate state of affairs, he introduces a new law, decreeing that all women will be public property from now on. At the end of the speech, the emperor sums up rewards available to those rendering their bodies to the service of the state, urging the gathered prostitutes to serve their country. Bruni, in short, presents Elagabalus as an emblem of the vices of imperial Rome and, by means of ironic inversion and historical parallel, uses him to comment on the city's moral climate in his own times.

Bruni was not the only author who was interested in the role of women during the reign of Elagabalus. Erasmus devoted one of his *Colloquia* – *Senatulus*, first published in 1529 – to the reinstitution of a women's senate, more than 13 centuries after Elagabalus had first established this governing body. The colloquium records the conversation between Cornelia, chairwoman of the senate, with several other women during the senate's first official session. Their discussion on protocol and fashion allows Erasmus to satirise both feminine vanity and the many moralists who, in his lifetime, concerned themselves with standards of dress and other things he deemed trivial. Elagabalus is only briefly mentioned. Cornelia defends the young ruler's reputation, but cannot conceal that he hurled the sacred fire of the vestals to the ground and that he was dragged by a hook and thrown into the sewer after his death. It is also mentioned that the emperor kept images of Moses and Christ in his domestic chapel, although this story runs counter to his alleged religious intolerance and was originally attributed to Severus Alexander.

Also worthy of note is the pamphlet *L'Isle des Hermaphrodites nouvellement descouverte* (1605) by Thomas Artus. The anonymous main character of the pamphlet describes how he accidentally arrives at the Island of the Hermaphrodites. He stumbles upon a lavish palace, in which he finds a book about the country's laws and customs, drawn up by 'Imperator Varius, Heliogabalus, Hermaphroditicus, Gomorricus, Eunuchus, semper impudicissimus' ('always the most shameless').[9] These laws and customs, given in full, deal with such diverse topics as religion, warfare, the justice system, banquets and art. Invariably, they go against conventional morality, advocating corruption and unbridled hedonism, and valuing the pursuit of profit above all else. The laws are followed by a poem, 'Contre les hermaphrodites', and two essays, in which the author of the pamphlet criticises the society he has just described. In the first of these, Elagabalus, 'this monster of nature', is mentioned as a ruler who despoiled the sea and the earth, and ruined all men.[10] Although the name Héliogabale only appears a few times in the pamphlet, the epithets mentioned above and his role as lawmaker make it obvious that Artus regarded him as a fitting ruler for the anti-utopian society he described.

As Claude-Gilbert Dubois has remarked, the Island of the Hermaphrodites was meant to evoke the image of the French king Henry III (1574–89) and his court. The laws and customs of the hermaphrodites are very much concerned with appearance, and turn every action into a rite or ceremony, parodying the pomp and aesthetic mannerism of the Baroque French state. Hermaphroditism, as opposed to androgyny, signified ambivalence, lack of unity. More specifically, when applied to political morality, it was a metaphor for the ambiguity of opportunistic politicians who tried to pass off their self-serving motives as conforming to moral and religious principles. Through his description of the Island of the Hermaphrodites, whose core values are desire and licence, Artus denounces the excessive sensuality and egoistical economic liberalism he perceived in the France of his time.[11] Elagabalus, as the Isle's founding father, is associated with these abuses, as well as with an overabundance of splendour and formalised, aesthetic manners.

Visual representations of the emperor are quite rare before the nineteenth century. One example is a seventeenth-century woodcarving in the church of S. Pietro Martire, on the island of Murano, near Venice (but originally placed in the Scuola di S. Giovanni Battista). It depicts 32 statues of 'bad' historical figures, standing among 20 panels which represent the life of St John the Baptist. One of these figures is Elagabalus, who, together with the other statues, emphasises the need for redemption which St John embodies. Again, the emperor is used as a bad example.

In 1802, an anonymous French author – possibly Pierre-Jean-Baptiste Chaussard – published the epistolary novel *Héliogabale ou esquisse morale de la dissolution romaine sous les empereurs*. The work consists of letters by, among others, Mammaea, mother of Severus Alexander, the jurist Ulpian, Sylvinus, Alexander's teacher, and Elagabalus himself. Through these letters, the author presents Elagabalus as a tyrant who cares nothing for the law, nor for his subjects. Many scandalous anecdotes from the ancient sources are mentioned, sometimes even with footnotes referring to Cassius Dio, Herodian or the *Vita Heliogabali*. The teacher Sylvinus longs for 'the restoration of the ancient institutions of freedom', urging his pupil, Alexander, 'at least temper the absolute power for the good of all and for yourself. Let something of the republic breathe forth into the empire.' Elsewhere, Marcus Aurelius is praised for respecting 'liberty, the first right of man'.[12] Thus, the novel explicitly propagates the values of the French Revolution, depicting Elagabalus as the paragon of all that is wrong with absolute rulership.

From the 1830s onwards, the ordeals of early Christians became a very popular theme in historical fiction. This tradition was initiated by Edward Bulwer-Lytton, whose novel *The Last Days of Pompeii* (1834) recorded the imprisonment and escape of a Christian community in the doomed city, with the pagan hero converting to Christianity in the end.[13] Many authors followed Bulwer-Lytton's example, describing the persecutions, death sentences and salvations of Christians in first-century Pompeii and other times and places.

The followers of Christ regularly make an appearance in Elagabalus's *Nachleben* from the nineteenth century onwards. However, only seldom is the emperor portrayed as actively prosecuting Christians – probably because ancient literature never suggests that he did. In Touissant Cabuchet's play *Héliogabale* (1837) – the first part of his *Trilogie sur le Christianisme* – Héliogabale is confronted with the Christian views of his aunt and wife(!) Mamméa. In line with Cabuchet's conviction that the spiritual and the material had to be in balance within both state and individual, she tries to persuade the emperor to let go of his luxurious, hedonistic lifestyle. Her nephew does not want to listen, asserting, 'I am born for pleasure: it's my god who orders me that.'[14] He does not understand Mamméa's religion. Still, he is not intolerant of her views, and even proposes to convert himself, as long as she agrees not to abandon him. Only when Mamméa refuses this offer, the emperor comes to consider her and her son Alexianus as his enemies.

The British novel *The Sun God* (1904), written by Arthur Westcott, shows Elagabalus as much more hostile towards Christians. Westcott describes how a Christian family in Rome tries to weather the reign of the priest-emperor. Elagabalus is portrayed as a cruel, child-sacrificing monster to which several family members fall victim. He is handsome, but also effeminate, licentious, luxurious, and completely under the sway of his lover, Hierocles. Even at 17, he has already earned a reputation 'such as even Nero or Caligula might have blushed to own'.[15]

Luxury, licentiousness and cruelty are also displayed by the eponymous villain of Émile Sicard and Déodat de Séverac's musical piece *Héliogabale*, performed in Béziers, southern France, in 1910. Sicard and Séverac pit the emperor against the Christians in Rome, who beg God to relieve them from their suffering. As Séverac remarked in a letter to a friend, 'the interesting thing [about Heliogabalus] is the contrast between paganism collapsing into Oriental perversity and Christianity at its dawn.'[16]

*Héliogabale* was inspired by *L'Agonie* (1888), a novel by Jean Lombard which will be discussed in detail in Chapter 6. In turn, the musical piece may have served as a source of inspiration for the French director Louis Feuillade, who produced the short, silent film *L'Orgie romaine* in 1911.[17] Although the film does not make any reference to Christianity, it is similar to Sicard's and Séverac's piece in presenting Elagabalus as a depraved tyrant.[18] In one of the first scenes, we see the emperor (played by Jean Aymé) lying on a couch, while slaves paint the nails of his fingers and toes. When one of them makes a mistake, he is mercilessly thrown to the lions. Elagabalus wears extravagant clothes and moves and acts in an effeminate manner. He surrounds himself with luxury and courtesans. As in the *Vita Heliogabali*, the emperor is fond of cruel practical jokes, showering his banquet guests with flower petals and setting a pack of lions loose on them. The composition of the former scene is reminiscent of Lawrence Alma-Tadema's famous painting *The Roses of Heliogabalus* (1888) (see Fig. 15), on which it may well have been based.

A more recent image of Elagabalus as evil tyrant is provided by British author Neil Gaiman. His online comic *Being an Account of the Life and Death of the Emperor Heliogabolus* (*sic*) (1991–92), made in just 24 hours, is clearly based on the *Historia Augusta*. Gaiman remarks that 'in his four years as emperor [...], Heliogabolus did lots of interesting things. Not nice things; but nonetheless interesting.' The author lists many of these things – smothering banquet guests in a rain of flowers, driving a chariot pulled by naked women, instigating the world's first 'penocracy', etcetera – with unabashed fascination and a large dose of humour. His Heliogabolus is a spoiled teenager with limitless power and a cruel imagination. As Gaiman succinctly states, 'Heliogabolus was just a weird kid with a thing about animals and big dicks.'[19]

Elagabalus appears as an utterly malign character in the French comic series *La Dernière prophétie* (2002–7) by Gilles Chaillet. The series is set in the time of Constantine, but has long flashbacks to the Severan age. In the second volume, *Les Dames d'Emèse*, we are introduced to Elagabalus. The boy is portrayed as a religious fanatic from a distinctly 'Oriental' background. We witness his reign of terror in the third volume, *Sous le signe de Ba'al*. Elagabalus imposes his foreign god on Rome and honours the deity with many sacrifices – animals and probably even people. Interestingly, the emperor is presented as the symbolical predecessor of Constantine, who is called 'a new Heliogabalus'.[20] Thus, this twenty-first-century comic-book series echoes the implicit comparison made by the *Vita Heliogabali*. Chaillet confirms the idea of Elagabalus as the enemy of pagan, rather than Christian, religion and accuses the emperor of displaying the same religious intolerance as fourth-century Christianity. For him, as for the author of the *Historia Augusta*, both Elagabalus and Constantine are villains.

Things seem to have come full circle – but future portrayals of Elagabalus as 'evil tyrant' will undoubtedly give other interpretations of his despotic character, continuing to explore the field's endless possibilities.

THE 'EVIL TYRANT': SELECTED WORKS

## Elagabalus in Aureli and Cavalli's Eliogabalo *(1667)*

Francesco Cavalli (1602–76) was one of the greatest opera composers of his time. When the *impresario* of the SS. Giovanni e Paolo theatre in Venice commissioned him to write the score for *Eliogabalo*, another success seemed imminent. The libretto of the opera, due to be put on stage in the Venetian carnival season of 1667–68, was written by Aurelio Aureli (ca. 1630–ca. 1708), one of the city's foremost librettists. Aureli's text – itself the revision of the text of an anonymous author – recorded the last days of the 'evil' emperor Eliogabalo, whose bad reign and selfish intrigues led to his murder and the ascent of his noble and virtuous successor, Alessandro. Like many of Aureli's plots, *Eliogabalo* was inspired by historical events, but did not stay true to its sources, elaborating on them and changing them into something substantially different. Nevertheless, it is evident that its 'historical' core was ultimately based on the *Historia Augusta*, which provides the opera with many specific scenes and details. Aureli did not read the *Vita Heliogabali* directly, but used the Italian translation of Pedro Mexía's *Historia imperial y cesarea* (1545), a Catalan work which borrowed from the *Historia Augusta*.[21]

The result of Cavalli's and Aureli's combined efforts did not please Giovanni Carlo and Vincenzo Grimani, who owned the SS. Giovanni e Paolo theatre. These two young brothers – 19 and 15 years old respectively – abruptly fired the theatre's *impresario* in 1667 and took matters into their own hands. They dismissed Cavalli and replaced him with Giovanni Antonio Boretti, a much younger composer, who wrote an entirely new score for the piece. Aureli was ordered to make some revisions to the text. It was this second version of *Eliogabalo* which was eventually performed, while Cavalli's original score was never heard in the opera houses of Venice.[22] The reasons for this are not entirely clear. Cavalli's musical style may simply have gone out of fashion, but this begs the question why the composer was hired in the first place.

In this chapter, we will concern ourselves with Aureli's original, unrevised libretto for *Eliogabalo*. The plot of the opera is constructed around emperor Eliogabalo's amorous escapades. After he has raped the noblewoman Eritea, the lustful ruler sets his eye on Flavia Gemmira, the fiancée of his virtuous cousin Alessandro. Eliogabalo makes several attempts to murder Alessandro and seduce Flavia, but does not succeed in either goal. Moreover, the emperor is unaware that his escapades have invoked the anger of his praetorian prefect, Giuliano, who is Flavia's brother and Eritea's lover. Giuliano wants to kill Eliogabalo, but is stopped by Alessandro, who argues that only heaven is allowed to punish a sinner. Eliogabalo still meets with a deservedly gruesome end when he tries to rape Flavia and is killed by his own soldiers. Alessandro succeeds him and takes Flavia as his empress. On this happy note, the opera ends.

Aureli leaves his audience in no doubt that Eliogabalo is the villain of the piece. In the first scene of the first act, the emperor passionately declares his love to Eritea, the noblewoman he has raped. He repeats his promise to marry her, but no sooner has she left than he exclaims, 'Which promises? Which oath? Which vows? The oath that I do not observe acquires name and pomp, illustrious is a law when I break it.' He then proceeds to plot the seduction of his next victim, Flavia Gemmira. Obviously, we are dealing with a tyrant who has no concern for others and lives only for his own pleasure. The law means nothing to Eliogabalo, nor does loyalty: 'Persistence and loyalty / are a slavish chain / for the cowardly people.' The emperor considers himself a god, remarking that he is no less powerful than Jupiter and even identifying himself with the thunder god. Elsewhere, he threatens to hit his praetorian prefect with a lightning bolt, stating that Jupiter has no jurisdiction in his realm.[23] This last quote seems to have been inspired by Elagabalus's alleged ambitions in the *Historia Augusta* to have no god worshipped other than his own. However, in Aureli's opera the emperor himself has become this god – possibly because both ruler and god are called Heliogabalus in the *Vita Heliogabali*.

Whatever the literary origins of Eliogabalo's hubris, he inspires only fear and hatred in his subjects. Flavia calls the emperor a 'shameless tyrant who rebels against Heaven' and Eritea considers him a 'brute' and a 'lustful tyrant'. The soldiers want him dead because he mocks them, underpaying them while living in great luxury himself. This *luxuria* theme probably also stems from the *Historia Augusta*. Of course, Eliogabalo is completely oblivious to these grievances, remarking, 'When this age will cherish the fame and glory I give it with my life, it will even surpass the Golden Century.'[24]

Gender plays an important role in the characterisation of Eliogabalo. The role was written for a soprano, which means it must have been intended for a woman or a *castrato*. It is hard to determine what this meant, since so many male roles in opera were sung by *castrati*. In fact, the role of the opera's hero, Alessandro, is a soprano too. Undoubtedly, the ambiguity between 'female' voice and 'male' body had a certain appeal, but it does not necessarily follow that the characters in question were supposed to be effeminate.[25] Still, both the words 'effeminato' and 'molle' ('soft') are attributed to Eliogabalo, while the latter word is also used to describe his perfume.[26] In this case, then, the character's 'female' voice *does* signify effeminacy.

A striking difference with the *Vita Heliogabali* is that Aureli's emperor is not primarily interested in men. If Eliogabalo has any homosexual tendencies, no reference is made to them, except perhaps that one of his minions is called Zotico. However, nothing indicates that this man is the emperor's lover, as is the case with Zoticus in the *Vita Heliogabali*. Hierocles is missing completely from the opera. Instead, *Eliogabalo* presents its titular character as a voracious womaniser who expresses the wish to merge all the beautiful women of Rome into one and possess a thousand beauties simultaneously.[27] As Jean-François Lattarico points out, the emperor is modelled after the *effemminato*, a recurring type in seventeenth-century Venetian opera. *Effemminati* characters are primarily driven by amorous, especially erotic, motives. After 1660, the term gets the connotation of *mollizia*, or the abuse of power to satisfy one's lust. Such behaviour was considered incompatible with the values of civic society. The members of this society defined themselves as masculine, in opposition to the effeminacy of lustful tyrants, like Eliogabalo.[28]

An episode which deserves special interest is that of the women's senate, which takes place in scenes XIV–XVI of the first act. In order to seduce Flavia, Eliogabalo has gathered the most beautiful women of Rome in the senate house. Dressed up as a woman, he makes a speech to them, calling them his fellow soldiers and telling them they now form a senate. Blindfolded, the women have to guess who embraces them. Whoever guesses right will win an important political office. Aureli has combined several anecdotes from the *Vita Heliogabali* in this episode: the women's senate, the accounts of Elagabalus's corrupt and absurd appointment policy, and the scene in which the emperor dresses up as a woman to address the gathered harlots of Rome as his 'fellow soldiers'. The reference to prostitution is emphasised when one of the women suggests that they all pay Eliogabalo 'the tithe of Amor'. The emperor is thus portrayed not only as a woman, but as a *depraved* woman, who is either a harlot – as is implied by 'fellow soldiers' – or a pimp.

We cannot be certain how much of this innuendo could be picked up by contemporary audiences, who will likely have been unfamiliar with the *Historia Augusta*, but it is telling that the senate episode was reduced to only seven lines in the Aureli/Boretti version of *Eliogabalo*. Calcagno points out that prostitution was a widespread phenomenon in Venice, and that the selling of political appointments was frequently practised by Venetian senators. Both themes were often touched on in clandestine political pamphlets – and often in combination, as happens in Aureli and Cavalli's *Eliogabalo*. The opera's concealed criticism of contemporary morals may well have offended Giovanni Carlo, the elder Grimani brother, who would eventually become a member of the Venetian senate himself.[29] Hence, the episode of the women's senate had to be drastically shortened to take out its sting.

Only a couple of lines in the opera seem even to hint that Eliogabalo is an 'Oriental'. When discussing why the emperor's soldiers abandoned him, Flavia says it was mostly 'because they could not bear guarding him in that unworthy flock of shameless women, [him being] barbaric in his dress, barbaric in his deeds, in triumphant form, breathing only lewdness and soft perfume'. The line is reminiscent of a passage in Herodian, who also remarks that the soldiers were disgusted at the emperor's effeminate appearance. If so, this is one of the very few details which indicate that Aureli's opera was ultimately based on sources other than the *Historia Augusta*. In another scene, Eliogabalo is described as 'weak, effeminate, love-drunk and lustful'. These characteristics were associated with the 'East' in antiquity, but if Aureli attempts to make the same connection, he does not do so explicitly. The god Elagabal is never mentioned in the opera, although the emperor at one time talks about erecting a Colossus for the sun. Clearly, the 'Oriental' background and 'Oriental' religion of Elagabalus are of little relevance in *Eliogabalo*.[30]

As in the *Vita Heliogabali*, the emperor finally dies at the hands of his own soldiers. Although this seems a fitting end for such a tyrant, the ending was drastically changed in the version composed by Boretti. Instead of dying, Aureli and Boretti's Eliogabalo repents his sins and continues to rule, helped by Alessandro. This is in accordance with the doctrine of the Society of Jesus, which had a big influence on the cultural life of Venice in the 1660s and taught that a rightful ruler may never be deposed, no matter how tyrannical his reign is. There are clues that the Grimani brothers supported the Society. Moreover, Aureli and Boretti's version of the opera would also be performed at the Jesuit college of Parma. It may have been conceived with this performance in mind.[31]

In 1687, the Grimani brothers would reject yet another version of the opera. This version, also written by Aureli, made no allusions to prostitution or the distribution of political appointments, but *did* contain Eliogabalo's off-stage murder. It was eventually staged at the Teatro Sant'Angelo. Apparently, not all Venetians had problems with tyrannicide.

### *Elagabalus in Tysens's* Bassianus Varius Heliogabalus *(1720)*

Gysbert Tysens (1693–1732) was one of many people in eighteenth-century Amsterdam who tried to earn a living by writing. He was the son of a craftsman and was born and raised in the city centre, where he would live until his death. During his short life, Tysens produced and published a great number of literary works, albeit of dubious quality. Most of these were probably commissioned by booksellers, although it is highly likely that he also accepted assignments from private individuals. Many of Tysens's poems were written for special occasions, such as weddings or funerals. Others lashed out at those who had caused him or his clients harm. These vitriolic poems may have been spread by leaflets before they appeared in books of poetry, and seem to have been very popular. However, the bulk of Tysens's work consists of plays: six tragedies and 27 comedies, in which he often criticises contemporary phenomena, such as the popular money lotteries and the so-called 'wind trade' in usually worthless financial documents.[32]

*Bassianus Varius Heliogabalus, of de uitterste proef der standvastige liefde*, was published in 1720 by Hendrik Bosch. As with most of Tysens's tragedies, it was inspired by antiquity. We do not know which sources the author used for this piece, but it appears to contain elements from Cassius Dio, Herodian and the *Historia Augusta*. All of these were available to Tysens, either in French (which he could read) or in Dutch. However, the play was rejected by the Amsterdamse Schouwburg and would never be staged. Nor is there any record of his other plays ever being performed in Amsterdam. Although we cannot exclude the possibility that his works were performed at fairs, it seems likely that the author intended them primarily to be read. Many of his plays seem to have served as pamphlets, allowing Tysens to mock and criticise the abuses and events of his day.

Overall, the quality of *Bassianus Varius Heliogabalus* is poor. It consists of endless monologues, in unimpressive rhyme, while all the action takes place off-stage. As in *Eliogabalo*, the plot revolves around the emperor thwarting the love of his cousin Alexander. Both of them are in love with Marcia, the daughter of a nobleman. Marcia loves Alexander, but pretends to love the emperor, in order to save her beloved from Heliogabalus's wrath. When the tyrant discovers this deceit, he has the two of them locked up; only if Marcia agrees to marry him will he spare them. The would-be lovers refuse, and Alexander is dragged off to be executed. However, at the last moment drums and trumpets sound: the people of Rome have risen against Heliogabalus and murdered him. Alexander now takes the throne and is finally able to marry Marcia.

Tysens paints Heliogabalus as a cruel and bloodthirsty tyrant, who rules with a 'steel fist' and kills everybody who dares to oppose him. Various characters in the play describe the emperor in outspoken negative terms. Among other things, he is called 'a Barbarian, and Executioner, and Pest of the Roman states', 'that degenerate Prince', and 'a tyrant [...] who finds lust in tyranny and all horrors'.[33] Just like his counterpart in *Eliogabalo*, Heliogabalus does not care for the law, nor for his subjects:

Let all the Roman people freely rise against me
By one single stroke of this feared fist
All that rebelling Rabble will be ground to dust:
What? should I be Emperor, and abide laws myself?
No, it only suits me to give them to others.[34]

The gods, too, should not count on the emperor's respect. At one point, Heliogabalus remarks to Marcia, 'I fear neither your revenge, nor that of the people, nor that of the Gods.' He claims to laugh at the gods' hatred, and boasts that he could overturn their thrones if they made him angry. Time and time again it is mentioned that the emperor has violated the temples of Rome. We also learn that he has forced a vestal virgin to marry him. Only to his own god does Heliogabalus pay respect: 'being less a priest than a cruel Murderer', he honours the deity with child sacrifices.[35]

Interestingly, the emperor is not presented as *completely* evil. At the start of the fourth act, when Alexander and Marcia are imprisoned, Tysens has him nearly repent his hideous crimes. Unexpectedly, Heliogabalus urges his hubris and cruelty to abandon him, expressing the wish to reign well and justly. He exclaims, 'How my soul is kicked about, swaying to and fro!/Here my revenge spurs me, there my honour!' Unfortunately, his mother urges him to be ruthless, and the emperor's doubts vanish as suddenly as they appear. However, we should note that Heliogabalus expresses love for Marcia during his short bout of self-reflection, stating that he does not want to live without her. Earlier, he had already told Alexander that both their hearts had been wounded by love for the noblewoman.[36] Although this does not stop him from trying to destroy what he cannot get, Heliogabalus's feelings for Marcia seem genuine. This distinguishes him from Aureli's Eliogabalo, who cared absolutely nothing for the women he pursues.

It is interesting to note that Tysens, like Aureli, chooses to portray Elagabalus as interested in women. In fact, there is nothing in the play to indicate that the emperor might also be attracted to members of his own sex. Hierocles, Zoticus, or other male lovers are completely absent. Possibly, Tysens chose to ignore the emperor's homosexual contacts because that would only distract from his feelings for Marcia, which are central to the plot. Tysens was certainly not afraid to tackle the subject of homosexuality, since he would write two long-winded poems against sodomy in 1730.[37]

In contrast to *Eliogabalo*, there are also hardly any references to the emperor's effeminacy. The part of Heliogabalus would have been played by a man, since women were not allowed on the stage. Although his dress is twice described as 'effeminate', the emperor does not involve himself in cross-dressing. In only one instance, the word 'effeminate' is applied to his person rather than to his clothes. However, there is also talk about the emperor's 'steel fist' and of him treading on the necks of the gods – expressions which evoke the image of a brutish, 'masculine' person.[38] Of course, we do not know how an actor would have dressed up for the role of Heliogabalus – if he would have worn extensive make-up and earrings, for instance – but from the text alone, it seems that little emphasis was put on the tyrant's effeminate characteristics.

The 'Oriental' background of Heliogabalus receives a bit more attention, but not much. The word 'barbarian' is repeatedly used to describe him, but the word seems to carry the notion of 'brute' rather than 'foreigner'. Although much emphasis is put on Heliogabalus's disrespect for Roman religion – mocking the gods, violating the temples and marrying a vestal – we learn nothing of the god he worships himself.

The name Elagabal is never mentioned, nor is it made clear that he is a Syrian god; the only thing we get to know is that he requires human sacrifices. In short, the play establishes Heliogabalus as an enemy of Rome and Roman religion, but hardly as an 'Oriental'. Only twice does Tysens explicitly oppose Rome to the 'East'. In one instance, Alexander remarks how Heliogabalus has 'cravenly betrayed' Roman bravery with his 'effeminate dress and Asian splendour / of purple, gold and silk, and other adornments'. At another instance, Alexander says that the emperor 'with effeminate dress smudges the Roman name, / and violates Numa's law in Assyrian clothes'. Note that the only two parts of the play which describe Heliogabalus's dress as effeminate identify it as Asian or Assyrian, explicitly linking effeminacy to the 'East'.[39]

Considering Tysens's love for criticising contemporary persons and events, we may wonder whether the evil tyrant he presents us with in *Bassianus Varius Heliogabalus* is meant to remind us of anyone in particular. Frits Naerebout suggests Louis XIV, the 'Sun King', but adds that he is not at all certain whether the play carries any such specific message. Since Louis XIV had died five years before the play was published, it seems unlikely that Tysens intended it as a criticism of the French monarch. Insofar as *Bassianus Varius Heliogabalus* was conceived to make a point, rather than just to entertain, it should probably be read as a charge against tyranny and the excesses of absolute rule in general.

### Elagabalus in Krasiński's Irydjon *(1836)*

At the time *Irydjon* was written, most of the territory that is modern-day Poland was ruled by Russia. Many intellectuals and soldiers had fled the country after a crushed rebellion in 1831, finding refuge in Paris. There, unhindered by censorship, they developed a peculiar brand of Romantic literature, which had an extremely activist character and portrayed Poland as an innocent nation, prey to the sins of others – Russia in particular. Many of these authors favoured Polish messianism: the idea that Poland was destined to play a leading (although not necessarily military) role in the liberation of suppressed countries. This biblically inspired ideology had strong moral and mystical components, providing people with hope that better times would come.[40]

Zygmunt Krasiński (1812–59) did not live in exile, but spent a lot of time in Paris. He was the son of Count Wincenty Krasiński, a nobleman and general very loyal to the tsar. The younger Krasiński did not share his father's convictions. He regarded Poland as an enslaved nation, and longed for his country to be reborn in a new world – a theme which features prominently in his work. Because of the anti-Russian streak in his poems and plays, Krasiński published them anonymously, which earned him the nickname the 'Anonymous Poet' of Poland. As a literary figurehead of resistance against Russian dominance, Krasiński had a big influence on the spiritual life of his homeland, but did not greatly affect the poetry of subsequent generations.

*Irydjon* was a play which was meant to be read rather than performed. The introduction and conclusion are not written in dramatic form, but in narrative prose. In its style as well as its historical background, Krasiński was heavily indebted to the French author François-René de Chateaubriand, whose *Études historiques* (1831) supplied him with the idea of paganism, Christianity and barbarism as three opposed but coexisting systems in ancient Rome. In all likelihood, the author read Cassius Dio, Herodian and the *Vita Heliogabali* in translation. Details from all three of these sources can be found scattered throughout the play. An extensive footnote, in which Krasiński elaborates on Heliogabalus, is based on the book *Il Vivere: Les contes de Samuel Bach* (1836) by Théophile de Ferrière.[41] However, the image of the emperor in this note is rather different from that in *Irydjon* itself, which makes it likely that Krasiński read Ferrière's work only after he had finished his play.

The titular hero of *Irydjon* – Iridion, in the English translation – is a nobleman of Greek and German descent, combining the alleged intellect of the former with the alleged strength and energy of the latter. Greece, which he considers his home country, symbolises contemporary Poland, while the Roman Empire obviously stands for the Russian oppressor. Iridion senses that Rome has entered a time of decay, and secretly strives to bring about its fall. Assisted by the mysterious Masinissa, an old friend of his father, he has gained much support among the soldiers. At the beginning of the play, he gives his sister, Elsinoe, to Heliogabalus, allowing him to get close to the ruler and feign friendship. Everything is now prepared for Iridion to strike, except for one thing: in order to ensure his victory, he needs the support of the Christians, who live in the catacombs of Rome. By deceiving the Christian maiden Cornelia, with whom he is in love, Iridion succeeds in winning the Christians over to his plan. However, at the last moment, when the fighting has already begun, they desert him, staying true to their ideals of love and peace.

As a result, Iridion fails: Heliogabalus is dead, but he is replaced by a new ruler, Alexander. Rome still stands. The old Masinissa – who is actually Satan in disguise – offers Iridion a bargain: in return for his soul, the defeated hero will enter a centuries-long sleep, and awaken to see Rome in ruins. Iridion accepts, which brings us to the conclusion of the play in contemporary Rome. In the Coliseum, before the cross which is placed there, heavenly powers battle with Masinissa for the awakened man's soul. The prayers of Cornelia and his love for Greece earn Iridion another chance: he is to go to Poland – described as the 'land of graves and crosses' – to help the oppressed people there to bear their burden.[42] Only by working in the spirit of love, not hatred, will he ultimately gain salvation.

Although Heliogabalus is portrayed in an unfavourable light, he is not the main villain in *Irydjon*. That role is reserved for Masinissa, whom Krasiński describes as 'the element of all-evil' and 'the Satan of all centuries' in a letter to a friend.[43] Significantly, Iridion does not strive so much to bring down Heliogabalus, but Roman dominion itself. After the emperor's death, he remarks, 'The worm which crawled upon the ground, the dust which has been shaken from my sandals, have lingered in my memory longer than the recollection of that man.' Nevertheless, Heliogabalus is an important figure, precisely because he embodies the tyranny of Rome – and thus, in a hardly concealed allegory, that of Russia. He is called a 'tyrant' and utters the cruel phrase, 'O if this whole people had but a single head which it were possible to strike off with one blow!' He threatens to throw his minions to the leopards, unscrupulously has slaves killed once they have finished their work for him and wishes to 'slay […] the law itself!'[44]

However, this version of Elagabalus is a lot less dominating and fear-inspiring than his counterparts in *Eliogabalo* and *Bassianus Varius Heliogabalus*. Instead of forcing himself on the beautiful Elsinoe, he showers her with gifts and begs for her love. In return, she calls him a 'baby, nourished on the brains of birds' and a 'servant of the Praetorians'.[45] Eutychian, the Praetorian prefect, confirms the latter remark by openly joking about killing the emperor, to which Heliogabalus responds, 'Have pity on me!' When all is said and done, he is a pathetic figure, a weakling who has to rely on the mercy of others. One character remarks that the populace loves Heliogabalus for his mock naval battles and the praetorians worship his prodigality, but immediately adds that the praetorians are actually on Alexander's side and the populace 'loves Caesar until it murders him'.[46] Monica Gardner describes the character as 'a half crazy vicious boy, a whipped cur at the feet of the beautiful Elsinoe, [...] clinging in terror for his life to the false friend [Iridion] who is betraying him'.[47] This is a far cry from Tysens's steel-fisted villain. Krasiński's Heliogabalus is a tyrant, but a weak, degenerate one, iconic of the decay to which Rome has fallen prey. He reminds us of the play's opening statement: 'Already the ancient world is drawing to its close – all that had life in it is decaying, dissolving, and going mad – gods and men are going mad.'[48]

The gender characteristics of the emperor underline his weakness. Whereas Iridion displays many traits which could be considered typically masculine, like strength, self-confidence and resoluteness, Heliogabalus is portrayed as effeminate in appearance and behaviour. At one point, the ruler throws himself on Iridion's neck and exclaims, 'Take this kiss from Caesar! – Is it not true that my lips are fragrant and my brow smooth as that of the most charming of maidens?' Elsewhere, he describes himself as 'the Apollo of Delos', boasting that 'once a whole legion claimed me Caesar for the smoothness of my cheeks'.[49] Although there seems to be a clear homosexual subtext to these statements, Heliogabalus directs the latter remark at Elsinoe, in an attempt to persuade her to stay with him. The emperor is clearly besotted with this beautiful maiden. His love for Iridion's sister is a recurring feature of the play, while any male lovers are completely absent. So, as in *Eliogabalo*, Elagabalus is presented as an effeminate figure, but his homosexual affairs are suppressed, allowing his courting of women to take centre stage.

An aspect which contrasts *Irydjon* to both Aureli's opera and Tysens's play is the remarkable emphasis which Krasiński puts on the emperor's 'Oriental' background. When Heliogabalus first appears on stage, the script states that he wears 'the robes of a high priest'. A gigantic statue of Mithras is standing in the background, while music is gradually fading and 'priests and soothsayers' are passing out of the room.[50] It is interesting that Krasiński chooses to name Mithras as the emperor's god, instead of Elagabal, although the characteristics of the cult seem similar to those mentioned in the ancient sources; i.e. it is a sun cult, celebrated with typical 'Oriental' extravagance. When Elsinoe, herself the daughter of a German priestess, scorns the Mithras cult, she explicitly opposes the religious practices of the 'East' to her proud German background:

> The daughter of the ice has naught but contempt for soft, dissolute gods, drowning in the smoke of incense, enveloped in the notes of flutes,

besprinkled with the blood of timorous deer or of babes, and the diamond sun that glitters on thy silken breast will not match the sun upon the snows of the North.[51]

Iridion urges the emperor to found a new empire in Syria, where he will 'pass sweet days, enveloped by the smoke of aloes and myrrh, and lulled by the notes of zither and flute', adding that nobody 'will dare deride thy Chaldaean mitre or mock at the flowing sleeves of thine oriental mantle!' The 'East' is thus associated with luxury and pleasure. This can also be seen in the scenery instructions, in which, for instance, an altar consecrated to Mithras is surrounded by 'carvings and costly vessels', with 'in the background a curtain ornamented with precious stones, suspended between two golden columns'. Throughout the play, reference is made to anecdotes in the *Historia Augusta*, including such samples of luxury as Elagabalus's mock naval battles, his consumption of exotic dishes and his 'suicide tower', built to ensure that he would die a luxurious death. Last but not least, the emperor wants to impose his own religion on Rome, swearing to Mithras that he will cast 'all the gods of Rome, shackled in chains', before his altars.[52]

The clear opposition between 'East' and 'West' in Krasiński's play reflects contemporary European ideas about the 'Orient'. As Edward Said has pointed out, a new kind of 'Orientalism' emerged in the eighteenth century. Whereas 'Asia had once represented silent distance and alienation' and Islam 'militant hostility to European Christianity', the West's increasing contacts with both the Near and the Far East contributed to new, more secular images. Increasingly, European scholars and artists thought in terms of different 'types' of people, characterised by distinct, innate traits. In opposition to 'the European', there was 'the Asian'. Polish intellectuals in Paris and elsewhere branded Russia an 'Asian' country, preying upon the 'European' Poland.[53]

Heliogabalus's reign in *Irydjon* could be interpreted in a similar vein. More important, however, seems the connection between the 'East' and decay. In a footnote to *Irydjon*, Krasiński says of the historical Elagabalus that 'in him Oriental myths were embodied', and 'in him paganism descended to the lowest round of the ladder, in him it was plainly shown that it was rotten and that it would never yield any more fruit, for it was manifested in him in all its power and extent – and to no purpose.'[54]

Heliogabalus in *Irydjon* is based on these notions. In the play's introduction, Krasiński remarks that the 'masters of the souls of thousands' and the 'soldiers of the legions' have vanished, making way for 'hitherto unknown' figures, 'neither beautiful like demigods, nor strong like the giants of the times of the Titans; but fantastic, glittering with gold, with garlands on their brows, with goblets in their hands'.[55] Clearly, the luxurious, 'Oriental' Heliogabalus is one of these figures. He represents the decadence that is gnawing at Rome, causing its decline. It is only a matter of time before the empire will collapse and the oppressed people will be free again – just as Poland would one day be free from Russian dominance.

## Conclusion

In the works of Aureli and Tysens, Elagabalus plays the role of main antagonist. He is presented as an evil tyrant who considers himself above the law, is preoccupied with his own desires and completely ignores the well-being of others, inspiring nothing but hatred and fear in the hearts of his subjects. Considering that both works were written in republics, in times when most of Europe was under the sway of absolute rulers, it is hardly surprising that they deal with the dangers of handing supreme rule to just one man. The Elagabalus in *Irydjon* also possesses many traits of an evil tyrant, but is considerably weaker than his seventeenth- and eighteenth-century counterparts. He does not feature as the main villain of the play, and can perhaps even be pitied, since he knows himself to be surrounded with enemies and relies in vain on his false friend, Iridion.

Aureli, Tysens and Krasiński have made use of all three major literary sources on Elagabalus, either directly or indirectly. They present their audiences with quotes and anecdotes which derive from ancient texts. Nevertheless, their images of the emperor do not always correspond with those of Cassius Dio, Herodian and the *Historia Augusta*. The effeminacy which these authors attribute to Elagabalus is present in *Eliogabalo* and *Irydjon*, but can hardly be traced in Tysens's play. Except for the occasional obscure allusion, all three works ignore the alleged homosexual contacts of the emperor. Instead, Elagabalus is portrayed as a womaniser, his lust / love for women playing a major part in all three plots. The ruler's 'Oriental' nature is hardly touched upon by Aureli and Tysens. The latter emphasises that Elagabalus is an enemy of the gods of Rome, but does not explicitly place this element in an 'East versus West' context. Only in *Irydjon* does the 'Oriental' nature of the emperor and his sun cult feature prominently.

One could argue that the villains in *Eliogabalo* and *Bassianus Varius Heliogabalus* might as well have been other 'tyrants', such as Nero or

Caligula, without the need to make any major alterations to the way they are portrayed. In contrast, the weak, cruel, Mithras-worshipping boy in *Irydjon* could have been no emperor but Elagabalus, since he possesses the unique combination of religious fanaticism and an emphatically 'Oriental' nature. By highlighting these particular traits, Krasiński presents us with Elagabalus as a tyrant, rather than with a tyrant who happens to be Elagabalus. Moreover, he is the only one of the three authors who puts emphasis on the decline of Rome and presents Elagabalus as exemplary for this decay. In doing so, Krasiński anticipates developments in the *Nachleben* from ca. 1850 onwards, when a new image of Elagabalus would emerge: that of the Decadent emperor.

# 6

# THE DECADENT EMPEROR

Elagabale! Elagabale! ah! l'avoir connu! avoir vécu à son ombre prodigieuse et mirifique!

Luis d'Herdy (pseud.), La Destinée (1900)

Following in the footsteps of such scholars as Barthold Georg Niebuhr and Theodor Mommsen, nineteenth-century ancient historians and classicists developed a more critical attitude towards the study of ancient Greece and Rome than their humanistic predecessors. The term *Altertumswissenschaft*, first coined by the historian Friedrich August Wolf in the early nineteenth century, described a field of study in which ancient texts were subjected to a critical, methodological analysis and were increasingly compared with other sources, such as coins, inscriptions, statues and other archaeological remains. By the middle of the nineteenth century this approach, which had largely originated in the German-speaking world, spread to other countries as well. Consequently, scholarly images of Elagabalus began to change. They became more independent from the works of ancient authors, although many of the old prejudices remained, and several new ones were introduced.

In the field of literature, Elagabalus became an iconic figure for authors of the Decadent movement. This movement, which reached its peak in France and England at the end of the nineteenth century, was fascinated with decay, death, the artificial and the unnatural. Between 1850 and 1914 – when World War I brutally ended the 'long nineteenth century' – an impressive number of works featured Elagabalus as a main character, especially in France. Rather than just being an evil tyrant, as he had been before 1850, the Decadent emperor was emphatically connected to such notions as androgyny, 'Orientalism', *ennui* and decay. Moreover, this period saw the emergence of the first positive images of Elagabalus – a trend which would continue in the twentieth and twenty-first centuries.

The first part of this chapter will give a general overview of scholarly and literary images of Elagabalus in the period under discussion. First, I will give a brief overview of the emergence and development of *Altertumswissenschaft* in the period 1810–1914, paying special attention to the images of Elagabalus which emerged from this new academic approach. I will continue with a short exposition on the most important Decadent authors, books and themes, in the course of which I will deal briefly with several works which focus on the young emperor.

In the second part of this chapter, we will take a closer look at some of the images of Elagabalus. Once again, I have selected three works to be discussed in more detail. The first is Jean Lombard's novel *L'Agonie* (1888), a French work which has been labelled a 'decadent ancient novel *par excellence*' by David.[1] Although the novel is not very well known nowadays, it inspired several other Decadent authors to write about Elagabalus, and is therefore well worthy of our attention. The second work is the lyric cycle *Algabal* (1892) by the German poet Stefan George. George is counted among the most eminent German poets of his generation, and *Algabal*, a complex lyric cycle which contains many Decadent themes, is widely regarded as one of his best and most intriguing works. Finally, we will look at the Dutch novel *De berg van licht* (*The Mountain of Light*), published in three volumes in 1905 and 1906. The author of this novel, Louis Couperus, is arguably the greatest Dutch novelist of his generation and certainly the most prominent representative of the Decadent movement in the Netherlands. Together, the three selected works represent literature in three different languages and cover both the late nineteenth and the early twentieth centuries. All contain themes and metaphors which may be labelled Decadent, but the images they present of Elagabalus are far from identical.

## THE 'DECADENT EMPEROR': A GENERAL OVERVIEW

### Elagabalus in historiographical works, 1810–1914

As we have seen in Chapter 5, the German scholar Friedrich August Wolf (1759–1824) conceptualised *Altertumswissenschaft*, advocating a thorough, critical analysis of ancient texts as the basis for the study of antiquity.

His ideas gained ground in the first decades of the nineteenth century. In 1810, they received a decisive boost from the German (originally Danish) historian Barthold Georg Niebuhr (1776–1831).

Having recently been appointed as a member of the Prussian Academy and historiographer of the Prussian court, Niebuhr was invited to give a lecture at the opening of the University of Berlin. In this lecture, which was about Roman history, he set the tone for the study of antiquity in general and his further academic career in particular. Niebuhr seriously and systematically questioned the validity of ancient texts, arguing that the ancient historian should not simply rely on their authority, but develop a keen eye to distinguish between possibilities, probabilities and truths. In his *Römische Geschichte* (1811–32), a three-volume work about the history of Rome from its foundation to 272 BCE, he studiously employed this principle, making an intensive analysis of the literary sources. Niebuhr's work, and the series of lectures upon which it was based, had a huge influence on contemporary scholars and following generations. Theodor Mommsen would later praise him as the first ancient historian 'who has dared to test the study of history by the logic of the facts'.[2]

Although Niebuhr's *Römische Geschichte* did not cover the reign of Elagabalus, his lectures on the period after 272 BCE were later reworked to two additional volumes. In the few pages dedicated to him, the priest-emperor does not receive a favourable treatment: 'He had an instinct for everything which degrades human nature', we read. In fact, Niebuhr assures his audience, the comparison with Elagabalus puts Nero and Caligula in a positive light. The crimes and vices of the young tyrant are not elaborated upon, except that he lost himself in the 'most insane indulgences'.[3] Nowhere does Niebuhr seem to question the hostile accounts of the ancient authors.

*Altertumswissenschaft* was not limited to the study of ancient texts, however. It combined the hitherto separate fields of *Altertumskunde* – the study of ancient cultures by means of single texts and material remains – history and philology. Increasingly, scholars started to take the historical context of ancient texts into account, comparing them with other sources, such as coins and inscriptions. The period 1800–50 saw the start of systematic excavations of archaeological sites, which earned archaeology a place next to philology. In the course of the century, an increasing number of non-literary sources were published in great collections and became accessible to historians.

A famous example is the *Corpus inscriptionum Latinarum*, which is still of immeasurable value to students of Greek and Latin inscriptions today. The instigator of this work, the German scholar Theodor Mommsen (1817–1903), is without doubt the greatest figure in the study of ancient history in the nineteenth century. In his vast academic oeuvre, comprising over one and a half thousand publications, Mommsen unlocked a great number of ancient sources, including coins, inscriptions, late classical and early medieval texts, and sources on Roman law. To the last of these fields, he made enormous contributions, demonstrating its vital importance for the understanding of Roman history and society. Largely due to his work, the study of Roman state affairs and Roman history experienced a methodological deepening in the second half of the nineteenth century.

Like Niebuhr, Mommsen wanted to write a great work about the whole of Roman history. However (again as with Niebuhr), his *Römische Geschichte*, published in three volumes from 1854 to 1856, was never completed. The third volume ended with the rise of Julius Caesar. In 1885, a fifth volume was published about the Roman provinces in the imperial period, but the intermediate volume about imperial Rome was never written. It was only in 1992 that this lacuna was partially filled by the publication of notes, taken by students, of Mommsen's lectures on this theme. Elagabalus is mentioned only once or twice in passing, which might indicate that Mommsen did not deem the emperor worthy of comment. Moreover, the scholar's unfavourable portrayal of Caracalla as 'a miserable man without value', whose untimely death should be considered good fortune, stays very close to the (hostile) literary sources.[4] This makes it likely that Mommsen's portrayal of Elagabalus would have been equally negative, if not more so.

Gradually, the principles of German *Altertumswissenschaft* also spread to other Western countries. In Britain, the study of ancient Greece received much attention. The greatest scholar in this field was George Grote (1794–1871), whose *History of Greece* was published from 1846 to 1856. Noting that there were not enough verifiable data to distinguish between legend and history in early Greece, Grote was the first to argue for a clear distinction between legendary and historical Greece. Francis John Haverfield (1860–1919), another eminent British scholar, mainly concerned himself with Roman Britain. Under his guidance, archaeology enjoyed unprecedented expansion. The finds of numerous excavations – many of them organised on scientific principles – significantly contributed to the study of Roman Britain. As a result, both fields of research rapidly professionalised.

In France, the historian Fustel de Coulanges (1830–89) broke with the prevailing French tradition of Romantic, nationalistic historiography. Declaring that 'history is a science' and should not be confused with virtue, he was obsessive in his efforts for objectivity. By using historical methods which he considered impeccable, Coulanges claimed to have found definite answers to many problems in ancient history. His countryman René Cagnat (1852–1937) specialised in Latin epigraphy and Roman Africa. He founded *L'Année Épigraphique*, which to the present day publishes new-found inscriptions and makes them accessible to numerous scholars.

An important development in nineteenth-century studies of antiquity was the increasing attention paid to so-called 'Oriental' cultures. Inspired by the fascination with the 'Orient' in Romanticism, travelogues of eastern countries and especially Napoleon's expedition to Egypt, scholars no longer focused only on classical Greece and Rome, but also became interested in the cultures and languages of the ancient Near East. The German historian Johann Gustav Droysen (1808–84) had been the first to take this path. His countryman Eduard Meyer (1855–1930) followed in his footsteps, taking a great interest in the interactions between the ancient Near East and the West, and acquainting himself with Hebrew, Arabic, Persian, Turkish, Egyptian and Sanskrit. It was Meyer's aim to write a 'universal' history of antiquity, which would include the history of the ancient Near East as well as that of Greece and Rome. Although he never managed to take his *Geschichte des Altertums* (1884–1902) further than the time of Alexander the Great, Meyer is still regarded as one of the great scholars of universal history. Since the field of ancient history became ever larger and more specialised in the late nineteenth and twentieth centuries, no ancient historian has managed to pursue universal history on an even remotely equal scale. In addition, Meyer made important contributions to the theory and methodology of the study of ancient history.

The stronger focus on the 'Orient' and 'Oriental' cultures in nineteenth-century scholarship does not necessarily imply more appreciation of these cultures. In the climate of growing anti-Semitism in the late nineteenth and early twentieth centuries, many scholars – particularly in Germany – described the peoples and cultures of the ancient Near East in openly hostile and derogatory terms. According to Johann Schiller, who published his *Geschichte der römischen Kaiserzeit* in 1883, Elagabalus's 'Oriental' upbringing made him 'spiritually insignificant, without any value, a resigned enemy of every serious activity'.[5] As Gibbon had done more than a century earlier, Schiller condemned Elagabalus as the worst ruler in the history of the Roman Empire. In his own words,

> Never was the emperorship held in such contempt as under this unripe, mad boy [...] The emperor played the role of Oriental despot with diadem, also outwardly at court, and desired to be worshipped. What has been handed over from Elagabalus's activity only stains the pages of history, and his reign is verily a witches' Sabbath of fornication, excesses and luxury.[6]

In his work *Abhandlungen zur römischen Religion*, published in 1909, Alfred von Domaszewski branded not just the reign of Elagabalus, but the entire period of Severan rule 'the late revenge of the Semites on Greco-Roman culture, whose chains it had silently worn for centuries'. In describing this supposed culture clash, he made it clear on whose side he stood. Like Schiller, von Domaszewski identified himself with the 'Western' values of Greece and Rome, which he saw as corrupted by 'Oriental' influences. As he comments with a profound sense of drama, 'It is therefore the night of barbarism which covers the Greco-Roman world since Septimius Severus.'[7]

In *La Religion à Rome sous les Sévères* (1886), the French historian Jean Réville likewise imagines 'East' and 'West' as two diametrically opposed cultures, continually striving for dominance. His hostility towards the 'East' is often phrased in biblical terms. For instance, he remarks about Elagabalus,

> There was actually nothing Roman nor Occidental any longer in the person of Elagabalus, or in that of his mother Soaemias. In them, the old spirit of Canaan, against which the prophets of Israel rose with such vigour, affirmed itself once again in a supreme exuberance before disappearing from history.[8]

A bit further, Réville speaks about the 'Syrian mind, which he characterises as 'frivolous and light, burning with passion but listless to effort, keen on novelties but superficial, sly and subtle but without solidity'. Not surprisingly, he regards Elagabalus's rise to the Roman throne as a disastrous defeat for the 'Western' world: 'This time, the triumph of the East was complete.' For the next years, Rome would experience all the turpitudes of an 'Oriental' court: extravagant vice; eunuchs and harems; disordered luxury; the dominant influence of women and boudoir favourites; and, last but not least, 'the complete absence of preoccupation with the public good and the egoistic concentration of all government activity on the sovereign's wellbeing'.[9] In other words, Elagabalus was a bad emperor *because* he was (and behaved like) an 'Oriental'.

Franz Cumont, author of *Les Religions orientales dans le paganisme romain* (1906), acknowledges that hostile ancient authors may have misrepresented the religious reforms of Elagabalus. Nevertheless, he gives a very negative portrayal of Syrian religion, 'who sacrificed to the divinity the life of men and the decency of women', commenting that it had been stuck 'at the moral level of uncivilizable and bloodthirsty tribes'. No wonder, then, that when Elagabalus tried to impose the cult of Elagabal on Rome, 'his obscene and atrocious rites provoked an enraged upheaval of the Roman conscience'.[10]

Of course the element of 'Orientalism' in nineteenth-century descriptions of Elagabalus was hardly new. It can already be found in the ancient literary sources, especially Herodian, and in the condemning words of Gibbon, with many of the same topoi appearing. But in the course of the nineteenth century, 'the European' and 'the Asian' became fixed categories in Western thought, each determined by their own, unchangeable characteristics. The anti-Orientalism in turn-of-the-century Europe can be regarded as the culmination of this practice: supported by academia, it attributed to the 'Asian' all the traits which were supposed to be *not* Western and, therefore, wrong. In the words of Said, 'an Oriental man was first an Oriental and only second a man'.[11]

Despite the great interest in the 'Orient', no nineteenth-century historians concerned themselves overmuch with Elagabalus. As we have seen, the emperor received little attention in the great Roman histories. Moreover, no monographs were written on him in the nineteenth century. In part, this was probably because the reign of the priest-emperor was not deemed particularly relevant or important in the larger history of the Roman Empire. However, we must also consider that many scholars were likely to find the sexually explicit stories in Cassius Dio, Herodian, and particularly the *Historia Augusta*, too scandalous to stake their reputation on. This is especially true for stories concerning homosexuality. Only in the early twentieth century do the first monographs on Elagabalus start to appear. In other circles, however, the emperor was already well known by that time.

*Decadent debaucheries, 1850–1914*

In mid-nineteenth-century France, the growing power and materialism of the bourgeoisie caused resentment among a number of artists. They could not identify themselves with the Romanticism of bourgeois art, and rejected its conservative, moralistic tone. In reaction, they advocated a different kind of art, which did not primarily stand in the service of bourgeois society and morals, but existed for its own sake: *l'art pour l'art*. Théophile Gautier (1811–72) was one of the first and most important authors to embrace this new principle. He drew attention to the beauty of artificial, artistically made objects, and proclaimed it the highest aim of the artist to make useless things for sophisticated, refined people. The principle of art for art's sake was also embraced by his friend Charles Baudelaire (1821–67), who found beauty in things normally considered ugly and unpleasant. Baudelaire was influential not only in France, but also in England, where the *l'art pour l'art* movement soon gained ground. Here, it found its most distinguished voice in the work of the essayist and literary critic Walter Pater (1839–94). By deliberately dissociating art from bourgeois morality, Gautier, Baudelaire, Pater and other French and English authors paved the way for the artistic category which has become known as Decadence.

The literary developments of the nineteenth century did not leave the image of Elagabalus unaffected. In Gautier's novel *Mademoiselle de Maupin* (1835), the emperor is briefly mentioned. Rather than portraying him as a despicable emblem of vice, as had been customary up to that time, Gautier presents the reader with a far more charming, dream-like image. One of his protagonists sighs,

> I, too, would like to build a bridge over the sea and pave the waves; I've dreamed of burning cities to light my parties; I've wished to be a woman to experience new pleasures. – Your gilded house, O Nero! is nothing but a muddy stable next to the palace I've raised; my wardrobe is better appointed than yours, Heliogabalus, and well differently splendid. – My circuses are more braving and bloodier than yours, my perfumes ranker and more penetrating, my slaves more numerous and better built; I too have hitched nude courtesans to my chariot, I've walked on men with a heel just as disdainful as yours.[12]

As we see, the traditional cruelty and splendour of Elagabalus are still present in this image, but the usual tone of moral disapproval is completely absent. On the contrary, the emperor becomes a fascinating figure; although he is not 'nice', we would love to meet him (or at least observe him from a safe distance). Something similar occurs in Gustave Flaubert's novel *La Première Éducation sentimentale* (1845). In this work, the protagonist, Henry, longs for the voluptuous sensuality of ancient Rome, which allegedly throve under Elagabalus (who is associated with India) and a number of other usually abhorred Romans, such as Nero. These new interpretations of Elagabalus and other hitherto condemned historical figures by Gautier and Flaubert would set the tone for many later nineteenth- and early twentieth-century works featuring Elagabalus and other 'bad' emperors.

It is hard to define where *l'art pour l'art* ends and Decadence begins – if such a distinction should be made at all. Ever since the Baron de Montesquieu's *Considérations sur les causes de la grandeur des Romains et de leur décadence* (1734), the word 'décadence' had been associated with the decline of the Roman Empire. Exactly a century after Montesquieu's study, the French author and literary critic Désiré Nisard published *Études de moeurs et de critique sur les poètes latins de la décadence*. In this book, he compared contemporary Romantic French poetry with late Latin poetry, arguing that both were characterised – among other things – by a fascination with decline, a strong emphasis on style, and a penchant towards subtlety on the one hand and the reprehensible and the shocking on the other. Thus, 'décadence' was connected to the field of literature. Despite its negative connotations, some authors adopted it as an honorific. In his introduction to Baudelaire's volume of poetry, *Les Fleurs du mal* (published posthumously in 1857), Gautier called his deceased colleague a 'poet of decadence'.[13]

The exact meaning of the term 'Decadence' is debated to the present day. The movement, if such it can be called, lacked coherence, with many 'Decadent' authors and books displaying only some, or occasional, Decadent elements. I will follow Ellis Hanson in her definition of Decadence as 'a late-romantic movement in art and literature that raised the aesthetic dictum of "art for art's sake" to the status of a cult, especially in the final decades of the nineteenth century'.[14] Hanson mentions several characteristics of Decadence, such as 'an elaborate, highly artificial, highly ornamented, often tortuous style' and a thematic preoccupation with art, continuing,

> Most notoriously, the decadents cultivated a fascination with all that
> was commonly perceived as unnatural or degenerate, with sexual

perversity, nervous illness, crime, and disease, all presented in a highly
aestheticised context calculated to subvert or, at any rate, to shock
conventional morality.[15]

We should also note that Decadent literature contains several recurring
sexual themes, such as the *femme fatale*, androgyny and homosexuality.

The novel *À Rebours* (1884) by Joris-Karl Huysmans marks the
culmination of Decadent literature in France and England at the end
of the nineteenth century. Often considered to be the quintessential
Decadent novel, *À Rebours* is 'less a source of new beginnings than a
catalogue of mature achievements, crystallising all those themes and
forms in which other, often more gifted, artists had already begun to
express the unease of the age'.[16] Its protagonist, Des Esseintes, is a typical
dandy – that is, a flamboyant – and possibly aristocratic – figure who
distances himself from the masses by means of his affected, aesthetic
pose. The novel concentrates on his inner life and interests. Elagabalus,
'the amazing high priest of Emesa', is mentioned in the musings of the
protagonist. The Roman ruler is described as one of the emperors who
brought about a time 'when the Roman Empire trembled on its
foundations, when the follies of Asia and the filth of paganism filled it to
its brim'. Rather than condemning the emperor, however, Des Esseintes is
delighted with the contrast between Elagabalus and Tertullian, a
contemporary Christian author. While the former led a life
of luxury and debauchery, the latter preached abstinence and sobriety –
ideals which are diametrically opposed to Des Esseintes's own. He
reflects that 'soon after, the Latin language, having reached its supreme
maturity under Petronius, was starting to disintegrate'.[17] As this passage
underlines, it is not virtue but decay which primarily interests the
Decadent author. Elagabalus's bad reputation made him the perfect
embodiment of this theme.

From the *fin-de-siècle* – broadly speaking, the last two decades of
the nineteenth century – to the outbreak of World War I, a striking
number of novels, poems and stories focus on the priest-emperor. This is
especially true in France, where Decadence had originated and made its
biggest impact. Like his notorious predecessor Nero, Elagabalus is
imagined as an amoral artist, who behaves in a histrionic manner and
regards the whole world as a stage on which to perform. As David has
remarked in her study on Decadence and Latin antiquity, 'Heliogabalus
is the pure product of aestheticism at all costs'. Ruling an empire as a
goal in itself means as little to him as morality. In the words of David,

'Politics burnt on the altar of the aesthetic: can one imagine a more fabulous dream for the aesthetes and dilettantes of the fin-de-siècle?'[18]

The rising interest in the 'Orient' may also have stimulated French authors to write about Elagabalus. Much more emphatically than in works dating from before the nineteenth century, the young ruler is portrayed as an 'Oriental'. In the Decadent novel *La Dernière nuit d'Héliogabale* (1889), Louis Jourdan speaks about

> Heliogabalus, [...] this young Syrian who, dragging the Asian morals and customs behind him, had made his entrance in the capital of the empire in a chariot sparkling with gems and gilt, crowned with the satraps' mitre, dressed in a woman's gown, and carrying in his hands the symbolic representation of the god Helios, the black stone of Emesa.

The emperor's Syrian descent, 'Oriental' luxury, the cult of Elagabal and the feminine appearance of its high priest are all combined in this passage. As in some of the academic works of the period, Elagabalus's 'foreign' background is explicitly opposed to Rome. When the emperor attempts to violate a Roman noblewoman, she exclaims, 'Syrian, you abuse a citizen.' This exclamation is illustrative for the whole reign of the Syrian monarch, as sketched in the novel: during the rule of Elagabalus, with his 'Syrian eunuchs' and his 'barge train of an Asian king', the 'East' reigns supreme, violating the values and traditions of Western Rome.[19]

Jourdan's Elagabalus is more than just another bloodthirsty tyrant, however. The emperor is cruel, but he combines his cruelty with a deep love for the aesthetic. This becomes apparent in a scene where Ariste, one of Elagabalus's minions, performs a dance for him. The dance fails miserably and the poor courtier is condemned to death. However, as an act of mercy, the emperor grants him a 'luxurious' death (probably inspired by the 'luxurious suicide' anecdote in the *Historia Augusta*): he will be strangled by three beautiful women. This combination of beauty and cruelty is typical for the Decadent movement. We see it as well in *The Roses of Heliogabalus* (1888), a painting by the British–Dutch painter Lawrence Alma-Tadema. It depicts a scene from the *Historia Augusta* in which the emperor smothers his banquet guests in an avalanche of flowers (Fig. 15).

The notion of Elagabalus as an artist can also be found in Louis Didier's novel *La Destinée*, published in 1900 under the pseudonym Luis d'Herdy. *La Destinée* is not set in Roman times, but in contemporary

France. The protagonist is young Maurice, who has fled from his domineering father to live in Paris and become a writer. While reading many books to find inspiration for a new novel, Maurice stumbles across the figure of Elagabalus. He is immediately enchanted by 'this grandiose emperor, this incomparable artist. For artist he had been! the greatest of his time and many others, without doubt.' In an animated conversation with his landlady, Maurice mentions just about every anecdote from the *Vita Heliogabali*; the novel spreads them over many pages. Maurice rejects the negative image of Elagabalus presented by Jean Lombard – discussed in detail later in this chapter – and calls the emperor 'a great man misunderstood, so alluring! So appealing!'[20] We cannot be certain to what extent the fictional young man is speaking for Didier himself, but it seems clear that the author of *La Destinée* shares his protagonist's fascination, or even admiration, for Elagabalus. Maurice feels for the long-dead ruler, who suffered from

> the unappeasable sorrow of one whose power has no limits but the very limits assigned to human possibilities, but who, maddened by desires bigger yet than his singular ability, ceaselessly hurls himself with a dour face against the bounds of the permitted, in hot and vain pursuit of the undoable.[21]

This, too, is a typically Decadent theme: the desire to cross every border, to accomplish the unaccomplishable, to go against the grain (*À Rebours!*) and triumph over nature, law, and even reality itself – in short, the desire to be larger than life. 'More than the grand and the grandiose, the colossal and the gigantic are the measure of the Decadence,' David remarks.[22] Many Decadents imagined Elagabalus as answering to this desire for the surpassing and the impossible, rejecting reality in favour of his fantasies. That did not prevent them from portraying him as a cruel, tyrannical megalomaniac, however. Didier, in the voice of Maurice, is one of the very few to portray him sympathetically.

Auguste Villeroy, author of the play *Héliogabale* (1902), follows Jourdan in portraying the emperor as the embodiment of the 'East', set on dominating the 'West'. In fact, this theme is even more prominent in *Héliogabale* than in *La Dernière nuit*. 'It must not be / That a Barbarian ever set foot on the Sacred Road', the prefect Julien warns his soldiers in the first act – it would mean slavery to the atrocious vices of the Orient! One of these vices is incest, as becomes clear from a later passage, in which Elagabalus considers marrying his mother. 'The Orient,

whence I come, is full of such examples / Incest is god over there,'
the emperor remarks. There is no mention of him having any male
lovers, although there seems to be a clear queer subtext in the comment of
the soldiers that their emperor is 'soft and white like a girl'. Elagabalus's
feminine characteristics are emphasised again in a later scene, in which
a crowd of Romans taunt their despised ruler: 'What is your sex? Are
you a priestess, empress?'[23]

Throughout the play, Elagabalus is looking for someone he can
love, and who will love him in return. Having been turned down by the
vestal Julia, he exclaims, 'And all besides Caesar are happy! They all love!
They are loved! Yes, all!' Frustrated, the young ruler declares war on Eros
himself. Proclaiming himself 'unsexed', he hails a new order, in which
Love has no place:

> Slaves of Venus, the Universe is dead! Make way
> For the Androgyne, for the Hermaphrodite, for the race
> Which shall not know Love.[24]

Here, Elagabalus phrases the ideal of androgyny – a popular theme
at the time. Many esoteric theories of the nineteenth century granted a
special place to the androgyne. The best known example of this occurs
in the work of Joséphin Péladan (1858–1916), a self-proclaimed mystic
whose ideas and striking appearance made him (in)famous throughout
France and abroad. According to Péladan, who mixed his personal ideas
with Catholicism, Adam had originally been androgynous, but had been
split in a male and female part by God, so that he could desire and love
himself. In Péladan's view, it was man's ultimate quest to regain this
original, androgynous state.

However, not everybody looked so favourably upon androgyny:
according to the famous Austro-German psychiatrist Richard von
Krafft-Ebing and many others in the medical world, it was the physical
manifestation of a pathological condition, namely homosexuality.
Whereas many nineteenth-century thinkers, mystics and artists lauded
the androgyne for combining the best of both sexes, the figure gained
an increasingly negative reputation during the *fin-de-siècle*, when it was
often associated with moral ambiguity, mental exhaustion, narcissicism
and perversity.[25]

Elagabalus was often interpreted as an androgyne. Considering
the accusations of effeminate appearance and behaviour which ancient
authors brought against the young ruler, this is hardly surprising. An

emperor who used make-up, referred to himself as 'empress' and longed to have a vagina implanted in his body could not fail to attract the attention of an age so obsessed with the merging of the sexes. In an article about Elagabalus in the *Jahrbuch für sexuelle Zwischenstufen* of 1901, Ludwig von Scheffler-Weimar described the emperor as a 'pathological individual' and an 'imperial hermaphrodite', meaning that 'he was of female psyche yet bodily a man'.[26]

The 1906 painting *Lui* by Gustav-Adolf Mossa illustrates this nicely. It shows a very feminine looking Elagabalus holding a mirror and applying make-up (see Fig. 16). (Its counterpart *Elle* shows a femme fatale on a heap of male bodies, so the weak, effeminate man is contrasted with a strong, 'masculine' woman.) Several decades earlier, Jean Richepin had already written a short story about a young man who, wearing female dress and make-up, committed suicide in a public toilet. According to the youth's suicide note, his life and death had been inspired by Elagabalus: 'I'm eighteen years old and have extraordinary passions. I was born to be an emperor in the age of Roman decadence. But the current era is not kind to dreamers. That's why I'm leaving. Not having been able to live like Heliogabalus, I've at least wanted to die like him, in the latrines.'[27]

It seems possible that the emperor indeed served as some sort of inspirational model for homosexual and gender-ambiguous men of the time. He certainly acquired that role in the twentieth century, as we will see in the next chapter.

In Henry Mirande's novel *Élagabal*, which reached its fourth edition in 1910, Elagabalus is described as feminine. The young emperor is said to have 'effeminate eyes in his androgyne's face' and longs to be the wife of his male lover, Hierocles. Like many Decadent authors, Mirande stresses the beauty of the young ruler, describing the portrait he sends to the senate as 'that of a perfectly beautiful adolescent, such as one that Apelles could have imagined to portray a marvellous child Apollo'. Unfortunately, the boy's beauty is spoiled by his use of make-up, which grants him 'an air of Oriental unmanliness'. This last remark is probably based on Herodian, who also condemns the emperor's use of make-up. We should note that Mirande, unlike Villeroy, does not connect androgyny to a higher state of being. Still, he seems to relish Elagabalus's 'radiant ephebic beauty', vividly describing several scenes in which the young emperor appears (almost) naked.[28] During one such scene, in which the boy is dancing, Mirande remarks that he could have been taken for a young courtesan. Androgyny, in this context, signifies moral ambiguity.

Mirande's Elagabalus suffers from *ennui* – a state of listless melancholy, which makes him sigh to a friend,

> You see, my friend, I don't know which bad spirits drive me; I want everything, perhaps because everything disgusts me. I dream of new pleasures, of impossible passions. I'm jealous at Nero who set fire to Rome and, with cythara in hand, admired the flames while singing a poem. I long for better and even worse: I invent new beverages and when I bring the desired cup to my lips, it makes me sick; I need to have the whole world by my side, even though these people tire me out; I need noise most of all to keep me from thinking of that which may await me tomorrow – I'm bored![29]

*Ennui* is a recurring theme in Decadent images of Elagabalus, as is his desire to outdo his personal example, Nero. David describes the Decadent monarch as a 'melancholy hero suffering from an incurable *ennui*', who is characterised by 'the thirst for appreciation and the satisfaction of a limitless narcissism'.[30] The emperor's listless disposition has been captured by the English painter Simeon Solomon, whose painting *Heliogabalus, High Priest of the Sun* (1866) shows an androgynous youth in splendid 'Oriental' dress, staring at nothing with a lacklustre expression on his face (see Fig. 14). Possibly, Elagabalus's *ennui* in Decadent art and literature originates from a passage in Gibbon, who wrote of the young ruler that 'the inflammatory powers of art were summoned to his aid: the confused multitude of women, of wines, and of dishes, and the studied variety of attitudes and sauces, served to revive his languid appetites.'[31]

The notion of *ennui* fits well with the idea of degeneration, which was very popular in *fin-de-siècle* Europe. Numerous experts in the fields of psychiatry, anthropology, sexology and criminology argued that the human race had somehow exhausted itself, leading to moral and physical decline on a grand scale. This degeneration – a reversal of Darwin's idea of progressive evolution – was regarded as the cause of rising criminality, alcoholism, sexual perversions and other evils of the modern age. Although humanity's decline was causally linked to negative influences from the environment, such as hectic city life, the aforementioned vices were usually supposed to be innate deviations, determined by biological factors. For instance, the Italian criminologist Cesare Lombroso published *L'uomo delinquente* (1876), a study in which he explained how 'born' criminals could be recognised by their physical features, such as hawk-like noses. The Austro–Hungarian Max Nordau, inspired by Lombroso, was the author of the popular book *Entartung*

(1892). In this polemic study, he argued that many writers and artists – including Friedrich Nietzsche, Émile Zola and the Decadents – suffered from the same diseases as criminals, prostitutes and anarchists: they were morally insane, imbecilic and demented. From 1870 onwards, 'bad' Roman emperors were likewise defined in pathological terms.[32]

Considering this background, it is hardly surprising that Decadent authors portrayed Elagabalus as a pathological case too. Instead of presenting us with a villain who is simply evil for evil's sake, Mirande and others imagine the emperor as a perverse, degenerate boy whose senses are so dulled that almost nothing can revive them – except the most cruel and debauched practices.

The period of Decadence could be said to end with the outbreak of World War I, if not earlier. For the *Nachleben* of Elagabalus, this breach is very clear. In the decades following 1914, only a handful of fictional works feature the priest-emperor. One of these still contains many Decadent themes and ideas, however. The novel in question is *Héliogabale: Orgies romaines*, co-written by Maurice Duplay and Pierre Bonardi, and published in 1935. Like many works from the period 1850–1914, the novel takes place against the background of an empire in decline: 'the habits in the capital of the Empire were so obscene that one cannot be surprised by the licence which governed the camps – especially in Asia.' Elagabalus embodies this decline, as becomes clear when he is compared to his younger cousin, Severus Alexander: 'the former prematurely crumpled, wretched, effeminate, the latter fit, his gaze direct and fresh, firm of step, already virile'. When the emperor laughs, 'the decadence of Rome, the Latin degeneration' are said to express themselves. Elagabalus is also portrayed as androgynous: he is said to have a double nature, with a body that is 'at the same time virile and effeminate'.[33] The authors give no indication that this double-sexed state has any spiritual, transcendent connotations.

In all of the works discussed above, Christianity plays only a minor role, if any. In Villeroy's *Héliogabale*, Christians make several appearances. They even have the final word. When Roman soldiers are celebrating that they have triumphed over Elagabalus, a Christian admonishes them: 'Until the day that the cross of the living God who bleeds / Will in his turn shut out your eagle and your signs.'[34] Mirande's *Élagabal* also ends on a Christian note, with one of the characters exclaiming, 'Glory to Christ!'[35] However, neither of these works focuses on Christianity, or mentions the persecution of Christians. The same is true for Duplay and

Bonardi's *Héliogabale*, which also occasionally refers to Christianity. Rather than emphatically propagating a Christian message, as was the case with Krasiński's *Irydjon*, the authors prefer to focus on Elagabalus and his vices.

Whether or not they presented him in a positive light, all Decadent authors were fascinated with the imagined ambiguity of the priest-emperor. In Elagabalus, they found a figure on the crossroads of 'East' and 'West', polytheism and Christianity, masculinity and femininity, extreme youth and fatigue, the sublime and the base – contrasting pairs whose combinations delighted them. It need not surprise us, therefore, that the young ruler became an icon of Decadence.

THE 'DECADENT EMPEROR': SELECTED WORKS

### Elagabalus in Lombard's L'Agonie *(1888)*

Jean Lombard (1854–91) led a short but very productive life. He was born into a poor family in Toulon, a French town on the Mediterranean coast. The family soon moved to Algeria, where Lombard lived for ten years before returning to France. At age 14, he came into the service of a jeweller in Marseille. These first-hand experiences with poverty and simple wage labour were an undoubted impetus to his socialist ideals. In 1878, the young man entered politics at the Congrès de Marseille. He apparently did well; not much later, he became the secretary-general of the Congrès de Lyon. Lombard did not limit his activities to politics, however: he also was a prolific writer. He wrote two studies on the democratic doctrine, three novels, and published prose, poetry and many articles in a number of journals and magazines, concerning himself with literary and political doctrines, social philosophy and many other subjects. In addition, he was the head editor of two socialist journals and editor of the *Marseille Républicaine*.[36]

Lombard's novels – *L'Agonie*, *Byzance* and *Loïs Majourès* – were not very widely read during his lifetime. Nevertheless, they influenced several Decadent authors. Louis Didier, Louis Couperus and others writing about Elagabalus mention *L'Agonie* in their works. Ironically, Lombard did not consider himself a Decadent author at all, and explicitly distanced himself from the movement. He accused Decadents and Symbolists of 'false sentimentality' and an 'overly subtle aesthetic', arguing for 'a social, healthy, true literature' instead.[37] In his novels, he devoted much attention to the fate of oppressed minorities, and advocated the same socialist values for which he pleaded in his non-fictional writings. However, his novels also contain many Decadent elements. This is especially true for *L'Agonie,* set on the stage of Elagabalus's decaying Rome. As David has remarked, the refined, artistic writing style of the novel is strongly reminiscent of Huysmans's *À Rebours.*[38] Moreover, in *L'Agonie,* Lombard discusses several themes which are typically Decadent: sexual incertitude, androgyny and artificiality.

Contrary to most other works discussed in this chapter, Elagabalus is not the protagonist, or even the main villain, of *L'Agonie.* The novel does not primarily focus on life at the imperial court – although we get to see our share of that – but on Madeh, a young priest of Elagabal, and on a large group of pagans and Christians living in Rome. Together with his master and lover, Atillius, Madeh travels from Syria to the capital. Under the sway of Elagabalus and his sun god, the city has turned into a stage for endless orgies and caprices. The ultimate goal of the adherents of the Elagabal cult is to become androgyne. As the supposed embodiment of this sacred state, the emperor gives himself to both men and women. In contrast, the jealous Atillius keeps Madeh to himself and forbids him to have sex with women. When the young man cannot suppress his desires and sleeps with his master's sister, Atillia, the angry Atillius rejects him and sends him out into the streets.

Madeh is adopted by a group of Christians. These are eastern Christians, who – as opposed to the Christians of western origin – support the cult of Elagabal, regarding its decadence as a necessary stage for the rise of Christ, and organise orgies among themselves. Lombard devotes much attention to the opposing views of the different Christian factions and their interaction with pagans. Many of his characters also appear at court, where they interact with the imperial family. Throughout the novel, there is a sense of impending doom, underlined by invocations of Babylon and the Apocalypse. Finally, the soldiers revolt against Elagabalus. In the ensuing slaughter, not only the emperor and his mother, but also Madeh, Atillius, Atillia and most of the Christians are brutally killed. The last words of the novel are spoken by a humble pork vendor, who advises another minor character that it is better to keep a low profile and not choose sides in religious and political conflicts.

Seen through the eyes of Lombard's cast of commoners, Elagabalus remains a distant figure, with whom they hardly interact directly. The story is never focused through the character of the priest-emperor. Still, he has a significant role as the fulcrum of all the debaucheries and decadence to which Rome has fallen prey. The spectators usually see him in a grand, lavish décor, dressed in splendid garb:

> under a spanning canopy of a heavy golden cloth, held up by four high spears, fixed in the earth and tilted, there flops a sumptuously immobile humanity, an obnoxiously stupid figure of fifteen years, crowned with a straight tiara wrought of pearls, gems and metals, worn atop streams of hair, black, over a whiteness of feminine shoulders shining out from a rich silken undertunic, iridescent like mother of pearl. And it is there, where Elagabalus lies on panther skins spreading his naked legs, showing his youthful virility, that with a flabellum made of a big lotus leaf, curled at the end, a black eunuch with purplish skin, white teeth and dumbly rolling white eyes fans him tranquilly.[39]

Because Lombard almost exclusively describes Elagabalus in this manner – seen from a distance in highly stylised dress, in a highly stylised environment – we never really perceive him as a person of flesh and blood. The emperor is an icon for the splendour and decadence of the 'East', transposed to Rome. Elagabalus hardly has any dialogue during the novel, but all his acts are public, from honouring the god Elagabal to having sexual intercourse with his minions. Despite his young age, the emperor is already past his prime. In one scene, spectators see him 'displayed on his bed, with the moist traces of rape on his robe of purple silk; tiara on head, eyes circled with black, terrible, bored; his features fine, drawn'.[40] Rome itself is in a similar state: exhausted, lacklustre and defiled by all the sex and violence within its walls.

Throughout the novel, Lombard mentions many details from the ancient sources, especially from the *Historia Augusta*. Like Alma-Tadema, he is drawn towards the story of the flower avalanche, describing the extravagant luxury and refined cruelty with which Elagabalus smothers his banquet guests. The emperor shows the same ruthlessness towards the multitudes of Rome, releasing lions to chase them from his palace, followed by praetorians who slaughter all those who remain behind. When the crowd cries out against him in the circus, he reveals his member in contempt. In one scene, he even sacrifices children to Elagabal. All of this makes it clear that we are dealing with a completely immoral person, a tyrant who places no value whatsoever on the lives of his subjects.

However, even Elagabalus becomes aware of the growing resentment against him, and realises his end may be near. As in the *Vita Heliogabali*, he makes plans for a luxurious suicide, 'as his extraordinary life must have such an extraordinary end, without equal in the centuries to come'.[41] Here, once more, we have the Decadent desire for the grand and fantastic, the wish to outdo all others, even future generations. Driven to despair, Elagabalus wants to turn even his own death into a work of art – an ambition in which he fails miserably.

As has been touched upon above, Lombard connects the Elagabal cult to an ideal of androgyny. The black stone, interpreted as a phallic symbol, represents the principle of Life, which was originally androgynous: 'At the beginning of All, unisexual Life engendered and gave birth to itself; the world was incapable of Happiness since the separation of the sexes; also, Perfection consisted of fusing the generating force within Unity.'[42]

Of course, no such ideas can be found in the sources on the historical Elagabal cult. The interpretation put forth by Lombard rests on the nineteenth-century concept of the androgyne as a mystical ideal, transcending the ordinary world of sexual opposites. Elagabalus, as the high priest of Elagabal, is supposed to fulfil this ideal, merging both sexes in one body. After he has married his lover, Hiéroklès, the Roman people rejoice: 'The Emperor is androgynous like destiny! [...] He is rich in both sexes, honour to him!' Elsewhere, the monarch is compared to 'The First Force'. According to the teachings of the cult, he has to give himself to all lovers, both male and female, 'for the dark and unexplained mystery of creation'.[43]

Impressive as this may sound, it later turns out to be wrong. To understand the true meaning of the androgynous ideal in *L'Agonie*, we have to consider Madeh, the young sun priest who also strives for androgyny. Atillius, Madeh's master and lover, wants to keep his protégé completely to himself. He compares his love for the young man to 'a black flower, with a black calyx, with black bud, whose shadow, like a cut-off phallus, clouds his brain'.[44] A black flower is an oft-used Decadent symbol for the unnatural and the artificial. Atillius rejects the 'natural' love of man and woman in favour of 'artificial Love', which he regards as the only path to androgyny. As David points out, the monstrous or black flowers – which are mentioned several times in the course of the novel – signify asexuality and death.[45] By focusing mainly or even exclusively on homosexual contacts, both Madeh and Elagabalus have chosen a dead end.

Gradually, Madeh seems to realise this. He feels that his sexuality has been twisted by the 'monstrous flowers' of his master's love and tries to escape their choking grasp. A revelatory key passage near the end of the novel hints to the reader that it is not the carnal union of man with man which will bring forth the true androgyne, but (spiritual) brotherly love. Lombard's androgynous ideal should be seen in the context of a radically socialist utopia: it points to a future world of absolute equality, in which even the differences between the sexes will be meaningless.[46]

Like many contemporary novels, *L'Agonie* puts great emphasis on the differences between the 'Orient' and the 'Occident', imagining them as polar opposites. During the reign of the priest-emperor, Rome is 'subjugated by the Orient'. Mention is made of Elagabalus's orgies and follies, his 'efforts to immerse the Occident in the pompous Orient to bring it out more dazzling, as from a bath of passions, crimes and gold'. From the start, the Roman people reject the 'Oriental customs' of their oppressor, regarding people from the 'East' as barbarians with 'inferior spirits'.[47] Elagabalus himself is the *summum* of all this: he is dressed in the splendour of an 'Oriental' priest, surrounds himself with the most extravagant riches and is constantly engaging in sexual escapades and unscrupulous cruelties, without even an attempt at rational behaviour.

The Christian community in Rome is also divided into 'Orientals' and 'Occidentals'. As has been noted, the Christians from the East actually support the emperor. They consider him an instrument of God, who brings Rome 'more and more into Vice, Crime and excrements', and thus unwittingly prepares the city for its salvation by Christ. In contrast, the western Christian Atta sides with Julia Mammaea and urges her to root out all eastern Christians when her time finally comes. His ruthless attitude is diametrically opposed to the religious beliefs of the 'Orientals', who consider all gods as aspects of (or variations on) one divine entity. The significance of this becomes clear at the end of the novel, when the delirious Atillius holds his beloved Madeh to be an androgyne. He exclaims, 'You, you see, you are the Kreistos, the T-symbol, the Immortal Vestal, Osiris, Zeus, everything!'[48]

In Lombard's ideal androgynous world, the differences between gods and religions have become as moot as the differences between the sexes. The decline of the Roman Empire in *L'Agonie* does not just signify an end – it also signifies a new beginning. By dragging Rome down with him, the depraved Elagabalus helps to set the stage for a new and better world. As David puts it, 'Here, the death throes of the Roman world lead not to the mournful pleasure which is customary for Decadence. They carry the germs of a rebirth within them.'[49]

### Elagabalus in George's Algabal *(1892)*

Stefan George (1868–1933) is counted among Germany's most famous poets, although his legacy is not undisputed. Born in 1868 in Büdesheim (near the Belgian border) as the son of a tavern holder, George started publishing volumes of poetry in 1890 and launched an influential art journal, *Blätter für die Kunst*. George never finished his studies, nor did he settle anywhere for a long period of time. From contempt for bourgeois life, he travelled through Europe all his life, staying with friends.

George's poems were meant for a small intellectual elite. They were written in a very stylised language, with many archaic, esoteric and invented words, complex syntactical and grammatical constructions, and idiosyncratic spelling, punctuation and typography. To make them even less accessible to the masses, George's first volumes of poetry were only printed in small numbers. At the start of his career, the poet was a typical proponent of *l'art pour l'art*, regarding art as an autonomous terrain which should not be infiltrated by other spheres of life, such as morality or politics. After the turn of the century, he went even further, advocating a 'strong aestheticism' which placed art above everything else. He gathered a select group of talented young men around him, who became his disciples. The members of this 'George Kreis' were meant to become the heralds of a new age in German culture and intellectual pursuit, based on the spirit of ancient Greece. Through his art, George attempted to forge a new religion, characterised by aestheticism and the transcendence of traditional morality.

The lyric cycle *Algabal* (1892) belongs to George's earlier work, written well before the founding of his *Kreis*. It follows on two earlier cycles, *Hymnen* (1890) and *Pilgerfahrten* (1891), with which it forms a union. *Hymnen* is about a poet who has averted himself from the world, but is still distracted by sensual desires. In *Pilgerfahrten*, the poet goes on a quest better to understand himself and his poetic mission. *Algabal* closes the arc. The lyric cycle concentrates on its eponymous protagonist, whose name is an altered form of 'Elagabalus'. It consists of three sections. The first section, 'Im Unterreich', describes the emperor's secluded life in a submarine garden which is completely artificial, constructed from metal, jewels and other objects and fabrics. The second section, 'Tage', elaborates on Algabal's nature and character, while the last, 'Die Andenken', has the emperor muse on his past. Each section consists of a number of short poems which do not form a continuing narrative, but evoke moods and impressions.

George had read Dio's and Herodian's accounts of Elagabalus, as well as the *Vita Heliogabali*. In all likelihood, he was also familiar with the images of Elagabalus by such authors as Gautier and Huysmans. As we will see, *Algabal* contains many elements that are typically Decadent. According to Jens Rieckmann, the lyric cycle has become 'one of the canonical works of decadence'.[50]

The submarine garden in which Algabal spends his days is of key importance for the understanding of his character. George gives an elaborate description of this artificial world. Interestingly, many of its details resemble features of Linderhof and Neuschwanstein.[51] These palaces, built by King Ludwig II of Bavaria (1845–86), contained advanced mechanisms to simulate natural phenomena, including machines to generate rainbows and waves. Here, the king could reside in a carefully constructed world of his own imagination, secluded from the mundane lives of his subjects. The same is true of Algabal's garden. George ends his description with these lines:

> Of the creation where only he awakens and manages
> Noble novelty sometimes gladdens him,
> Where no will prevails except his
> And where he commands the light and the weather.[52]

Algabal, in other words, is presented as an artist, who has withdrawn from the 'real' world to live in an environment which is entirely his own creation, and entirely under his control. Ernst Morwitz, a member of the George Kreis, describes the emperor as someone who, like George himself, 'must create the air he can breathe in'.[53]

Algabal is the embodiment of *l'art pour l'art*. He is the artist who regards art as an autonomous domain, not subject to morality, politics and other spheres of life. Beauty means everything to him. A clear example of this is the passage in which the emperor sees a beautiful priestess in the market, 'the most beautiful of the line of white sisters'. He marries her, but later sends her away, because it turns out her beauty is imperfect: 'Like the others she had a blemish.'[54] The unnamed woman is obviously inspired on the vestal Aquilia Severa, but the story of the blemish comes from Elagabalus's marriage to Julia Paula, who, according to Cassius Dio, was cast out for the same reason. However, whereas Dio mainly seems to present the story as an example of the emperor's frivolity and capriciousness, George uses it to demonstrate the absolute, unattainable standard of beauty his protagonist desires.

The longing for the unattainable also emerges in other passages of *Algabal*. Early on in the lyric cycle, it becomes clear that the emperor is not satisfied with his artificial garden. Something is missing. 'But how do I breed you in [this] sanctuary,' Algabal sighs, 'dark big black flower?'[55] The exact meaning of this phrase has been the subject of much debate. The black flower – a negation of the blue flower, the Romantic symbol for longing – could be interpreted as Algabal's desire to generate life from the sterile landscape. Jeffrey Todd regards it as 'a work of art that is wholly the creation of the artist', that is art which has not been inspired by nature or God, but rests solely on its human conception.[56] Considering George's doctrine of art as an autonomous field, this seems the most compelling interpretation, although there are many alternatives.

Cruelty is part of Algabal's character: 'I want the people to die and groan,' the young man remarks.[57] However, the cruelties and excesses of Algabal are not the focus of the poem, nor are they condemned by the poet. 'The emperor's immorality, in light of Christian morality, is significant not as immoralism, but shows instead that he operates outside Judeo–Christian moral categories altogether,' Todd remarks.[58] Like the decadent artist, Algabal transcends traditional morality. Elevated far above his subjects, the emperor functions as a mediator of fate, dealing out death and blessing as if he were a god. His cruelty is, in fact, the cruelty of life itself: 'I do what life does to me / And should I hit them with rods until they bleed: / They have corn and they have fighting games.'[59]

Despite this attitude, the concept of 'sin' is not absent from *Algabal*. George uses the word 'sinful' when the emperor thinks back to the time when he lost his virginity to a woman, an experience which he considers to be the destruction of his most beautiful dream.[60] Immoral behaviour, in George's view, is behaviour which goes against the imagination and the aesthetic. Art determines morality, rather than the other way around. For instance, when the emperor poisons two sleeping children, this is not a crime, but an act of mercy: he saves them from the disillusion of waking up.

The second edition of *Algabal* was dedicated to the late King Ludwig II of Bavaria, to whom George professed love and whom he called Algabal's younger brother. Indeed, many parallels can be drawn between George's emperor and the Bavarian king. Both came to power when they were young and beautiful; both lived in isolated splendour and showed little interest in affairs of state; and both died tragic, untimely deaths (although the latter can only be assumed for Algabal: the emperor's demise is not included in the lyric cycle). As has already been noted, Ludwig's palaces served as inspiration for Algabal's submarine garden. Moreover, the Bavarian king had the reputation of being averse to the world of rational politics and industry, turning to poetry, art and history instead. George, following Paul Verlaine, admired him as a monarch-artist.[61]

*Algabal* contains several hints at homosexuality. The first is the lyric cycle's dedication to King Ludwig II, who had been notorious throughout Europe for his homosexual tastes and behaviour. George himself was, in all likelihood, homosexual as well, which may have been another reason for his fascination with Ludwig. However, the German poet was never outspoken about his sexual preference, an attitude reflected in his work. Algabal's sexuality is deliberately presented as ambiguous. The young ruler displays an interest in women, but these women are often portrayed as treacherous seductresses. In one telling passage, singing Attic girls can no longer enchant Algabal: he longs for the 'flute players from the Nile', who bring him to ecstasy with their phallic instruments.[62]

There are also hints that the emperor is striving for androgyny. After he has secretly caroused among the common people, Algabal looks into a mirror and sees 'almost the face of a sister' – almost, but not quite. The emperor's god is called 'twoformed', which seems to indicate that the deity is a hermaphrodite. If Algabal is indeed striving for a double-sexed state, his regret about having slept with a woman for the first time gains an extra dimension: the act has distracted him from his devotion to his hermaphroditic god and is an acknowledgement of the fact that he is 'a man like all others', who needs a woman 'as a complement to himself'.[63]

The 'Oriental' background of Algabal is mentioned, but does not receive much attention – certainly not when we compare the lyric cycle to many other *fin-de-siècle* works, such as *L'Agonie* and Villeroy's *Héliogabale*.

The emperor recalls 'how many spears whistled / When I wrestled for the crown in the East', and laments his lost childhood in his 'home town' (which is not specified as Emesa). The god he worships is called Zeus, but that may just be the 'Occidental' name for an 'Oriental' deity. The procession towards Zeus's temple – situated in the east, as the poem explicitly states – is certainly of 'Oriental' splendour. The emperor's escort is opened by dancers in alluring dresses, while boys scatter sand, silver dust and dead flowers. In another passage, Algabal twice calls upon 'Syrians', who are said to be wise and sing chants, and are therefore probably priests or magicians.[64] Nowhere in the lyric cycle does there seem to be an explicit opposition between 'East' and 'West'.

George's Algabal has been interpreted as a self-portrait of the poet, 'one of George's masks'.[65] Although this interpretation seems plausible, it remains speculative. All we can say for certain is that the emperor is presented as an exemplary figure. Rather than embodying moral decay, as in most other Decadent incarnations of Elagabalus, Algabal symbolises the kind of artist George aspired to be: a mysterious, secluded figure, living in the autonomous domain of art and elevated far above conventional morality. As we have seen, the emperor was not only modelled after Elagabalus, but probably also after the 'monarch-artist' Ludwig II. The resulting image is that of a ruler who values beauty over power, and a priest for whom art is an alternative form of religion.

### Elagabalus in Couperus's De berg van licht *(1905–6)*

The Decadent movement did not have many adherents in the Netherlands. Of all major Dutch authors, Louis Couperus (1863–1923) is perhaps the only one whose work contains significant Decadent influences. Born in The Hague as the youngest of eleven children, Couperus spent part of his childhood in the Dutch Indies. In 1878, he published his first novel, *Eline Vere*, as a feuilleton in the journal *Het Vaderland*. Many more novels, volumes of short stories and travel journals would follow, leading to an impressive oeuvre of almost fifty works. Couperus married his niece, Elisabeth, but the couple never had any children. It is possible that the celebrated author – whose reputation as a dandy was frowned on by some of his Dutch contemporaries – was a closet homosexual. Many of his works contain themes and passages which are undeniably homoerotic.

Although not all of his novels were well received during his lifetime, Couperus is nowadays regarded as one of the greatest authors in

Dutch literary history. A fascination with decay, the concept of the degeneration of the human race and the idea of an all-powerful, inescapable Destiny are recurring themes in his work. *De berg van licht*, published in 1905 and 1906 in three volumes, contains all of these. The novel is set in the time of Elagabalus and portrays the rise and fall of the priest-emperor, who functions as the novel's protagonist. Most of the story is focused through him.

The first volume, set in the East, describes how Bassianus – as the character is initially called – serves his god in Emesa and rises to power through the machinations of his ambitious grandmother. The second and third volume show Antoninus – now called by his imperial name – in Rome, where he soon loses his initial popularity and eventually comes to a gruesome end, as was his Destiny. Couperus was obviously familiar with the accounts of Cassius Dio, Herodian and the *Historia Augusta*, and had also read Lombard's *L'Agonie*:

> Of all the emperors, I have always been most struck by the figure of the beautiful sun priest, who was proclaimed emperor because the army was in love with him, and because he can dance so beautifully. [...] Everybody who wrote about him has slandered him, even Lombard. The boy was a spoiled Child and certainly hysterical in his male-femaleness, but he was not just 'debauched' and nothing else. He was brilliant, and an artist in all he did.[66]

These words, written by Elisabeth Couperus-Baud on behalf of her husband in a leaflet to promote *De berg van licht*, give a clear indication of the way the priest-emperor is portrayed in Couperus's novel. Rather than presenting him as a vile, morally repulsive character, the author chooses to present Elagabalus as a beautiful, charismatic boy with considerable talents. That is not to say that the picture is completely positive. As the word 'hysterical' indicates, the protagonist of *De berg van licht* is a neurotic figure. Couperus describes the boy's soul as the 'utter bloom of an overcivilisation which is ceasing to flower'. The 'hysteria of his sensuality' is partially a blood heritage, but has been 'sharpened by too much colour-fragrant weakness and luxury, too much adoration, and even too much mysticism', resulting in a boy who is overtly sensitive and prone to excesses, but also 'graceful, [...] artfully, full of talent, brilliant and divine'.[67] This fits well with contemporary ideas about 'overcivilisation', which on the one hand was supposed to lead to neurotic, degenerate individuals, but on the other hand also heightened the senses, stimulated artistic abilities and gave people a keen eye for beauty.

Like many emperors in Decadent literature, Couperus's Antoninus is an actor who regards the whole world as his stage. According to senator Gordianus, the young ruler is 'not a boy and not an emperor, but [...], brilliantly, everything', a 'life artist, who continued with his endless recreations', ranging from an idol of divine beauty to a general in Antioch to a tempting Venus.[68] When he is still high priest in Emesa, Bassianus already knows how to appeal to the crowd. His divine beauty and dancing bring the spectators to such ecstasy that children get trampled to death without anybody noticing – even the screaming mother forgets her loss in an instant and is carried away by the spectacle. When the boy has been proclaimed emperor, his beauty and charisma gather many to his banners:

> They proclaimed him, they streamed towards him, because he was adorable, that Priest-of-the-Sun. Those tens of thousands of souls, from north and south: Romans and people from Asia Minor, but also Germans, Gauls, Brits, Sarmatians, Pannonians: they worshipped, in the South, the beauty, the ancient, almighty, ruling beauty, which two centuries of expanding Christianity had not yet been able to smother.[69]

In Rome, Antoninus initially has a similar effect on the people, dazzling them with his beauty and the splendid roles he plays. He surrounds himself with luxury and lives larger than life, dragging all of Rome with him in his orgies, games and ecstatic worship of the sun. Even senator Gordianus, an icon of moderation, admires him for his audacious lifestyle: he considers Antoninus 'adorable, excessive as only a god could be'. The emperor himself regards his orgies as a way to get closer to the divine. For him, feasting and sex are ways to reach 'the highest pleasure, that of the gods'. He scorns the 'pigs' who throw up behind the pillars and break expensive glasswork, not understanding what an orgy is really about.[70] Thus, the excessive banquets for which ancient authors scorned Elagabalus are given a new meaning: they are supposed to be life-celebrating events which should elevate the participants to a higher, divine level (although the opposite occurs).

Antoninus's initial triumph does not last long. At the start of the second part, when we first see the emperor in Rome, the first signs of his impending downfall already present themselves. 'How little he seemed changed,' Couperus tells us: the 'dancing child from Emessa' has developed 'for those not expecting it, a very striking perversity'. He has become a 'spoiled child' whose 'mystical aureole' has diminished and who flirts with those around him – not only because his priestly office requires him to offer his body to the world, as the author points out, but also for 'playful pleasure'.[71] The boy's frivolous nature gets the better of him, distracting him from fulfilling his duties as emperor and high priest of Helegabalus (as Couperus calls the sun god). Antoninus mocks the giant Maximinus when that man comes to offer his service to him, turning the future emperor into an enemy. The cruel streak which he already possesses at the start of the novel grows worse. He violates the temple of the vestals and forces the vestal virgin Severa to marry him – a deliberate insult to Rome, where he does not feel at home – and is present at the sacrifice of a baby, in whose entrails his future is read. The constant orgies also take their toll. The emperor starts to look tired, 'as if, unfortunately, the haze of his youth had been erased', and his eyes express sadness and bitterness.[72] Worst of all, Antoninus falls into the hands of Hierocles, portrayed as a violent, terrifying character, all cruelty and ambition. Despite himself, the emperor cannot stop loving this man, who embodies the Destiny to which he will succumb.

The decline and fall of Antoninus in *De berg van licht* can be properly understood only if we regard them in the context of 'East' versus 'West'. Time and time again, Couperus emphasises that his protagonist is an 'Oriental': 'And immediately, in Emessa, Bassianus had felt that in his blood he was no Roman, but Syrian, Asian and Oriental. Hardly grown from the tenderness of childhood, an air, atmosphere, strangely familiar, had immediately surprised him in Emessa, which he breathed in smilingly.'[73]

All through his stay in the capital, Antoninus keeps longing for the 'East', which he associates with 'a sultry smile, which floated towards him in the air around him, smile of sympathy and greeting; warm kiss of familiar lusts; embrace, mysterious and mystical'. Congruent with contemporary Western ideas, these terms characterise Syria as an exotic, mysterious and lascivious place, standing in sharp contrast to the more rational, moderate city of Rome. Only in the 'sensual-mystical-fragrant East,' Couperus assures us, would the soul of Antoninus still have been able to 'open in splendour'; transplanted to the capital, she would 'poison herself, and all whom she enchanted...'[74] Indeed, the soldiers and people of Rome soon grow tired of the excesses of their emperor, feeling offended by his violations of Roman law and tradition.

Androgyny, or rather the lack thereof, also plays a role in Antoninus's demise. The priest Hydaspes, who is the boy's mentor in Emessa, hopes his pupil may be the 'Chosen Soul'. Bassianus's attractive ephebe body, 'a costly vase full of beauty' which is compared to the beauty of Ganymede, Hylas, Hermaphroditos and Bacchus, combines both male and female characteristics. 'Bassianus, oh my Bassianus, are you not like that?' Hydaspes exclaims. 'Not too feminine, not too masculine, both sexes in balance, fused together in harmony...'[75] He instructs the boy to strive for androgyny in mind and body, to be both 'Adam' and 'Heva'. Only by finding and maintaining this holy balance can Bassianus reach back to the divine light from which all has come into being and which itself is sexless. Maarten Klein has argued that this theology is very similar to the ideas of Péladan, which may have inspired the author. Caroline de Westenholz has explored other possibilities, arguing that Couperus's interpretation of the Elagabal cult goes back to Gnosticism, Hermeticism, alchemy and, ultimately, ancient Shivaism.[76]

Unfortunately, emperor Antoninus is not able to maintain the holy balance: his sexual preference is for men, not women, which makes him feel more comfortable in the feminine role of 'Heva'. When he marries the charioteer Hierocles, he plays the bride. 'Man in form, he already felt like a woman, and had married his Husband... [...] Heva, Heva he was, but he had to be both: Adam-Heva...'[77] In an attempt to restore the balance, Antoninus marries Severa, but the act is moot: she does not instil any love or passion in him, as Hierocles does. Ironically, while the emperor's soul becomes increasingly feminine, his body grows into that of a man. This further disturbs the androgynous balance and underlines that Antoninus is not Hydaspes's Chosen Soul after all.

In the end, the Romans are fed up with their effeminate, 'Oriental' ruler. Antoninus and his mother are brutally killed in an uprising of the soldiers. The novel ends with a speech by Severus Alexander, made to the senate when he accepts the imperial office. Couperus does not hide his lack of sympathy for the new ruler, contrasting the boy's dullness and hesitant way of speaking with the audacity and brilliance of his predecessor. 'like you, Eminence, I will NEVER forget his adorability!' senator Gordianus whispers to grandmother Moeza.[78]

It has often been suggested that Couperus identified himself with Elagabalus, presenting the beautiful emperor as a protagonist to voice his own secret homosexual desires. 'Behind Heliogabalus, the author himself is continually hiding,' Theo Bogaerts remarks – a hypothesis which is confirmed by Frédéric Bastet. Klein disagrees, rightly arguing that we cannot identify the author with his work in such a straightforward manner.[79]

Nevertheless, it seems clear that Couperus idealised Elagabalus to some extent, even though he also attributed several negative characteristics to the boy-emperor. When Alexander makes his speech at the end of the novel, there are many 'gloomily dressed, monk-like, slavishly cheering Christians' among the crowd. Senator Gordianus is 'wistfully aware [...] of an Ancient Beauty which, alas, withered [...] and an Ancient Piety, which soon gives way...'[80] More than anything else, these last lines of De berg van licht summarise what Elagabalus meant to Couperus.

### Conclusion

Of the three works discussed in detail in this chapter, Lombard's Elagabalus comes closest to the interpretation of the emperor as an evil tyrant. However, the emphasis on the depraved ruler as a symbol of the decay of Rome, as well as other typically Decadent elements, set this image apart from those discussed in the previous chapter. The Elagabalus of L'Agonie has relatively little 'screen time' and does not serve as a villain who thwarts the protagonists of the novel. Rather, he is an icon, embodying the filth and depravity to which mighty Rome has fallen. The Antoninus of De berg van licht offers a striking contrast: here, we have a figure who does not remain a distant icon, but whom we get to know intimately. Few, if any, interpretations of the priest-emperor throughout the centuries have reached a similar level of psychological depth. Moreover, rather than embodying the decay of pagan Rome and setting the stage for the glorious rise of Christianity, Couperus's Antoninus approaches these themes from the opposite angle: he is the last symbol of an 'Ancient Beauty' and 'Ancient Piety' which will forever vanish as the Empire converts to the one, true God of the Bible. His orgies are not meant to be degraded excesses, but celebrations of life and expressions of devotion to Helegabalus. In addition, his 'Oriental' background does not merely make him effeminate and perverse, but also provides him with a mystical streak and artistic talent – characteristics which, on the whole, are presented as positive.

The contrast becomes even clearer when we consider the ways in which Lombard and Couperus address the concept of androgyny. The

Elagabalus in *L'Agonie* is clearly misguided in his efforts to reach this divine state. Rather than engaging in lascivious homosexual acts, he should strive for a world where all people are brothers and sisters, that is completely equal. Antoninus in *De berg van licht* also fails in finding and maintaining a balance between the sexes in himself, but this is due to his innate homosexuality and the growth of his ephebe body into that of a man. Nowhere in the novel does Couperus hint that the theology of the Helegabalus cult itself is wrong: Antoninus simply does not turn out to be the Chosen Soul. However, that should not distract us from the fact that the boy's effeminacy – introduced as an insult in the ancient sources – is presented as a positive trait. As with Elagabalus's 'Oriental' background and his orgies, Couperus gives a twist to this negative topos, making it, at least partially, into something positive.

The Algabal of George's poem is a different character. In contrast to the emperors in *L'Agonie* and *De berg van licht* he is not, or only barely, connected to decay; nor to the antagonism between 'East' and 'West' which is so emphatically present in the two novels. Like the Antoninus of Couperus, George's Algabal is an artist. The emperor shares the poet's conviction that life should be in the service of art rather than the other way around. In a similar vein, Couperus highly appreciated the artistic abilities of his protagonist, as well as his 'pagan' *joie de vivre* and piety. Lombard's Elagabalus lacks such positive traits. Nowhere in *L'Agonie* do we get the impression that the author has any sympathy for the emperor: on the contrary, he is presented as an opposing force to the radical social equality which this French politician and writer preached.

All three portraits of Elagabalus contain Decadent elements. However, despite their similarities, the differences are considerable. For Lombard, the young ruler was an icon of decay; for George, the embodiment of art for art's sake; for Couperus, the last representative of pagan beauty and piety. Within the Decadent movement, the interpretation and appreciation of Elagabalus gained more variety than it had possessed in the *Nachleben* of earlier times. As we will see in the next chapter, his trend of widening possible meanings would continue in the twentieth and twenty-first centuries.

# 7

# THE MODERN PRINCE

Mais c'est ici au contraire qu'Héliogabale montre tout ce qu'il est; un esprit indiscipliné et fanatique, un vrai roi, un rebelle, un individualiste forcené.

Antonin Artaud, *Héliogabale ou l'anarchiste couronné* (1934)

In the twentieth century, the study of antiquity was characterised by an increasing degree of specialisation. With more and more sources being found, catalogued and published, many scholars chose to concentrate on specific, relatively small subjects, working them out in depth rather than presenting grand narratives spanning centuries. This led to the first monographs on the reign of Elagabalus. In the decades following World War II, propaganda, representation and ideology started to draw scholarly attention. Ronald Syme (1903–89) was among the first to examine the ways in which emperors sent messages to influence their subjects, but it was Paul Zanker's *Augustus und die Macht der Bilder* (1987) which really put representation and ideology on the agenda of ancient historians. The complicated relation between image and reality continues to occupy scholars to this day, and has encouraged some of them to look at Elagabalus from a new angle.

In the fields of art and literature, the twentieth century brought many innovations. After its infancy in the last decade of the nineteenth century, film quickly developed into a fully fledged art form. Comics rose to great popularity, and many new genres of music were invented. New media such as radio, television and, later, the Internet provided

180

artists with a distribution network of unprecedented scale. Combined with mass production and the increase in wealth of the population, especially after World War II, films, books, music and other art forms became available to almost everyone in the Western world. Elagabalus turns up not only in novels, plays and paintings, but also in films, comics and pop songs. The priest-emperor seems to have sparked little attention in the interbellum years, with Antonin Artaud's *Héliogabale ou l'anarchiste couronné* (1934) as a notable exception. During the second half of the twentieth century, however, he once again captured the attention of authors and artists, and in the first years of the twenty-first century, there appears to be even a small boom of art and literature concerning him.

Once again, the first part of this chapter will provide a general overview of images of Elagabalus in scholarly and literary works. Since attempting even a brief account of the developments of modern classical scholarship would be too ambitious a task here, I will restrict myself to a few important trends in the twentieth- and twenty-first-century study of antiquity and their effects on scholarly images of Elagabalus. As a starting point, I have chosen the year 1903, since this is when the first monograph on the emperor appeared. In the next subsection, several twentieth and twenty-first century pieces of art and literature on Elagabalus will be briefly discussed. As already stated in Chapter 6, I regard the outbreak of World War I as the breaking point with the *fin-de-siècle*.

The second part of the chapter will provide a closer look at some of the images of Elagabalus. Again, three works will be discussed in detail. The first of these is Artaud's *Héliogabale ou l'anarchiste couronné* (1934), mentioned earlier. This French essay has attracted several later writers and artists to the colourful young ruler, and has probably been more influential than any other item in the emperor's fictional afterlife. The other two works are written in English. Alfred Duggan's *Family Favourites* (1960) is a British novel, Martin Duberman's *Elagabalus* (1973) an American play. The latter represents a new and interesting development, namely that of the young ruler as a modern gay role model. The three selected works are spread over three countries, two genres and several decades. They present very different images of Elagabalus, testifying to the diversity of the emperor's fictional afterlife in the twentieth and twenty-first centuries.

THE 'MODERN PRINCE': A GENERAL OVERVIEW

*Elagabalus in historiographical works, 1903 to the present*

In the twentieth century, the great work of collecting, cataloguing and publishing ancient sources such as coins, inscriptions and papyrus texts continued. The ever-increasing amount of available source material allowed scholars to focus their attention on small, specific subjects and to examine these in depth. Non-literary sources provided a welcome addition to ancient texts, putting their reliability into perspective. However, the first academic work on Elagabalus was still very much text-centred. In *Héliogabale raconté par les historiens grecs et latins* (1903), Georges Duviquet collected the most important literary accounts of the reign of the priest-emperor, although he also gave some short descriptions of coins, medallions and inscriptions. Duviquet does not draw any conclusions from the sources he has put together, but the famous literary critic Remy de Gourmont, who wrote a preface to the book, voices his opinion on Elagabalus.

According to Gourmont, the young ruler was 'the emperor of extravagance', but that was only to be expected from an adolescent boy. He notes that Elagabalus was not cruel, that the empire was at peace and that his reign was a time of plenty. On the other hand, Gourmont stresses that the emperor was not a Roman. He counts him among the 'Oriental emigrants, corrupted by the hostility of nature, withered by the continuous fire of the sun', thus expressing disdain for the 'Orient' and its people. He regards Elagabalus as a monotheist, striving for religious unity, 'very much closer to Christianity than to Aryan paganism'. Likewise, the emperor is described as a 'Jew-like Syrian'. The overall verdict is quite mild: although Gourmont mentions that Elagabalus did not concern himself much with governing, he is said to have been, 'in his own way, a worthy emperor'.[1]

The next work, *Studies in the Life of Heliogabalus* (1908) by Orma Butler, also dismisses some of the stories in the ancient sources, while retaining part of the hostile rhetoric. Although this book is primarily concerned with the *Vita Heliogabali*, rather than with Elagabalus himself, it contains an extensive section on the reign of the priest-emperor. Butler does not base her conclusions exclusively on literary accounts, but also makes use of coins, inscriptions and prosopography. She asserts that 'one can not accept without question the sweeping statements of some of the writers who claim that [Elagabalus] was always hateful to the people.' However, she makes no attempt to portray the emperor in an objective way, but adopts many of the negative opinions of the ancient authors. For instance, she speaks about the 'fantastic fanaticism and incomprehensible folly' with which Elagabalus devoted himself to Elagabal, criticising the 'barbaric splendour' of his dress and condemning the double marriage of emperor and god as 'the climax of his folly'. The emperor, according to Butler, had a 'cowardly nature' and a 'selfish spirit', and surrounded himself with 'evil counsellors' and 'unworthy favourites'. His effeminacy is not emphasised, but his Syrian background tempts the author to remark, 'Considering the facts that Heliogabalus was an Oriental, and that he lived in an age of extreme superstition, it is not at all strange that he turned to those who practised magic.'[2] In short, Butler's use of non-literary sources did not prompt her to overcome ancient and contemporary prejudice.

A very different, and rather surprising, image of Elagabalus is provided by John Stuart Hay in *The Amazing Emperor Heliogabalus* (1911). Hay seems wary that the subject of his book may be frowned upon. In the preface, he writes about the *Vita Heliogabali*:

It is written in Latin, and has never been translated into English, to the writer's knowledge, nor has he any intention of undertaking the work at this present or any other time, as he has no desire to land himself, with the printers and publishers, in the dock at the Old Bailey, in an unenviable, if not an invidious and notorious position.[3]

This indicates that, in 1911, the extravagances of Elagabalus could still be considered an unsavoury subject, with the potential to damage the reputation of the scholar who concerned himself with them. Nevertheless, Hay not only devoted a study to the controversial emperor, but even set out to salvage Elagabalus's reputation. Although he admits that 'the reign of Elagabalus is not a record of great deeds', nor 'an age of great men', he deems the splendour of the age unsurpassed, remarking that 'the glow of the purple reached its apogee' during the emperor's rule, which comprised the 'last years of imperial greatness'. As for Elagabalus himself, Hay describes him as 'an incredibly generous person, instinctively trusting, open-hearted and affectionate'. He admits that the boy had 'a congenital twist towards the evil tendencies of his age' – probably a reference to the emperor's homosexual contacts – but stresses that his negative image is an 'absurd, purely grotesque [...]

caricature', cooked up by his aunt Mammaea: 'and for 1800 years no one has had the audacity to look below the surface and unmask the deception.'[4]

Hay tries to give a psychological analysis of Elagabalus in the tradition of nineteenth-century medical authorities such as Krafft-Ebing. He speaks about the boy's 'hereditary sexuality, neurotic religion, and love of life', remarking that 'in the body of the man resided the soul with all the natural passions of a woman. He was what the world knew as a Psycho-sexual Hermaphrodite.' 'Orientalism' also plays a big part in Hay's characterisation of Elagabalus. Both the emperor's religion and his psychology are said to have developed 'under the eastern sky and surrounded by the pomp and colour of the Orient'. The young ruler possesses 'the weak softness of the Semitic races', and his reign is 'a record of enormous wealth and excessive prodigality, luxury and aestheticism, carried to their ultimate extreme, and sensuality in all the refinements of its Eastern habit'. Hay argues that Elagabalus was 'far nearer to the worship and doctrines of Jehovah than to those of any Western mode of thought'. He depicts the emperor as a monotheist who dreamt of 'the unification of churches in one great monotheistic ideal'. Contrary to Christianity, Hay assures us, the cult of Elagabal 'was never cruel, it never persecuted'. He regards religion in general as an 'effete neuroticism', but makes it clear that he would have much preferred the worship of Elagabal, 'the worship of life and light', to the 'obscure and impossible dogmas' of Christianity.[5] Apparently, what we have here is an author who was frustrated with the dominant religion of his times, and saw in Elagabalus a champion who could have directed history towards another, preferable, path.

After 1911, no new monographs on Elagabalus were published for several decades. Only in 1957 was the emperor once again deemed worthy of an extensive study. Roland Villeneuve published *Héliogabale, le César fou*. As the title indicates, this book does not even attempt to give an unbiased portrayal of Elagabalus. Although the author notes that 'his family charged him with every crime, his detractors did the rest', he does not approach the literary accounts with much scepsis. Like Hay, Villeneuve shows much interest in the emperor's psychology. He diagnoses that Elagabalus suffered from 'religious psychopathia', remarking, 'As the victim of a neuropathia dominated by a quasi-unconscious exhibitionism, he would probably have ended in dementia.' Artaud, whose surreal book on Elagabalus was apparently taken for a serious academic work by Villeneuve, is cited as an authority, as is Krafft-Ebing. In fact, many of Villeneuve's ideas seem to come straight out of the nineteenth century. For instance, the author remarks that Elagabalus's lack of sense of morality and justice was a sign of 'degeneration'. He also comments upon 'the Oriental origin and the lewd heredity' which he sees in marble busts of the emperor, concluding that they are 'closer to statues of Babylonian androgynes than to Greek ephebes, let alone Roman ones'. Equally curious is the remark that 'Heliogabalus perhaps believed he glimpsed that within the Androgyne, the denial of one sex and the absolute of both, supreme perfection resided.'[6]

Two later monographs, G.R. Thompson's unpublished PhD thesis 'Elagabalus, Priest-Emperor of Rome' (1972) and Robert Turcan's book *Héliogabale et le sacre du Soleil* (1985), do not add new perspectives to the existing corpus of studies on Elagabalus. Thompson characterises his subject as an emperor who 'was so occupied with sex and religion that he ignored the fact that he was the ruler of the Roman Empire'. He states that there was 'nothing Roman nor even occidental' about Elagabalus and his mother: 'In them arose the old spirit of Canaan against which the prophets of Israel rose with great energy.' Turcan is equally biased in his portrayal of the emperor, reporting scandalous stories from Cassius Dio, Herodian and the *Historia Augusta* as fact. When speaking about Elagabalus's concern for the prostitutes of Rome, he remarks that 'in our day, Heliogabalus would have created a ministry of Prostitution.'[7] Both authors subscribe to the idea that the emperor planned to unify the empire by instituting the cult of Elagabal as the universal religion. It was up to Martin Frey, author of *Untersuchungen zur Religion und zur Religionspolitik des Kaisers Elagabal* (1989), to look at the emperor's religious policy in more detail. His book is arguably the first monograph that subjects the years 218–22 to a serious critical analysis, making an effort to avoid stereotypes and prejudice. However, Frey is exclusively concerned with the cult of Elagabal and the role it played during Elagabalus's rule. He does not give an image of the priest-emperor himself.

A recent monograph on Elagabalus is Saverio Gualerzi's *Né uomo, né donna, né dio, né dea*, published in 2005. Gualerzi argues that the emperor's reputation was damaged not only because of his dubious morality and unrestrained display of luxury, but also because he refused to play the sociopolitical, sexual and religious roles traditionally expected of him. The author regards androgyny as a fundamental element of the Elagabal cult and argues that this caused tension with Roman religious tradition. He points out that Artaud had already said this in *L'Anarchiste couronné*, but historians had failed to pick it up. Amending this neglect, Gualerzi concludes that Elagabalus wanted to be associated with the divine and used his androgynous qualities to achieve this. As a result, the Roman people were dominated by 'two bizarre figures', namely the emperor and his divine protector, Elagabal, who were 'homonymous, similar, and of an indefinite and indefinable sexual nature: neither man nor woman; god nor goddess'.[8]

Most of the works discussed so far have concentrated on the reality of Elagabalus's reign; that is, they have tried to reconstruct what happened during the period 218–22 and what the motives and goals of the emperor were. However, the study of antiquity in the last decades has increasingly turned its gaze on another aspect: the imaginary. In his much-praised work, *The Roman Revolution* (1958), Ronald Syme called attention to the role of propaganda during the reign of Augustus, remarking, 'The Princeps, now a monopolist of the means of influencing opinion, used all his arts to persuade men to accept the Principate and its programme.'[9] The notion was picked up by Paul Zanker, who made Augustan propaganda the subject of his influential book, *Augustus und die Macht der Bilder* (1987). Jaś Elsner, the author of *Art and the Roman Viewer* (1995), focused on the audiences at which ideological messages were directed. In addition, scholars became increasingly aware that the images of emperors in ancient literature are likewise constructed to convey certain messages and ideas. A good example of this is Jaś Elsner and Jamie Masters's *Reflections of Nero* (1994), a volume devoted to the different portrayals of the last Julio-Claudian emperor in ancient literature and modern popular culture.

So far, the effects of these developments on the study of Elagabalus have been modest. As we have seen, Thompson and Turcan take much of the ancient accounts at face value. In contrast, Theo Optendrenk, author of *Die Religionspolitik des Kaisers Elagabal im Spiegel der Historia Augusta* (1969), is well aware that the *Vita Heliogabali* deliberately creates a negative image of Elagabalus. However, his primary concern is not with this image, but with the question of the extent to which stories about the emperor's religious policy are true. Only Michael Sommer's article 'Elagabal: Wege zur Konstruktion eines "schlechten" Kaisers' (2004) devotes itself entirely to the literary images of Elagabalus, rather than to the events of his reign or the reliability of the ancient texts. The self-representation of the emperor has been the subject of a handful of articles, most notably one by Erika Manders, who compares the coinage of Elagabalus to that of Severus Alexander.[10]

In general, though, most ancient scholars now seem aware that the negative image of Elagabalus is a construction and does not necessarily reflect historical reality. Moreover, the hostile rhetoric concerning 'Orientals', let alone Semites, has mostly gone out of scholarly fashion. As a result, the portrayal of Elagabalus in handbooks and reference books tends to be a lot more nuanced than it used to be. Compare, for instance, the 1939 edition of Volume XII of the *Cambridge Ancient History* with the revised edition of 2005. The 1939 edition condemns the emperor's promotion of Elagabal as 'an exhibition of childish egotism and of the contentiousness of Syrian *baal*-worship', remarking,

> The incongruity of a circumcised Augustus, who abstained from the flesh of swine to perform with a ritual purity the obscenities of a Syrian cult and who paraded in public tricked out in the effeminate finery prescribed by its ceremonial, offended a public opinion which was not exacting in morals but expected a traditional decorum from its rulers.[11]

In contrast, the 2005 edition – which devotes considerably fewer pages to the reign of the priest-emperor – formulates things much more neutrally:

> Eastern cults were acceptable in Rome, but the flaunting of the peculiar dress and rituals involved, and the appearance of the 'most mighty priest of the invincible Sungod' among the imperial titles, preceding *Pontifex Maximus*, were, at least, undiplomatic.[12]

As we see from this extract, Elagabalus is still being criticised. But the criticism concerns his 'undiplomatic' behaviour and decisions, rather than expressing moral disapproval. From a scandalous, effeminate pervert, Elagabalus has evolved into an emperor whose religious reforms were merely politically clumsy.

### Modern images, 1914 to the present

The American play *Heliogabalus, a Buffoonery in Three Acts* (1920), written by Henry Louis Mencken and George Jean Nathan, shows a clear break with the Decadent interpretation of Elagabalus dominant in *fin-de-siècle* Europe. Instead of a bored, degenerate boy of androgynous beauty, the emperor we meet in this play is a man nearing middle age. He has sat on the throne for about two decades and has no fewer than 11 wives. Like his counterpart in the ancient sources, Heliogabalus leads a life of pleasure and plenty. When he meets the beautiful Lucia, he immediately marries her, banishing his other spouses from the imperial bedchamber to spend all his time with her. Lucia is a devout Christian and wants the emperor to give up his hedonistic lifestyle. Heliogabalus initially tries to understand and follow her ideals, but soon grows weary of her chaste kisses, longing for more. His complaint formulates one of the key points of the play: 'Lucia, I can't understand you or this Christianity either. What's the idea of trying to make people miserable by forbidding them to do what they want to, and then, when they're unhappy about it, telling them they're awfully happy but don't know it?'[13]

Even Lucia has to admit that kissing may be more pleasant than praying. However, the play not only pokes fun at the over-zealous chastity of (some) Christians; the excessive hedonism of pagans such as Heliogabalus is also mocked. Due to heavy drinking, the emperor suffers from a stomach ache. The doctors treating him remark that Christianity makes an end to the old diseases of intemperance, but replaces them with new vices: a fasting Christian eats too little and sleeps too much. A better alternative, it is implied, would be the middle road, between the exaggerated morality of Christianity and the rampant excesses of paganism. Perhaps we can read this message as a reaction to moralising novels such as Arthur Westcott's *The Sun God* (1904), in which pious Christians fall victim to the cruelty of a pagan tyrant. *Buffoonery* presents a less black-and-white picture.

The tone of the play, as the word 'buffoonery' suggests, is light-hearted – a contrast with the heavy-handed tone of some Decadent pieces. There is no mention of the cult of Elagabal, nor are there any references to the emperor's 'Oriental' background, except for one remark that he was born in Syria. In fact, hardly anything in the play is reminiscent of Elagabalus as presented in the ancient sources. Mencken and Nathan's Heliogabalus is explicitly heterosexual and does not seem overtly interested in religion, although he remarks that he 'was originally designed for the church'.[14] He is presented as a remarkably smooth talker, an element which is absent from ancient accounts. Only his hedonism and his frequent outbursts of cruelty may recall the Elagabalus from the stories of Dio, Herodian and the *Historia Augusta*. However, the playwrights might as well have projected these characteristics on another notorious Roman emperor: it would have mattered little if the protagonist of *Buffoonery* had been Nero, Domitian or Caracalla.

The Heliogabalus in the play is often ruthless and capricious, but he can also be very amiable and charming, especially towards women he fancies. Mencken and Nathan present him as a comical, rather than a sinister, character. Finally, *Buffoonery* is unique in that it grants Elagabalus a happy ending: Lucia sets off to do God's work elsewhere, leaving the emperor free to devote himself to his eleventh wife, the fair Dacia.

From the 1920s to the 1950s, Elagabalus hardly featured in art and literature. Antonin Artaud was one of the very few who devoted a work to him. Perhaps this hiatus in the emperor's fictional afterlife was the result of the economic malaise of the 1930s, which caused a more serious and morally tight cultural climate. During the decade before and the years immediately following World War II, there may have been little room for such 'perverse' topics as the reign of Elagabalus. This changed in the 1960s, when the emperor once again inspired several authors. After Alfred Duggan's 1960 novel, *Family Favourites*, which will be discussed in detail later, Elagabalus appeared in *Child of the Sun* (1966), written by Kyle Onstott and Lance Horner. Serious and morally tight are adjectives which certainly do not apply to this novel, which is primarily concerned with Elagabalus's homosexual love life and may best be classified as an erotic gay novel. The emperor's relationships with Zoticus and, especially, Hierocles, take centre stage, but the authors find ample opportunity to include other male beauties, who are often described in vivid detail.

When we first meet Elagabalus – then called Varius – in Emesa, it seems the authors are setting him up to become the next tyrant of Rome. The boy likes to lash out at slaves with his whip, and nearly drowns a young man in the pool for his own sadistic amusement. At the same time, he is a 'snivelling sissy', who screams for his mother as soon as his cousin Alexianus starts beating him.[15] According to his aunt Mamaea, however, Varius is not to be blamed for what he is. She warns her son Alexianus,

> Blame him not. His grandmother, his own mother, Comazon, the priest Zenotabalus and that debauched Gannys are all conspiring to make him as evil as possible in order to gain their own ends. Varius could have been as fine a person as you are but he has been taught to think of nothing but the pleasures of his own young body.[16]

Time and time again, it is emphasised that Varius is trained to be a pawn, indoctrinated into 'the then fashionable vices of the East' and kept away from politics. His ambitious family plans to make him emperor, but does not want him actually to reign. 'Give him wine to drink and a man to bed with and he will be contented,' Maesa states smugly. As a result of the spoiling and indoctrination of those around him, Varius has become a 'simpering catamite' and a 'ridiculous little queen'; effeminate, vain, cruel, and interested only in pretty clothes and sex with men.[17]

Still, the boy proves capable of true love. He genuinely cares for the hunky Zoticus, whom he marries, and in Rome he immediately falls for the gorgeous charioteer Hierocles, the love of his life. This man changes Antoninus – as he is called after becoming emperor – for the better. 'My beloved [...] is a boy who has starved for love without ever knowing what love really is and now that he has found my love, he glories in it,' Hierocles explains to his mother. When he spends a week alone with the charioteer, Antoninus becomes 'less petulant, more mature', losing 'some of his mincing walk and airy affectations', and is 'coarsened a bit by Hierocles's masculinity', becoming 'handsomer'. In turn, Hierocles becomes 'more tender' in this 'week of miracles', so that 'there was a blending between the two of them, each taking from the other the needed qualities he did not possess.'[18] Thus, Antoninus becomes more masculine and Hierocles more feminine, both of them abandoning their stereotypical gender roles to come closer to each other. Nowhere in the novel do Onstott and Horner suggest that the relationship between the two is morally wrong or disgusting; on the contrary, it is consistently presented as genuine and affectionate, despite Antoninus's occasional unfaithfulness and Hierocles's tendency to jealousy and physical violence. *Child of the Sun* is the first novel to make the relationship of Elagabalus and Hierocles its main theme, and the first to put so much emphasis on the positive aspects of their love.

Later plays and novels would continue this tradition of Elagabalus as a positive gay character. Martin Duberman's 1973 play *Elagabalus*, which will be discussed in detail later, is about a modern-day homosexual who has taken the emperor as his idol. The Canadian play *Heliogabalus, a Love Story* (2002), by Sky Gilbert, presents Heliogabalus and Hierocles – or at least their postmodern reincarnations – as a modern gay couple, living together in an apartment in an unspecified city. Hierocles functions as the narrator of the play, recounting his life with the beautiful boy who claims to be Elagabalus reborn. Hierocles is a strong but gentle guy who speaks lovingly about his 'little emperor', 'prancing princelet' and 'favourite despot'.[19] He has a lot to put up with: Heliogabalus is very domineering and constantly claims attention, as symbolised by his much-too-large chair, whereas his much bigger partner has to settle for a much smaller one.

The play switches between modern times – scenes of the lovers living together – and antiquity – scenes from the reign of Elagabalus, such as the emperor addressing the harlots of Rome (a role imposed on the play's audience) and visiting his sexually voracious mother, Symiamira. The borders between past and present, between the ancient Heliogabalus and his reincarnation, are deliberately blurred, with one dialogue even starting in antiquity and continuing in the twenty-first century. The emperor is certainly not divested of negative characteristics. Sometimes, he acts like a tyrant, playing games of life and death with his subjects, although he claims that he does not 'kill people regularly', except in sacrifice to the God of the Sun. However, he can also be gentle and kind, especially to prostitutes, whom he regards as 'the most important people in the Roman Empire', since they are devoted to pleasure. His relation with the army – represented by three muscle-boys – is less amiable. The soldiers are not pleased with their emperor, 'a flaming queen who wore dresses and eyeshadow'. As Hierocles emphasises, this is not 'an ordinary case of straights against gays': the muscle-boys are gay themselves, but they are 'buddy fags' who do not go around flaunting their homosexuality.[20] Ultimately, *Heliogabalus* makes a plea for tolerance – not tolerance of homosexuality, but of people who do not play the gender roles which society allots them. Heliogabalus tells Hierocles,

> No, you don't understand. No one could ever understand what it's like to be a boy who looks and acts like a girl. I didn't want to be like this, I didn't try and be like this, but this is the way I am, and I'm perfectly happy with it, it's just that people, people treat me strangely, I walk into a room and they say it's a girl, it's a girl in a boy's body ulch. ughg. It's as if I have a disease. [...] I'm never going to make any real money, or any real future, nobody wants to listen to what I say nobody takes me seriously, do you understand what it's like? Not to be a masculine person in our culture?[21]

Jeremy Reed's novel *Boy Caesar*, published in 2004, also has the emperor question the dominance of the masculine ideal. The novel has two alternating narrative strands. One is concerned with Jim, a young gay man living in twenty-first-century London, who is writing a PhD thesis on Elagabalus. Jim is aware 'that Heliogabalus had become a fiction, a character in part invented by his biographers'. He wants to 'recreate Heliogabalus incontemporary terms', 'making him live now'. In his interpretation, the emperor 'had attempted to overthrow the system', substituting 'the heterodox with the unorthodox, the heterosexual ideal with its homosexual counterpart and the regenerate with the degenerate'.[22] This is confirmed in the other narrative strand, which describes the reign of Heliogabalus from the emperor's own point of view:

> His imagination had needed little prompting. Already he saw himself dragging it in front of the Senate. It was his plan to affront their machismo by insisting that women should be introduced into the governing body. He had it in mind to subvert the whole gender-bias on which Roman society was founded.[23]

However, the Heliogabalus in this narrative is not supposed to be 'genuine', not even in the context of the novel; we see him filtered through Jim's imagination. This becomes clear from the many obvious anachronisms in the text, such as references to AIDS, computer mouses, and other distinctly modern concepts. Jim imagines Elagabalus as an explicitly gay emperor who became 'the victim of a homophobic assassination'.[24] As in *Heliogabalus, a Love Story*, Elagabalus is presented as an ideologue, advocating acceptance of gay people and challenging traditional gender roles – causes to which he becomes a martyr. This reflects the struggle for gay rights in Europe and the US from the 1960s onwards. 'Orientalism' plays no significant part in these pieces: the authors are interested in the emperor's sexual contacts with men, his effeminacy and his cross-dressing, not in his Syrian background. Remarkably, both *A Love Story* and *Boy Caesar* mirror the ancient Elagabalus with a modern counterpart: Gilbert's play has Heliogabalus and Hierocles living together as a twenty-first-century couple, while Jim in Reed's novel meets a reincarnation of the emperor in Rome. In this way, a relatively unknown character from distant times is integrated into and made relevant for the gay subculture of the twentieth and twenty-first centuries.

Another interesting, distinctive image of Elagabalus is presented in the 2003 opera *Heliogabal*, scripted by the German author Thomas Jonigk and put to music by the Belgian musician Peter Vermeersch. Jonigk turns the emperor into an ancient pop star, complete with his own manager, the senator Claudius, who keeps track of the sale of Heliogabal posters and biographies. The opera starts with the body of the murdered Macrinus, displayed on a table; at the end, the dead Heliogabal occupies the same position. Stars come and go, is the message; they only last as long as they capture the imagination of the public, by whose whims they are made or broken.

In an introductory text for the opera, Jonigk states that 'having, like Michael Jackson once did, a fanbase of millions, the fourteen-year-old boy emperor Heliogabal has overwhelmed Rome.'[25] However, his popularity dwindles when he is accused of blasphemy, provocation, arrogance, political treason, nepotism, sexual excesses, prostitution and homosexuality. Jonigk remarks that superstars walk a tightrope: being too common bores the fans, being too extreme frustrates and alienates them. It is between these two extremes that idols have to find a middle ground.

Because of his young age, short reign, alleged good looks and supposedly flamboyant lifestyle, Elagabalus makes for a good protagonist to demonstrate these ideas. During much of the opera, Heliogabal seems to be on top of the world. Like an ancient Michael Jackson in his glory days, he is adored and worshipped by everybody. In reality, however, he is no more than a plaything, a doll, at the mercy of the capricious attention of the public and the cold calculations of his manager. 'Heliogabal – that's a worthwhile investment,' remarks Claudius, summarising exactly what the imperial superstar means to him. The boy's grandmother, Maesa, says to him, 'That's how an emperor must be. Like me. You are like me. Immortal. I through you and you through me.' However, when Heliogabal is killed, she is quick enough to support Alexander as the new star, exclaiming, 'Time for the emperor!' Significantly, Heliogabal himself has almost no speech in the piece. Although he is at the centre of everything, his opinion does not count. Only in a scene near the end does the boy open his mouth to tell the audience how he has been butchered by the Romans. The public which used to worship him has turned against him, looking for a new thrill. Thus, the young emperor becomes an example of the fleeting nature of fame: raised to the stars in an instant, plunged into infamy the next. As Jonigk concludes in his introductory text, 'That was the way it was for Heliogabal. And that is the way it is everywhere.'[26]

Since Elagabalus returned to the attention of artists and authors in the 1960s, he has never left. The fictional afterlife of the emperor in the past decades has been particularly rich and varied, with appearances in many genres and many countries. For instance, we encounter Elagabalus in the British novel *Family Favourites* (1960), the Italian movie *Necropolis* (1970), the French play *Héliogabale* (1971), the Italian ballet *Phaidra-Elagabalus* (1981), the German poem 'Bericht von der Ermordung des Heliogabal durch seine Leibgarde' (1999), the British pop song 'Heliogabalus' (2001), the Canadian play *Heliogabalus, a Love Story* (2002), the French comic series *La Dernière prophétie* (2002–7) and the American painting *Heliogabalus' Remorse* (2005). Apparently, the priest-emperor appeals to modern authors and artists from many different cultural and artistic backgrounds.

It would be too much to state that Elagabalus has become a popular figure, known and adored by the masses. Although he has found his way into several genres associated with popular culture, such as comics (Neil Gaiman's *Being an Account of the Life and Death of the Emperor Heliogabolus*; Gilles Chaillet's *La Dernière prophétie*), movies (*Necropolis*) and pop music (among others, the song 'Heliogabalus' on the album *Folktronic* by Momus), the emperor usually appears outside the mainstream, in art niches with a particular, limited audience. Franco Brocani's *Necropolis*, for instance, is described on the Internet Movie Database as a 'bizarre art movie' and has never captured the attention of large crowds.[27] However, the fact that mainstream audiences are not acquainted with Elagabalus does not mean we cannot regard the emperor as part of modern pop culture. According to cultural studies scholar Simon During, popular culture can be defined as 'all culture that is not regarded as, or does not consider itself, elite culture'. It includes mass-produced culture, but is also 'riddled with art niches'.[28]

Contrary to the *fin-de-siècle*, when most images of the emperor fitted (to a greater or lesser extent) into the Decadent tradition, twentieth and twenty-first century interpretations of Elagabalus show little coherence. The most influential twentieth-century author who wrote on the emperor was undoubtedly Artaud, whose essay on Elagabalus will be discussed later in this chapter. As we will see, Artaud imagined the emperor as a rebel against Roman society, prompting the Italian author Alberto Arbasino to write *Super-Eliogabalo* (1969). In this so-called anti-novel, which consists of loose fragments rather than a continuous narrative, Elagabalus is likewise imagined as a rebel. Arbasino, basing his text on the ancient literary sources and *L'Anarchiste couronné*, uses the emperor to present an ironical, critical view of the massive student protests of 1968. Artaud's name is mentioned in the works of Sky Gilbert and Jeremy Reed, and clearly influenced the French play *Héliogabale* (1971) by Pierre Moinot. His theories on theatre were a source of inspiration for the Italian theatre group Fanny & Alexander, whose 2006 play *Heliogabalus* portrays a young man trying to embody the myth of Elagabalus. The protagonist wants to devise a language without words, just as Artaud favoured *mise-en-scène* over textual theatre and wanted to subordinate words to physically articulate signs. Despite their connection to Artaud, however, the pieces mentioned above give quite distinct images of Elagabalus, with the rebellious, innovative character of the emperor as the only common factor.

Other works are just as diverse in their interpretations. As we have seen, several of the novels and plays from the 1960s onwards portray Elagabalus as a positive gay character. In Chaillet's *La Dernière prophétie*, the young ruler is an evil tyrant, cruel and bloodthirsty. Jonigk interprets him as an ancient Michael Jackson, whereas Moinot combines Artelian concepts with notions from Decadence, such as the accusation that the emperor embodies 'deformity, hideousness, degradation'.[29] Twentieth- and twenty-first-century images of Elagabalus cannot be classified as variations on a theme, such as the evil tyrant or the Decadent emperor. They branch out in many directions, turning the emperor into an anarchistic rebel, a pop star, a martyr for gay rights, and other interpretations never envisaged by the ancient authors. This diversity seems to fit with sociologist Frank Webster's ideas about postmodern society, which, he argues, no longer accepts the opinions of experts as the truth 'Against this the postmodern mentality celebrates the fact that there is no "truth", but only versions of "truth" which makes a nonsense of the search for "truth". In its stead the advocacy is for difference, for pluralism, for "anything goes".'[30]

From this statement, we could conclude that modern images of Elagabalus are no more than random evocations, void of meaning. This, however, would be taking things too far. Like their earlier counterparts, modern interpretations of the priest-emperor are taken out of context and adapted to make them relevant to contemporary issues, such as modern gender roles. The authors doing so still have points to make, which they may well feel are 'absolute' truths. Therefore, the increased diversity of images in the *Nachleben* of Elagabalus does not signify a loss of meaning; it only indicates that twentieth- and twenty-first-century authors and artists allow themselves more freedom to deviate from the sources.

Often, modern authors do not try to hide that the Elagabaluses they present to their audiences are fictional constructions. On the contrary, many of them play with this notion. Just as scholarship has become increasingly aware that much of our knowledge about Roman emperors does not rest on hard facts, but on consciously constructed images, modern literature often presents Elagabalus as a purposely constructed character. Jonigk's pop-star Heliogabal is an artificial idol, carefully designed by his manager. In Duberman's *Elagabalus* and Fanny & Alexander's *Heliogabalus*, we do not meet the eponymous ruler himself, but somebody who aspires to be like him – in other words, an imitation of the original. Likewise, Gilbert's play and Reed's novel both give us a modern reincarnation of the emperor. Moreover, the many anachronisms in Reed's description of the reign of the 'historical' Elagabalus make it clear that we see these episodes filtered through the mind of a twenty-first-century student: the emperor is the product of Jim's imagination. Arbasino's 'anti-novel' *Super-Eliogabalo* also makes extensive use of anachronisms. In all these cases, we are dealing with images drawing attention to their own artificiality.

The French philosopher and cultural theorist Jean Baudrillard argues that the twentieth century has seen such an increase in images – in art, popular culture, commercials, television – that they have started to form a reality of their own. Images are no longer thought to refer to reality, Baudrillard argues, but to other images. As a result, the underlying reality disappears, leaving only representations.[31] Elagabalus's fictional afterlife could be interpreted as a case in point. The illusion that we are reading a book or watching a play about the 'real' emperor is often deliberately broken by the author. Although elements from the ancient accounts are still used to portray Elagabalus, the pretence of authenticity is discarded. Like Jim, the PhD student in *Boy Caesar*, the works mentioned above acknowledge that they are recreating the emperor in contemporary terms, 'making him live now'.[32]

Since 2000, the attention for Elagabalus has been remarkably strong. In the last years, the emperor has played a significant role in at least four plays, one opera, two novels and one comic series. In addition, he has been depicted on the oil painting *Heliogabalus' Remorse* (2005) by Matt Hughes, has inspired Martin Bladh to a series of paintings (2007), has been the subject of Momus's song 'Heliogabalus' (2001) – in which the singer asserts to us that 'he was beautiful and sexy and completely without guilt' – and has inspired two musical albums: John Zorn's *Six Litanies for Heliogabalus* (2007) and Rorcal's *Heliogabalus* (2010).

Possibly all this attention for the emperor is caused by the growing number of people with a fast connection to the Internet, where information about him is easy to find. There are certainly many websites mentioning Elagabalus, as well as images of ancient coins and modern depictions. A quick search reveals the existence of 'Heliogabby's Homepage' and 'HelioGabby's Bath House', whose 'Electronic Library' features English translations of the relevant passages in Cassius Dio, Herodian and the *Historia Augusta*, as well as Gibbon's description of the young ruler's escapades and large chunks of Hay's *The Amazing Emperor Heliogabalus*. Elagabalus is also graced with an entry in 'Joan's Mad Monarch Series'.[33] Numerous other websites could be mentioned. At the start of the third millennium, it seems, the third-century emperor still fascinates.

THE 'MODERN PRINCE': SELECTED WORKS

*Elagabalus in Artaud's* L'Anarchiste couronné *(1934)*

The life and career of Antonin (originally Antoine) Artaud (1896–1948) are characterised by an alternation of energetic, creative peaks and deep personal tragedies. Born in Marseille as the son of a shipbuilder at the end of the nineteenth century, Artaud was a sickly, nervous child. He grew up to be an actor and writer, and co-founded the short-lived Alfred Jarry Theatre, which was to present a new, physical form of theatre, meant to give the audience a 'hysterical sensory overload'.[34] Artaud had to battle depressions and an opium addiction, and spent the final years of his life in several asylums, where he received electroshock treatment. He died in Paris in 1948, probably from an overdose of chloral.

The 'theatre of cruelty' is undoubtedly Artaud's greatest legacy. As he explained in *Le Théâtre et son double* (1938), a collection of his letters, manifestoes, lectures and articles, Artaud objected to the predominantly textual and psychological nature of European theatre. He rejected the idea that theatre should hold up a mirror to humanity; in his eyes, this only made it false, an illusion. Instead, he argued for 'le théâtre de la cruauté', which would subordinate text and the narrative, and would give a central place to the body and non-verbal signs: 'It is therefore necessary to create a metaphysics of the word, the gesture, the expression for the theatre, with the aim of tearing down its psychological and human pounding.'[35] Audiences had to be fully submerged in the performance, and would thereby break through the illusions conjured up by traditional theatre, seeing reality for what it was. They would reconnect with metaphysical primeval forces which, at the time, Artaud thought, were only to be found in the 'pure' theatre of the 'East'. As he states in his manifesto: 'Without an element of cruelty at the base of every spectacle, theatre is not possible. In the degenerate state we are in, we will return the metaphysical to the minds through the skin.'[36]

The term 'cruauté' does not primarily signify 'cruelty' in the sense of bloodthirst and sadism; it expresses that this is theatre without mediation, since it does not represent reality, but is a deed, an event in itself. Artelian cruelty, in the words of Stephen Barber, should be regarded as 'an elaborated version of the intentional and hostile Surrealism' which Artaud had promoted earlier in his career.[37] The term 'double' is also important: it indicates that the theatre should become the double of the primeval forces, and vice versa. Like many Artelian concepts, it is a contradictory term, since Artaud also wanted the theatre to coincide completely with these forces, eradicating duplicacy.

Artaud wrote *Héliogabale ou l'anarchiste couronné* (1934) when he was developing his ideas about the 'theatre of cruelty'. In his book, he applies these ideas to Elagabalus. The choice for this emperor was not his own: Artaud was commissioned to write the book by the publishing house Éditions Denoël-Steel. He took the job because he needed money, but soon warmed to the subject. *L'Anarchiste couronné* may best be classified as an essay, although it crosses genre boundaries and also contains elements of a novel, such as vivid invented descriptions of characters and places. The essay consists of three parts, followed by three short appendices with additional information on esoteric subjects.

It could be argued that *L'Anarchiste couronné* is more about the author's ideas concerning anarchy and androgyny than about Elagabalus: only the last third is devoted to the emperor and his reign. In the first part, Artaud gives his idiosyncratic interpretation of the background of the future ruler: he discusses Syria, Elagabalus's family and the cult of Elagabal. The small but crucial middle part concerns itself with 'la guerre des principes', the war which, according to the author, is being waged between opposing divine principles, such as the masculine and the feminine. Artaud connects this centuries-long metaphysical war to the worship of the sun, particularly Elagabal: 'And this war is wholly within the religion of the sun, and one finds it in some degree, sanguinary yet magical, in the religion of the sun practised at Emesa.' This, according to him, is the key to understanding the actions of Elagabalus: 'it's not so much in his own personal psychology, but rather in the religion of the sun that they [i.e. historians discussing the emperor] should have sought the origin of his excesses, his follies and his highly mystical lewdness.'[38]

Contrary to such authors as Louis Couperus – or John Stuart Hay, for that matter – Artaud is not interested in a psychological portrait of the emperor. To him, Elagabalus is the embodiment of opposing principles, whose constant struggle is described in the second part of the book. His Héliogabale is androgynous, 'flesh plump as a woman's, [...] features waxen-smooth', combining a male sex with female characteristics.[39] As Leslie Anne Boldt-Irons points out, androgyny in *L'Anarchiste couronné* depicts the coexistence of blended male and female principles in one being.[40] As in *Le Théâtre et son double*, Artaud seems fascinated with the double. Nearly every character in the book is doubled: Domna with Moesa, Gannys with Eutychian, Héliogabale with Alexandre, although the emperor scornfully regards his cousin as 'a poor imitation of himself'. An important appendix to *L'Anarchiste couronné* expresses the view that everything that exists is double at its source. However, a few lines further, Artaud states that 'beyond that there's only pure essence, unanalysable abstraction, the indeterminate absolute, "The Intelligible", finally', apparently contradicting his earlier statement.[41] This ambiguity about the original nature of reality – one or double – is maintained throughout the main text and is never resolved.

The androgyne represents the double united in unity: it is both male and female, yet one. The counterpart to androgyny, according to Artaud, is anarchy, the disorder that arises when separate principles are at war with one another, preventing unity. Intriguingly, Héliogabale is not only an androgyne, but also an anarchist: 'The initial anarchy was within him and ravaged his organism.'[42] The emperor is tormented by the polarities he embodies: not only man and woman, but also god and man, human king and sun king, the man crowned and uncrowned. Even his name, El-Gabal (or its variants), is made up out of the names of many gods or opposing principles.

200 THE CRIMES OF ELAGABALUS

'Héliogabale was a born anarchist, and one who ill bore with kingship, and all his acts as king were acts of the born anarchist, the public enemy of order, who is an enemy to public order,' Artaud states. He regards Héliogabale not as a madman, but as a rebel against 'the Roman polytheistic anarchy' and 'the Roman monarchy'. All his gestures are double-edged: they generate order and disorder, unity and anarchy, generosity and cruelty, etc. The author reinterprets many stories from the ancient sources, such as Herodian's account that Elagabalus walked backwards during a procession to keep facing his god. In *L'Anarchiste couronné*, this walking backwards is transferred to the scene where the emperor first enters Rome, to show that 'at the outset he's had himself buggered by the whole Roman empire'.[43] Accounts from the *Vita Heliogabali* about Elagabalus's licentious and excessive lifestyle become deliberate attempts to subvert the Roman order. Artaud remarks,

> To restore poetry and order to a world whose very existence is a threat to order, is to bring back war and the permanence of war; it is to bring in a state of enforced cruelty, to arouse a nameless anarchy, anarchy of things and appearances which awaken before sinking anew and melting into unity.[44]

What this passage seems to indicate is that anarchy, or war between the principles, is ultimately necessary to bring the opposing forces closer together and merge them completely, establishing unity. This is confirmed by an earlier passage: 'It was in order to cut short this separation of principles, to reduce their essential antagonism, that they [i.e. men] took up arms and fell upon one another.' Indeed, the emperor's 'marvellous ardour for disorder' is said to be 'merely the application of a metaphysical and superior idea of order – of unity, that is'.[45]

According to Artaud, Héliogabale, 'not content with taking the throne for a stage, [...] proceeded to take the very soil of the empire for a stage'. He introduces 'theatre and, through theatre, poetry to the throne of Rome, into the palace of a Roman emperor, and poetry, when it's real, is worthy of blood, it justifies the shedding of blood'.[46] What Héliogabale does, in other words, is to apply Artaud's ideas about the 'theatre of cruelty' to the governing of the Roman Empire. All his acts are deliberate attempts to break through the superficial order of Roman society and reveal the opposing principles which lie beneath it. His subjects (his audience) are actively involved in this 'play' and are 'cruelly' brought into contact with the metaphysical forces that their ruler unleashes. As Boldt-Irons remarks, this philosophy seems to indicate that Artaud favours anarchy over androgyny, war over harmony, since the latter holds the danger of inertia and non-being. However, she points out, we should not forget that Héliogabale becomes a martyr to his own cause: he cannot control the anarchy he has unleashed, and dies a gruesome death. Moreover, the emperor was ultimately striving for a superior, metaphysical unity.[47]

Artaud places great emphasis on Héliogabale's 'Oriental' background, especially in the first part of the book. He describes Syria as a place of 'sanguinary excesses' and 'violent spirituality', where blood, sperm and sweat flow freely. The land has 'a feeling for a certain natural magic', and 'an idea of the magic that is not natural'. The 'West', in contrast, has forgotten these things. It is the opposite of the 'East', its double; patriarchal where the 'East' is matriarchal; static where the 'East' is vibrant and dynamic. Addressing his readers directly, Artaud speaks about 'we people of the Occident', who associate ourselves with civilisation and regard all others as barbarians. However, he points out, 'all the ideas which enabled the Roman and Greek worlds not to die immediately, not to sink into a blind bestiality, came from precisely this barbarian fringe.'[48] Following Artaud, input from the 'East' allowed the 'West' to maintain contact with tradition.

On a superficial level, Héliogabale seems to undermine patriarchal authority: the emperor is an androgynous figure, brought up in a matriarchal society and dominated by four women. In his family, 'the men assumed all the malice and weakness, and the women the virility.'[49] Father figures, as John Stout points out, are either ineffective, absent or castrated (like Héliogabale's foster father, the eunuch Gannys).[50] In addition, the emperor 'banishes men from the senate and replaces them with women'. However, Artaud represents Elagabal as a phallic god, speaking about his 'vigorous prick', and notes that Héliogabale, 'the pederast king who wanted to be a woman, was a priest of the Masculine'.[51] So, just as the emperor is stimulating anarchy in order to achieve a new unity, he is undermining the patriarchal structure of Roman society in order to achieve the triumph of the phallic Elagabal. Stout concludes, 'Ironically, Artaud's Héliogabale dethrones the Father the better to reinstate His power in a new form.'[52]

David contrasts Elagabalus as portrayed in L'Anarchiste couronné with images of the emperor from Decadent authors, such as Lombard, Jourdan and Mirande. She remarks that Artaud rejected their interpretation of the young ruler as an extravagant, derailed soul, plagued by *ennui* and wishing to outdo Nero. The traditional signs of a decadent society – taverns and brothels, circus games, torture, orgies and sexual inversion – are absent from Artaud's Rome. Instead, the author of *L'Anarchiste couronné* concentrates exclusively on the sexual extravagance of the emperor himself, which is sacralised: it serves a higher purpose. 'Artaud is interested in deep motivations and in the consequences of an act dictated not by the individual fantasy of an esthete, but by a political and religious will,' David points out.[53] Artaud's Héliogabale may appear to incorporate the height of imperial Rome's decadence, but he also represents an element of regeneration. The author repeatedly states that Héliogabale let blood and sperm flow freely during his reign, but also notes that the young ruler hardly killed anyone, except for Gannys and the cronies of Macrinus. This remark stresses once again that the emperor's intentions are essentially benevolent. We could even compare him to Jesus Christ, who likewise set out on a spiritual mission to save mankind and was killed as part of his efforts.[54]

Ultimately, Artaud refuses to instill in his text one definite meaning. Stout remarks, 'The narrator's elaborately structured sentences and paragraphs move from one opposition or paradox to another, aggressively claiming the reader's assent while violating his or her sense of logic and order.'[55] By being deliberately self-contradictionary, the author applies the principles of anarchy to his own narrative. In a letter to a friend, Artaud stated that Héliogabale was a self-portrait: 'in the conception of the central figure [...] I have indeed described myself.' Since *L'Anarchiste couronné* hardly explores the psychology of the emperor, we can assume that Artaud was first and foremost referring to the values and ideas he shared with Héliogabale. Like the crowned anarchist, he probably considered himself 'a spirit undisciplined and fanatical, [...] a rebel, a crazed individualist' – pursuing contact with the roaring primeval forces behind the veil of everyday life.[56]

### Elagabalus in Duggan's Family Favourites *(1960)*

Alfred Duggan (1903–64), the son of a rich Argentinean landowner of Irish descent, was born in Buenos Aires. After his father's death, he and his family moved to England. Duggan was a productive writer, but only published his first novel – *Knight in Armour*, about the First Crusade – in 1947. A whole range of historical novels would follow. Without exception, these were set in antiquity or medieval times. Duggan had a preference for obscure historical periods and places, such as the founding of Rome or the autumn days of Roman Britain, since, he claimed, these required the least research. Evelyn Waugh admired Duggan's oeuvre, which he described as 'accurate and infused throughout with a dry irony that is peculiarly his own', commenting that the author's talent was 'certain to attract more and more admirers in the future and to establish him safely in a high place among the writers of his period'.[57]

In *Family Favourites* (1960), Duggan set out to describe the rise to power, the reign and the downfall of Elagabalus. The narrator of his story is Duratius, a praetorian guard who becomes closely acquainted with the emperor and his family. Five years after Elagabalus's death, while living in northern Britain, Duratius writes his memoirs for his two sons, 'so that when they are grown up they will know they come of good stock'.[58] He recounts how he first met Elagabalus after Macrinus was defeated in battle; since he was the first soldier to change sides and declare for the boy, he is rewarded with a job at court. Duratius trains the new emperor in swordfighting and, because of his frankness and sensible mind, soon wins the affection of Elagabalus and his grandmother, becoming a 'family favourite'. He travels with the imperial company to Rome and experiences the major events of the priest-emperor's reign up close. When Elagabalus is eventually murdered, Duratius is knocked out in the skirmish, but not killed. Instead, he is allowed to retire to a remote corner of the empire and live out his remaining days in peace, which brings the story full circle.

From the moment that Duratius first meets Elagabalus, he has a favourable impression of the boy. After the defeat of Macrinus, when the new emperor first addresses the troops who have just come over to his side, he says 'exactly the right thing', taking their loyalty for granted while at the same time reminding them of their privileged position. 'He was the kind of Emperor we needed,' Duratius notes.[59] Like all the soldiers, he is 'struck by the superhuman beauty of this marvellous boy', who 'radiated happiness and wellbeing'.[60] The picture he presents of Elagabalus is that of a brave, confident and intelligent young ruler, who does not fail to charm his subjects. After the reign of the uninspiring Macrinus, everybody has high expectations of Caracalla's heir. Duratius reminisces about those early days of Elagabalus's rule, when the imperial company was still in the East:

> Our ruler was all that could be desired, beautiful and intelligent and high-spirited and merciful. If he was not yet very wise that hardly mattered. The Emperor leads the army, but we were at peace with all our neighbours. [...] Best of all, we felt secure. Elagabalus did not turn against his friends, and if he tried to his grandmother would stop him. Throughout the world his rule was accepted; all the pretenders were dead, nowhere did a province rise in arms. During that autumn civilisation was at peace.[61]

Cruelty, Duratius stresses, is not part of Elagabalus's character. Whereas Cassius Dio claims that the emperor gloated over the dead body of Macrinus, Duggan has him take pity on his unfortunate rival. In *Family Favourites*, Elagabalus, having received word that the previous emperor has been captured, orders him to be killed immediately, 'to put him out of his misery'. The deed is done 'painlessly and without torture'. Moreover, Duratius assures his readers that Elagabalus 'never harmed any of his subjects' and 'had a kindly heart'. In contrast to Dio's account, in which the emperor is the first to strike a mortal blow against his tutor, Gannys, Duggan has Duratius do the killing: the soldier intervenes when Gannys draws his dagger in a heated argument with his young pupil. Duratius nearly beheads the man, after which Elagabalus finishes the job, cutting the head off completely from the body and holding it up. Amazed, he remarks, 'It's not difficult to kill a man, is it? But it's not nearly so much fun as I had expected.'[62]

Though Elagabalus in *Family Favourites* may not be an evil tyrant, that does not mean he is without flaws. Following the *Historia Augusta*, Duggan portrays the emperor as someone who is very fond of playing practical jokes and giving absurd orders. He serves his dinner guests fake food and orders the police and watchmen of Rome to gather a thousand pounds of cobwebs. As Duratius regretfully remarks, 'at seventeen he was still in love with the pranks that had amused him when he was fourteen.' Even so, the soldier concedes, it could have been a lot worse. The emperor's fondness for jokes is essentially harmless: 'He tried so hard to be a wicked debauchee, after the manner of Nero or Caligula; but it is difficult to earn a reputation for wickedness if you have sworn an oath never to give pain to an innocent subject.'[63] Other hobbies of the young ruler include acting and disguising himself to mix with the commoners. At the heart of these apparently frivolous pleasures lies a deep longing:

> 'No, I can't have everything,' he answered wistfully. 'But if only I could control my mind I might be able to *experience* everything. That's what I try to do. I want to be the Emperor, and the high priest of Elagabalus. But I want also to be a porter on holiday, and a poor man selling cabbages, and a virgin bride, and an ardent young husband, and a poor old harlot working when she's ill because the rent must be paid. I want to be all my subjects, a painted Briton and a black Ethiopian and a Cappadocian wrapped in yards and yards of linen trousers. I want to feel the whole civilised world beating in my heart.[64]

This is reminiscent of the Decadent notion of the emperor regarding the whole world as his stage, but there is an important difference: rather than regarding all his subjects as extras in a play starring himself, Duggan's Elagabalus wants to *be* them. His primary drive is not megalomanic self-indulgence, but a desire to experience all the shades of human life, from the high to the low, from the familiar to the exotic.

Contrary to most interpretations of Elagabalus, the emperor in *Family Favourites* is usually not at all effeminate or androgynous. Although his looks are stunning, 'his perfect beauty had in it nothing of the feminine; even the long embroidered gown could not conceal his manliness.' Duratius recalls how anxious the young ruler was to learn swordfighting from him – a 'manly' interest which the emperor certainly did not have in the accounts of ancient authors.[65]

Sexually, however, Duggan's Elagabalus is (almost) exclusively interested in men. 'I shall never touch a woman for my own pleasure,' he stubbornly declares, when his grandmother wants him to marry. For procreational purposes, he agrees to marry Julia Paula, but rather than spending his wedding night with her, he organises a private party for some intimate friends, including Duratius. At this party, the emperor plays the role of a woman: he appears dressed as a maiden bride, with his golden hair in elaborate curls, his arms depilated and powdered, wearing bracelets and a transparent silk veil. In this guise, he takes the charioteer Gordius for a husband. After sharing the latter's bed, he returns wearing a bridegroom's wreath, taking on the masculine role in a marriage with Hierocles. In contrast to just about any other interpretation of this character, Duggan's Hierocles is a frightened, effeminate boy, rather than a big, muscular man. He does not become the emperor's husband, but his wife. This emphasises that Elagabalus can choose to play a female role (as he did with Gordius), but that his homosexuality does not make him unmanly. In fact, the marriage with Gordius is the only instance where the emperor presents himself as feminine. Later, he even falls in love with a woman, Annia Faustina, although it is explicitly stated that 'his affection for Hierocles was unimpaired' by this.[66]

Although Duggan was a conservative Catholic, *Family Favourites* does not condemn the homosexual contacts of the emperor. Duratius's remark, 'I am a Gaul, with the Celtic distaste for unnatural love', does not stop him from appreciating the beauty and charms of the young ruler, albeit in a platonic way. The soldier feels that 'the Emperor's private life was his own affair, and it seems to me ridiculous to hold that it is more wicked to love boys than girls.' Elsewhere, he calls his master's homosexuality 'a fancy which nobody seriously condemns', which is 'at bottom harmless enough'.[67] Considering that this sentiment is repeated several times throughout the novel, and taking the generally positive portrayal of Elagabalus into account, no irony on the part of the author seems to be involved.

Stereotypes about the 'East' are also challenged, up to a point. When he first hears about Elagabalus, Duratius asks if he is a eunuch. When he sees the boy in person, his assumptions about 'Orientals' are challenged. Although Elagabalus 'did not look like a Roman neither did he resemble a feeble oriental. He seemed a fair servant of the gods, come down from Olympus to supervise their worship.' On the other hand, there is his foster father Gannys, 'a flashy, soft, handsome man who wore too much jewellery', who seems to embody precisely those characteristics which the soldier associates with the 'East': softness and luxury. Nevertheless, Elagabalus is an 'Oriental' through and through. He 'knew nothing of Roman etiquette or even of Roman daily life' and wears 'the most elaborate vestments' as high priest of Elagabal, causing Duratius to remark, 'There is a limit to what even an Emperor can wear as the dress of everyday without being considered mad; but what the high priest should wear had been decreed by the god long ago.'[68]

The soldier grows used to the emperor's outlandish appearance, but many Romans take offence. When Elagabalus first enters the capital and is greeted by the Roman elite, Duratius suddenly realises how scandalous the emperor and his entourage must appear to them:

Elagabalus in his splendid priestly robes looking 'more like an image than a human being', his mother and grandmother 'Syrians bedizened with facepaint such as only whores use in Rome'.[69]

Things only get worse from this point onwards. The Augusta does her utmost to make her imperial grandson fit into Roman society, but the senate does not accept him. 'I tried so hard to make them like us,' Moesa complains, '[...] and after all that they still despise us as Syrians and foreigners.' The emperor reacts angrily: 'They despise us, and we despise them. Henceforth they shall feel my contempt.' He vows to 'show these fusty pedants how their traditions are valued by the soldiers who rule the Empire, and by the Emperor who rules the soldiers'. The sun god Elagabal, kept in the background at first, is now proclaimed the ruling god of Rome. Resentment against Elagabalus grows when one Roman tradition after the other is violated. Ultimately, Moesa and her confident Eutychianus conspire to get rid of Elagabalus, whom they feel has become 'impossible'.[70] The young man is killed and replaced by the more malleable Alexander.

*Family Favourites* gives a favourable portrait of an oft-scorned emperor, seen through the gaze of a loving servant. Rather than describing a monster who gets what he deserves, Duggan interprets Elagabalus as a kind boy whose cultural background and deviant sexual orientation make him unacceptable to the conservative Roman elite. 'My dear lord will never take his rightful place among the gods,' Duratius finishes his account, '[...] But even if demons surround him his beauty and charm will make them his servants.'[71]

### Elagabalus in Duberman's Elagabalus *(1973)*

Martin Bauml Duberman (1930–) was born in New York City as the son of a Jewish garment manufacturer of Ukrainian descent. He studied at Yale and Harvard, earning a PhD in American history, and became Distinguished Professor of History at the City University of New York in 1971. Since he came out of the closet in 1970, Duberman has become an active proponent of the gay cause, taking a public stance against homophobia and making homosexuality a major theme of both his academic and his fictional work, which includes a historical novel and many plays.[72]

Seven of Duberman's plays have been collected in *Male Armor* (1975). Each of these plays is concerned with the construction of masculinity as an 'armour', used by men to protect themselves from their own sexuality and emotions. The last play in the volume is *Elagabalus*, originally performed in a different, but unpublished, version in 1973. Despite its title, the priest-emperor from Emesa does not make an appearance in the piece. Instead, the focus is on Adrian, a young homosexual who lives in contemporary New York with his new boyfriend, Danny. Adrian comes from a rich and ambitious family – an obvious parallel to the maternal family of Elagabalus. His Uncle Paul, who never appears onstage, is making a bid for a high, but unspecified position in Washington. Julia Donner, Paul's mother and the matriarch of the family, wholeheartedly supports her son's ambitions. Adrian, however, constitutes a problem: the young man refuses to adjust his behaviour to conventional social norms and causes scandalous rumours in Washington. He acts out the role of Elagabalus, copying scenes from the emperor's life in word and deed. Thus, we see the absent Elagabalus reflected in Adrian. Likewise, the people around him resemble figures from the imperial court: for instance, his mother and grandmother resemble Julia Soaemias and Julia Maesa respectively, while his boyfriend resembles Hierocles. However, only Adrian consciously models his life on that of his historical counterpart.

At the start of *Elagabalus*, Adrian is turning the knobs of a huge stereo system. According to the author's instructions, the young man is 'dressed in a loose-fitting, white linen shirt – just long enough to suggest a tunic', and wearing 'a large, cone-shaped black onyx ring' on his left hand. A voice from the stereo (Adrian's) declares, 'Elagabalus, you dance too much!', followed by statements that the army, the senate, and the people of Rome will not stand for it. It is the start of a self-made radio play on Elagabalus, which Adrian will keep expanding and revising throughout the piece. He seems obsessed with the third-century emperor, with whom he completely identifies. He worships his onyx ring as Baal, nicknames his boyfriend Hierocles, and often speaks in anachronisms and non-sequiturs. For instance, he remarks to Faustina, his Puerto Rican housekeeper, 'I do wish you spoke Aramaic. I'm so bad at Latin, my tutors despair.' To his mother, he says, 'Our line goes back to the Divine Severus.' And when Dominick, his grandmother's chauffeur, enters his apartment, Adrian enquires, 'Did you come by way of Tyre or northward from the Aegean? What news from the capital?'[73] He even takes up the plan to re-enact Elagabalus's marriages to Hierocles and Annia Faustina, intending to wed both Danny and Faustina in a double marriage, much to his grandmother's and Uncle Paul's dismay.

According to Duberman's instructions in the list of characters, Adrian has a manner of 'simplicity and guilelessness'. Indeed, the young man's lines in the play indicate a positive outlook on life and those around him. He accepts everybody for who they are, treating his stableboy and his Puerto Rican housekeeper with as much respect as he does everybody else. Adrian is impulsive, dynamic and full of energy, often surprising – and, in some cases, shocking – others with his wild, unconventional ideas and weird, unexpected remarks. His grandmother Julia, representing traditional morality, blames him for pressing 'too hard against the boundary of form', and even seems to question his sanity. Adrian laughingly reassures her: 'I do know that this is Nueva York, Gran'mère. *Not* Emesa.' Selena, his laid-back mother, has a better understanding of her son: 'Adrian is not delusional. It's a calculated conceit. The boy wants more than one life. So should we all.' In a later scene, she underlines this sentiment: 'One makes choices. Somewhere along the way. That's why I adore Adrian: his refusal to choose.'[74]

The idea that we are not necessarily stuck to one role in life is a key theme of *Elagabalus*. Similar to the emperor's wish in *Family Favourites* to experience the lives of all his subjects, it is Adrian's professed ambition to 'experience everything. However unpleasant.' 'You have to learn to play against type,' he tells Danny. 'That's how you discover there aren't any types.' In contrast to the other male characters in the play, Adrian refuses to play the traditional masculine role: rather than acting like a reserved, emotionless macho man, he follows his impulses and openly shows his affection for others. Danny, who is very much stuck in his 'male armour', reacts negatively towards his boyfriend's gestures of affection, wriggling free from a hug and responding to a spontaneous declaration of love with a matter-of-fact 'Pour the fuckin' coffee.'[75]

Significantly, Adrian does not fit the stereotype of the effeminate homosexual, either. In the character's description, Duberman stresses that the young man is 'strikingly beautiful, but has no trace in voice or gesture of what is called "effeminacy"'.[76] Adrian is meant to be a new sort of man, who defies traditional gender categories. That does not mean, however, that he is an ideal type who cannot be criticised. As the author expounds in the introduction to *Male Armor*,

I'm certain that many readers will find Adrian merely tiresome, in no way more appealing than the more obviously armoured men in the other plays. He may seem to choose and alternate his personae with greater freedom and from a far wider repertory than most people imagine is available to them, but his style, many may feel, is unfettered only in comparison with those around him. And perhaps not even then; for Adrian is driven by his own imperatives, ones derived from the newest social dicta about the necessity for androgyny, and profoundly reliant for their implementation on the privileges available to those with leisure and wealth.[77]

Nevertheless, Duberman points out, 'Adrian is playful and daring', and, unlike the other men in *Elagabalus*, 'he *is* moving toward an *un-armoured* territory, moving out so far that finally he's left with no protection against the traditional weaponry brought to bear against him.'[78] The main antagonists of the young man are Julia Donner and the invisible Uncle Paul, both of whom are presented in an unflattering light by the author. Julia, who is constantly criticising her grandson for his unconventional behaviour and regards her daughter's wild sex life with acid disapproval, turns out to be a hypocrite: while constantly striving to keep up the family's good name in public, she secretly engages in S&M with her chauffeur. As for Uncle Paul, he is so focused on his (unspecified) political goals that he has become a slave to his own ambitions. For the sake of his career, he has to act as the perfect traditional role model. Moreover, he perceives any unconventional behaviour by a family member as a threat which could damage his political chances, and which therefore needs to be suppressed. Uncle Paul never appears on stage because he is hardly a person at all; his every act is dictated by conventional morality. In the words of Adrian, 'Uncle Paul? Mon chère – il n'existe pas. He is too important to exist.'[79]

Julia Donner and Uncle Paul are ruthless in their ambitions, banishing Adrian's mother Selena to the countryside and going so far as to consider castrating the young man. When Uncle Paul decides against the idea, it is 'entirely on pragmatic grounds: Adrian would promptly decide he was Cleopatra and the wedding ceremonies would be shifted to a barge in the Hudson.' Ultimately, the young man succumbs to his family's pressure: he calls everybody together under the pretence that he will call off his double marriage to Danny and Faustina. When all are gathered in his apartment, Adrian and Danny, both wearing elaborate priestly costumes, perform a ceremony in honour of Baal. Adrian's self-made radio play is playing in the background, describing how the Romans slaughtered the

Carthaginians. The others gather around the young man, speaking to him in turn. Dr Anscombe, the family physician, tells him that 'the family will not stand for it'. Julia Donner, her chauffeur Dominick, and Danny repeat the phrase, speaking for the senate, the army and the people respectively. Each line is echoed by Adrian's voice on the stereo. At a piercing volume, it concludes, 'ELAGABALUS: YOU DANCE TOO MUCH!' Suddenly, Adrian plunges a knife into his groin, killing himself. His grandmother reacts with relief to this unexpected suicide: 'Every expert in the land will agree: self-mutilation is the one sure sign of madness.'[80] Only Faustina seems genuinely grief-stricken, mourning Adrian's death.

In Duberman's interpretation, both Elagabalus and Adrian are tragic victims of their conservative surroundings, in which there is no room for those who deviate from conventional standards. Considering the emperor's reputation as a controversial eccentric, full of weird but original ideas, it is not hard to see why Adrian has chosen him as a role model. The way in which Elagabalus is imagined in the play is primarily based on the *Historia Augusta*. Like the *Vita Heliogabali*, *Elagabalus* places much emphasis on the emperor's eccentricities, his homosexual preferences and his refusal to conform to traditional masculine standards (with the significant difference that, contrary to the ruler in the *Vita Heliogabali*, Adrian is *not* supposed to be effeminate). Moreover, both pieces somewhat downplay the importance of Elagabalus's 'Oriental' background. Adrian makes some references to the Syrian roots of his alter ego – for instance, by remarking, 'in Syria we prefer indirection in all matters' – but Duberman seems not overtly interested in portraying the emperor as a stereotypical 'Oriental'.[81] Only the elaborate costumes that Adrian and Danny wear in the final scene recall the notion of typical 'Oriental' splendour, as found in Herodian.

More important is the association of Adrian with Carthage, Rome's ancient enemy. Adrian explains to Danny how the Carthaginians were slandered by the Romans, who 'spread the lie that they sacrificed live babies', adding, 'Only Rome could invent such a story. Rome demanded three hundred children from Carthage as hostages – and then burnt the city to the ground anyway.' To him, Rome symbolises the enemy, the forces of convention and tradition. 'We should hire a scribe for tonight, Danny,' he declares before the final family gathering. 'Otherwise, our history, too, will be written by Rome. Another chapter in Carthaginian treachery. More babies burnt for Baal.'[82]

In the end, of course, this is exactly what happens: Adrian kills himself and his family is able to write him off as insane, thus preserving the precious family name. Nevertheless, as Duberman writes in his introduction, there is a positive element to Adrian's suicide. It is 'a choice *he* makes – in defiance, and in the conviction that Carthages will everywhere continue to rise against Rome.'[83]

## *Conclusion*

What is immediately striking about the images of Elagabalus in the works of Artaud, Duggan and Duberman is that all three authors present the emperor as a positive figure, deliberately deviating from the social *mores* of the Romans. Artaud's protagonist is an anarchist (in the author's idiosyncratic use of the term), martyring himself to stir up dormant energies in a stagnant society. The emperors in Duggan's and Duberman's works do not seek to stir up controversy per se, but likewise meet a violent end because they refuse to conform to the traditions and morals of the Roman establishment. The authors count this trait a point in the emperor's favour: Elagabalus's refusal to be put in a moral straightjacket establishes him as an independent individual who makes his own choices. He is not a Decadent figure, signifying decay – although Artaud's version preserves some Decadent elements – but rather an inspiring character, breaking free from the restraining bonds of society.

Of the three authors, only Artaud preserves the concept of Elagabalus as a cruel tyrant. However, the cruelty of the crowned anarchist serves a higher purpose and is therefore not objectionable. Duggan and Duberman present him as a kind, caring person who does not deserve his cruel fate, completely shattering the tyrant image. Nor do any of the authors hold the emperor's Syrian background against him, as some ancient sources do. For Artaud, the 'East' was a dynamic place which could vitalise the stagnant 'West', as Héliogabale attempts in *L'Anarchiste couronné*. Duggan devotes much attention to the clash between 'East' and 'West' in *Family Favourites*, but – despite some bemused remarks by his narrator, the Gallic Duratius – does not present one as better than the other. His Elagabalus perishes because the two cultures cannot understand and accept each other's different habits and morals. In Duberman's play *Elagabalus*, the emperor's Syrian background does not play a major role. Instead, Carthage is set up as the counterpart and opposition to Rome. Adrian, Elagabalus's modern representative, sympathises with the African city.

None of the authors present the homosexuality of the priest-emperor as a negative characteristic. For Artaud, the young man's effeminacy and affairs with men are just another means by which he deliberately goes against Roman morals. Duggan's narrator, Duratius, constantly stresses that he does not share the emperor's taste for men, but does not condemn it, advocating a tolerant attitude. Duberman goes even further, setting the young ruler up as an exemplary figure who has dared to shed his 'male armour'. Significantly, both Duggan and Duberman emphasise that Elagabalus is not effeminate, thereby challenging traditional gay stereotypes and proposing a more broadminded perspective.

In contrast to Couperus and George, Artaud, Duggan and Duberman do not let us experience things from the emperor's point of view. Artaud's Héliogabale hardly has any personality at all: he is a vehicle for the author's ideas concerning anarchy, cruelty and theatre, and his feelings are sparsely and distantly described. Duggan's Elagabalus is focused exclusively through Duratius, who reminisces about him years later. Nevertheless, the emperor in *Family Favourites* is a rounded character who comes fully alive to the reader. As for Adrian in *Elagabalus*, here we have the interesting complication that the young man is not actually Elagabalus, but merely aspires to be him; the emperor figures in the play only to the extent that he is interpreted and re-enacted by the protagonist.

The resulting images of Elagabalus in *L'Anarchiste couronné*, *Family Favourites* and *Elagabalus* are quite distinct from each other, but all three works reject the ancient sources' hostile approach to the emperor's Syrian background, homosexual preferences and alleged effeminacy. Rather than condemning the young man's failure to meet the moral standards and expectations of the Roman establishment, they call these standards and expectations into question. Whether as a crowned anarchist, a gay 'Oriental' or a new, 'unarmoured' type of man, Elagabalus is admired for his courage to make different choices – to rebel against a society which refuses to accept him.

# EPILOGUE

The figure of Elagabalus has long blurred fact with fiction. The many layers of images around the historical core, which already started to form in antiquity, have obscured our vision of the third-century emperor. Where does historical reality end and imagination begin? And how does one relate to the other?

As has been discussed in the first part of this book, the single most important aspect of Elagabalus's reign was the implementation of a distinctly foreign god at the head of the Roman pantheon. Although this was an unprecedented move which played a substantial part in the emperor's downfall, the emphasis on a personal god was in itself nothing new and would be a recurring element in the representation of third-century emperors. In any field other than religion, moreover, the reign of Elagabalus was characterised by continuity rather than change. The empire was still in the age of relative peace and stability which would start to crumble under Severus Alexander with the first attacks of the Persians. We should be careful, therefore, not to exaggerate the exceptional status of the years 218–22 within the larger scope of Roman imperial history.

Elagabalus's self-representation contains both traditional and innovative elements. The imperial administration sent out traditional messages and emphasised dynastic continuity, but also presented Elagabalus as the 'invincible priest-emperor' of Elagabal. After the young ruler's violent death and damnatio memoriae, these positive images were replaced with very negative representations in ancient literature. In the works of Cassius Dio and Herodian, as well as in the *Vita Heliogabali*, the traditional elements of Elagabalus's reign are largely ignored in favour of the strange and exceptional. The latter category not only includes the emperor's religious reforms and role as high priest of Elagabal, but first and foremost showcases the many stories about

215

his corruption, effeminacy and perverted, luxurious lifestyle. Such stories are part of a long tradition of 'character assassination' in ancient historiography and biography. They represent topoi which can also be found in the accounts of many other 'bad' rulers and should, for the most part, not be taken too seriously.

Nevertheless, the reputation of Elagabalus as an exceptional emperor has to a large extent been determined by these scandalous stories. In early-modern times, scholars and artists were much more concerned with the young ruler's alleged vices and excesses than with his priesthood of Elagabal. These vices and excesses continue to play an important role in artistic and literary works on Elagabalus to the present day. They can even be found in some modern historical studies, like Turcan's monograph.

Only in the nineteenth century did other aspects of the young ruler's reign come into focus. Historians and literary authors became interested in the emperor as an 'Oriental', whose rise to power and introduction of the Elagabal cult in Rome instigated a culture clash between 'East' and 'West'. While this interpretation has the merit that it acknowledges the emperor's religious reforms as an important and remarkable aspect of his reign, it tends to reduce Elagabalus to an icon of the 'East'; someone who embodies traits which the author deems typically 'Oriental' and has no affinity whatsoever with Roman culture and traditions. Moreover, many of these typically 'Oriental' traits concern the same vices and excesses that previous authors already attributed to the emperor.

It is hardly surprising that the three major ancient accounts of Elagabalus's reign have had such a determining influence on later scholarly and literary images of the young ruler. More difficult to answer is the question of how these later traditions of scholarship and literature have influenced each other. There is little to indicate that scholarly works on Elagabalus have had much impact on artistic interpretations, whether in early-modern or more recent times. Gibbon's *Decline and Fall*, widely read and full of evocative descriptions, may well have inspired many artists and authors, but there are not enough data to verify this. Considering the frequent use of names, anecdotes and other details from the ancient literary sources, it seems that most novelists, poets and playwrights found their inspiration chiefly in Cassius Dio, Herodian and the *Historia Augusta* themselves – at least until the twentieth century, when the first monographs on the priest-emperor became available. In addition, Decadent and modern authors were inspired by previous artistic works on Elagabalus, as can be deduced from explicit and implicit references. Modern plays and novels sometimes contain a short bibliography of historical studies, indicating that the author was probably familiar with them. However, if these studies played a determining role in the piece's conception, this seldom, if ever, becomes evident. We should be cautious in drawing any conclusions; but all in all, one cannot escape the impression that the most significant contribution of historiography to Elagabalus's *Nachleben* in art and literature has been to point artists and authors in the right direction, to make them aware of the priest-emperor's existence and introduce them to the ancient accounts documenting his reign.

Ironically, the reverse is easier to demonstrate: literary images of Elagabalus have directly and significantly influenced scholarly reconstructions of the emperor. I am referring to Artaud's *L'Anarchiste couronné*, which has repeatedly been mistaken for a scholarly work. Not only has this curious essay been used as a serious academic study in Villeneuve's *Le César fou*, it was also a major source of inspiration for Gualerzi's *Né uomo, né donna*. In this study, the author complains that other historians had not picked up Artaud's observations on the androgynous nature of the Elagabal cult, and proceeds to do so himself. Both Villeneuve and Gualerzi regard the striving for androgyny as a central aspect of Elagabalus's religious convictions – a notion that cannot be found in the ancient literary sources, nor in previous historical studies on the emperor, but *is* present in Artaud's essay, as well as in Decadent literature. Once again, fact blurs with fiction.

Ultimately, Elagabalus remains an elusive figure, an often inextricable tangle of history and imagination. From antiquity onwards, authors and artists have constantly remodelled the young ruler, using him as a vehicle to present their notions on gender, 'Oriental' people, monotheism, tyranny, androgyny, degeneration, anarchy and a whole range of other issues. Most remarkable in this respect is the development of Elagabalus's image from a depraved tyrant in ancient historiography to a positive, sometimes even exemplary figure in several modern artistic works. The imperial rebel we encounter in plays and novels from the last decades, celebrating his homosexuality and breaking free from traditional role models, seems a far cry from the debauched slave of his own lusts painted by the *Vita Heliogabali*. Yet both images consist of many of the same elements: a sexual preference for men, a predilection to dress and act as a woman, a dynamic sex life with many different partners. It is our *appreciation* of these things that has changed. To many modern readers, self-realisation and sexual liberty are more important than conforming to narrow moral conventions. This shift in values has brought about a change in meaning, turning an ancient exemplum malum into a modern role model. Even Elagabalus, it appears, can be a hero.

# THE NACHLEBEN OF ELAGABALUS IN ART AND LITERATURE: AN OVERVIEW

The following list consists of novels, plays, paintings and other literary and artistic pieces which feature or reference the emperor Elagabalus. Items marked with an asterisk devote considerable attention to Elagabalus and/ or the persons and anecdotes connected to him.

Some of the works on this list are hard to find. Whenever I thought this was useful and the information was available to me, I have included a reference to the (publicly accessible) location of the work in question. I do not make any claims with regard to the completeness of this list.

After the main list, I have attached a second overview of Elagabalus's *Nachleben*. This list categorises the same works by artistic form, referenced by date to the main list.

1407–8: Leonardo Bruni, *Oratio Heliogabali ad meretrices* (oration)*; Bibliothèque Nationale de France, no RES-J-2397

1529: Desiderius Erasmus, *Colloquia, Senatulus* (dialogue)*

1588: Jodocus van Winghe, *Heliogabal und die Weisen* (illustration)*

1605: Thomas Artus, *L'Isle des Hermaphrodites nouvellement descouverte* (pamphlet)

1666: Anonymous, woodcarving in the church of S. Pietro Martire on the island of Murano (originally in the Scuola di S. Giovanni Battista)

1667: Aurelio Aureli and Francesco Cavalli, *Eliogabalo* (opera)*

1667: Jean Le Pautre, *La Mort d'Héliogabale* (illustration)*; Bibliothèque Nationale de France, no ED-42(D)-FOL

1720: Gysbert Tysens, *Bassianus Varius Heliogabalus, of de uitterste proef der standvastige liefde* (play)*; Koninklijke Bibliotheek at The Hague, no 448 G 136; http://www. let.leidenuniv.nl/Dutch/Ceneton/Heliogabalus.html (accessed 6 October 2006)

1802: Anonymous (Pierre-Jean-Baptiste Chaussard?), *Héliogabale ou esquisse morale de la dissolution romaine sous les empereurs* (epistolary novel)*; Bibliothèque Nationale de France, no J-14970

1835: Théophile Gautier, *Mademoiselle de Maupin* (novel)

1836: Zygmunt Krasiński, *Irydjon* (play)*

1836: Edgar Allen Poe, 'Four beasts in one: the homo-camelopard' (short story)

1837: Touissant Cabuchet, *Héliogabale* (play)*; Bibliothèque Nationale de France, no YF-8479

1839: Edgar Allen Poe, 'William Wilson' (short story)

1845: Flaubert, *La Première Éducation sentimentale* (novel)

1849: Edgar Allen Poe, 'Mellonta Tauta' (short story)

ca. 1850: Anonymous, *Heliogabulus's Magic Tablets: A neverfailing key to the future fortunes of the enquirers*; University of Oxford, Bodleian Library, BOD Bookstack, Harding A 137 (5)

1855: N.-A.-François Puaux, *Dialogue des morts* (dialogue)*; Bibliothèque Nationale de France, no D2-10324

1866: Simeon Solomon, *Heliogabalus, High Priest of the Sun* (painting)*; in private possession(?)

1868: Théophile Gautier, 'Charles Baudelaire' (introduction to Charles Baudelaire's *Les Fleurs du mal*)

1873: Albert Castelnau, 'Alexandrie' (poem)*; Bibliothèque Nationale de France, no YE-17288

1876: Jean Richepin, 'Un empereur' (short story)*; Bibliothèque Nationale de France, no 8-Y2-638

1877: Ouida, *Ariadne, the Story of a Dream* (novel)

1879: William Gilbert and Arthur Sullivan, *The Pirates of Penzance, or The Slave of Duty* (play)

1882: Anonymous, *Le Temple de Phoebé ou les martyrs sous Julien l'Apostat* (novel); Bibliothèque Nationale de France, no 8-Y2-5391

1884: Joris-Karl Huysmans, *À Rebours* (novel)

1885: Auguste-Constant Bertrand, *L'Héliogabale et la Messaline du XIXe siècle, à Paris* (novel); Bibliothèque Nationale de France, no 8-Y2-8528

1887 Catulle Mendès, 'L'empereur et les papillons' (short story)*; Bibliothèque Nationale de France, no. 8-Y2-9999

1888: Lawrence Alma-Tadema, *The Roses of Heliogabalus* (painting)*; in private possession

1888: Jean Lombard, *L'Agonie* (novel)*

1889: Louis Jourdan, *La Dernière nuit d'Héliogabale* (novel)*; Bibliothèque Nationale de France, no 8-Y2-43006

1890: Oscar Wilde, *The Picture of Dorian Gray* (novel)

1891: Leo Reiffenstein, *Ein Gastmahl des Heliogabal* (painting)*

1892: Stefan George, *Algabal* (lyric cycle)*

1894: Louis Couperus, 'Brief uit Rome' (letter)*

1895: Georges Brandimbourg, 'Héliogabe' (short story)*; Bibliothèque Nationale de France, no M-945

1898: Henri Corbel, 'La danse au temple du Soleil' (poem)*; Bibliothèque Nationale de France, no 8-YE PIECE-5670

1898: Jean Richepin, 'Elagabal' (poem)*

ca. 1900: Anonymous, *Héliogabale XIX ou biographie du dixneuvième siècle de la France: dediée à la grande nation en signe de sympathie par un Allemand* (book with cartoons)*; Bibliothèque Nationale de France, no FOL-LA37-13

1900: Luis d'Herdy (pseud.), *La Destinée* (novel)*; Bibliothèque Nationale de France, no 8-Y2-52468

1901: Auguste Leroux, illustrations for the new edition of Lombard's *L'Agonie*

1902: Jean Lorrain, *Les Noronsoff: Coins de Byzance* (novel)

1902: Auguste Villeroy, *Héliogabale, drame en vers, en cinq actes* (play)*; Bibliothèque Nationale de France, no 8-Y-2350

1904: Jan de Redni, *Lentulus et Ascyltos. Roman de mœurs antiques* (novel)*; Bibliothèque Nationale de France, no 8-Y2-54387

1904: Arthur Westcott, *The Sun God* (novel)*

1905: Jacques d'Adelswärd-Fersen, *Messes noires. Lord Lyllian* (novel)

1905: Pol Loewengard, 'La prière d'Héliogabale' (poem)*; Bibliothèque Nationale de France, no. 8-YE-6470

1905–6: Louis Couperus, *De berg van licht* (novel)*

1906: Gustav-Adolf Mossa, *Lui* (painting)*; Musée des Beaux Arts Jules Cheret, Nice

1909: Jacques Nayral, 'Elagabal' (poem)*; Bibliothèque Nationale de France, no 8-YE-7456

1910: André Calmettes, *Héliogabale* (movie)*

1910: Henry Mirande, *Élagabal* (novel)*; Bibliothèque Nationale de France, no 8-Y2-58053

1910: Émile Sicard and Déodat de Séverac, *Héliogabale: Tragédie lyrique en 3 actes* (musical piece)*; Bibliothèque Nationale de France, no 8-RF-81187

1911: Louis Feuillade, *L'Orgie romaine* (movie)*; Dutch Film Museum at Amsterdam, tape Vv25, no 1 (0:00:00–0:09:35)

1914: Pierre Benoit, 'Héliogabale' (poem)*; Bibliothèque Nationale de France, no 8-Y2-64405 (19)

1920: Henry Louis Mencken and George Jean Nathan, *Heliogabalus, a Buffoonery in Three Acts* (play)*

1929: Paul Moinet, 'La Vie infâme d'Héliogabale' (short story)*; Bibliothèque Nationale de France, no B.M. *E-2011

1934: Antonin Artaud, *Héliogabale ou l'anarchiste couronné* (essay)*

1935: Maurice Duplay and Pierre Bonardi, *Héliogabale: Orgies romaines* (novel)*; Bibliothèque Nationale de France, no 8-Y2-83837

1958: Yukio Mishima, *Confessions of a Mask* (novel)

1960: Alfred Duggan, *Family Favourites* (novel)*

1966: Kyle Onstott and Lance Horner, *Child of the Sun* (novel)*

1969: Alberto Arbasino, *Super-Eliogabalo* (anti-novel)*

1970: Franco Brocani, *Necropolis* (movie)*

1971: Pierre Moinot, *Héliogabale* (play)*; Bibliothèque Nationale de France, no 16-Y-224 (105)

1972: Hans Werner Henze, *Heliogabalus Imperator* (musical piece)*

1973: Martin Duberman, *Elagabalus* (play)*

1973: Kurt Vonnegut, *Breakfast of Champions* (novel)

1974: Anselm Kiefer, *Heliogabal* (painting)*; Saint Louis Art Museum

1976–77: Frank Manley, 'Heliogabalus' (poem)*

1977: Emilio Locurcio, *L'Eliogabalo* (record)*

1981: Sylvano Bussotti, *Phaidra-Elagabalus* (ballet)*

1983: Anselm Kiefer, *Heliogabal* (painting)*

1984: Fulvio Caldini, *Aria di Eliogabalo* (musical piece)*

1989: Hélène Delprat, *Elagabal* (illustration)*; Bibliothèque Nationale de France, no DH-1 (DELPRAT, Hélène) -FT7

1989: Hélène Delprat, *Héliogabale* (series of illustrations)*; Bibliothèque Nationale de France, no DC-2076-FOL

1990: Devil Doll, *Eliogabalus* (musical album)*

1991–92: Neil Gaiman, *Being an Account of the Life and Death of the Emperor Heliogabolus* (comic)*; http://www.holycow.com/dreaming/stories/being-an-account-of-the-life-and-death-of-the-emperor-heliogabolous/ (accessed 13 July 2011)

1999: Durs Grünbein, 'Bericht von der Ermordung des Heliogabal durch seine Leibgarde' (poem)*

2001: Momus, 'Heliogabalus' (track on the musical album *Folktronic*)*

2001: Alain Pastor, *Héliogabale* (play)*

2002: Sky Gilbert, *Heliogabalus, a Love Story* (play)*

2002– 7: Gilles Chaillet, *La Dernière prophétie* (comic series)*

2003: Thomas Jonigk and Peter Vermeersch, *Heliogabal* (opera)*

2004: Jeremy Reed, *Boy Caesar* (novel)*

2005: Matt Hughes, *Heliogabalus' Remorse* (painting)*; http://www.matthughesart.com/caesar.htm (accessed 27 September 2007)

2006: Fanny and Alexander, *Heliogabalus* (play)*

2006: Emma Locatelli, *Le Scandaleux Héliogabale, empereur, prêtre et pornocrate* (novel)*

2007: John Zorn, *Six Litanies for Heliogabalus* (musical album)*

2007: Martin Bladh, *Heliogabalus* (series of paintings)*

2008: Shawn Ferreyra, *Elagabalus, Emperor of Rome* (play)*

2008: Chelsea Quinn Yarbro, *Roman Dusk* (novel)

2010: Rorcal, *Heliogabalus* (musical album)*

THE NACHLEBEN OF ELAGABALUS CATEGORISED BY ARTISTIC FORMS

**Images**
1588*
1666
1667*
1866*
1888*
1891*
1900*
1901*
1906*
1974*
1983*
1989*
1989*
2005*
2007*

**Operas**
1667*
2003*

**Other musical pieces**
1910*
1972*
1977*
1981*
1984*
1990*
2001*
2007*
2010*

**Plays**
1720*
1836*
1837*
1879
1902*
1920*

1971*
1973*
2001*
2002*
2006*
2008*

**Novels**
1802*
1835
1845
1877
1882
1884
1885
1888*
1889*
1890
1900*
1902
1904*
1904*
1905
1905–6*
1910*
1935*
1958
1960*
1966*
1969*
1973
2004*
2006*
2008

**Short stories**
1836
1839
1849

1876*
1887*
1895*
1929*

**Poems**
1873*
1892*
1898*
1898*
1905*
1909*
1914*
1976–77*
1999*

**Movies**
1910*
1911*
1970*

**Miscellaneous**
1407–8*
1529*
1605
ca. 1850
1855*
1868
1894*
1934*
1991–92*
2002–7*

# SEVERAN FAMILY TREE

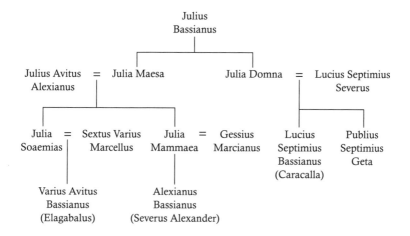

Julius
Bassianus

Julius Avitus  =  Julia Maesa     Julia Domna  =  Lucius Septimius
Alexianus                                        Severus

Julia  =  Sextus Varius    Julia  =  Gessius     Lucius      Publius
Soaemias     Marcellus    Mammaea   Marcianus   Septimius   Septimius
                                                  Bassianus     Geta
                                                  (Caracalla)

Varius Avitus       Alexianus
Bassianus           Bassianus
(Elagabalus)   (Severus Alexander)

SEVERAN FAMILY TREE

# NOTES

For full details of works cited, and for a list of abbreviations used, see Select bibliography.

## INTRODUCTION

1  No ancient text calls the emperor Elagabalus. Heliogabalus (a hybrid contraction of Helios, the Greek sun god, and the Latinised name for Elagabal) is first used by the fourth-century author Aurelius Victor. In this work, I will refer to the emperor as Elagabalus, which seems the most commonly used name nowadays in works in English.
2  E. Gibbon, *Decline and Fall*, vol. I, p. 168.
3  G.H. Halsberghe, *The Cult of Sol Invictus*, pp. 80, 103–4.
4  J.S. Hay, *The Amazing Emperor*, pp. vi–vii; G.R. Thompson, *Elagabalus*, pp. 160–61.
5  M. Frey, *Untersuchungen*, pp. 43–44.
6  A new monograph on Elagabalus, entitled *The Emperor Elagabalus: Fact or fiction?* has been published in 2010 by Leonardo de Arrizabalaga y Prado. Unfortunately it appeared too late to be discussed in this study. My review of Prado's book is available on www.sehepunkte.de.
7  O.J. Hekster, *Commodus*.
8  J. Elsner and J. Masters (eds), *Reflections of Nero*.
9  L. de Blois, 'Emperor and empire', pp. 3405–15.
10 G. Alföldy, 'Herodian's person', pp. 241–42, 259–61, 263–65.
11 De Blois, 'Emperor and empire', pp. 3415–31; H. Sidebottom, 'Herodian's historical methods and understanding of history'.
12 A. Scheithauer, 'Die Regierungszeit des Kaisers Elagabal', p. 356.
13 R. Syme, *Ammianus and the Historia Augusta*, pp. 211, 219.
14 R. Syme, *Historia Augusta Papers*, p. 43.

CHAPTER 1

1   Herodian, *Ab excessu divi Marci* V, 3/1. Unless specified otherwise, all the translations from ancient texts are based on the Loeb editions, sometimes with slight alterations.
2   Herodian V, 3/8.
3   Cassius Dio, *Historia Romana* LXXIX, 31/2.
4   *ILS* 467, 5843: 'divi Antonini filius, divi Severi nepos'.
5   H.-G. Pflaum, *Les Carrières procuratoriennes équestres*, no 290.
6   Cassius Dio LXXX, 2/2–3: 'αὐτοκράτορα καὶ Καίσαρα, τοῦ τε 'Αντωνίνου υἱὸν καὶ τοῦ Σεουήρου ἔγγονον, εὐσεβῆ τε καὶ εὐτυχῆ καὶ Αὔγουστον, καὶ ἀνθύπατον τήν τε ἐξουσίαν τὴν δημαρχικὴν ἔχοντα'.
7   *CIL* VI, 2001, 2009, 2104; *ILS* 466.
8   The name III Gallica has been erased from several inscriptions: *ILS* 2657, 5865, 9198.
9   *BMC* V, Elagabalus, nos 10–15, 105–9; nos 274–76.
10  Cassius Dio LXXX, 6/2–3.
11  Ibid., 4/2; 21/2; *CIL* VI, 866; *ILS* 505, 2420, 9014.
12  *CIL* VI, 31776a, 31776b, 31875; B.P.M. Salway, 'A fragment of Severan history'.
13  Herodian V, 5/6–7.
14  H.R. Baldus, 'Das "Vorstellungsgemälde"', pp. 471–76.
15  *BMC* V, Elagabalus, nos 138–42. Although no coins with Jupiter as 'conservator Augusti' can be dated after 219 with certainty, one coin type showing the Roman god on a throne can certainly be dated to 220 (*BMC* V, Elagabalus, no 178); *BMC* V, Elagabalus, nos 273, 284–88.
16  Eutropius, *Breviarium ab urbe condita* VIII, 22. The equites singulares dedicated an altar to the emperor 'ob reditum domini nostri' on 29 September 219 (*ILS* 2188). This would suggest that Eutropius is wrong, but Alexandrian coins indicate that Elagabalus married Julia Paula before 29 August. Presumably the marriage took place in Rome.
17  Herodian V, 6/1. As Joseph Vogt has pointed out, Julia Paula already appears as empress on Alexandrian coins from the second year of Elagabalus's reign. Since Alexandrian years started on 29 August, Elagabalus and Julia Paula must have married before 29 August 219: J. Vogt, *Die alexandrinischen Münzen*, p. 177.
18  *BMC* V, Elagabalus, nos 151–53, 218–22A; nos 126–27.
19  *ILS* 470, 476; *AE* 1956, no 144.
20  *RIC* IV.II, Elagabalus, nos 400–1.
21  M. Grant, *The Severans*, p. 4. Grant's comment concerns the Severan period in general.
22  *CIL* VI, 866; XIV, 2809.
23  Cassius Dio LXXX, 4/2; 21/2.

24 For a detailed survey of the members of the senate between 218 and 222, see Thompson, *Elagabalus*, pp. 220–25b.

25 P.M.M. Leunissen, *Konsuln und Konsulare*, p. 226; Cassius Dio LXXIX, 22/4–5; K.H. Dietz, *Sentatus contra principem*, pp. 249–51.

26 Herodian V, 7/6.

27 *CIL* XIV 3553.

28 Pflaum, *Les Carrières procuratoriennes équestres*, nos 257, 297. It is probable, but not certain that these appointments should be dated in the reign of Elagabalus.

29 Aurelius Victor, *Historiae abbreviatae* 24/6; *Vita Ant. Heliog.* 16/4.

30 T. Honoré, *Ulpian, Pioneer of Human Rights* (2nd edition, Oxford, 2002) pp. 26–29.

31 Leunissen, *Konsuln und Konsulare*, p. 356; *ILS* 2188, 2411; *AE* 1965, no 49.

32 Leunissen, *Konsuln und Konsulare*, pp. 366, 368; *ILS* 466; *AE* 1917/18, no 44.

33 R. Duncan-Jones, *Money and Government*, pp. 217, 215 (n. 11), 227.

34 *HA, Vita Ant. Heliog.* 17/8–9; *LTUR* V s.v. 'Vicus Sulpicius' (C. Lega) pp. 192–94; *LTUR* I s.v. 'Amphiteatrum' (R. Rea), pp. 30–35. A complete list of Elagabalus's alleged building activities is given in H.W. Benario, 'Rome of the Severi', *Latomus* 17 (1958) pp. 712–22, at pp. 719–20. For a more recent overview, check the index to *LTUR*.

35 *CIL* II, 4766–4769; III, 3713; VII, 585, 1045; VIII, 10,124, 10,127, 10, 160, 10,267, 10,295, 10,297, 10,304, 10,308, 10,347, 22,438, 22,482, 22, 504, 22,543; XIII, 9117, 9138.

36 Duncan-Jones, *Money and Government*, pp. 82 (Fig. 5.10), 249 (table A.1).

37 Herodian V, 6/6; *LTUR* V s.v. 'Circus Varianus' (C. Paterna), pp. 237–38. The *Historia Augusta* mentions Elagabalus making preparations for a chariot-race at the Gardens of Spes Vetus (*HA, Vita Ant. Heliog.* 13/5, 14/5).

38 J.H. Oliver, 'On the edict of Severus Alexander (P. Fayum 20)', *The American Journal of Philology* 99 (1978) pp. 474–85, at p. 478. The cities still had to pay the levies they were due for Elagabalus's ascension and Alexander's adoption as Caesar.

39 Zosimus I, 11/1: 'μάγοις τε καὶ ἀγύρταις' (my translation). The *Historia Augusta* mentions that the emperor was surrounded by 'magi' (*Vita Ant. Heliog.* 8/2).

40 Frey, *Untersuchungen*, p. 80. See for instance Cassius Dio LXXIX, 16/3; LXXX, 8/1; *CIL* XVI, 139–41.

41 *BMC* V, Elagabalus, nos 225–28, 332, 359–360, 364§; nos 230–33, 333–34; nos 209–13, 330, 350, 368.

42 Ibid., nos 197–200.

43 *CIL* VI, 708, 2269; *CIL* VI, 2129, 2130, 2270.

44 *BMC* V, Elagabalus, nos 93*, 408, 424–26, 430, 431.

45 Herodian V, 5/8; *LTUR* III, s.v. 'Elagabalus, templum: Heliogabalium' (F. Coarelli), pp. 10–11.

46 H. Broise and Y. Thébert, 'Élagabal et le complexe religieux de la Vigna Barberini'; Y. Thébert et al., 'Il santuario di *Elagabalus*: un giardino sacro'. Recent Catalan excavations on the Palatine have added to our knowledge of the Elagabal temple: R. Mar, *El Palati*, pp. 208–17.

47 Cassiodorus, *Chronica* (ed. Mommsen 1961) p. 145: 221. 'Gratus et Seleucus conss. Heliogabalum templum Romae aedificatur'; Hieronymus, *Chronica* (ed. Helm 1913), p. 214.

48 Chausson, '*Vel Iovi vel Soli*', pp. 705–11. Chausson argues that 'aedes Orci', presumably the location of the Palatine temple (*HA, Vita Ant. Heliog.* 1/6) should be read as 'aedes Beli' and concerns the second, suburban temple. An alternative location for this sanctuary would be near the imperial dwelling 'Ad Spem Veterem': *LTUR* III, s.v. 'Elagabalus, neos' (F. Coarelli), p. 10.

49 *CIL* VI, 50 = *IGUR* 117; *CIL* VI, 51 = *IGUR* 118; Chausson, '*Vel Iovi vel Soli*', pp. 705–11.

50 A. Scheithauer, *Kaiserliche Bautätigkeit in Rom*, p. 194 (n. 70); *BMC* III, Trajan, no 863; *LTUR* III, p. 384 (Fig. 9).

51 Broise and Thébert, 'Élagabal et le complexe religieux', p. 746. Previous authors argued for an already existing temple: F. Villedieu, 'Constructions impériales', pp. 731–35; J.-P. Morel, 'Stratigraphie et histoire sur le Palatin', pp. 190–206.

52 Frey, *Untersuchungen*, p. 89.

53 *RIC* IV.II, Elagabalus, nos 46–53.

54 Cassius Dio LXXX, 11/2: 'πολλάκις'.

55 Herodian V, 5/8–10.

56 Ibid., 6/6–8.

57 Lucian, *De Dea Syria*, p. 58.

58 *RIC* IV.II, Elagabalus, nos 225–27; no 228; no 231.

59 Vogt, *Die alexandrinischen Münzen*, vol. I, p. 176.

60 Frey, *Untersuchungen*, pp. 89–90. Imperial portraits from 221 CE show the emperor with long sideburns (*BMC* V, Elagabalus, Pl. 90/9–12) or even with a full beard (Pl. 90/13; 90/15; 97/4). The bronze medallion is depicted in F. Gnecchi, *I medaglioni romani*, vol. II, Pl. 97/2.

61 Cassius Dio LXXX, 9/3.

62 Herodian V, 6/3–5; Cassius Dio LXXX, 12/1–2¹.

63 *SEG* IV, 164; *AE* 1974, no 371 adn.; H. Seyrig, 'Le culte du soleil', p. 370; Frey, *Untersuchungen*, pp. 50–51.

64 Herodian V, 6/5.

65 Halsberghe, *The Cult of Sol Invictus*, pp. 89–91.

66 F. Studniczka, 'Ein Pfeilercapitell', Pl. XII.

67 Frey, *Untersuchungen*, pp. 50–54.

68 Ibid., pp. 91–93.

69 M. Pietrzykowski, 'Die Religionspolitik', p. 1817.

70 *BMC* V, Elagabalus, no 176‡; nos 39–43; nos 44–60.

71 *HA, Vita Ant. Heliog.* 3/4–5.

72 Ibid., 7/4; 6/7.

73 *BMC* V, Elagabalus, nos 246–50, 440, 446‡; nos 251–55. As has been remarked, both Juno Regina and Venus Caelestis appear on the coins of Julia Soaemias (nos 39–43; nos 44–60), but it is impossible to date these coins exactly.

74 *CIL* VI, 2001 (which records that Alexander joined the 'sodales' Antoniniani in 221); *BMC* V, Elagabalus, no 452 (Alexander as Caesar and 'PONTIFEX'); *CIL* VI, 2105, 2106 (the acta Arvalium of 220 and 221).

75 R. Haensch, 'Pagane Priester des römischen Heeres im 3. Jahrhundert nach Christus', pp. 215–17; *CIL* VI, 30/685; R.O. Fink (ed.), *Roman Military Records on Papyrus*, no 50, col. i, lines 2, 9; col. ii, frag. b, line 2.

76 R.O. Fink, A.S. Hoey and W.F. Snyder, 'The Feriale Duranum', p. 141. The *Vita Severi Alexandri* (1/2) and Aurelius Victor (23/3) erroneously assume that Alexianus had already been adopted as Caesar in 218, a notion which coins and inscriptions clearly disprove.

77 *ILS* 9058: 'imperatoris Caesaris Marci Aurelii Antonini Pii Felicis Augusti filius, divi Antonini Magni Pii nepos'; *ILS* 483, 2009, 4340, 5854.

78 Dušanić, 'Severus Alexander as Elagabalus' associate', p. 490.

79 Ibid., pp. 489–95.

80 *CIL* XVI, 140; *AE* 1964, no 269; *Corpus Iuris Civilis, Codex Iustinianus* IV, 44/1; VIII, 44/6; IX, 1/3.

81 *BMC* V, Elagabalus, nos 266–67, 452.

82 Herodian V, 7/4–5.

83 Honoré, *Ulpian*, p. 27. Paul, too, was restored by Alexander.

84 *BMC* V, Elagabalus, nos 452*, 453; no 456.

85 Cassius Dio LXXX, 19/1a.

86 *CIL* XVI, 140; *AE* 1964, no 269.

87 Fink, Hoey and Snyder, 'The Feriale Duranum', pp. 86 (n. 285), 88–89.

88 Cassius Dio LXXX, 20/1–2.

89 *HA, Vita Ant. Heliog.* 16/5–17/3; 17/7. Only later is it mentioned that Julia Soaemias was killed together with her son (18/2).

90 R. Syme, *Emperors and Biography*, p. 118.

91 *M. Chr.*, no 241, lines 12–13; *P. Lips.* no 9, line 16; *P. Turner*, no 38, col. i, lines 14–15; *GBMC*, Lydia, Sardes, nos 175–79; Bithynia, Nicomedia, nos 57–59.

92 *LTUR* III, s.v. 'Iuppiter Ultor' (F. Coarelli), pp. 160–61, 384 (Fig. 9), 439 (Fig. 108). The theory seems valid, not just because of the similarities of both temples on coins and medallions, but also because the temple of Elagabal obviously had to be either rededicated to another god or

destroyed. Jupiter's epithet, 'the Avenger', may have been directed against the overthrown 'usurper god' Elagabal.

CHAPTER 2

1 A. von Domaszewski, *Abhandlungen zur römischen Religion*, p. 148; *RIC* IV.II, p. 23; Halsberghe, *The Cult of Sol Invictus*, pp. 101–2.

2 F. Millar, *The Roman Near East*, p. 308.

3 Galen, *De simplicium medicamentorum temperamentis ac facultatibus*, IX, 8.

4 H. Seyrig, 'Antiquités syriennes 53 (1$^{re}$ partie)', pp. 227–36, 240–44, nos 3, 6.

5 G.R.D. King, 'Archaeological fieldwork at the citadel of Homs, Syria', p. 45.

6 A. Kropp, 'Earrings, *nefesh* and *opus reticulatum*'.

7 Herodian V, 3/2: 'τὸ γένος Φοίνισσα, ἀπὸ Ἐμέσου καλουμένης οὕτω πόλεως ἐν Φοινίκῃ'.

8 Heliodorus, *Aithiopica* X, 41/4: 'ἀνὴρ Φοῖνιξ Ἐμισηνός' (my translation).

9 Cicero, *Ad familiares* XV, 1/2: 'phylarcho Arabum'; Cassius Dio L 13/7: ''Αραβίων τινῶν βασιλέα'.

10 Flavius Josephus, *Antiquitates Iudaicae* XVIII, 135.

11 Cicero, *Ad familiares* XV, 1/2: 'quem homines opinantur [...] amicumque esse rei publicae nostrae'.

12 *IGL Syr.* 2760 (= *ILS* 8958 = *CIL* III, 14387a): 'rex magnus, philocaesar and philorohmaeus [*sic*]'.

13 *IGL Syr.* 2212.

14 J. Starcky, 'Stèle d'Elahagabal'.

15 Ibid., p. 503. It is worth noting that Arsu was worshipped in Palmyra, but 'LH' GBL was not, as far as we know.

16 *GBMC*, Syria, Emisa, nos 15 (Pl. XXVII, 12), 16 (Pl. XXVII, 13), 17 (Pl. XXVII, 14).

17 Herodian V, 3/5.

18 *AE* 1910, no 141.

19 Herodian V, 3/4.

20 *GBMC*, Syria, Emisa, nos 15 (Pl. XXVII, 12), 16 (Pl. XXVII, 13; without stairs), 17 (Pl. XXVII, 14), 24 (Pl. XXVIII, 2; without stairs); Avienus, *Descriptio orbis terrae* 1083–90.

21 *AE* 1910, nos 133, 141; *AE* 1962, no 229; J.E. Bogaers, 'Sol Elagabalus', p. 153.

22 Incerti auctoris, *Epitome de Caesaribus* 23/1.

23 A.R. Birley, *Septimius Severus*, p. 118.

24 Herodian V, 3/6.

25 Ibid., 5/4.

26 *BMC* V, Elagabalus, nos 441–46 (Pl. 97, 4), 446§, 449 (Pl. 97, 6); R. Krumeich, 'Der Kaiser als syrischer Priester', pp. 110–12.

27 Tertullian, *Apologeticus* 9,1/3.
28 J.L. Lightfoot (ed.), *On the Syrian goddess*, pp. 527–28. The infamous passage in Lucian reads 'ἐς πήρην ἐνθέμενοι χειρὶ κατάγουσιν' (*De Dea Syria* 58).
29 Cassius Dio LXXX, 11/1; 11.
30 See for instance, Thompson, *Elagabalus*, p. 161; Halsberghe, *The Cult of Sol Invictus*, p. 80.
31 Herodian V, 6/4.
32 Julian, *Orationes* IV, 150 C–D. At Palmyra, Azizos was identified with Ares, but could also be associated with a Hermes figure (T. Kaizer, *The Religious Life of Palmyra*, pp. 122–24).
33 *IGL Syr.* 2218.
34 *IGL Syr.* 2089: 'τῇ κυρίᾳ Σημέᾳ'.
35 Lucian, *De Dea Syria* 33.
36 Lightfoot (ed.), *On the Syrian goddess*, pp. 540–47.
37 Cassius Dio LXXIX, 30/2; *AE* 1921, no 64; *AE* 1962, no 229; H.-G. Pflaum, 'La carrière de C. Iulius Avitus Alexianus', pp. 298–314.
38 H. Halfmann, 'Zwei Syrische Verwandte', pp. 221, 224.
39 Ibid., pp. 222–23.
40 Cassius Dio LXXIX, 30/4: 'ὑπό τε γήρως καὶ ὑπ' ἀρρωστίας'.
41 *AE* 1932, no 70: 'inter mulieres equestres'.
42 *ILS* 478 (= *CIL* X, 6569).
43 *ILS* 8687 (= *CIL* XV, 7326).
44 Pflaum, *Les Carrières procuratoriennes équestres*, no 237; Birley, *Septimius Severus*, pp. 304–6.
45 Halfmann, 'Zwei Syrische Verwandte', pp. 226–34. Halfmann's reconstruction is confirmed by: B.E. Thomasson, *Fasti Africani*, pp. 179–80.
46 *Corpus Iuris Civilis, Digesta* I, 9/12 (Ulpianus).
47 Cassius Dio LXXIX, 30/3.
48 Herodian V, 7/4: 'τοῦ δωδεκάτου ἐπιβαίνοντα'. See note 1 at Herodian V, 7/2 for the probable date.
49 *AE* 1962, no 229.
50 Aurelius Victor 23/1; *HA, Vita Ant. Heliog.* 2/3.
51 *IGR* IV, 1287. Caracalla is assumed to have gone through Thyatira in 215, but John Scheid argues that the emperor already arrived in Nicomedia in December 213, rather than 214. See J. Scheid, 'Le protocole arvale de l'année 213 et l'arrivée de Caracalla à Nicomédie'.

CHAPTER 3

1  J. Elsner, *Imperial Rome and Christian Triumph*, p. 53.

2  Herodian V, 4/4.

3  K. Fittschen and P. Zanker, *Katalog der römischen Porträts*, vol. I, no 97. The four specimens are: Copenhagen, Ny Carlsberg Glyptotek 756a, inv. 2073 (Beilagen 81a, 82a–d); Gotha, Landesmuseum, no number (Beilagen 81c–d); Paris, Louvre MA 1077 (Beilage 81b); Rome, Musei Capitolini, Magazzino di Via Portico d'Ottavia, no number (Pl. 119).

4  *ILS* 471, 475, 9058; *AE* 1964, no 269; 1967, no 653; 1991, no 1542.

5  *BMC* V, Elagabalus, nos 7–9, 346§, 346, 346¶, 346.

6  *HA, Vita Sev. Alex.*, 9/4.

7  *ILS* 424, 454.

8  *ILS* 469; *AE* 1910, no 157.

9  *ILS* 475, 9058.

10  Cassius Dio LXXX, 1/2.

11  *RIC* IV.II, Elagabalus, no 124.

12  *BMC* V, Elagabalus, nos 10–15, 105–09; nos 15–16, 128–37; *BMC* V, Elagabalus, nos 274–76.

13  *BMC* V, Elagabalus, nos 17–22, 110–13; nos 37–37†, 169–70; nos 30–37, 121–25.

14  Bergmann, *Studien zum römischen Porträt*, pp. 22–24; Fittschen and Zanker, *Katalog der römischen Porträts*, vol. I, no 98. Fittschen and Zanker mention two specimens which can be identified with certainty: Musei Capitolini, Stanza degli Imperatori 55 inv. 470 (Pl. 120–21); Oslo, Nasjonalgalleriet 600, inv. 1433 (Beilagen 83a–d). Next to these, Bergmann mentions a third one: Thessaloniki, Mouseio Archeologika inv. 855 (Pl. 1, 3–4). Fittschen and Zanker list the Saloniki bust as a possible Elagabalus type 2, together with two other specimens (117 [n. 11]).

15  *AE* 1989, no 731.

16  *RIC* IV.II, Elagabalus, nos 1–8, 11–16, 25–26, 165, 169, 171A, 280–282, 284–86, 292–95; *BMC* V, Elagabalus, nos 195–96, 347, 365.

17  *BMC* V, Elagabalus, nos 126–27; nos 189–94; nos 264–65, 452‡, 452§; nos 143–47.

18  *CIL* VIII, 10,304, 10,308.

19  *BMC* V, Elagabalus, nos 151–53.

20  Ibid., no 364; nos 223–24.

21  Ibid., nos 155–61.

22  Ibid., nos 138–42.

23  Ibid., text, ccxxxiv.

24  Ibid., nos 70–75, 389–90; nos 79–83, 396–401; *RIC* IV.II, Elagabalus, no 263; no 251.

25 *RIC* IV.II, Elagabalus, nos 400–401; *BMC* V, Elagabalus, nos 39–43; nos 66–68, 295; nos 176‡, 177, 323–25.

26 Baldus, 'Das "Vorstellungsgemälde"', p.471; *BMC* V, Elagabalus, no 104; nos 138–42.

27 *AE* 1986, no 684; 1991, no 1542.

28 *BMC* V, Elagabalus, nos 273, 284–87.

29 Ibid., no 288; *BMC* V, Septimius Severus and Caracalla, no 132; *BMC* IV, Marcus Aurelius and Commodus, no 1637†.

30 E. Manders, 'Religion and coinage', p.136.

31 Baldus, 'Das "Vorstellungsgemälde"', p.476.

32 *BMC* V, Elagabalus, nos 291–92, 315.

33 *ILS* 473, 475, 2008, 9058. The exception to the rule is *ILS* 1329, which has 'pontifex maximus' first.

34 *BMC* V, Elagabalus, nos 256–63, 268–70, 338–40, 341, 441–46, 446§, 449, 454–55; *BMC* V, Elagabalus, nos 209–13, 330, 350, 368; nos 225–28, 359–60; nos 230–33, 333–34. Like 'sacerdos amplissimus', 'summus sacerdos' could be regarded as an alternative version of 'pontifex maximus'.

35 L. Dirven, 'The emperor's new clothes', p.26; Herodian V, 3/6; 5/3–4; *BMC* V, Elagabalus, nos 256–63 (Pl.90, 13–15); *RIC* IV.II, Elagabalus, nos 88 (Pl.II, 13), 146 (Pl.II, 20), 147.

36 Cassius Dio LXXIX, 3/3. For a discussion of 'German clothing', see: A.T. Croom, *Roman Clothing and Fashion*, pp.139–41.

37 *BMC* I, Augustus, nos 38–39 (uncertain objects in quadriga on no 39), 55.

38 *BMC* V, Elagabalus, nos 197–98. The *RIC* has a third type (IV.II, Elagabalus, no 176); *BMC* V, Elagabalus, nos 199–200, 240–45, 439, 446†, 447–48; *BMC* V, Elagabalus, nos 199–200.

39 *BMC* V, Elagabalus, nos 332–34, 444–45, 454–57†.

40 E. Krengel, 'Das sogenannte "Horn" des Elagabal', pp.53–56. For the horn, see *BMC* V, Elagabalus, nos 332–34, 444–45, 454–57†.

41 During the vegetation festival in honour of the mountain god near the Hethitic city of Zippalanda, the king was offered the penis of a sacrificial bull magically to give him strength: V. Haas, *Hethitische Berggötter und hurritische Steindämonen*, pp.56–58.

42 Dirven, 'The emperor's new clothes', p.25. The author also points out that not all coins showing the emperor sacrificing to Elagabal depict the 'horn' (p.25 [n.27]). Krengel herself notes that the 'horn' disappears from coins at the beginning of 222, which she explains as a concession to the increasingly disgruntled soldiers ('Das sogenannte "Horn"', pp.62–64).

43 *BMC* V, Elagabalus, nos 209–13, 225–28, 230–33, 256–63, 268–70; nos 330, 332–33, 338–41; *BMC* V, Elagabalus, nos 197–200, 240–45.

44 Ibid., nos 439, 446†, 447–48; nos 350, 359–60, 364§, 368, 441–46, 446§, 449, 454–55, 455, 456†.

45  Ibid., *Text*, p.ccxxxviii.
46  Ibid., Elagabalus, nos 271, 340, 341; nos 197–98.
47  Ibid., nos 104, 273, 284–87; Baldus, 'Das "Vorstellungsgemälde"', p.471.
48  *BMC* V, Elagabalus, no 188; nos 337, 437; nos 450–51; nos 271, 340, 341.
49  *ILS* 473, 475, 2008, 9058; *BMC* V, Elagabalus, nos 240–63, 268–71.
50  *BMC* V, Elagabalus, nos 452, 266–67 (nos 266–67 without patera); *BMC* V, Elagabalus, nos 452, 453.
51  Cassius Dio LXXIX, 29/2: 'ὑφ' οὗ οὐδὲν ὅ τι οὐ κακὸν καὶ αἰσχρὸν ἐγενέτο'; Herodian V, 8/8: 'ἀσχημονοῦντα βασιλέα'.
52  Cassius Dio LXXX, 11/1; LXXX, 9/3: 'ἐκφανέστατα παρανομήας'; LXXX, 12/1: 'γελοιότατον'; Herodian V, 7/8.
53  Herodian V, 3/10: 'εἴτε πλασαμένη εἴτε καὶ ἀληθεύουσα'.
54  *CIL* VI, 2104; *CIL* VI, 2067, 523; *CIL* VI, 2105, 2106.
55  Philostratus, *Vitae Sophistarum* II, 31/625.
56  M. Meckler, 'Prostituierte als Kaiser/Kaiser als Prostituierte; der römische Kaiser Elagabal bei Philostrat, *Erotischer Brief* Nr 19' (unpublished text, kindly made available to me by its author).
57  Philostratus, *Epistulae*, no 19; no 72.
58  C. Bruun, 'Roman emperors in popular jargon: searching for contemporary nicknames (I)', in L. de Blois et al. (eds), *Impact of Empire III*, pp.69–98, at p.95.
59  *Epitome de Caesaribus* 23/23 'appellatus est' (my translation).
60  *ILS* 470; *AE* 1938, no 117; 1967, no 361; *AE* 1910, nos 133, 141; Bogaers, 'Sol Elagabalus und die Cohors III Breucorum', p.153.
61  *ILS* 467, 469, 472, 476, 5843, 6878; *AE* 1888, no 180; 1910, no 157; 1978, no 842; 1983, no 778; 1984, no 432; *ILS* 469; *AE* 1910, no 157; R. Ziegler, *Städtisches Prestige und kaiserliche Politik. Studien zum Festwesen in Ostkilikien im 2. und 3. Jahrhundert n. Chr.* (Düsseldorf, 1985), at p.36 no B13.
62  *AE* 1992, no 1491; 1999, no 1355; *AE* 1995, no 1641; *ILS* 5793; *AE* 1995, no 1641; 2001, no 938.
63  *GBMC*, Palestine, Aelia Capitolina, nos 85–90; L. Kadman, *Corpus nummorum Palaestinensium*, vol. I: *The Coins of Aelia Capitolina*, nos 148–49, nos 151–52; A. Geißen, *Katalog alexandrinischer Kaisermünzen*, vol. 3: *Marc Aurel – Gallienus (Nr. 1995–3014)*, nos 2336, 2373; R. Ziegler, *Kaiser, Heer und städtisches Geld*, no 395; A. Dupont-Sommer and L. Robert, *La Déesse de Hiérapolis-Castabala (Cilicie)*, nos 41, 103–4; M.J. Price, 'Greek imperial coins', pp.121–34, no 11; R.E. Hecht, 'Some Greek imperial coins in my collection', pp.27–35, no 25; *GBMC*, Samaria, Neapolis, nos 101–2.
64  *GBMC*, Cilicia, Anazarbos, no 18.
65  *AE* 1985, no 976; *AE* 1972, no 600.
66  L. Robert, 'Monnaies grecques de l'époque impériale', *Revue Numismatique* 18 (1976), pp.25–56, at pp.51–52, Pl. II, 7; Cabinet de Paris, Lydie, no 1285; *GBMC*, Lydia, Sardes, no 170; Cabinet de Paris, Lydie, nos 1282, 1284.

67  L. Robert, 'Deux concours grecs à Rome', *CRAI* (1970) pp. 6–27, at pp. 24–25; see p. 24 (n. 4) for the Greek text of the inscription; Robert, 'Monnaies grecques', pp. 53–54; *HA, Vita Ant. Carac.* 11/6–7: 'sibi vel Iovi Syrio vel Soli – incertum id est'; Dupont-Sommer and Robert, *La Déesse*, p. 82 (n. 4); T. Mikocki, 'Sub specie deae', *Les impératrices et princesses romaines assimilées à des déesses, Étude iconologique* (Rome 1995), s.v. 'Faustina Minor' (pp. 63–66), nos 367–69, 376–78 (pp. 202–6); Robert, 'Monnaies grecques', p. 54; Dupont-Sommer and Robert, *La Déesse*, pp. 51–53, 81–82; C. Bosch, *Die kleinasiatischen Münzen der römischen Kaiserzeit*, p. 233 nos 431–33.

68  R. Ziegler, 'Der Burgberg von Anazarbos in Kilikien und der Kult des Elagabal in den Jahren 218 bis 222 n. Chr.', *Chiron* 34 (2004), pp. 59–85 at pp. 61–2, 76–80; Idem, *Kaiser, Heer und städtisches Geld*, no 395; *GBMC*, Palestine, Neapolis, nos 101–2.

69  *AE* 1985, no 976; 1972, no 600; L. Robert, 'Monnaies grecques de l'époque impériale', *Revue Numismatique* 18 (1976), pp. 51–52, Pl. II, 7.

70  *GBMC*, Lydia, Sardes, nos 170–74; Bosch, *Die kleinasiatischen Münzen der römischen Kaiserzeit*, p. 231 nos 428–30; *GBMC*, Cilicia, Anazarbus, nos 17–25 (AMK); *GBMC*, Cilicia, Anazarbus, nos 19–20.

71  *GBMC*, Lydia, Sardes, nos 175–79; *GBMC*, Bithynia, Nicomedia, nos 57–59; *GBMC*, Cilicia, Anazarbus, nos 27–28, 30. Apparently, news of Elagabalus's damnatio did not reach Anazarbos until 223 (nos 26, 29).

72  *P. Oxy.* XLVI, no. 3298, i, line 2 ("Ἀντωνεῖνος ὁ κόρυφος'); no 3299, line 2 ('ἀνόσιος Ἀντωνίνος μικρός'). According to Adam Lukaszewicz, 'κόρυφος' should rather be translated as 'virgin-raper' ('Antoninus the ΚΟΡΥΦΟΣ (note on *P. Oxy.* XLVI, 3298.2)'.

73  *RIC* IV.II, p. 23.

74  Hekster, *Commodus*, pp. 103–11, 146–54, 191–95; S. Berrens, *Sonnenkult und Kaisertum*, pp. 39–51.

75  Thompson, *Elagabalus*, p. 161. Halsberghe seems to imply the same when stating, 'It is as if the years of Elagabalus' rule were the shining event whose rays were later to give meaning and direction to religious life' (*The Cult of Sol Invictus*, p. 136).

76  Halsberghe, *The Cult of Sol Invictus*, pp. 135–62.

CHAPTER 4

1  See, for instance: Xenophon, *Agesilaos*; Plato, *Epistulae* VI and VII; Isocrates, *Evagoras* and *Ad Nicoclem*; Pliny, *Panegyricus*; Dio Chrysostom, *Orationes* I–IV.

2  De Blois, 'Emperor and empire', p. 3394.

3  Cassius Dio LXXIX, 29/2; LXXX, 7/2.

4  Cassius Dio LII, 14/1–40/2.

THE CRIMES OF ELAGABALUS

Cassius Dio LXXX, 7/2–3.

6 Cassius Dio LXXIX, 40/3: 'παιδαρίου'.

7 Cassius Dio LXXX, 4/1: 'τοὔνομα ἔκ τε μίμων καὶ γελωτοποιίας'; LXXX, 4/1–2: 'ἐν τοῖς παρανομωτάτοις'; LXXX, 21/2; C. Edwards, 'Beware of imitations: theatre and the subversion of imperial identity', in Elsner and Masters (eds), *Reflections of Nero*, p. 83–97, at p. 83.

8 Cassius Dio LXXX, 15/3.

9 Dio Chrysostom, *Orationes* III, pp. 87, 89.

10 Cassius Dio LXXX, 3/3: 'μιαιφονώτατα'; 8,1.

11 Ibid., 5/4.

12 Ibid., 5/2.

13 B. Isaac, *The Invention of Racism in Classical Antiquity*, pp. 335–51.

14 M. Gambato, 'The female-kings', pp. 227–30.

15 Diodorus Siculus, *Bibliotheca historica* II, 23/1–2.

16 Cassius Dio LXXX, 14/3–4.

17 L. Larsson Lovén, '*Lanam fecit*', pp. 85–95.

18 Diodorus Siculus II, 23/1. It was a commonplace in Greco–Roman literature that sexual indulgence sapped a man of his strength and made him like a woman, unable to take part in public life (C. Edwards, *The Politics of Immorality*, p. 86).

19 Cassius Dio LXXX, 14/3: '"Οτι ἐν τῷ δικάζειν τινὰ ἀνήρ πως εἶναι'; LXXX, 5/5; 9/1; LXXX, 16/4.

20 Ibid., 11/1; 16/7; p. 471.

21 Diodorus Siculus II, 23/3.

22 Ibid.

23 Athenaeus, *Deipnosophistae* XII, 529d.

24 Cassius Dio LXXX, 12/22: 'πολλῷ καὶ ποικίλῳ κόσμῳ διαπρέπων'.

25 Ibid., 13/1.

26 Ibid., 13/2. As Edwards notes, it is an oft-recurring paradox in Roman literature that effeminate men are supposed to be sexually passive, taking the 'female' role, but at the same time have a great, 'manly', urge for sex (Edwards, *The Politics of Immorality*, pp. 81–84).

27 Cassius Dio LXXX, 11/1; 11.

28 Ibid., 12/1: 'τὸ γελοιότατον [...] καθάπερ καὶ γάμου παίδων τε δεομένῳ'.

29 Ibid., 11/2.

30 M. Sommer, 'Wege zur Konstruktion', pp. 104–5, 107.

31 Cassius Dio LXXX, 9/4.

32 Ibid., 7/2.

33 Herodian I, 3/1.

34 Herodian V, 8/8: 'ἀσχημονοῦντα βασιλέα'.

35 Ibid., 3/9–10.

36 Ibid., 5/1.

37 Ibid., 7/1.
38 Ibid., 7/6–7; 7/8: 'πάντων δὲ οὕτως τῶν πάλαι δοκούντων σεμνῶν ἐς ὕβριν καὶ παροινίαν ἐκβεβακχευμένων'.
39 Ibid., 6/1.
40 Ibid., 6/10; 7/8; 7/7.
41 Ibid., 5/3–4. It is interesting to note that, while Dio's Elagabalus works with wool (LXXX, 14/4), Herodian's version looks down on wool as a cheap material.
42 Herodian V, 7/2: 'βακχείαις καὶ ὀργίοις'.
43 Ibid., 6/6–8.
44 Ibid., 7/4; 7/5; 7/5–6.
45 Sommer, 'Wege zur Konstruktion', pp. 107–8.
46 Herodian V, 7/8.
47 A. Scheithauer, *Kaiserbild und literarisches Programm*, pp. 36–42.
48 *HA, Vita Ant. Heliog.* 18/1.
49 *HA, Vita Sev. Alex.* 9/4.
50 *HA, Vita Ant. Heliog.* 1/5; 2/1; 9/2: 'nomen [...] Antonini pollueret, in quod invaserat'; 33/8: 'tam vita falsum fuisse quam nomine'.
51 Ibid., 20/1; 11,1.
52 Ibid., 12/1–2.
53 Ibid., 8/1–2.
54 Ibid., 12/3.
55 Ibid., 31/7.
56 Ibid., 5/4–5; 23/5; 7/2.
57 *HA, Vita Sev. Alex.* 23/7: 'tertium genus hominum'; 66/3; 18/3.
58 *HA, Vita Ant. Heliog.* 33/6.
59 Ibid., 21/5; Suetonius, *Vita Neronis* 31/2.
60 *HA, Vita Ant. Heliog.* 33/1: 'spinthrias veterum malorum vinceret, et omnis apparatus Tiberii et Caligulae et Neronis norat'.
61 Ibid., 7/1–3.
62 Ibid., 3/4–5.
63 Ibid., 6/7.
64 Ibid., 6/6–8.
65 T. Optendrenk, *Die Religionspolitik*, pp. 16–17.
66 *HA, Vita Sev. Alex.* 29/2; 12/4; F. Paschoud, 'L'intolérance chrétienne vue et jugée par les païens', *Cristianesimo nella storia* 11 (1990) pp. 545–77, at pp. 566–71.
67 S.C. Zinsli, 'Gute Kaiser, slechte Kaiser', pp. 117–38. See also R. Turcan, 'Héliogabale précurseur de Constantin?', pp. 38–52.
68 *HA, Vita Sev. Alex.* 7/4.
69 Ausonius, *De XII Caesaribus* 24, pp. 97–100.
70 *Epitome de Caesaribus* 23, pp. 2–3.
71 Eutropius VIII, 22.

72 Syncellus, *Ecloga chronographica* 673/14: 'φονικώτατος σφόδρα' (translation taken from W. Adler and P. Tuffin [eds], *The Chronography of George Synkellos*, p.515). Among Syncellus's sources were Dexippus, Eusebius and Eutropius (pp.lx–lxi).

73 *Epitome de Caesaribus* 23/10–11: 'in se convertens muliebri nomine Bassianam se pro Bassiano iusserat appellari' (my translation).

74 Syncellus 673/13–14, translation taken from Adler and Tuffin (eds), *The Chronography of George Synkellos* (translation taken from p.515).

75 Philostratus, *Epistulae*, no 19.

76 Aurelius Victor 23/2: 'impurius ne improbae quidem aut petulantes mulieres fuere' (my translation); Eutropius VIII, 22: 'probis se omnibus contaminavit; impudicissime et obscenissime' (my translation); *Epitome de Caesaribus* 23/8 (my translation).

77 Orosius, *Historiae adversus paganos* VII, 18/5 (my translation); Zosimus I, 11/1 (my translation); John of Antioch, *Historica chronica* 138 (my translation); Herodian V, 7/7.

78 Philostratus, *Epistulae*, no 19.

79 John of Antioch 136, 138; 137: 'τούς τε θεοὺς αὐτοῦ' (my translation).

80 Julian, *Caesares* 313A: 'ἐκ τῆς Ἐμέσης παιδάριον'.

81 Theodoros Skoutariotes, *Synopsis Chronica* 33/31–34/2: 'ἐλλόγιμος ἄριστος, ὀξὺς ἐν πολέμοις, σώφρων, ταχὺς, πάντας θεραπεύων καὶ ὑπὸ πάντων μετὰ λόγου φιλούμενος' (translation taken from E. Jeffreys, M. Jeffreys, R. Scott et al. [eds], *The Chronicle of John Malalas* [Melbourne, 1986], p.158 [n.25]).

82 Theodoros Skoutariotes 31/18–22.

83 Malalas, *Chronographia* XI, 281. See p.158 (n.25). For the original Greek, see L.A. Dindorf (ed.), *Ioannis Malalae Chronographia* (Bonn, 1831), 281/11–17.

CHAPTER 5

1 G. Boccaccio, *Famous Women* (ed. and transl. V. Brown, Cambridge, MA/ London, 2001) s.v. 'Symiamira, woman of Emesa' (XCIX), pp.421–26, at XCIX, 11: 'ignavum filium'; 10: 'cum hostes reipublice et illecebres iuvenes exteri atque incogniti urbis et orbis teneant principatum'; L. Bruni, *History of the Florentine People*, vol. I, p.38.

2 N. Machiavelli, *The Prince*, p.112.

3 J. de Brune, *Banket-werck van goede gedachten*, pp.232–33.

4 L.-S. Le Nain de Tillemont, *Histoire des empereurs*, vol III, p.147: 'une suite continuelle de crimes contre a pudeur, contre l'humanité, et contre toutes sortes de loix'. My thanks to Jason Hartford for his help with translations from French.

5 Gibbon, *Decline and Fall*, vol. I, pp.168, 167; 164.

6  Ibid., p. 166.

7  Ibid., pp. 166; 167, 166; 170.

8  R.R. Bolgar, *The Classical Heritage and its Beneficiaries*, p. 328.

9  T. Artus, *L'Isle des Hermaphrodites*, p. 81.

10  Ibid., p. 171: 'ce monstre de la nature'.

11  C.G. Dubois (ed.), *L'Isle des Hermaphrodites*, pp. 18–20; 30–31; 40; 9.

12  Anonymous, *Héliogabale ou esquisse morale*, p. 103: 'la rétablissement des institutions antiques de la liberté'; 'tempérez du moins le pouvoir absolu par intérêt pour tous et pour vous-même. Laissez transpirer quelque chose de la république dans l'empire'; p. 356: 'la liberté, le premier droit de l'homme'.

13  E.M. Moormann, 'Jews and Christians at Pompeii in fiction and faction', in S. Mucznik (ed.), *Assaph 2005–06: Studies in Art History*, vols 10–11: *Kalayos: Studies in Honour of Asher Ovadiah* (Tel Aviv, 2006), pp. 53–76, at pp. 53, 60–61.

14  T. Cabuchet, *Héliogabale* II/2 (p. 95): 'Je suis né pour le plaisir: c'est mon dieu qui m'ordonne cela.'

15  A. Westcott, *The Sun God*, p. 19.

16  D. de Séverac, *La Musique et les lettres: Correspondance rassemblée et annotée par Pierre Guillot* (Sprimont, 2002), lettre 418, p. 338: 'l'intérêt [d'Héliogabale] est le contraste entre le paganisme dégringolant dans la perversité orientale et le christianisme à son aurore.' Quoted from: A. d'Hautcourt, 'Peinture ou théâtre?', p. 116.

17  L. Feuillade (dir.), *L'Orgie romaine* (1911); also known as *Héliogabale, a Roman Orgy* and *Die Löwen des Tyrannen*. A copy of the film (with texts in German) can be found in the Dutch Film Museum at Amsterdam, tape Vv25, no 1 (0:00:00–0:09:35).

18  For speculation on Feuillade's inspiration by Sicard's and Séverac's *Héliogabale*, see Hautcourt, 'Peinture ou théâtre?', p. 115. Hautcourt also argues that *L'Orgie romaine* was probably an answer to the movie *Héliogabale* (1910) by André Calmettes, a competitor to Feuillade (p. 114).

19  N. Gaiman, *Heliogabolus*, pp. 13–14.

20  G. Chaillet, *Le Dernière phrophétie*, vol. 3: *Sous le signe de Ba'al*, p. 48: 'un nouvel Héliogabale'.

21  M. Calcagno, 'Censoring *Eliogabalo*', p. 364. Mexía's novel was translated into Italian by Ludovico Dolce under the title *Le vite de gli imperadori romani da Giulio Cesare sino a Massimino*; this translation was first published in 1558.

22  Calcagno, 'Censoring *Eliogabalo*', p. 357. In 2004, Cavalli's version of *Eliogabalo* saw its first performance ever at De Munt/La Monnaie in Brussels.

23  A. Aureli, *Eliogabalo* I, 2 : 'Che promesse? Che fé? Che giuramenti? La fé che non osservo acquista nome e pompa, decoro della legge è ch'io la rompa.'; I, 14: 'Constanza e fedeltà/è una servil catena/della plebea viltà.'; II, 10. All English translations are my own.

24 Ibid., III, 13: 'impudico tiranno al Ciel ribelle'; I, 16: 'crudel'; II, 3: 'tiran lascivo'; II, 4: 'Nella gloria del tempo quand'a bearsi questo secol giunga, solo perché col viver mio l'onoro gli cederà la destra il secol d'oro.'

25 M. Reynolds, 'Ruggiero's deceptions, Cherubino's distractions', in C.E. Blackmer and P.J. Smith (eds), *En Travesti: Women, gender subversion, opera* (New York, 1995), pp.132–51, at pp.136–38.

26 A. Aureli, *Eliogabalo* I, 11; I, 6: 'molli'.

27 Ibid., I, 2. This remark is possibly a parody of a quote in Suetonius, in which an annoyed Caligula wishes that the Roman people had but one neck (so that he could cut its head off) (*Vita Caligulae* 30/2).

28 J.-F. Lattarico, 'Aantekeningen bij de *effemminato* antiheld in de Venetiaanse opera van de 17de eeuw', in I. Dumont and S. van Renterghem, *Eliogabalo*, pp.139–49, at pp.141, 146.

29 Ibid., pp.362–69.

30 A. Aureli, *Eliogabalo* I, 6: 'perché non potero soffrire d'accompagnarlo in mezzo a indegne schiere di femmine immodeste, barbaro di vestir barbaro d'opre, in forma trionfante lascivie solo e molli odor spirante'; Herodian V, 7/8; A. Aureli, *Eliogabalo* I, 11; I, 14.

31 Calcagno, 'Censoring *Eliogabalo*', pp.360–61.

32 B. van der Zijde, 'Gysbert Tysens (1693–1732). Een broodschrijver in de achttiende eeuw', *Mededelingen van de Stichting Jacob Campo Weyerman* 19 (1996), pp.65–78, at pp.65–69.

33 G. Tysens, *Bassianus Varius Heliogabalus* I, 1, line 28: 'stále vuist'; I, 1, line 52: 'een Barbaar, en Beul, en Pest der Roomse státen'; I, 1, line 107: 'die ontaarde Vorst'; I, 1, lines 136–37: 'een dwing'land [...] die lust in tiranny en alle gruuw'len vind'.

34 Ibid., I, 7, lines 320–24: 'Laat vry al 't Roomse volk zig tegens my verheffen,/Door éénen enk'len slag van deez' gevreesde vuist,/Word al dat muitend Graauw gelyk tot stof vergruist:/Hoe? zoude ik Keizer zyn, en zelf naar wetten léven?/Neen, 't voegd my die alleen aan anderen te géven.'

35 Ibid., II, 7, line 691: 'Ik dugt de wraak van u, van 't volk, nog van de Goôn'; I, 7, line 373; III, 4, lines 1077–78; I, 7, line 371; I, 8, lines 381–83; lines 397; IV 8, line 1655; III, 3, lines 945–47; line 946: 'Min Priester zynde, als wel een wréde Moordenaar'.

36 Ibid., IV, 2, lines 1373–74: 'Hoe word myn ziel gesold, geslingerd heen en weêr!/Hier prikkeld my myn wraak, daar prikkeld my myne eer!'; IV, 1, line 1302; I, 7, line 355.

37 F.G. Naerebout, 'Iron-fisted Varius' (unpublished text, kindly made available to me by its author).

38 Tysens, *Bassianus Varius Heliogabalus* III, 3, line 950: 'verwyfd Gewaad'; IV, 8, line 1661: 'verwyfd gewaad'; IV, 3, line 1416: 'een verwyfden Beul'; I, 1, line 28: 'stále vuist'; III, 3, line 944.

39 Ibid., I, 1, line 52: 'een Barbaar'; I, 2, line 161: 'een wreè Barbaar'; III, 3, lines 950–52: 'Die met verwyfd Gewaad en Asiaanse pragt/Van Purper, goud en zyde, en verd're praalsieráden,/De roomse dapperheid lafhartig heeft verráden'; IV, 8, lines 1661–62: 'Die met verwyfd gewaad den roomsen Naam besmet,/En in 't Assiries kleed schent Vader Numa's wet'.

40 J. Krzyżanowski, *A History of Polish Literature*, pp. 224–25.

41 Z. Krasiński, *Iridion*, pp. 248–57 (n. 13).

42 Ibid., 'Conclusion' (p. 236). This reading is based on the English translation of *Irydjon*.

43 The letter, written to Gaszynski on 6 June, 1837, is quoted in M.M. Gardner, *The Anonymous Poet*, p. 149. Masinissa was a Numidian king and ally of the Romans in the third and second centuries BCE. It is unclear to me why Krasiński uses the name.

44 Krasiński, *Iridion* III (p. 195); III (p. 196); I (p. 66). Undoubtedly based on Suetonius, who attributed a similar phrase to Caligula (*Vita Caligulae* 30/2); I (p. 64); I (p. 88); I (p. 89).

45 Ibid., I (p. 62); I (p. 62). The first quote is a reference to Elagabalus eating the brains of thrushes and flamingoes in the *Vita Heliogabali* (20/6).

46 Ibid., I (p. 64); I (p. 69).

47 Gardner, *The Anonymous Poet*, p. 147.

48 Krasiński, *Iridion*, 'Introduction' (p. 27).

49 Ibid., I (p. 61); I (p. 97).

50 Ibid., *Iridion* I (p. 60).

51 Ibid., I (pp. 60–61).

52 Ibid., I (p. 95); III (p. 155); I (p. 95). See also I (p. 92).

53 E.W. Said, *Orientalism*, pp. 91, 113–23; C. Miłosz, *The History of Polish Literature*, p. 200.

54 Krasiński, *Iridion*, p. 256 (n. 13).

55 Ibid., 'Introduction' (p. 28).

CHAPTER 6

1 David, *Antiquité latine*, p. 479: 'roman antique décadent par excellence'.

2 Th. Mommsen, *Reden und Aufsätze* (republished by O. Hirschfeld, Berlin, 1905) p. 199. Quoted from K. Christ, *Von Gibbon zu Rostovtzeff*, pp. 48–49: 'der [...] es gewagt hat die Geschichtswissenschaft an der Logik der Tatsachen zu prüfen.'

3 G.B. Niebuhr, *Römische Geschichte*, vol. V: *Römische Geschichte von dem ersten punischen Krieg bis zum Tode Constantins: Zweiter Band*, p. 366: 'Er hatte eine Leidenschaft für alles was die menschliche Natur entehrt'; 'wahnsinnigsten Schwelgereien'.

4 Th. Mommsen, *Römische Kaisergeschichte*, pp. 396–97, MH.II.312–313: 'ein geringfügiger, nichtswürdiger Mensch'.

5 J.H.K.F.H. Schiller, *Geschichte der römischen Kaiserzeit*, vol. I, p. 762: 'geistig unbedeutend, ohne jede Würde, ein abgesagter Feind jeder ernsthaften Thätigkeit'.

6 Ibid., vol. I, pp. 762–63: 'Nie wurde das Kaisertum in gleicher Weise herabgewürdigt, wie unter diesem unreifen, tollen Knaben [...] Der Kaiser trat auch äusserlich am Hofe ganz als orientalischer Despot mit dem Diadem auf und verlangte die Adoration. Was von Elagabals Thätigkeit überliefert wird, beschmutzt lediglich die Blätter der Geschichte, und seine Regierung ist ein wahrer Hexensabbat von Unzucht, Ausschweifungen und Luxus.'

7 Von Domaszewski, *Abhandlungen*, p. 148: 'die späte Rache der Semiten an der griechisch-römischen Kultur, deren Fesseln sie durch Jahrhunderte stumm getragen hatte'; p. 213: 'Die Nacht der Barbarei ist es denn auch, die seit Septimius Severus die griechisch-römische Welt bedeckt.'

8 J. Réville, *La Religion à Rome sous les Sévères*, p. 240: 'Il n'y a, en effet, plus rien de romain ni d'occidental en la personne d'Elagabal ou de sa mère Soaemias. En eux le vieil esprit de Canaan, contre lequel les prophètes d'Israël se sont élevés avec tant d'énergie, s'affirme encore une fois dans un débordement suprême avant de disparaître de l'histoire.'

9 Ibid., p. 241: 'esprit syrien'; 'frivole et légère, ardente à la passion mais indolente à l'effort, avide de nouveautés mais superficielle, rusée et subtile mais sans consistance'; p. 240: 'Cette fois le triomphe de l'Orient était complet'; p. 247: 'l'absence complète de préoccupation du bien public et la concentration égoïste de toute l'activité gouvernementale sur le bien-être du souverain'.

10 F. Cumont, *Les Religions orientales*, p. 177: 'qui sacrifiait à la divinité la vie des hommes et la pudeur des femmes'; 'au niveau moral de peuplades insociables et sanguinaires'; 'ses rites obscènes et atroces provoquèrent un soulèvement exaspéré de la conscience romain'.

11 Said, *Orientalism*, p. 231.

12 Th. Gautier, *Mademoiselle de Maupin*, p. 175: 'Moi aussi je voudrais bâtir un pont sur la mer et paver les flots; j'ai rêvé de brûler des villes pour illuminer mes fêtes; j'ai souhaité d'être femme pour connaître de nouvelles voluptés. – Ta maison dorée, ô Néron! n'est qu'une étable fangeuse à côté du palais que je me suis élevé; ma garde-robe est mieux montée que la tienne, Héliogabale, et bien autrement splendide. – Mes cirques sont plus rugissants et plus sanglants que les vôtres, mes parfums plus âcres et plus pénétrants, mes esclaves plus nombreux et mieux faits; j'ai aussi attelé à mon char des courtisanes nues, j'ai marché sur les hommes d'un talon aussi dédaigneux que vous.'

13 D. Borchmeyer and V. Žmegač (eds), *Moderne Literatur in Grundbegriffen* (2nd edition, Tübingen, 1994) s.v. 'Décadence' (D. Borchmeyer), pp. 69–76, at pp. 69–70; R. Bauer, *Die schöne* Décadence, pp. 21–41.

14 E. Hanson, *Decadence and Catholicism*, p. 2.

15 Ibid., pp. 2–3.

16 J. Birkett, *The Sins of the Fathers*, p. 61. For more on Huysmans, see M. Smeets, *Huysmans l'inchangé: Histoire d'une conversion* (Amsterdam, 2003); Idem (ed.), *Joris-Karl Huysmans* (Amsterdam, 2003).

17 J.-K. Huysmans, *À Rebours*, p. 120: 'l'étonnant grand-prêtre d'Émèse'; 'pendant que l'Empire romain branlait sur ses bases, que les folies de l'Asie, que les ordures du paganisme coulaient à pleins bords'; p. 121: 'puis la langue latine, arrivée à sa maturité suprême sous Pétrone, allait commencer à se dissoudre'.

18 David, *Antiquité latine*, p. 233: 'Héliogabale est le pur produit de l'esthéticisme à tout prix'; p. 239: 'Le politique immolé sur l'autel de l'esthétique: image-t-on rêve plus fabuleux pour les esthètes et dilettantes de la fin du siècle?'

19 L. Jourdan, *La Dernière nuit d'Héliogabale*, p. 12: 'Héliogabale, [...] ce jeune Syrien qui, traînant à sa suite les moeurs et les coutumes asiatiques, avait fait son entrée, dans la capitale de l'empire, sur un char étincelant de gemmes et de dorures, coiffé de la mitre des satrapes, vêtu d'une robe de femme, et portant dans ses mains la symbolique représentation du dieu Hélios, la pierre noire d'Émèse'; p. 40: 'Syrien, tu outrages une citoyenne'; p. 15: 'eunuques syriens'; p. 58: 'cortège de roi asiatique'.

20 d'Herdy (pseud.), *La Destinée*, p. 172: 'cet empereur merveilleux, cet incomparable artiste. Car, artiste, il le fut! le plus grand de son temps et de bien d'autres sans doute'; p. 140: 'un grand incompris, combien séduisant! combien sympathique!' Lombard is explicitly mentioned.

21 Ibid.,: '[...] l'inapaisable détresse de celui, dont la puissance n'ayant pour limites que les limites mêmes assignées aux possibilités humaines, mais affolé de désirs plus grands encore que son insolite pouvoir, sans cesse heurta, d'un front douloureux, les bornes du permis, en une ardente et vaine poursuite de l'irréalisable.'

22 David, *Antiquité latine*, p. 258: 'Plus que le grand et le grandiose, le colossal et le gigantesque sont la mesure de la Décadence'.

23 A. Villeroy, *Héliogabale*, p. 29: 'Il ne faut pas/Qu'un Barbare dans la Voie Sacrée fasse un pas'; p. 56: 'L'Orient, d'où je sors, est plein de ces exemples;/L'Inceste est dieu là-bas'; p. 31: 'doux et blanc comme une fille'; p. 92: 'Quel est ton sexe? Es-tu prêtresse, impératrice?'.

24 Ibid., p. 110: 'Et tous plus que César sont heureux! Tous ils aiment! Ils sont aimés! Oui, tous!'; p. 116: 'in-sexué'; p. 118: 'Esclaves de Vénus, l'Univers est mort! Place/A l'Androgyne, à l'Hermaphrodite, à la race/Qui ne connaîtra pas l'Amour'.

25 L. Rado, *The Modern Androgyne Imagination: A failed sublime* (Virginia, 2000), pp. 1–25. For more on the 'crisis of masculinity' in the *fin-de-siècle*, see G.L. Mosse, *The Image of Man: The creation of modern masculinity* (New York, 1996), pp. 77–106; A.J.L. Busst, 'The image of the androgyne', pp. 39–75.

26 L. von Scheffler-Weimar, 'Elagabal, pp.231–64, at pp.244, 252, 255: 'pathologisches Individuum'; 'kaiserliche Hermaphrodit'; 'er war mit weiblicher Psyche doch körperlich eben Mann'. The case of the adjectives and nouns in some of these quotations has been adjusted.

27 J. Richepin, 'Un empereur', p.67: 'J'ai dix-huit ans et des passions extraordinaires. J'étais né pour être empereur du temps de la décadence romaine. Mais l'époque actuelle n'est pas bonne pour les fantaisistes. C'est pourquoi je m'en vais. N'ayant pu vivre comme Héliogabale, j'ai au moins voulu mourir comme lui, dans des latrines.'

28 H. Mirande, *Élagabal*, p.82, 13: 'yeux efféminés dans sa face d'androgyne'; p.81: 'celui d'un adolescent parfaitement beau, tel qu'un Apelle en pouvait imaginer pour peindre un merveilleux Apollon enfant'; 'un air d'émasculisme oriental'; pp.10–11: 'radieuse beauté d'éphèbe'.

29 Ibid., pp.202–3: Vois-tu, ami, je ne sais quels mauvais génies me poussent; j'ai envie de tout, peut-être parce que tout me dégoûte. Je rêve des jouissances nouvelles, des voluptés impossibles. Je suis jaloux de Néron qui embrasa Rome et, la cythare à la main, contemplait l'incendie en chantant un poème. Je souhaite mieux et pis encore: j'invente des breuvages nouveaux et, quand je porte à mes lèvres la coupe désirée, elle, m'écoeure; j'ai besoin d'avoir du monde à côté de moi, bien que ces gens me fatiguent; il me faut du bruit surtout, pour m'empêcher de penser à ce qui m'attend demain peut-être. – Je m'ennuie!'

30 M.-F. David, 'Figure du désordre', p.153: 'héros mélancolique souffrant d'un incurable ennui'; 'la soif de reconnaissance et la satisfaction d'un narcissisme illimité'.

31 Ibid., pp.153–54 (n.16); Gibbon, *Decline and Fall*, vol.I, p.167.

32 David, *Antiquité latine*, pp.223–35.

33 M. Duplay and P. Bonardi, *Héliogabale*, p.3: 'les moeurs étaient si dissolues dans le capitale de l'Empire, qu'on ne pouvait s'étonner de la licence qui régnait dans les camps – et surtout en Asie'; p.216: 'le premier, précocement fripé, avachi, efféminé, le deuxième sain, le regard direct et frais, la démarche ferme, déjà viril'; p.25: 'la décadence de Rome, la décomposition latine'; pp.138–39; p.4: 'à la fois viril et efféminé'.

34 Villeroy, *Héliogabale*, p.136: 'Juqu'au jour où la croix du Dieu vivant qui saigne/A son tour chassera votre aigle et vos enseignes.'

35 Mirande, *Élagabal*, p.375: 'Gloire à Chrestos!'

36 É. Bellot, *Jean Lombard*, pp.34–37.

37 Lombard in a letter to Louis-Xavier de Ricard, quoted from M.-F. David, 'Présentation', in J. Lombard, *L'Agonie*, pp.7–27, at p.7 (n.2): 'fausse sentimentalité'; 'esthétique bien subtile'; 'une littérature sociale, saine, vraie'.

38 David, 'Présentation', p.7.

39 Lombard, *L'Agonie*, p. 86: '[…] sous un dais plafonné à d'une dense étoffe d'or soutenue par quatre hautes piques fichées en terre et inclinées, s'affale une humanité somptueusement immobile, une fastueuse figure de quinze ans, coiffée d'une tiara droite, tissée de perles, de gemmes, de métaux, portée sur des échappées de cheveux longs, noirs, par-dessus une blancheur d'épaules féminines transparant sous une riche subucula de soie qui s'irise comme de la nacre. Et c'est là, en un écartement de jambes nues, Elagabalus couché sur des peaux de panthères et montrant sa virilité jeune qu'évente tranquillement, d'un flabellum fait d'une grande feuille de lotus ployée à la pointe, un eunuque noir à peau blète, aux dents blanches, aux yeux blancs roulant niaisement.'

40 Ibid., p. 180: 'étalé sur son lit, avec, sur sa robe de soie pourpre, des traces humides du viol; la tête tiarée, les yeux cerclés de noir, terribles, ennuyés; les traits fins, tirés.'

41 Ibid., p. 332: 'tant sa vie extraordinaire devait avoir une extraordinaire fin, sans exemple dans les siècles à venir.'

42 Ibid., p. 45: 'Au commencement de Tout, la Vie unisexuelle engendrait et enfantait d'elle-même; le monde était en impuissance de Bonheur depuis la séparation des sexes; aussi, la Perfection consistait-elle à fondre la force génératrice dans l'Unité.'

43 Ibid., p. 178: 'L'Empereur est androgyne comme le destin! […] Il est riche des deux sexes, honneur à lui!'; p. 184: 'La Force Première'; 'pour le ténébreux et inexpliqué mystère de la création'.

44 Ibid., p. 207: 'une fleure noire, au calice noir, aux sépales noirs, dont l'ombre, en phallus découpée, enfumait son cerveau.'

45 David, 'Présentation', pp. 11–12.

46 Ibid., pp. 15–16. The androgyne was often used as a symbol of social equality: Busst, 'The image of the androgyne', pp. 12–38.

47 Lombard, *L'Agonie*, p. 80: 'subjuguée par l'Orient'; p. 164: 'tentatives d'immerger l'Occident dans le pompeux Orient pour l'en ressortir, plus éclatant, comme d'un bain de voluptés, de crimes et d'or'; p. 79: 'mœurs orientales'; 'esprits inférieurs'.

48 Ibid., p. 436: 'de plus en plus dans le Vice, le Crime et les excréments'; p. 476: 'Toi, vois-tu, tu es le Kreistos, le symbole du T, la Vesta Immortelle, Osiris, Zeus, tout!'

49 David, 'Présentation', p. 10: 'L'Agonie du monde romain ne conduit pas ici à la délectation morose dont est coutumière la Décadence. Elle porte en elle des germes de renaissance.'

50 J. Rieckmann, 'Introduction', in Idem (ed.), *A Companion to the Works of Stefan George* (New York, 2005), pp. 1–22, at p. 8.

51 H. Naumann, 'Stefan Georges "Algabal"'. George visited Linderhof in 1891, but never went to Neuschwanstein. However, as Christophe Fricker points

out, he may have familiarised himself with its architecture through drawings and paintings ('Ludwig II', p. 443).

52  S. George, *Algabal*, p. 91: 'Der schöpfung wo er nur geweckt und verwaltet/Erhabene neuheit ihn manchmal erfreut,/Wo ausser dem seinen kein wille schaltet/Und wo er dem licht und dem wetter gebeut.' My thanks to Marco Mattheis for his help with the English translations of Stefan George.

53  E. Morwitz, *Stefan George: Poems*, p. 18.

54  George, *Algabal*, p. 118: 'die schönste aus der weissen schwestern zug'; 'Sie hatte wie die anderen ein mal.'

55  Ibid., p. 96: 'Wie zeug ich dich aber im heiligtume / [...] Dunkle grosse schwarze blume?'

56  J. Todd, 'Stefan George and two types of aestheticism', p. 131.

57  George, *Algabal*, p. 107: 'Ich will daß man im volke stirbt und stöhnt'.

58  Todd, 'Stefan George and two types of aestheticism', pp. 132–33.

59  George, *Algabal*, p. 107: 'Ich thue was das leben mit mir thut/Und träf ich sie mit ruten bis aufs blut:/Sie haben korn und haben fechterspiele.'

60  Ibid., p. 120: 'sündig'.

61  Fricker, Ludwig II, pp. 442–43.

62  George, *Algabal*, p. 106: 'Flötenspieler vom Nil'; R. Kiefer and B. Jungheim, *Der Krieg der Prinzipien*, pp. 13–19.

63  George, *Algabal*, p. 107: 'beinah einer schwester angesicht'; p. 101: 'zwiegestalt'; Todd, 'Stefan George and two types of aestheticism', p. 135.

64  George, *Algabal*, pp. 102, 114: 'wie viele speere pfiffen/Als ich im Osten um die krone rang'; 'heimat'; p. 111: 'Syrer'.

65  Todd, 'Stefan George and two types of aestheticism', p. 132.

66  L.M.A. Couperus, *De berg van licht*, pp. 441–42: 'Tusschen de keizers heeft mij het meest altijd getroffen de figuur van het mooie zonnepriestertje, dat tot keizer werd uitgeroepen, omdat het Leger verliefd op hem was en omdat hij zoo mooi kan dansen. [...] Niemand die over hem schreef, of hij heeft hem gelasterd, zelfs Lombard. Het jongetje was een bedorven Kind en zeker hysteriesch in zijn man-vrouwelijkheid, maar hij was niet enkel 'liederlijk' en meer niet. Hij was geniaal, en artiest in alles wat hij deed.' All the quoted translations of Couperus are my own.

67  Ibid., p. 80: 'de uiterste bloem eener ùitbloeiende overbeschaving'; p. 79: 'hysterie zijner sensualiteit'; 'verscherpt door te veel kleur-geurige weekheid en weelde, te veel adoratie, en zelfs te veel mystiek'; p. 98: 'sierlijk [...], kunstig, talentvol, geniaal en goddelijk'.

68  Ibid., p. 227: 'geen knaap en geen keizer, maar [...], geniaal-weg, àlles'; p. 228: 'een levensartiest, die voortging met zijn eindelooze herscheppingen'.

69  Ibid., pp. 89–90: 'Zij riepen hem uit, zij stroomden hem toe, omdat hij aanbiddelijk was, dien Priester-der-Zon. Die tienduizende zielen,

noordelijke en zuidelijke: Romeinen en Klein-Aziaten, maar ook Germanen, Galliërs, Britten, Sarmaten, Pannoniërs: zij eeredienden, in het Zuiden, de schoonheid, de antieke, almachtige, overheerschende schoonheid, die twee eeuwen van zich uitbreidend Christendom nog niet hadden kunnen versmoren.'

70 Ibid., p.298: 'aanbiddelijk, buitensporig als alleen een god zijn kon'; p.311: 'de hoogste genieting, die der goden'; 'zwijnen'.

71 Ibid., pp.148–49: 'Hoe weinig, hij scheen veranderd'; 'dansende kind van Emessa'; 'eene, wie dit niet verwachtte, zeer treffende perversiteit'; 'bedorven kind'; 'mystieke aureool'.

72 Ibid., pp.278–79: 'als of, helaas, het waas van zijn jeugd was gewischt'.

73 Ibid., p.22: 'En dadelijk, te Emessa, had Bassianus gevoeld, dat hij geen Romein was in bloed, maar Syriër, Aziaat en Oosterling. Nauwlijks ontwassen der prilheid van kinderjeugd, had hem dadelijk in Emessa verrast een lucht, atmosfeer, vreemd bekend, die hij glimlachend inademde'.

74 Ibid., p.23: 'een zoele glimlach, die in de lucht om hem aandreef, glimlach van sympathie en begroeting; warme kus van bekende wellusten; omhelzing, mysterieus en mystiek'; p.80: 'sensueel-mystiek-geurige Oosten'; 'in pracht […] ontluiken'; 'vergiftigen zìch, en allen, die zij bekoorde…'.

75 Ibid., p.30: 'Uitverkoren Ziel'; 'een kostbare vaas vol schoonheid'; p.31: 'Bassianus, o mijn Bassianus, ben je zoo niet? Niet te vrouwelijk, niet te mannelijk, de beide seksen in evenwicht versmolten tot een harmonie…'

76 M. Klein, *Noodlot en wederkeer*, pp.157–62, 170–72; C. de Westenholz, 'Heliogabalus en de Vlam van de Lust'.

77 Couperus, *De berg van licht*, p.253: 'Man van vorm, voèlde hij zich al vrouw, en had hij gehuwd zijn Gemaal… […] Heva, Heva was hij, maar beiden moest hij zijn: Adam-Heva…'

78 Ibid., p.421: 'als U, Eerwaarde, vergeet ik zijn aanbiddelijkheid NOOIT!'

79 Th. Bogaerts, *De antieke wereld van Louis Couperus* (Amsterdam, 1969), p.82: 'Achter Heliogabalus gaat de auteur voortdurend zelf schuil.'; F.L. Bastet, *Louis Couperus*, pp.324–326; Klein, *Noodlot en wederkeer*, pp.6–9.

80 Couperus, *De berg van licht*, pp.421–22: 'somber gekleede, monnikachtige, slaafsch jubelende Christenen'; p.422: 'zich weemoediglijk bewust… van een Antieke Schoonheid, die, helaas, verwelkte… en een Antieke Vroomheid, die weldra wijkt…'

CHAPTER 7

1  R. de Gourmont, 'Préface', in G. Duviquet (ed.), *Héliogabale raconté*, pp. 7–27, at pp. 8–9: 'l'empereur de l'extravagance'; pp. 7–8: 'émigrants orientaux, corrompus par l'hostilité de la nature, desséchés par le feu continu du soleil'; p. 7: 'bien plus près du christianisme que du paganisme aryen'; 'Syrien judaïsant'; p. 9: 'à sa manière, un digne empereur'.

2  O. Butler, *Studies in the Life of Heliogabalus*, pp. 75; 72, 86; 104, 72, 98; 135.

3  Hay, *The Amazing Emperor*, pp. ix–x.

4  Ibid., pp. 1–2, 244, 200–201; 232; 229, 201, 172.

5  Ibid., pp. 230; 93; 242, 1–2; 286; vi–vii; 98; 51, 273.

6  R. Villeneuve, *Le César fou*, p. 161: 'sa famille le chargea de tous les crimes, ses détracteurs firent le reste'; p. 82: 'psychopathie religieuse'; 'Victime d'une névropathie dominée par un exhibitionnisme quasi inconscient, il aurait probablement fini dans la démence'; p. 82: 'la dégénérescence'; p. 75: 'l'origine orientale et l'hérédité voluptueuse'; 'plus proche de statues d'androgynes babyloniennes, que des éphèbes grecs, voire romains'; p. 76: 'Héliogabale [...] crut peut-être entrevoir que dans l'Androgyne, négation d'un sexe et absolu des deux, résidait la perfection suprême.'

7  Thompson, *Elagabalus*, pp. 206, 146; R. Turcan, *Héliogabale*, p. 176: 'de nos jours, Héliogabale aurait créé un ministère de la Prostitution.'

8  S. Gualerzi, *Né uomo, né donna*, p. 88: 'due figure bizzarre, omonime, simili, e dal genere sessuale indefinito e indefinibile: né uomo, né donna; né dio, né dea.'

9  R. Syme, *The Roman Revolution*, p. 458.

10  Sommer, 'Wege zur Konstruktion'; Manders, 'Religion and coinage'.

11  S.N. Miller, 'The army and the imperial house', p. 55.

12  B. Campbell, 'The Severan dynasty', in A.K. Bowman, P. Garnsey and A. Cameron (eds), *The Cambridge Ancient History*, vol. XII: *The Crisis of Empire, A.D. 193–337* (2nd edition, Cambridge, 2005), pp. 1–27, at p. 21.

13  H.L. Mencken and G.J. Nathan, *Heliogabalus*, II (p. 129).

14  Ibid., II (p. 77).

15  K. Onstott and L. Horner, *Child of the Sun*, p. 30.

16  Ibid., p. 30.

17  Ibid., pp. 9, 48, 54.

18  Ibid., pp. 157, 175.

19  S. Gilbert, *Heliogabalus, a Love Story*, p. 2. Thanks are due to the author for kindly providing me with a copy.

20  Ibid., pp. 24, 7, 26.

21  Ibid., p. 29.

22  J. Reed, *Boy Caesar*, pp. 30–31; 79, 68.

23  Ibid., pp. 13–14.

24 Ibid., p. 70.
25 Th. Jonigk, 'Erst Superstar, dann Staatsfeind', in Idem and P. Vermeersch (eds), *Heliogabal*, p. 4: 'wie Michael Jackson einst eine millionenschwere Fangemeinde, hat der vierzehnjährige Jungkaiser Heliogabal Rom im Sturm genommen.'
26 Jonigk and Vermeersch (eds), *Heliogabal*, II, 1 (p. 39): 'Heliogabal – das ist eine Investition, die sich lohnt'; III, 2 (p. 43): 'So muß ein Kaiser sein. Wie ich. Du bist wie ich. Unsterblich. Ich durch dich und du durch mich'; VI, 6 (p. 69): 'Zeit für den Kaiser!'; Jonigk, 'Erst Superstar, dann Staatsfeind': 'So war es für Heliogabal. Und so ist es überall.'
27 http://www.imdb.com/title/tt0188093 (accessed 30 August 2007).
28 S. During, *Cultural Studies: A critical introduction* (London, 2005), pp. 197, 199.
29 P. Moinot, *Héliogabale*, p. 48: 'la difformité, la hideur, la dégradation'.
30 F. Webster, *Theories on the Information Society* (2nd edition, London/New York, 2002), p. 234.
31 See, for instance J. Baudrillard, *Simulacres et simulation* (Paris, 1981). For a summary of Baudrillard's ideas on this matter, see Webster, *Theories*, pp. 243–48.
32 Reed, *Boy Caesar*, p. 79.
33 http://members.aol.com/heliogabby/ (accessed 11 April 2008); http://members.aol.com/heliogabby/private/hgbath.htm (accessed 11 April 2008: currently closed for renovation); http://members.aol.com/heliogabby/private/hglib.htm (accessed 11 April 2008; J. Bos, 'Joan's Mad Monarch Series', s.v. 'Elagabalus of Rome': http://www.xs4all.nl/~kvenjb/madmonarchs/elagabalus/elagabalus_bio.htm (accessed 11 April 2008).
34 S. Barber, *Antonin Artaud*, p. 38.
35 A. Artaud, *Le Théâtre*, p. 96: 'Il s'agit donc, pour le théâtre, de créer une métaphysique de la parole, du geste, de l'expression, en vue de l'arracher à son piétinement psychologique et humain.'
36 Ibid., pp. 98–99: 'Sans un élément de cruauté à la base de tout spectacle, le théâtre n'est pas possible. Dans l'état de dégénérescence où nous sommes, c'est par la peau qu'on fera rentrer la métaphysique dans les esprits.'
37 Barber, *Antonin Artaud*, p. 52.
38 A. Artaud, *L'Anarchiste couronné*, p. 92: 'Et cette guerre est tout entière dans la religion du soleil, et on la trouve au degré sanglant mais magique dans la religion du soleil, telle qu'elle se pratiquait à Emèse'; p. 93: 'plus haut que dans sa psychologie personelle, c'est dans la religion du soleil qu'ils auraient cherché l'origine de ses excès, de ses folies et de sa haute crapule mystique'. All English translations of *L'Anarchiste couronné* are taken from A. Lykiard (transl.), *Heliogabalus or, The Crowned Anarchist* (London, 2003).
39 Ibid., p. 99: 'les chairs rondes d'une femme, un visage de cire lisse'.
40 L.A. Boldt-Irons, 'Anarchy and androgyny', p. 867.

41 Artaud, *L'Anarchiste couronné*, p. 180: 'une mauvaise effigie de lui-meme'; p. 188: 'en dehors de cela il n'y a que l'essence pure, l'abstrait inanalysable, l'absolu indéterminé, "l'Intelligible" enfin'.

42 Boldt-Irons, 'Anarchy and androgyny', pp. 866–67; Artaud, *L'Anarchiste couronné*, p. 133: 'la première anarchie est en lui, et elle lui ravage l'organisme'.

43 Artaud, *L'Anarchiste couronné*, p. 136: 'Héliogabale est un anarchiste né, et qui supporte mal la couronne, et tous ses actes de roi sont des actes d'anarchiste-né, ennemi public de l'ordre, qui est un ennemi de l'ordre public'; p. 165: 'l'anarchie polythéiste romaine'; 'la monarchie romaine'; p. 162: 'il se fait d'abord enculer par l'empire romain'.

44 Ibid., p. 138: 'Ramener la poésie et l'ordre dans un monde dont l'existence même est un défi à l'ordre, c'est ramener la guerre et la permanence de la guerre; c'est amener un état de cruauté appliqué, c'est susciter une anarchie sans nom, l'anarchie des choses et des aspects qui se réveillent avant de sombrer à nouveau et de se fondre dans l'unité.'

45 Ibid., p. 92: 'C'est pour en finir avec cette séparation des principes, pour réduire leur antagonisme essentiel, qu'ils ont pris les armes et se sont rués les uns contre les autres'; p. 155: 'merveilleuse ardeur au désordre'; 'rien que l'application d'une idée métaphysique et supérieure de l'ordre, c'est-à-dire de l'unité.'

46 Ibid., p. 153: 'non content de prendre le trône pour un tréteau, [...] prend la terre meme de l'empire pour un tréteau'; p. 154: 'le théâtre et par le théâtre la poésie sur le trône de Rome, dans le palais d'un empereur romain, et la poésie, quand elle est réelle, ça mérite du sang, ça justifie que l'on verse le sang.'

47 Boldt-Irons, 'Anarchy and androgyny', pp. 876–77.

48 Artaud, *L'Anarchiste couronné*, p. 70: 'excès sanglants'; 'spiritualité violente'; p. 45: 'le sentiment d'une certaine magie naturelle'; 'une idée de la magie qui n'est pas naturelle'; p. 16: 'nous, gens d'Occident'; 'toutes les idées qui ont permis aux mondes Romain et Grec de ne pas mourir tout de suite, de ne pas sombrer dans une aveugle bestialité, sont justement venues de cette frange barbare'.

49 Ibid., p. 20: 'les hommes ont pris toute la méchanceté et la faiblesse, et les femmes la virilité'.

50 J.C. Stout, 'Modernist family romance', p. 420.

51 Artaud, *L'Anarchiste couronné*, p. 157: 'chasse les hommes du Sénat et il met à leur place des femmes'; p. 41: 'vigoureuse verge'; p. 95: 'le roi pédéraste et qui se veut femme, est un prêtre du Masculin'.

52 Stout, 'Modernist family romance', p. 421.

53 David, 'Figure du désordre', p. 157: 'Artaud s'intéresse aux motivations profondes et aux conséquences d'un acte dicté non point par la fantaisie individuelle d'un esthète, mais par une volonté politique et religieuse'.

54 Thanks are due to Jason Hartford for pointing this comparison out to me.

55  Stout, 'Modernist family romance', p. 422.

56  A. Artaud, *Oeuvres complètes d'Antonin Artaud*, vol. VII, pp. 187–88: 'dans la conception de la figure centrale […] je me suis moi-même décrit.' Letter to Jean Paulhan (20 August 1934); Idem, *L'Anarchiste couronné*, p. 181: 'un esprit indiscipliné et fanatique, […] un rebelle, un individualiste forcené'.

57  Ibid., pp. 627, 626.

58  A. Duggan, *Family Favourites*, p. 2.

59  Ibid., pp. 78–80.

60  Ibid., pp. 78–80.

61  Ibid., p. 102.

62  Ibid., pp. 93, 191, 135, 118.

63  Ibid., pp. 238, 216.

64  Ibid., p. 184.

65  Ibid., pp. 59–60, 87.

66  Ibid., pp. 106, 222.

67  Ibid., pp. 168, 161, 181.

68  Ibid., pp. 60; 84; 107, 124.

69  Ibid., pp. 144–45.

70  Ibid., pp. 189, 245.

71  Ibid., p. 247.

72  R.M. Pettis, 'Duberman, Martin Bauml', in GLBTQ, *an Encyclopedia of Gay, Lesbian, Bisexual, Transgender, & Queer Culture*: http://www.glbtq.com/social-sciences/duberman_mb_ssh,2.html (accessed 20 September 2007).

73  M.B. Duberman, *Elagabalus*, pp. 279–352, at scene I (p. 284); I (p. 283–284); II (p. 290); III (p. 304); III (p. 308).

74  Ibid., p. 281; I (p. 287); III (p. 300); IV (p. 314).

75  Ibid., I (p. 286); V (p. 324); II (p. 290, 294).

76  Ibid., p. 281.

77  M.B. Duberman, *Male Armor*, p. xiii.

78  Ibid., p. xiv.

79  Duberman, *Elagabalus*, VI (p. 334).

80  Ibid., IV (p. 315); VI (p. 350); VI (p. 351).

81  Ibid., VI (p. 341).

82  Ibid., VI (p. 332).

83  Duberman, *Male Armor*, p. xiv.

# SELECT BIBLIOGRAPHY

ABBREVIATIONS

| | |
|---|---|
| *AE* | *L'Année épigraphique* |
| *ANRW* | *Aufstieg und Niedergang der römischen Welt* |
| *BMC* | *Coins of the Roman Empire in the British Museum* |
| *CIL* | *Corpus inscriptionum Latinarum* |
| *CRAI* | *Comptes rendus de l'Académie des Inscriptions et Belles-Lettres* |
| *GBMC* | *A Catalogue of the Greek Coins in the British Museum* |
| *HA* | *Historia Augusta* |
| *IGL Syr.* | *Inscriptions grecques et latines de la Syrie* |
| *IGR* | *Inscriptiones Graecae ad res Romanas pertinentes* |
| *IGUR* | *Inscriptiones Graecae urbis Romae* |
| *ILS* | *Inscriptiones Latinae selectae* |
| *JRS* | *The Journal of Roman Studies* |
| *LTUR* | *Lexicon topographicum urbis Romae* |
| *M. Chr.* | *Grundzüge und Chrestomathie der Papyrusurkunde* |
| *MEFRA* | *Mélanges de l'École Française de Rome* |
| *P. Bub* | *Die verkohlten Papyri aus Bubastos* |
| *PIR* | *Prosopographia imperii Romani* |
| *P. Lips.* | *Griechische Urkunden der Papyrussammlung zu Leipzig* |
| *P. Oxy.* | *The Oxyrhynchus Papyri* |
| *P. Turner* | *Papyri: Greek and Egyptian, edited by various hands in honour of Eric Gardner Turner on the occasion of his seventieth birthday* |
| *RIC* | *The Roman Imperial Coinage* |
| *SEG* | *Supplementum epigraphicum Graecum* |

255

I: ANCIENT SOURCES

NB. Literary sources have been excluded from this list. The notes refer to the translations I have used whenever this is relevant.

Bosch, C., *Die kleinasiatischen Münzen der römischen Kaiserzeit. II. Einzeluntersuchungen. Vol. 1. Bithynien. 1. Hälfte* (Stuttgart, 1935) (no other volumes have appeared)

Cagnat, R. et al., *L'Année épigraphique* (Paris, 1888–)

— *Inscriptiones Graecae ad res Romanas pertinentes*, 4 vols (Paris, 1903–27)

Dessau, H., *Inscriptiones Latinae selectae*, 3 vols (Berlin, 1892–1916)

Fink, R.O. (ed.), *Roman Military Records on Papyrus* (Cleveland, 1971)

Fink, R.O., A.S. Hoey and W.F. Snyder, 'The Feriale Duranum', *Yale Classical Studies* 7 (1940), pp. 1–222

Fittschen, K. and P. Zanker, *Katalog der römischen Porträts in den Capitolinischen Museen und den anderen kommunalen Sammlungen der Stadt Rom*, 4 vols (Mainz, 1983–85)

Frösén, J. and D. Hagedorn (eds), *Die verkohlten Papyri aus Bubastos*, 2 vols (Opladen, 1990–98)

Geißen, A., *Katalog alexandrinischer Kaisermünzen der Sammlung des Instituts für Altertumskunde der Universität zu Köln*, 5 vols (Opladen, 1974–83)

Gnecchi, F., *I medaglioni romani*, 3 vols (Milan, 1912)

Grenfell, B.P., A.S. Hunt et al., *The Oxyrhynchus Papyri* (London, 1898–)

Hecht, R.E., 'Some Greek imperial coins in my collection', *The Numismatic Chronicle*, 7th series, 8 (1968), pp.27–35

Hondius, J.J.E. et al., *Supplementum epigraphicum Graecum* (Leiden/Amsterdam, 1923–)

Jalabert, L., R. Mouterde et al., *Inscriptions grecques et latines de la Syrie* (Paris, 1929–)

Kadman, L., *Corpus nummorum Palaestinensium*, 4 vols (Jerusalem, 1956–61)

Leber, P.S., *Die in Kärnten seit 1902 gefundenen römischen Steininschriften* (Klagenfurt, 1972)

Mattingly, H. and R.A.G. Carson, *Coins of the Roman Empire in the British Museum*, 6 vols (London, 1923–62)

Mattingly, H., E.A. Sydenham et al., *The Roman Imperial Coinage*, 10 vols (London, 1923–94)

Mercklin, E. von, *Antike Figuralkapitelle* (Berlin, 1968)

Mitteis, L. (ed.), *Griechische Urkunden der Papyrussammlung zu Leipzig* (Leipzig, 1906)

Mitteis, L. and U. Wilcken (eds), *Grundzüge und Chrestomathie der Papyrusurkunde*, 2 vols (Leipzig/Berlin, 1912)

Mommsen, T., W. Henzen et al., *Corpus inscriptionum Latinarum* (Berlin, 1863–)

Moretti, L., *Inscriptiones Graecae urbis Romae*, 4 vols (Rome, 1968–90)

Parsons, P.J. and J.R. Rea (eds), *Papyri: Greek and Egyptian, edited by various hands in honour of Eric Gardner Turner on the occasion of his seventieth birthday* (London, 1981)

Poole, R.S. et al., *A Catalogue of the Greek Coins in the British Museum*, 29 vols (London, 1873–1927)

Price, M.J., 'Greek imperial coins: some recent acquisitions by the British Museum', *The Numismatic Chronicle*, 7th series, 11 (1971), pp. 121–34

Thirion, M., *Le Monnayage d'Élagabale (218–22)* (Brussels/Amsterdam, 1968)

Vogt, J., *Die alexandrinischen Münzen: Grundlegung einer alexandrinischen Kaisergeschichte*, 2 vols (Stuttgart, 1924)

## II: MODERN LITERARY WORKS (1350–PRESENT)

NB. Some of these works are hard to find. I have added a reference to their location when I thought this would be useful.

Adelswärd-Fersen, J. d', *Messes noires. Lord Lyllian* (Paris, 1905)

Anonymous (P.-J.-B. Chaussard?), *Héliogabale ou esquisse morale de la dissolution romaine sous les empereurs* (Paris, 1802); available at the Bibliothèque Nationale de France, no. J-14970

Arbasino, A., *Super-Eliogabalo* (2nd edition, Turin, 1978)

Artaud, A., *Héliogabale ou l'anarchiste couronné* (Paris, 1934)

— *Le Théâtre et son double* (Paris, 1938)

— *Oeuvres complètes d'Antonin Artaud*, 26 vols, ed. P. Thévenin (Paris, 1956–94)

Artus, T., *L'Isle des Hermaphrodites nouvellement descouverte*, in C.-G. Dubois (ed.), *L'Isle des Hermaphrodites* (Geneva, 1996), pp. 47–187

Aureli, A., *Eliogabalo*, in I. Dumont and S. van Renterghem (eds), *Eliogabalo* (Brussels, 2004), pp. 153–265

Benoit, P., 'Héliogabale', in P. Benoit, *Diadumène: Poèmes* (2nd edition, Paris, 1921), p. 49; available at the Bibliothèque Nationale de France, no 8-Y2-64405 (19)

Brandimbourg, G., 'Héliogabe', in Idem, *Croquis du vice* (Paris, 1895); available at the Bibliothèque Nationale de France, no M-945

Bruni, L., *Oratio Heliogabali ad meretrices*, in M. Aldo and T. Andrea (eds), *Historiae Augustae scriptores* (Venice, 1519), pp. 291–95; available at the Bibliothèque Nationale de France, no RES-J-2397

Cabuchet, T., *Héliogabale*, in Idem, *Trilogie sur le Christianisme* (Paris/Lyon, 1837), pp. 63–171; available at the Bibliothèque Nationale de France, no YF-8479

Captijn-Müller, C. and H. Schneeweiß (transl.), *Heliogabal: Der Sonnenkaiser* (Berlin, 1998)

Castelnau, A., 'Alexandrie', in Idem, *Sonnets historiques* (Paris, 1873), pp. 53–54; available at the Bibliothèque Nationale de France, no YE-17288

Chaillet, G., *La Dernière prophétie*, 4 vols (Grenoble, 2002–7)

Corbel, H., 'La danse au temple du Soleil', in Idem, *Sonnets romains* (Paris, 1898), pp. 41–42; available at the Bibliothèque Nationale de France, no 8-YE PIECE-5670

Couperus, L.M.A., *De berg van licht*, in Idem, *Volledige werken Louis Couperus*, vol. 24 (Amsterdam/Antwerp, 1993)

Duberman, M.B., *Male Armor: Selected plays, 1968–1974* (New York, 1975)

— *Elagabalus*, in Idem, *Male Armor: Selected plays, 1968–1974* (New York, 1975), pp. 279–352

Duggan, A., *Family Favourites* (2nd edition, London, 2007)

Dumont, I. and S. van Renterghem (eds), *Eliogabalo* (Brussels, 2004)

Duplay, M. and P. Bonardi, *Héliogabale: Orgies Romaines* (Paris, 1935); available at the Bibliothèque Nationale de France, no 8-Y2-83837

Dupont-Sommer, A. and L. Robert, *La Déesse de Hiérapolis-Castabala (Cilicie)* (Paris, 1964)

Erasmus, D., *The Colloquies of Erasmus*, ed. and transl. C.R. Thompson (Chicago/ London, 1965)

Flaubert, G., *La Première Éducation sentimentale* (Paris, 1993)

Gaiman, N., *Being an Account of the Life and Death of the Emperor Heliogabolus* (1991–92); available online at http://www.holycow.com/dreaming/stories/being-an-account-of-the-life-and-death-of-the-emperor-heliogabolous (accessed 13 July 2011)

Gautier, T., *Mademoiselle de Maupin* (Paris, 1973)

George, S., *Algabal*, in Idem, *Hymnen. Pilgerfahrten. Algabal* (2nd edition, Berlin, 1899)

Gilbert, S., *Heliogabalus, a Love Story* (unpublished, 2002)

Grünbein, D., 'Bericht von der Ermordung des Heliogabal durch seine Leibgarde', in Idem, *Nach den Satiren* (Frankfurt am Main, 1999), pp. 26–29

Herdy, L. d' (pseud.), *La Destinée* (Paris, 1900); available at the Bibliothèque Nationale de France, no 8-Y2-52468

Huysmans, J.-K., *À Rebours* (Paris, 1977)

Jonigk, Th. and P. Vermeersch, *Heliogabal*, in Idem and P. Vermeersch (eds), *Heliogabal* (2003), pp. 35–69

Jourdan, L., *La Dernière nuit d'Héliogabale* (Paris, 1889); available at the Bibliothèque Nationale de France, no 8-Y2-43006

Krasiński, Z., *Iridion*, ed. and transl. G.R. Noyes (London, 1927)

Loewengard, P., 'La priere d'Héliogabale' in Idem, *Les Fastes de Babylone* (Paris, 1905), p. 54; available at the Bibliothèque Nationale de France, no. 8-YE-6470

Lombard, J., *L'Agonie* (Paris, 2002)

Manley, F., 'Heliogabalus', *Poetry* 129 (1976–77), pp. 81–82

Mencken, H.L. and G.J. Nathan, *Heliogabalus, a Buffoonery in Three Acts* (2nd edition, Whitefish, MT, 2005)

Mendès, C., 'L'empereur et les papillons', in Idem, *Pour lire au couvent* (Paris, 1887) pp. 185–87; available at the Bibliothèque Nationale de France, no. 8-Y2-9999

Mirande, H., *Élagabal* (4th edition, Paris, 1910); available at the Bibliothèque Nationale de France, no 8-Y2-58053

Moinet, P., 'La Vie infâme d'Héliogabale', in Idem, *En marge de l'histoire* (Paris, 1930), pp.33–42; available at the Bibliothèque Nationale de France, no B.M. *E-2011

Moinot, P., *Héliogabale* (Paris, 1971); available at the Bibliothèque Nationale de France, no. 16-Y-224 (105)

Nayral, J., 'Elagabal', in Idem, *A l'ombre des marbres* (Paris, 1909), pp. 39–40; available at the Bibliothèque Nationale de France, no 8-YE-7456

Onstott, K. and L. Horner, *Child of the Sun* (London, 1966)

Pastor, A., *Héliogabale* (Nice, 2001)

Reed, J., *Boy Caesar* (London, 2004)

Richepin, J., 'Un empereur', in Idem, *Les Morts bizarres* (Paris, 1876), pp.63–67; available at the Bibliothèque Nationale de France, no 8-Y2-638

— 'Elagabal', Idem, *Contes de la Décadence romaine* (2nd edition, Paris, 1994), pp.225–32

Sicard, E. and D. de Séverac, *Héliogabale: Tragédie lyrique en 3 actes, en vers* (Béziers, 1910); available at the Bibliothèque Nationale de France, no 8-RF-81187

Tysens, G., *Bassianus Varius Heliogabalus, of de uitterste proef der standvastige liefde* (Amsterdam, 1720); available at the Koninklijke Bibliotheek at The Hague, no 448 G 136; also available online at http://www.let.leidenuniv.nl/Dutch/Ceneton/Heliogabalus.html (accessed 6 October 2006)

Villeroy, A., *Héliogabale: Drame en vers en cinq actes* (Paris, 1902); available at the Bibliothèque Nationale de France, no 8-Y-2350

Westcott, A., *The Sun God* (London, 1904)

III: MODERN SCHOLARLY WORKS (1350–PRESENT)

Adler, W. and P. Tuffin (eds), *The Chronography of George Synkellos: A Byzantine chronicle from the creation* (Oxford/New York, 2002)

Alföldy, G., 'Herodian's person', in Idem (ed.), *Die Krise des Römischen Reiches: Geschichte, Geschichtsschreibung und Geschichtsbetrachtung: Augewählte Beiträge* (Stuttgart, 1989), pp.240–72

Ando, C., *Imperial Ideology and Provincial Loyalty in the Roman Empire* (Berkeley/Los Angeles/London, 2000)

Baldus, H.R., 'Das "Vorstellungsgemälde" des Heliogabal: Ein bislang unerkanntes numismatisches Zeugnis', *Chiron* 19 (1989), pp.467–76

— 'Zur Aufnahme des Sol Elagabal-Kultes in Rom, 219 n. Chr.', *Chiron* 21 (1991), pp. 175–78

Barber, S., *Antonin Artaud: Blows and bombs* (London, 1993)

Baron, H. (ed.), *Leonardo Bruni Aretino: Humanistisch-philosophische Schriften* (2nd edition, Berlin, 1969)

Bastet, F.L., *Louis Couperus: Een biografie* (3rd edition, Amsterdam, 1989)

Bauer, R., *Die schöne* Décadence: *Geschichte eines literarischen Paradoxons* (Frankfurt am Main, 2001)

Beard, M., J. North and S. Price (eds), *Religions of Rome*, 2 vols (2nd edition, Cambridge 1999)

Bellot, É., *Jean Lombard. Sa vie, ses oeuvres* (2nd edition, Paris, 1904)

Bergmann, M., *Studien zum römischen Porträt des 3. Jahrhunderts n. Chr.* (Bonn, 1977)

Bernheimer, C., *Decadent Subjects: The idea of decadence in art, literature, philosophy, and culture of the* fin de siècle *in Europe*, T.J. Kline and N. Schor (eds) (Baltimore/London 2002)

Berrens, S., *Sonnenkult und Kaisertum von den Severern bis zu Constantin I (193–337 n. Chr.)* (Stuttgart, 2004)

Birkett, J., *The Sins of the Fathers: Decadence in France 1870–1914* (London, 1986)

Birley, A.R., *Septimius Severus: The African emperor* (London, 1971)

Blois, L. de, 'Volk und Soldaten bei Cassius Dio', *ANRW* II, 34.3 (1997), pp. 2650–76

— 'Emperor and empire in the works of Greek-speaking authors of the third century AD', *ANRW* II, 34.4 (1998), pp. 3391–443

— et al. (eds), *Impact of Empire III: The Representation and Perception of Roman Imperial Power: Proceedings of the third workshop of the international network Impact of Empire (Roman Empire, c.200 BC–AD 476)* (Amsterdam, 2003)

Boccaccio, G., *Famous Women*, ed. and transl. V. Brown (Cambridge, MA/ London, 2001)

Bogaers, J.E., 'Sol Elagabalus und die Cohors III Breucorum in Woerden (Germania Inferior)', *Oudheidkundige mededelingen uit het Rijksmuseum van Oudheden te Leiden* 74 (1994), pp. 153–61

Boldt-Irons, L.A., 'Anarchy and androgyny in Artaud's *Héliogabale ou l'anarchiste couronné*', *The Modern Language Review* 91 (1996), pp. 866–77

Bolgar, R.R., *The Classical Heritage and its Beneficiaries* (Cambridge, 1954)

Bowersock, G.W., 'Herodian and Elagabalus', *Yale Classical Studies* 24 (1975), pp. 229–36

Broise, H. and Y. Thébert, 'Élagabal et le complexe religieux de la Vigna Barberini', *MEFRA* 111 (1999), pp. 729–47

Brune, J. de, *Banket-werck van goede gedachten* (Middelburg, 1657); available at the University Library of Leiden, no 1019 G 14 (M.C.); also available online at http://www.let.leidenuniv.nl/Dutch/Renaissance/JohandeBrune Banketwerk.html (accessed 26 October 2006)

Bruni, L., *History of the Florentine People*, 3 vols, ed. and transl. J. Hankins (Cambridge, MA/London, 2001–7)

Busst, A.J.L., 'The image of the androgyne in the nineteenth century', in I. Fletcher (ed.), *Romantic Mythologies* (London, 1967), pp. 1–95

Butcher, K., *Roman Syria and the Near East* (London, 2003)

— *Coinage in Roman Syria: Northern Syria, 64 BC–AD 253* (London, 2004)

Butler, O.F., *Studies in the Life of Heliogabalus* (New York, 1908)

Calcagno, M., 'Censoring *Eliogabalo* in seventeenth-century Venice', *Journal of Interdisciplinary History* 36 (2005–6), pp. 355–77

Chausson, F., '*Vel Iovi vel Soli*: quatre études autour de la Vigna Barberini (191–354)', *MEFRA* 107 (1995), pp. 661–75

Christ, K., *Von Gibbon zu Rostovtzeff: Leben und Werk führender Althistoriker der Neuzeit* (Darmstadt, 1972)

Corbeill, A., 'Dining deviants in Roman political invective', in J.P. Hallett and M.B. Skinner (eds), *Roman Sexualities* (Princeton, 1997), pp. 99–128

Croke, B., 'Malalas, the man and his work', in E. Jeffreys, B. Croke and R. Scott (eds), *Studies in John Malalas* (Sydney, 1990), pp. 1–25

Croom, A.T., *Roman Clothing and Fashion* (Gloucestershire, 2000)

Cumont, F., *Les Religions orientales dans le paganisme romain* (2nd revised edition, Paris, 1909)

— 'Une dédicace à des deux Syriens trouvée à Cordoue', *Syria* 5 (1924), pp. 342–45

David, M.-F., 'Héliogabale, figure du désordre', *Roman 20–50: Revue d'étude du roman du XXe siècle* 21 (1996), pp. 149–61

— *Antiquité latine et Décadence* (Paris, 2001)

Dietz, K.H., *Sentatus contra principem: Untersuchungen zur senatorischen Opposition gegen Kaiser Maximinus Thrax* (Munich, 1980)

Dirven, L., 'The emperor's new clothes: a note on Elagabalus' priestly dress', in S.G. Vashalomidze and L. Greisiger (eds), *Der Christliche Orient und seine Umwelt: Gesammelte Studien zu Ehren Jürgen Tubachs anläßlich seines 60: Geburtstag* (2nd edition, Wiesbaden, 2007), pp. 21–36

Domaszewski, A. von, *Abhandlungen zur römischen Religion* (Berlin/Leipzig, 1909)

— *Geschichte der römischen Kaiser*, 2 vols (2nd edition, Leipzig, 1914)

Dubois, C.G. (ed.), *L'Isle des Hermaphrodites* (Geneva, 1996)

Duncan-Jones, R., *Money and Government in the Roman Empire* (Cambridge, 1994)

Dušanić, S., 'Severus Alexander as Elagabalus' associate', *Historia: Zeitschrift für alte Geschichte* 13 (1964), pp. 487–98

Duviquet, G. (ed.), *Héliogabale raconté par les historiens grecs et latins* (Paris, 1903)

Edwards, C., *The Politics of Immorality in Ancient Rome* (Cambridge, 1993)

— 'Unspeakable professions: public performance and prostitution in ancient Rome', in J.P. Hallett and M.B. Skinner (eds), *Roman Sexualities* (Princeton, 1997), pp. 66–95

Elsner, J., *Art and the Roman Viewer: The transformation of art from the pagan world to Christianity* (Cambridge, 1995)

— *Imperial Rome and Christian Triumph* (Oxford, 1998)

Elsner, J. and J. Masters (eds), *Reflections of Nero: Culture, history and representation* (London, 1994)

Emont, N., 'Les aspects religieux du mythe de l'androgyne dans la littérature de la fin du XIXe siècle', in F. Monneyron (ed.), *L'Androgyne dans la littérature* (Paris, 1990), pp. 38–49

Frey, M., *Untersuchungen zur Religion und zur Religionspolitik des Kaisers Elagabal* (Stuttgart, 1989)

Fricker, C., 'Ludwig II in Stefan Georges "Algabal"', *Weimarer Beiträge* 52 (2006), pp. 441–48

Gambato, M., 'The female-kings: some aspects of the representation of eastern kings in the Deipnosophistae', in D. Braund and J. Wilkins (eds), *Athenaeus and His World: Reading Greek culture in the Roman Empire* (Exeter, 2000), pp. 227–30

Gardner, M.M., *The Anonymous Poet of Poland: Zygmunt Krasiński* (Cambridge, 1919)

Gibbon, E., *The History of the Decline and Fall of the Roman Empire*, 3 vols, ed. D. Womersley (London, 1994)

Gilman, R., *Decadence: The strange life of an epithet* (New York, 1979)

Glover, J., *Cavalli* (London, 1978)

Grant, M., *The Severans: The changed Roman Empire* (London/New York, 1996)

Greenslade, W., *Degeneration, Culture and the Novel 1880–1940* (Cambridge, 1994)

Groag, E., A. Stein et al., *Prosopographia imperii Romani saec. I, II, III*, 7 vols so far (2nd revised edition, Berlin/Leipzig, 1933–)

Gualerzi, S., *Né uomo, né donna, né dio, né dea: Ruolo sessuale e ruolo religioso dell'Imperatore Elagabalo* (Bologna, 2005)

Haas, V., *Hethitische Berggötter und hurritische Steindämonen* (Mainz, 1982)

Haensch, R., 'Pagane Priester des römischen Heeres im 3. Jahrhundert nach Christus', in L. de Blois, P. Funke and J. Hahn (eds), *The Impact of Imperial Rome on Religions, Ritual and Religious Life in the Roman Empire: Proceedings of the fifth workshop of the international network Impact of Empire (Roman Empire, 200BC–AD476)* (Leiden/Boston, 2006), pp. 208–18

Halfmann, H., 'Zwei Syrische Verwandte des severischen Kaiserhauses', *Chiron* 12 (1982), pp. 217–35

Halsberghe, G.H., *The Cult of Sol Invictus* (Leiden, 1972)

Hanson, E., *Decadence and Catholicism* (Cambridge, MA/London, 1997)

Hargreaves, T., *Androgyny in Modern Literature* (Basingstoke/New York, 2005)

Hautcourt, A. d', 'Peinture ou théâtre? Louis Feuillade, Héliogabale et le cinéma français en 1911', *Journal of Inquiry and Research* 84 (2006), pp. 107–23

Hay, J.S., *The Amazing Emperor Heliogabalus* (London, 1911)

Hekster, O.J., *Commodus: An emperor at the crossroads* (Amsterdam, 2002)

Horstmann, A., 'Die "Klassische Philologie" zwischen Humanismus und Historismus: Friedrich August Wolf und die Begründung der modernen Altertumswissenschaft', *Berichte zur Wissenschaftsgeschichte* 1 (1978), pp. 51–70

Icks, M., 'Priesthood and imperial power: the religious reforms of Heliogabalus, 220–222 AD', in L. de Blois, P. Funke and J. Hahn (eds), *The Impact of Imperial Rome on Religions, Ritual and Religious Life in the Roman Empire: proceedings of the fifth workshop of the international network Impact of Empire (Roman Empire, 200 BC–AD 476)* (Leiden/Boston, 2006), pp. 169–78

— *Heliogabalus: geschiedenis, droom en nachtmerrie: Historische achtergronden bij* De berg van licht (The Hague, 2006)

— 'Empire of the sun? Civic responses to the rise and fall of Sol Elagabal in the Roman Empire', in O.J. Hekster, S. Schmidt-Hofner and C. Witschel (eds), *Ritual Dynamics and Religious Change in the Roman Empire: Proceedings of the eighth workshop of the international network Impact of Empire (Heidelberg, 5–7 July, 2007)* (Leiden/Boston, 2009), pp. 111–120

— 'Heliogabalus, a monster on the Roman throne: the literary construction of a "bad" emperor', in I. Sluiter and R.M. Rosen (eds), *KAKOS: Badness and anti-value in classical antiquity* (Leiden, 2008), pp. 477–88

Isaac, B., *The Invention of Racism in Classical Antiquity* (Princeton/Oxford, 2004)

Kaizer, T., *The Religious Life of Palmyra: A study of the social patterns of worship in the Roman period* (Stuttgart, 2002)

— 'Kingly priests in the Roman Near East?', in O. Hekster and R. Fowler (eds), *Imaginary Kings: Royal images in the ancient Near East, Greece and Rome* (Munich, 2005), pp. 177–92

Keilson-Lauritz, M., *Von der Liebe die Freundschaft heißt: Zur Homoerotik im Werk Stefan Georges* (Berlin, 1987)

Kenney, E.J., *The Classical Text: Aspects of editing in the age of the printed book* (Berkeley, 1974)

Kiefer, R. and B. Jungheim, *Der Krieg der Prinzipien: Über Georges 'Algabal' und Artauds 'Heliogabal'* (Aachen, 1981)

Kimbell, D., *Italian Opera* (Cambridge, 1991)

King, G.R.D., 'Archaeological fieldwork at the citadel of Homs, Syria: 1995–1999', *Levant* 34 (2002), pp. 39–58

Klebs, E., H. Dessau and P. de Rohden, *Prosopographia imperii Romani saec. I, II, III*, 3 vols (Berlin, 1897–98)

Klein, M., *Noodlot en wederkeer: De betekenis van de filosofie in het werk van Louis Couperus* (Maastricht, 2000)

Kolb, F., *Literarische Beziehungen zwischen Cassius Dio, Herodian und der Historia Augusta* (Bonn, 1972)

Krengel, E., 'Das sogenannte "Horn" des Elagabal – Die Spitze eines Stierpenis. Eine Umdeutung als Ergebnis fachübergreifender Forschung', *Jahrbuch für Numismatik und Geldgeschichte* 47 (1997), pp. 53–72

Kropp, A., 'Earrings, *nefesh* and *opus reticulatum*: self-representation of the royal house of Emesa in the first century AD', in T. Kaizer and M. Facella (eds), *Kingdoms and Principalities in the Roman Near East* (Stuttgart, 2010) pp. 199–216

Krumeich, R., 'Der Kaiser als syrischer Priester: Zur Repräsentation Elagabals als *sacerdos dei Solis Elagabali*', *Boreas* 23–24 (2000–1), pp. 107–12

Krzyżanowski, J., *A History of Polish Literature* (Warsaw, 1978)

Larsson Lovén, L. '*Lanam fecit*: woolworking and female virtue', in L. Larsson Lovén and A. Strömberg (eds), *Aspects of Women in Antiquity: Proceedings of the first Nordic symposium on women's lives in antiquity* (Göteborg, 12–15 June 1997) (Jonsered, 1998)

Leunissen, P.M.M., *Konsuln und Konsulare in der Zeit von Commodus bis Severus Alexander (180–235 n. Chr.): Prosopographische Untersuchungen zur senatorischen Elite im römischen Kaiserreich* (Amsterdam, 1989)

Levick, B., *Julia Domna: Syrian empress* (London/New York, 2007)

Lightfoot, J.L. (ed.), *Lucian: On the Syrian goddess* (New York, 2003)

Lukaszewicz, A., 'Antoninus the ΚΟΡΥΦΟΣ (Note on *P.Oxy.* XLVI 3298.2)', *The Journal of Juristic Papyrology* 22 (1992), pp. 43–46

Lukkenaer, W.J., *De omrankte staf. Couperus' Antieke werk deel 1: van 'Dionysos' t/m 'Herakles'* (Katwijk, 1989)

Machiavelli, N., *The Prince*, ed. and transl. G. Bull (12th edition, Suffolk, 1974)

Manders, E., 'Religion and coinage: Heliogabalus and Alexander Severus: two extremes?', *Talanta: Proceedings of the Dutch Archaeological and Historical Society* 36–37 (2004–5), pp. 123–38

Mar, R., *El Palati: La formació dels palaus imperials a Roma* (Tarragona, 2005)

Marasco, G. (ed.), *Greek and Roman Historiography in Late Antiquity: Fourth to sixth century AD* (Leiden/Boston, 2003)

Marsh, D., 'Mamma Roma, City of Women: Leonardo Bruni's *Oration to the Prostitutes*', in R. Schnur et al. (eds), *Acta Conventus Neo-Latini Abulensis: Proceedings of the Tenth International Congress of Neo-Latin Studies, Avila 4–9 August 1997* (Tempe, 2000), pp. 413–21

Matern, P., *Helios und Sol. Kulte und Ikonographie des griechischen und römischen Sonnengottes* (Istanbul, 2002)

Millar, F., *A Study of Cassius Dio* (Oxford, 1964)

— 'The Roman *coloniae* of the Near East: a study of cultural relations', in H. Solin and M. Kajava (eds), *Roman Eastern Policy and Other Studies in Roman History* (Helsinki, 1990), pp. 7–58

— *The Roman Near East, 31 BC– AD 337* (Cambridge, MA, 1993)

Miller, S.N., 'The army and the imperial house', in S.A. Cook et al. (eds), *The Cambridge Ancient History*, vol. XII: *The Imperial Crisis and Recovery, AD 193–324* (Cambridge, 1939), pp. 1–56

Miłosz, C., *The History of Polish Literature* (2nd edition, Berkeley/Los Angeles/ London, 1983)

Mommsen, Th., *Römische Kaisergeschichte: Nach den Vorlesungs-Mitschriften von Sebastian und Paul Hensel*, ed. B. and A. Demandt (Munich, 1992)

Monneyron, F., *L'Androgyne décadent: Mythe, figure, fantasmes* (Grenoble, 1996)

Montaigne, M. de, *Les Essais*, ed. J. Balsamo, M. Magnien and C. Magnien-Simonin (Paris, 2007)

Moormann, E.M. and W. Uitterhoeve, *Lexikon der antiken Gestalten: Mit ihrem Fortleben in Kunst, Dichtung und Musik*, transl. M. Pütz (Stuttgart, 1995)

Morel, J.-P., 'Stratigraphie et histoire sur le Palatin: la zone centrale de la Vigna Barberini', *CRAI* 85 (1996), pp.173–206

Morwitz, E., *Stefan George: Poems* (2nd edition, New York, 1946)

Moussli, M., 'Griechische Inschriften aus Emesa und Laodicea ad Libanum', *Philologus* 127 (1983), pp.254–61

Naumann, H., 'Stefan Georges "Algabal": Ein Hinweis zum Unterreich-Zyklus', in *Castrum Peregrini* 134–35 (1978), pp.122–24

Niebuhr, G.B., *Römische Geschichte*, 3 vols (Berlin, 1811–32); later extended with two additional volumes, ed. L. Schmitz, transl. G. Zeiss (Jena, 1844–45)

Noreña, C., 'The communication of the emperor's virtues', *JRS* 91 (2001), pp.146–68

Optendrenk, Th., *Die Religionspolitik des Kaisers Elagabal im Spiegel der Historia Augusta* (Bonn, 1969)

Oswald, Jr, V.A., 'The historical content of Stefan George's *Algabal*', *The Germanic Review* 23 (1948), pp.193–205

— 'Oscar Wilde, Stefan George, Heliogabalus', *Modern Language Quarterly* 10 (1949), pp.517–25

Palacio, M.J. de, 'Jacques d'Adelswärd-Fersen et la figure d'Héliogabale', *Romantisme* 113 (2001), pp.117–26

Pfeiffer, R., *History of Classical Scholarship from 1300 to 1850* (Oxford, 1976)

Pflaum, H.-G., *Les Procurateurs équestres sous le Haut-Empire romain*, 2 vols (Paris, 1950)

— *Les Carrières procuratoriennes équestres sous le Haut-Empire romain*, 5 vols (Paris, 1960–82)

— 'La carrière de C. Iulius Avitus Alexianus, grand'père de deux empereurs', *Revue des études latines* 57 (1979), pp.298–314

Pietrzykowski, M., 'Die Religionspolitik des Kaisers Elagabal', *ANRW* II, 16.3 (1986), pp.1806–25

Prado, L. de Arrizabalaga y, *The Emperor Elagabalus: Fact or fiction?* (Cambridge, 2010)

Radnóti, A., 'C. Julius Avitus Alexianus', *Germania* 39 (1961), pp.383–412

Réville, J., *La Religion à Rome sous les Sévères* (Paris, 1886)

Rieckmann, J., 'Introduction', in Idem (ed.), *A Companion to the Works of Stefan George* (New York, 2005), pp.1–22.

Riikonen, H., *Die Antike im historischen Roman des 19. Jahrhunderts: Eine literatur- und kulturgeschichtliche Untersuchung* (Helsinki, 1978)

Rink, A., 'Algabal – Elagabal: Herrschertum beim frühen Stefan George', *Weimarer*

Roller, L.E., *In Search of God the Mother: The cult of Anatolian Cybele* (Berkeley – Los Angeles – London 1999)

Rosand, E., *Opera in Seventeenth-Century Venice: The creation of a genre* (Berkeley/ Los Angeles/Oxford, 1991)

Said, E.W., *Orientalism: Western conceptions of the Orient* (4th edition, London, 1995)

Salway, B.P.M., 'A fragment of Severan history: The unusual career of ...atus, praetorian prefect of Elagabalus', *Chiron* 27 (1997), pp. 127–54

Scheffler-Weimar, L. von, 'Elagabal: Charakterstudie aus der römischen Kaiserzeit', *Jahrbuch für sexuelle Zwischenstufen* 3 (1901), pp.231–64

Scheid, J., 'Le protocole arvale de l'année 213 et l'arrivée de Caracalla à Nicomédie', in G. Paci (ed.), *Epigrafia romana in area adriatica: Actes de la IXe Rencontre franco-italienne sur l'épigraphie du monde romain, Macerata, 10–11 Novembre 1995* (Macerata 1998), pp. 439–51

Scheithauer, A., *Kaiserbild und literarisches Programm: Untersuchungen zur Tendenz der Historia Augusta* (Frankfurt am Main, 1987)

— 'Die Regierungszeit des Kaisers Elagabal in der Darstellung von Cassius Dio und Herodian', *Hermes* 118 (1990), pp. 335–56

— *Kaiserliche Bautätigkeit in Rom* (Stuttgart, 2000)

Schiller, J.H.K.F.H., *Geschichte der römischen Kaiserzeit*, 2 vols (Gotha, 1883–87)

Seyrig, H., 'Antiquités syriennes 53: Antiquités de la nécropole 'd Émèse (1re partie)', *Syria* 29 (1952), pp. 204–50

— 'Antiquités syriennes 53 (suite): Antiquités de la nécropole d'Émèse', *Syria* 30 (1953), pp. 12–24

— 'Antiquités syriennes 76: Caractères de l'histoire d'Émèse', *Syria* 36 (1959), pp. 184–92

— 'Antiquités syriennes 95: Le culte du Soleil en Syrie à l'époque romaine', *Syria* 48 (1971), pp. 337–73

Sidebottom, H., 'Herodian's historical methods and understanding of history', *ANRW* II, 34.4 (1998), pp. 2775–836

Sommer, M., 'Elagabal: Wege zur Konstruktion eines "schlechten" Kaisers', *Scripta Classica Israelica: Yearbook of the Israel Society for the Promotion of Classical Studies* 23 (2004), pp.95–110

Starcky, J., 'Stèle d'Elahagabal', *Mélanges de l'Université Saint-Joseph* 49 (1975–76), pp.503–20

Steinby, E.M. (ed.), *Lexicon topographicum urbis Romae*, 6 vols (Rome, 1993–2000)

Stout, J.C., 'Modernist family romance: Artaud's *Héliogabale* and paternity', *The French Review* 64 (1991), pp.417–27

Studniczka, F., 'Ein Pfeilercapitell auf dem Forum', *Mitteilungen des Deutschen Archäologischen Instituts: Römische Abteilung* 16 (1901), pp.273–82

Sullivan, R.D., 'The dynasty of Emesa', *ANRW* II, 8 (1977), pp. 198–219

Syme, R., *The Roman Revolution* (5th edition, Oxford, 1967)

— *Emperors and Biography: Studies in the Historia Augusta* (Oxford, 1971)

— *Historia Augusta Papers* (Oxford, 1983)

— *Ammianus and the Historia Augusta* (Oxford, 1986)

Thébert, Y., et al., 'Il santuario di *Elagabalus*: un giardino sacro', in F. Villedieu (ed.), *Il giardino dei Cesari: Dai palazzi antichi alla Vigna Barberini, sul Monte Palatino* (Rome, 2001), pp. 83–106

Thomasson, B.E., *Fasti Africani: Senatorische und ritterliche Amtsträger in den römischen Provinzen Nordafrikas von Augustus bis Diocletian* (Stockholm, 1996)

Thompson, G.R., *Elagabalus: Priest-Emperor of Rome* (unpublished PhD thesis, University of Kansas, 1972)

Tillemont, L.-S. Le Nain de, *Histoire des empereurs et des autres princes qui ont regné durant le six premiers siecles de l'Eglise*, 6 volumes (1st revised edition, Venice, 1732–39)

Todd, J.D., 'Stefan George and two types of aestheticism', in J. Rieckmann (ed.), *A Companion to the Works of Stefan George* (New York, 2005), pp. 127–43

Turcan, R., *Héliogabale et le sacre du soleil* (Paris, 1985)

— 'Héliogabale précurseur de Constantin?', *Bulletin de l'Assocation Guillaume Budé* 47 (1988), pp. 38–52

Varner, E.R., *Mutilation and Transformation*: damnatio memoriae *and Roman imperial portraiture* (Leiden/Boston, 2004)

Villedieu, F., 'Constructions impériales mises au jour à l'angle nord-est du Palatin: résultats des fouilles de l'École française de Rome sur le site de la Vigna Barberini', *CRAI* 84 (1995), pp. 719–36

Villeneuve, R., *Héliogabale, le César fou* (Paris, 1957); republished in a slightly revised edition as *Le Divin Héliogabale: César et prêtre de Baal* (Paris, 1984)

Vogt, J., *Die alexandrinischen Münzen: Grundlegung einer alexandrinischen Kaisergeschichte*, vol. I (Stuttgart, 1924)

Walters, J., 'Invading the Roman body: manliness and impenetrability in Roman thought', in J.P. Hallett and M.B. Skinner (eds), *Roman Sexualities* (Princeton, 1997), pp. 29–43

Westenholz, C. de, 'Heliogabalus en de Vlam van de Lust: Heilig sensualisme in *De berg van licht*', article in 5 parts, *Arabesken* 12 (2004), no 23, pp. 4–15; 13 (2005) no 25, pp. 19–27; no 26, pp. 23–33; 14 (2006) no 27, pp. 30–41; no 28, pp. 23–30

Williams, C.A., *Roman Homosexuality: Ideologies of masculinity in classical antiquity* (New York/Oxford, 1999)

Young, G.K., 'Emesa and Baalbek: where is the temple of Elahagabal?', *Levant* 35 (2003), pp. 159–62

Zanker, P., *Augustus und die Macht der Bilder* (Munich, 1987)

Ziegler, R., *Kaiser, Heer und städtisches Geld: Untersuchungen zur Münzprägung von Anazarbos und anderer ostkilikischer Städte* (Vienna, 1993)

Zinsli, S.C., 'Gute Kaiser, slechte Kaiser: Die eusebische Vita Constantini als Referenztext für die Vita Heliogabali', *Wiener Studien* 118 (2005), pp. 117–38

# INDEX